MUSEUMS-*Positionen*
MUSEUM *Positions*

MUSEUMS-*Positionen*

BAUTEN UND PROJEKTE IN ÖSTERREICH
BUILDINGS AND PROJECTS IN AUSTRIA

Herausgeber
Editor

AUGUST SARNITZ

Residenz Verlag

Diese Publikation erscheint anläßlich der Wanderausstellung *Museums-Positionen* im Auftrag des Bundesministeriums für auswärtige Angelegenheiten.

Ausstellungsorganisation:
Bundesministerium für auswärtige Angelegenheiten:
Peter Marboe, Leiter der Kulturpolitischen Sektion
Georg Jankovic, Leiter der Ausstellungsabteilung

Ausstellungskommissär, Ausstellungsgestaltung, Katalogredaktion und Koordination:
August Sarnitz

Katalog-Übersetzung:
Peter Waugh

Katalog-Gesamtherstellung:
Residenz Verlag, Salzburg und Wien

© 1992 Bundesministerium für auswärtige Angelegenheiten
© 1992 für die Texte bei den Autoren

Alle Rechte vorbehalten
Satz: Fotosatz Rizner, Salzburg
Repros: Ludwig, Zell am See
Printed in Austria by Welsermühl, Wels
ISBN 3-7017-0781-2

Video zur Ausstellung »Museums-Positionen«
Konzept: Herbert Link, August Sarnitz
Regie: Herbert Link

This catalogue was published in conjunction with the touring exhibition *Museum Positions* and was commissioned by the Austrian Federal Ministry for Foreign Affairs.

Organisation of the exhibition:
Austrian Federal Ministry for Foreign Affairs:
Peter Marboe, Director of the Department for Cultural Policy
Georg Jankovic, Director of the Exhibition Section

Commissioner for the exhibition, exhibition design, catalogue editor and coordination:
August Sarnitz

English translations:
Peter Waugh

Overall production of the catalogue:
Residenz Verlag, Salzburg und Wien

© 1992 Austrian Federal Ministry for Foreign Affairs
© 1992 the authors

All rights reserved
Set by Fotosatz Rizner, Salzburg
Reproduction: Ludwig, Zell am See
Printed in Austria by Welsermühl, Wels
ISBN 3-7017-0781-2

Video produced for the exhibition "Museum Positions"
Concept: Herbert Link, August Sarnitz
Directed by Herbert Link

Inhalt / Contents

Vorwort

Eine neue Wendezeit ist angebrochen, nicht nur in der politischen Landschaft Europas, sondern auch in der Reflexion über das kulturelle Erbe und das Selbstverständnis der kulturellen Institutionen. Als ein integrierter Bestandteil des kulturellen Umfeldes gelten die Museen als jene Institutionen, welche zeitübergreifend tätig sind. Die historischen Dimensionen dokumentieren sich in der Parallele zur politischen Entwicklung. In diesem Sinn ist Kultur gerade auch heute, wo wir uns um die Schaffung eines neuen Europas bemühen, Überbringerin einer entscheidenden Botschaft.

Damit ist sie natürlich auch eine politische Kraft – ein Phänomen, das die Polis prägt, die Bemühungen zwischen den Menschen und deren Verhältnis zueinander.

Jede Reflexion über die österreichischen Museen als »Botschafter österreichischer Kultur« zeigt die heterogene Struktur der bestehenden Museen auf. Die Ausstellung *Museums-Positionen*, geplant in den Jahren 1990–1992, versteht sich als ein österreichischer Beitrag zu einer internationalen Diskussion.

Die Kulturkonzepte von Städten wie Frankfurt und Paris haben zum Beispiel den Stellenwert des Museums neu definiert: als Spannungsfeld zwischen postindustrieller Arbeit und postindustrieller Freizeit.

Die österreichische Museumslandschaft wird sich in den nächsten Jahren grundlegend verändern. Es geht aber nicht nur darum, ob jedes der vielen Museumsprojekte auch tatsächlich sofort realisiert wird, sondern es stellt sich vielmehr die Frage, wie das einzelne Museum seine »Position« innerhalb der kulturellen Diskussion definieren will. Neben den baulichen Maßnahmen geht es aber somit in erster Linie um

Konzepte, Strukturen und *Ideen:* das Museum als intelligentes Kulturprodukt der Wendezeit.

Zehn österreichische Museen – zehn österreichische Positionen – wurden für diese Ausstellung vom Ausstellungskommissär, Herrn Architekt Dozent August

Foreword

We have entered a new era, one of change, not only in the political landscape of Europe, but also in the way in which we view our cultural heritage and the way in which cultural institutions view themselves.

As institutions which are active in fields which transcend temporal periods, museums form a well-integrated part of our cultural surroundings. Their historical dimensions are documented by the parallels which exist to political developments. In this sense, the arts have a decisive message to deliver today, when we are attempting to create a new Europe.

As such, the arts are, of course, also a political force – a phenomenon which exerts an influence on the *polis,* on the efforts involved in human transactions and on people's relations with one another.

Any reflection about the role of Austrian museums as 'messengers of Austrian culture' reveals the heterogeneous structure of the existing museums. The exhibition *Museum Positions*, planned between 1990-1992, can be regarded as an Austrian contribution to an international discussion.

The cultural concepts of cities such as Frankfurt and Paris, for example, have redefined the value attached to the museum as a field of tension between post-industrial work and post-industrial leisure.

The Austrian museum scene will undergo fundamental changes in the next few years. Yet it is not only a question of whether each one of these museum projects will in fact be realised in the immediate future; for the question also arises of how the individual museum will define its 'position' within the context of the cultural discussion. Thus, in addition to questions concerning building measures, it is also primarily a matter of *concepts, structures* and *ideas:* the museum as an intelligent cultural project in this time of change.

The commissioner for this exhibition, the architect Dr. August Sarnitz, has chosen ten Austrian museums, ten Austrian positions, as providing a representative selection of those buildings which are at present being planned.

Sarnitz, ausgewählt, stellvertretend für die große Anzahl der in Planung befindlichen Bauwerke.

Als »work in progress« werden Einblicke in die gegenwärtige, aktuelle Situation geliefert: einige dieser Bauten sind bereits fertiggestellt, ein großer Teil der Projekte befindet sich in in lebhafter Diskussion. Die Zeit des letzten »fin de siècle« hat in Österreich die großen kulturellen Institutionen entstehen lassen; es bleibt zu wünschen, daß die Zeit des fin de millénaire die großen Projekte vollenden wird.

Die Wanderausstellung »Museums-Positionen« will vermitteln, aufzeigen und auffordern: ein Bild der österreichischen Arbeiten auf diesem Gebiet vermitteln, die neuen Konzepte auch gegenüber dem ausländischen Publikum und den Fachleuten aufzeigen und so zu einer internationalen Diskussion auffordern.

Dr. Alois Mock
Bundesminister für
auswärtige Angelegenheiten

In presenting 'work in progress' the exhibition provides insights into the actual situation today: some of these buildings have already been completed, many of them are the subject of great discussion. The last *fin de siècle* saw the emergence of great cultural institutions in Austria; it only remains to hope that the *fin de millénaire* will see the completion of these great projects.

The travelling exhibition *Museum Positions* seeks to communicate, demonstrate and stimulate: to communicate a picture of Austrian work in this field, to demonstrate new concepts to a foreign public and to specialists abroad, and, in doing so, to stimulate international discussion.

Dr. Alois Mock
Federal Minister for
Foreign Affairs

Museums-Positionen

August Sarnitz

Museum Positions

August Sarnitz

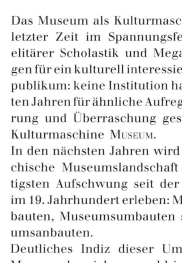

Christo, *Whitney Museum of American Art Packed*, 1971

Das Museum als Kulturmaschine steht in letzter Zeit im Spannungsfeld zwischen elitärer Scholastik und Mega-Ausstellungen für ein kulturell interessiertes Massenpublikum: keine Institution hat in den letzten Jahren für ähnliche Aufregung, Verwirrung und Überraschung gesorgt wie die Kulturmaschine Museum.

In den nächsten Jahren wird die österreichische Museumslandschaft ihren wichtigsten Aufschwung seit der Gründerzeit im 19. Jahrhundert erleben: Museumsneubauten, Museumsumbauten sowie Museumsanbauten.

Deutliches Indiz dieser Umwälzung im Museumsbereich – sowohl im internationalen Museumsboom als auch in den Publikationen – sind die »Retrospektiven« und »Sonderschauen« zu großen Themen der Kunstgeschichte, seien es nun einzelne Künstler oder thematische Zusammenfassungen. Das Museum selbst hingegen ist selten Gegenstand der Betrachtung, wenn es nicht sogar ganz vernachlässigt wird. Der Ort, an dem »kulturelle Ereignisse« stattfinden, wird größtenteils ebenso aus der Betrachtung der bildenden Kunst ausgeblendet wie der *Genius loci*. Das Museum als *Kunstverpackung*, als Metapher des Kulturbetriebes, erscheint aber zumindest ebenso relevant wie der Inhalt selbst. Gäbe es das »Kunsthistorische Museum« in Wien nicht, würde nicht nur ein baulicher Rahmen für die Kunstwerke fehlen, sondern ebenso eine auratische Atmosphäre, in der sich der Kunstgegenstand mit dem äußeren Rahmen der Kunstbetrachtung zu einer erlebnisreichen Einheit verbindet. Die in Thomas Bernhards Roman »Alte Meister« erwähnten Werke hängen nicht irgendwo, sondern im Kunsthistorischen Museum in Wien. Somit gilt auch der literarische Hinweis, daß ein Museumsbau selbst Teil eines kulturellen Erbes ist.

Eine Ausstellung über die österreichischen Museen will mehr sein als nur ein Überblick über zehn aktuelle Projekte von besonderem Interesse: sie ist eine Untersuchung über das Potential der öffentlichen

Recently, the museum as a cultural machine has found itself caught between the esotericism of scholarship and megaexhibitions for a mass public; no institution has aroused quite so much excitement, confusion and surprise over the past few years as the cultural machine of the Museum.

Over the next few years, the Austrian museum scene will be experiencing its most important upswing since the *Gründerzeit* of the last century, with the construction of new museum buildings, alterations to existing buildings and even extensions to museums.

A clear indication of this radical change in the museum sector – seen both in the international museum boom and in publications – is provided by the 'retrospectives' and 'special shows' about great subjects in art history, whether devoted to individual artists or to more general themes. By contrast, the museum itself is seldom regarded as an object of study in its own right – and is usually neglected completely. In the fine arts, the place where cultural events are held has, to a large extent, disappeared as an element of art appreciation, as has the *genius loci*. Yet as 'art packaging', as a metaphor for the art business, the museum ought to be regarded as being at least as relevant as its contents. Without the Kunsthistorische Museum in Vienna it is not only the architectural setting for the works of art that would be missing: so too would that aura-like atmosphere in which the art object merges with the external setting of art appreciation, creating a unity rich in experiential value. Thomas Bernhard's 'old Masters' are not hanging in any museum, they are hanging in the Kunsthistorische Museum in Vienna. Thus literature too provides a reminder that a museum building is itself part of a cultural heritage.

This exhibition about Austrian museums aims to be more than just a survey of ten current projects of special interest: it aims to investigate the ability of public institu-

Hand, sich in Sachen Kultur zu artikulieren und sich der öffentlichen Sache – der *res publica* – als politisches, kulturelles und architektonisches Phänomen anzunehmen.

Eine Ausstellung über Museums-Positionen in Österreich zielt deshalb in Ergänzung zu den großen Kunstausstellungen auf das spezifische Thema der baulichen Situation und die von Fachleuten erarbeitete Museumskonzeption. Der Gegensatz zwischen *Museum als Rahmen* und *Museum als Vermittler* sollte Ausgangspunkt einer Dokumentation sein. Ohne baulichen Rahmen ist eine Kulturvermittlung nicht im direkten Kontakt, sondern nur über die Medien durchführbar.

Das kulturelle Erbe Mitteleuropas erwartet in Zukunft zwei überregionale Impulse: Erstens durch die Öffnung der Grenzen gegenüber den ehemaligen »Oststaaten« und deren politischer, wirtschaftlicher und kultureller Entwicklung und zweitens durch die Integrationsbestrebungen Westeuropas zu einem gemeinsamen Wirtschaftsraum.

Unter diesen überregionalen und historisch relevanten Veränderungen ergibt sich für die kulturpolitische Situation in Österreich ein neuer Sachverhalt in bezug auf sein kulturelles Erbe: Die Aktivierung neuer Kulturträger und die Re-Aktivierung bestehender kultureller Einrichtungen. Sowohl durch die »Museumsmilliarde« für die Bundesmuseen als auch durch die Investitionen der Länder wurde dieser Erneuerungsprozeß begonnen. Der Ministerrat bewilligte ein Investitionsprogramm zur baulichen Sanierung in der Höhe von mehreren Milliarden Schilling, das Aktionsbudget der Museen wurde angehoben und das Personal aufgestockt.

In den letzten Jahren hat das Museum als Kulturträger nicht nur an Bedeutung gewonnen, sondern ist nolens volens auch in das größere Umfeld der gesamtwirtschaftlichen Diskussion um die »Umwegrentabilität« geraten – Museen als »Freizeitkapital«, Museen als »Urlaubsprogramm«.

Angesichts dieser Sachlage hat sich das traditionelle Bild der Museen grundsätzlich geändert. Aus dem konservativen Branchenbekenntnis Sammeln, Bewahren, Ausstellen ist eine besucherorientierte

tions to act on behalf of the arts and support the public cause – the *res publica* – as a political, cultural and architectural phenomenon.

This exhibition about museums in Austria therefore aims at complementing large-scale art exhibitions by concentrating on the specific theme of the architectural situation and the specialists' concept of the museum. The dialogue between the museum as a setting and the museum as a mediator should form the starting point for any documentation. Without an architectural setting, culture cannot be mediated in the form of direct contact, but can only be communicated via the media.

In the future, the cultural heritage of Central Europe can expect two trans-regional impulses: firstly, from the opening of the borders with the former Eastern bloc countries and the subsequent political, economic and cultural development of the latter; and secondly from Western Europe's attempts to achieve self-integration within a common economic area.

For the cultural and political situation in Austria, these trans-regional and historically relevant changes are bringing about a new situation with regard to the country's cultural heritage: the activation of new cultural media and the re-activation of existing cultural establishments. This process of renewal was initiated with the so-called 'museum millions' for the Austrian Federal Museums and with investments by the Austrian Provinces. The Austrian Cabinet approved an investment programme of several billion shillings for architectural redevelopment, the museums' operational budgets were raised and the number of employees increased.

In the past few years, the museum as a vehicle of culture has not only gained in importance, but has – *nolens volens* – also become involved in a larger area of discussion, one which concerns the economy as a whole: that of 'indirect returns' – museums as 'leisure-time capital', museums as part of a 'holiday programme'.

Taking this situation into account, the traditional picture of the museum has fundamentally changed. Out of the sector's conservative creed of Collect, Preserve, Exhibit a visitor-oriented exhibition policy

Wien, Plan der Ringstraße, ca. 1914
Vienna, general plan, ca. 1914

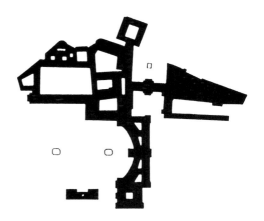

Filiberto Lucchese, Plan der Hofburg, ca. 1914,
Wien
Filiberto Lucchese, plan of the Hofburg,
ca. 1914, Vienna

Ausstellungspolitik geworden, die auch in den österreichischen Museen Fuß gefaßt hat beziehungsweise im Zusammenhang mit deren geplanter Umstrukturierung steht.

Die meisten der bestehenden österreichischen Bundesmuseen verdanken ihre Entstehung der Gründung durch die Habsburger während der Monarchie. Im Kräftespiel der vorigen Jahrhunderte waren die Museen Kultureinrichtungen eines mitteleuropäischen Vielvölkerstaates, dessen Charakter sicherlich mehr durch Heterogenität und Vielfalt als durch Homogenität und Uniformität geprägt war. Infolgedessen waren die Intentionen für die Sammlungsschwerpunkte in den Museumsbereichen entsprechend einer repräsentativen Mannigfaltigkeit ausgerichtet. Sowohl die im Kunsthistorischen Museum als auch die in der Graphischen Sammlung Albertina aufbewahrten Werke können in ihrer Vielfalt als Beispiele internationaler Museumsbestände von höchster Qualität bezeichnet werden.

Durch die geänderte politische Situation in den ehemaligen »Oststaaten« werden die verschütteten Querverbindungen und Vernetzungen des österreichischen Kulturraumes sichtbar. Der Zusammenhang der Städte Prag, Dresden, Leipzig, Budapest – um nur einige zu nennen – mit Wien wird dann besonders augenscheinlich, wenn man die Sammlungsschwerpunkte der Museen dieser einzelnen Städte vergleicht.

10 Museen – 10 Positionen werden anhand von Modellen, Photos und Zeichnungen dargestellt. Zu Wort kommen Museumsdirektoren, Museumsfachleute, Architekten und Architekturkritiker. Die Ausstellung versteht sich als ein Beitrag zu den in Umwälzung und Umstrukturierung befindlichen Museen: als »work in progress« werden Aspekte aufgezeigt und Sachverhalte transparent gemacht.

Die Kriterien für die Wahl dieser Museen in Österreich basieren zum einen auf der Qualität der einzelnen Sammlungen und zum anderen auf ihrer Relevanz und Beispielhaftigkeit innerhalb der Museumslandschaft. Als besondere Auswahlkriterien gelten die geplanten oder gerade abgeschlossenen Umbautätigkeiten – re-

has developed, and this is also gaining ground in Austrian museums, and, in some cases, is already in the process of restructuring them.

The origins of most of the existing Austrian federal museums can be traced to their foundation by the Habsburg monarchy. In the political power game of the previous century the museums were the cultural establishments of a multi-national Central European state, characterised more by its heterogeneity and multiplicity than its homogeneity and uniformity. As a result of this, the intentions behind the museums' collecting policies in their respective fields were oriented towards a representative multiplicity. In their variety, both the Kunsthistorische Museum and the Graphische Sammlung Albertina could be described as examples of museums with international collections of the very highest quality.

With the changed political situation in the former Eastern countries, the buried cross-references and inter-relatedness of the former Austrian cultural area are becoming increasing visible once again. Vienna's connections with the cities of Prague, Dresden, Leipzig and Budapest – to name but a few – become particularly obvious when one compares the main emphasis of the museum collections in the individual cities.

10 museums and 10 positions are presented, with the aid of models, photographs and drawings. Museum directors, museum specialists, architects and architectural critics express their views. The exhibition has been conceived as a forum for those museums which are at present undergoing radical change and restructuring, and documents various aspects of the work in progress.

The selective criteria for choosing the museums were based, on the one hand, on the quality of the individual museum, and, on the other, on its relevance and exemplary role within the Austrian museum scene. In order to achieve an objective temporal framework, an important selective criterion was that of whether a museum's planned or recently completed rebuilding activities involved new designs. The method of selection strove for diversity

spektive Neuplanungen –, um einen gegenständlichen Zeitbezug zu erzielen. Methode der Auswahl war, die Vielfältigkeit und die Eigenständigkeit der einzelnen Museen mit dem Prinzip der Qualität als oberstem Kriterium zu verbinden. Aus der großen Anzahl existierender Museen eine repräsentative und gerechte Auswahl zu treffen, scheint nicht nur schwierig, sondern fast unmöglich: sie ist deshalb prinzipiell als »pars pro toto« zu verstehen – die nicht genannten Sammlungen werden in ihrer Qualität und Bedeutung in keiner Weise in Frage gestellt.

Eine Intention der Auswahl war es, nicht nur die Situation der Bundes- und die der Landesmuseen zu berücksichtigen, sondern auch die unterschiedlichen Größenverhältnisse im Sinne der Gegebenheiten: Ausstellungshalle der Stadt Wien; Jüdisches Museum der Stadt Wien; Kunsthistorisches Museum, Wien; Kunsthaus Bregenz; Museumsquartier Messepalast, Wien; Niederösterreichisches Landesmuseum, St. Pölten; Österreichisches Museum für angewandte Kunst; Wien; Österreichisches Theatermuseum, Wien; Technisches Museum, Wien; Trigon Museum, Graz.

and independence in the individual projects, while applying the principle of quality as the overriding criterion. The task of making a representative selection from all the many existing museums was not only difficult but almost impossible: the choice should therefore principally be understood as *pars pro toto* – those museums which have not received mention here have in no way been called into question as far as their quality and importance is concerned.

In making the following selection we wanted to take account not only of the situation of the federal and regional museums, but also of the differences which exist with respect to actual size. Museums involved: the Kunsthalle of the City of Vienna; the Jewish Museum of the City of Vienna; the Kunsthistorische Museum, Vienna; the Kunsthaus, Bregenz; the Museumsquartier Messepalast, Vienna; the Lower Austrian Provincial Museum, St. Pölten; the Austrian Museum for the Applied Arts, Vienna; the Austrian Theatre Museum, Vienna; the Technical Museum, Vienna; the Trigon Museum, Graz.

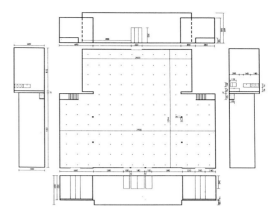

Secession Wien, Grundriß Ausstellungsraum
Secession Vienna, floor plan of exhibition hall

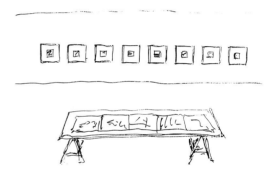

August Sarnitz, Entwurfsskizze, Ausstellungsgestaltung *Museums-Positionen*
August Sarnitz, sketch for the design of the exhibition *Museum Positions*

Museumspositionen – oder von der Verteidigung des Museums gegen seine Anhänger

Dieter Ronte

Museum Positions – or, of the Defence of the Museum against its Supporters

Dieter Ronte

Jenny Holzer, Installation im Solomon
R. Guggenheim Museum, New York,
Dezember 1989 – Februar 1990
Jenny Holzer, Installation at the Solomon
R. Guggenheim Museum, New York,
December 1989 – February 1990

Ein Museum ist ein Museum ist ein Museum ist ein Museum. Dennoch sind die Museen nicht gleich; aber doch sind Museen Museen. Sie dienen der Forschung und der Präsentation. Ihre verschiedenen Museumstypen haben sich bis heute nicht überholt, ganz im Gegenteil. Das breite Angebot von Museumstypen und ihre Varianten haben sich vermehrt. Das 20. Jahrhundert, besonders die Zeit nach dem Krieg, tendierte zum Festhalten, zum Sichern, zum Absichern: dazu braucht die Gesellschaft Museen. Das heißt: Museen heute sind bedeutsam, nicht nur in der Vergangenheit, sondern auch für die Zukunft. Museen sind Datenbanken der Naturwissenschaften, der Kulturgeschichte und der Kunst, sie sind Zeichen des Bewußtseins einer Gesellschaft, ihrer Verantwortung gegenüber der Vergangenheit, ihrer Aufmerksamkeit für die Gegenwart, ihrer Beachtung der Zukunft.

Strukturelle Bindungen des Museumswesens galten seit ihrer Gründung im 19. Jahrhundert mehrheitlich dem Museumswesen selbst und den darin dargestellten Wissensbereichen und somit der Darstellung von Wertinhalten. Die Museen hatten Vorbildfunktion, auch wenn sie unterschiedliche Optionen in der Benutzung offen ließen. Die frühen Bindungen der Museen galten den Benutzern, dennoch waren diese nicht der Maßstab aller Dinge im Museum, sondern eben die Wissensbereiche, die Bindungen an die Paradigmata von Wissenschaft und Wertinhalt.

In der Tat haben die letzten zwanzig Jahre am Bewußtsein des Museums gerüttelt. Es hat auch Veränderungen gegeben; doch im Prinzip sind die Museen unflexibel geblieben – so schwerfällig wie die Physis einer Sammlung. Es klingt fast paradox, wenn wir heute feststellen, daß jene Museen, die die ganzen Selbstfindungsprozesse nicht mitgemacht haben, weil sie in ihrer Tra-

A museum is a museum is a museum is a museum. And yet museums are not all the same; still, museums *are* museums. They serve the ends of research and presentation. Even today, the great variety in the different types of museums has not been superseded. Quite the contrary: the wide range of different types of museum, and their variants, has increased. The 20th century, especially the post-war period, has been inclined to cling, to protect, to safeguard things: for that, society needs museums. Which means that museums today are important not only for the past but also for the future. Museums are databanks of natural science, cultural history and art, they are signs of a society's awareness, its responsibility towards the past, its attention to the present, its respect for the future.

More often than not, the museum system has, ever since it was first developed in the 19th century, generally been committed to the museum system itself and to the areas of knowledge represented within it, and thus to the representation of value content. Museums served as models, even if different options were left open as far as their use was concerned. In the early days, museums were committed to the users, although it was not the latter who were the measure of all things in the museum, but rather the areas of knowledge, the commitments to the paradigms of science and value content.

And, in point of fact, the past twenty years have shaken the awareness of the museum. There have also been changes; yet in principle the museums have remained inflexible – as ponderous as the physis of an exhibition. It sounds almost paradoxical if we declare today that those museums which did not take part in the whole process of self-discovery because they remained static in their own tradition, have survived that process best of all. For the museum –

dition statisch in sich selbst ruhend waren, diesen Prozeß am besten überstanden haben. Denn das Museum, das gilt für damals wie für heute wie für morgen, ist jener Ort, in dem der Besucher wissenschaftlich geprüfte Daten im Bereich von Naturalien und Artefakten abrufen und erleben kann. Wichtig ist, daß er im Museum mit dem Original konfrontiert wird, also nicht mit der second hand reality. Hier liegt der eigentliche Grundgedanke – nicht die Bildungsexplosion – für den vermehrten Besucherandrang in den Museen. Nach 1968, 1969 verdoppelten sich in den großen Museen schlagartig die Besucherzahlen.

Man kann darüber diskutieren, ob die Museen sich wirklich dieser aufbrausenden Neugier gestellt haben. Nachweisbar sind strukturelle Veränderungen: die waren notwendig, von der Eingangshalle, dem Foyer, bis zu den Toilettenanlagen; fraglich aber ist es, ob sie sich auch in ihrer inneren Struktur geändert haben.

Denn welche Möglichkeiten gäbe es da? In eine postmoderne Gesellschaft, in der keine Wertungen mehr vorgenommen werden, sondern alle Dinge gleichwertig nebeneinandergestellt werden, ist ein sogenannter Enzyklopädismus eingezogen, der zum Beispiel Begriffe wie Freiheit oder Autobahn in der gleichen Länge enzyklopädisch behandeln würde. Wir werten nicht mehr, wir setzen keine Prioritäten mehr. Die Toleranz überholt sich selbst. Umgesetzt in den Bereich des Museums würde dies heißen, daß zum Beispiel das Kunstmuseum enzyklopädisch arbeitet, das heißt, strenggenommen, alphabetisch. Da das Internationale weiterhin gefragt ist, würde es im Museum des 20. Jahrhunderts zum Beispiel bei Josef Albers beginnen und bei Ossip Zadkine enden. Der Besucher wüßte genau, daß alle Daten über Picasso, Pablo, etwa nach zwei Dritteln der Gesamtstrecke abzurufen sind. Dieses Museum hätte am besten eine Zwangswegeführung, damit die alphabetische Ordnung eingehalten wird. Klar und präzise gliedert sich die Sammlung, die Lücken werden spielend übergangen, Dinge stehen nebeneinander, die durch den Zufall des Alphabets zusammengeführt wurden. Daniel Spoerri hat in seinen künstlichen Museen des Zufalls (Musée sentimentale) diese Po-

and this applies to the past just as it does to the present or the future – is that place where the visitor can summon and experience scientifically verified data in the field of natural objects and artefacts. What is important is that, in the museum, he is confronted with the original, i.e. not with a second-hand reality. It was this fundamental idea – and not the education explosion – which was really behind the increased throng of visitors to museums. Visitor figures double at a stroke in the large museums after 1968, 1969.

It is debatable whether museums have really responded to this surge of interest. What can be ascertained are structural changes. These were necessary: from the entrance hall and the foyer, to the toilet facilities. However, it is questionable whether museums have also changed as far as their inner structure is concerned. For what possibilities did they have? In a post-modern society, where value-judgements are no longer made and everything is placed on an equal footing with everything else, the so-called encyclopaedism which has emerged, which would treat terms such as 'freedom' or 'the motorway', for example, in the same encyclopaedic manner. We no longer make any value-judgements, we no longer order our priorities. Tolerance outstrips itself. Translated into the museum sector, this would mean that the museum of art, for example, worked encyclopaedically, i.e. strictly speaking, alphabetically. Since the international scene is still in demand, in the Museum of the 20th Century it would begin, for example, with Albers, Josef and end with Zadkin, Ossip. The visitor would know exactly that all data about Picasso, Pablo, could be called up after about ⅔ of the total distance. At best, this museum would have a compulsory route, so that people would keep to the alphabetical order. The collection is organised in a clear and precise manner, the gaps are easily passed over, those things stand next to each other which have been brought together by alphabetical chance. Daniel Spoerri has already attempted this position in his artificial museums of chance (Musée sentimentale). All the conflicting apparently irreconcilable elements which frequently give the

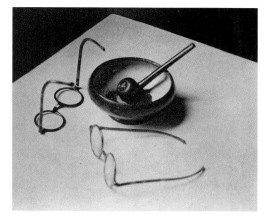

André Kertész, *Mondrians Brillen und Pfeife*, Paris, 1926
André Kertész, *Mondrian's Glasses and Pipe*, Paris, 1926

Man Ray, *Pablo Picasso*, Paris, 1932

sitionen bereits versucht. Das Gegeneinander, das scheinbar nicht miteinander Vereinbare, das der bildenden Kunst oft kohärent ist, würde sich im Zusammenspiel gegenseitig ausreizen. Dennoch wäre Logik und Ordnung gegeben.

Da Museen neben ihren klassischen Aufgaben aber – und hier liegt eine eklatante Veränderung ihrer Verhältnisse vor – also neben dem Sammeln, Konservieren, Präsentieren und Vermitteln – noch die Aufgabe hinzugewonnen haben, Geld zu verdienen, das heißt für einen budgetären Ausgleich selbst zu sorgen, kämen auch andere Gliederungsversuche in die Diskussion. Zum Beispiel die kapitalistische Ordnung. Das Museum, bleiben wir doch beim Kunstmuseum, beginnt mit den billigen Bildern, kommt dann mit den etwas teureren weiter, steigert sich also von Saal zu Saal in den Versicherungssummen der Bilder, die ihrerseits ein Spiegel der Marktwerte sind. Natürlich bedeutet dies, daß nach jedem Saal der Eintritt erhöht wird. Der Massenandrang vor Pablo Picasso würde somit verhindert, da bis zu Picasso so viel Geld zu zahlen wäre, daß die Einsamkeit vor dem Bilde gesichert ist. Der Ökonom würde sagen: Der Preis reguliert die Knappheiten. Durch eine hohe Preisgestaltung würden Knappheiten, zum Beispiel an Besucherraum, abgeschafft: Knappheiten auch in der Bekanntschaft mit dem Bild. Zugleich aber würden ausreichende, für wenige Erlesene konzipierte kulturelle Räume gewonnen werden, in denen der sogenannte Kunstgenuß nach erfolgtem Obolus besonders intensiv sein kann. Der Preis wäre so hoch anzusetzen, daß die Allgemeinheit den besonderen Besucher vor dem besonderen Werk nicht mehr stört.

Beide Präsentationstypen wären da konsequent und logisch, auch der Allgemeinheit sicherlich verständlich zu machen. Sie würden zwar nicht mehr den wissenschaftlichen Paradigmen, den Bindungen des Museums an seine Inhalte entsprechen, aber doch deutlich machen, daß die Inhalte im Museum dazu da sind, im Zuge der Vermittlung sich selbst zu finanzieren, das Institut mit zu tragen, sich selbst einzuspielen.

Es ist die gleiche Ordnung, die darin be-

visual arts its coherency, would be constantly outdoing one another in such an ensemble. Yet logic and order would be given.

However, in addition to the classical responsibilities of museums (and here there is a striking change in their circumstances) – i.e. besides collecting, conserving, presenting and mediating – they have now also acquired the task of earning money, i.e. of ensuring their own budgetary solvency. As a result, other organisational experiments would also come up for discussion. For example, the capitalistic order. The Museum (let us keep to the museum of art) begins with the cheap pictures, then continues with something more expensive, and thus from room to room there is a constant increase in the insurance sums commanded by the paintings, which in their turn reflect the market values. Naturally, this means that the entry price increases after each room. The throng of the crowd in front of Pablo Picasso would in this way be prevented, since by the time one reached Picasso there would be so much money to pay that solitude in front of the picture would be guaranteed. The economist would say that price regulates scarcity. By having high prices, some scarcities would be abolished; for example, a scarcity of space for visitors, or a scarcity of familiarity with the picture. At the same time, however, there would be enough cultural space available for what is less select, since the so-called enjoyment of art can be particularly intensive once the corresponding obulus is paid. The price would be set so high that the public at large would not disturb the special visitor in front of the special work of art.

Both these kinds of presentation would therefore be consistent and logical, and could even be made comprehensible for the general public. It would, indeed, no longer correspond to scholarly paradigms, to the museum's commitment to its collections; yet it would make it clear that the contents of the museum are there to finance themselves in the course of mediation, to bear part of the responsibility for the institute, to bring in the takings.

It is the same kind of order as that which would consist in improving the finances of

stehen würde, die Finanzen des Museums dadurch zu verbessern, daß Dinge verkauft werden, die scheinbar nicht von besonderem Wert und überflüssig sind. Das Museum als Dokumentation, als Datenbank der Geschichte hätte damit überlebt. Es wäre statt dessen immer aktuell, es wäre immer anders, es müßte sich permanent umgruppieren, die Bilder müßten täglich neu befragt werden, neue Versicherungssummen festgelegt werden, Bilder müßten verschoben werden, weil zum Beispiel in der Gruppe zwischen O und P ein neues Bild einzieht, ein neuer Künstler sein Platzrecht beansprucht. Der Generationenstreit wird alphabetisch oder finanziell geordnet geführt.

Die ursprüngliche Wirkung von Museen wäre damit hinfällig. Die Museen wären nicht mehr jene Institute, die mit wissenschaftlicher Methodik, also streng fachlich orientiert, ganz bestimmte und von anderen Institutionen nicht oder nur selten solcherweise behandelte Fragengruppen angehen. Das Institut Museum als Fachinstitut hätte ausgespielt, denn die geprüften Fakten wären dann auch nicht mehr das, was der Besucher sucht.

Die Verwaltung des Großteils des geistigen Besitzes der Menschheit als Orte von Präsentation wäre zwar im Prinzip durch das Museum weiterhin gewährleistet, aber die Allgemeinheit könnte nicht mehr mit fachlichem Wissensgut sowie mit gewachsenem Kunst- und Kulturgut in einer geklärten Ordnung im Sinne von Bildungsgut konfrontiert werden. Das Museum würde sich auf lange Sicht dem kurzlebigen Tagesgeschehen hingeben anstatt ihm enthoben zu sein, um der menschlichen Gemeinschaft Aussagen mit Maßstabfunktionen vorzustellen. Das Museum würde sich in fataler Weise jenem Zustand nähern, den Soziologen schlichtweg mit Disneyland bezeichnen. Neue Museumsbauten nähern sich dem Container- beziehungsweise Silogedanken als Hülle für Entertainment. Konsequenterweise sollten die Renditeberechnungen der Gebäude – zum Beispiel beim Centre Beaubourg - diese relativen Kurzlebigkeiten einer Immobilie inkludieren. Auf ein Neues! Alle zehn Jahre ein anderer Bau. Das Museum als Markenname.

the museum by selling things which are apparently not of any special value and are superfluous. The museum as a documentary record, as a databank of history, would survive. It would be always up-to-date, it would always be different, it would have to be permanently regrouped, the pictures would have to be considered anew every day, new insurance sums would have to be fixed; and pictures shifted around, because, for example, in the group between O and P a new picture was moving in, a new artist was demanding his right to a place. The conflict between the generations would be carried on according to alphabetical or financial order.

The original effect of museums would then be invalid. Museums would no longer be institutions which, proceeding by means of the scholarly method (i.e. in a rigorously specialised way), dealt with quite definite groups of questions which were not – or only rarely – dealt with in the same way by other institutions. As a specialist institution, the museum would be finished, for the verified facts would then also no longer be what the visitor wanted.

The administration of the greater part of the intellectual possessions of mankind in places of presentation would indeed continue to be guaranteed by the museum in principle, yet the general public could no longer be confronted by specialist knowledge or by well-developed artistic and cultural assets with a definite system, in the sense of a cultural tradition. In the long term, the museum would surrender to the ephemeral events of everyday life instead of remaining above them and presenting the human community with statements which serve as standards. The museum would come fatally close to that state which sociologists simply designate as 'Disneyland'. New museum buildings are approaching the container or silo concept as an exterior form for entertainment. Logically, calculations of the rentability of the buildings – e.g. in the case of the Centre Beaubourg – should include the relatively short-lived nature of real estate. To the next one! Every ten years another building. The museum as a brand name.

This change in the direction of Disneyland, this Disneyland-isation of the museum

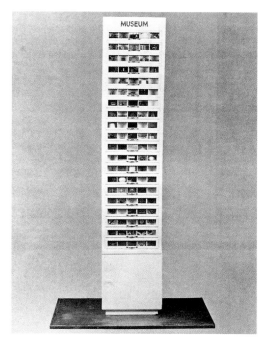

Michael Levin, *The Modern Museum*, Tel Aviv, 1983

Claes Oldenburg, Fassadenentwurf für das
Museum der zeitgenössischen Kunst, Chicago,
in Form einer geometrischen Maus, 1967
Claes Oldenburg, Proposal for the façade of the
Museum of Contemporary Art, Chicago, in the
shape of a geometric mouse, 1967

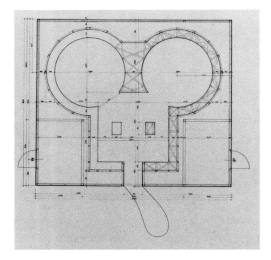

Claes Oldenburg, Architektenplan für ein Maus
Museum auf der Documenta 5, 1972
Claes Oldenburg, Architect's Plan for the Maus
Museum at Documenta 5, 1972

Diese Wende zum Disneyland, diese Disneylandisierung des Museumswesens, findet in der Tat seit langem statt. Es gibt immer wieder nur einen Begriff, der zur Rechtfertigung herangezogen wird: das Geld. Kultur unter dem Diktat des McDonald-Prinzips. Schneller Konsum, schneller Wechsel, ständig frische Ware. Humboldt verkümmert im Kleinhirn. In dem Moment, in dem die Gesellschaft das Museum an den Pranger seiner Finanzierbarkeit stellt, stellt sie das Museum selbst in Frage. Errungenschaften der Französischen Revolution, daß die Bürger ein Recht auf Kultur haben, ohne staatliche Zwangsbeglückungen, werden wieder über die finanzielle Schiene geläutert. Das Museum verschreibt sich einem Populismus, es ist nicht mehr theoriebildend, nicht mehr theorievermittelnd, es folgt der postmodernen These, daß »Theorie Terrorismus« ist (J.-F. Lyotard). Es stellt sich die Frage, wie lange das Publikum solch eine Trendwende von Museum akzeptiert. Es ist vorauszusehen, daß diese Leichtigkeit des Seins, die auch unser Museum mehr und mehr durchzieht, irgendwann abgelehnt wird. Das Museum ist nicht die Stätte von Ereigniskultur, diese sollten wir dem Theater, der Oper, der Operette, dem Musical, den Experimentierbühnen überlassen.

Das Museum der Moderne spiegelt immer noch jener schöne Satz des Begründers des Museum of Modern Art, Mr. Barr jun.: »Das Museum ist ein Labor, das Publikum ist eingeladen, an den Experimenten teilzunehmen.«

Experimente aber sind nicht mehr möglich, wenn Populismus betrieben wird. Die Sucht nach Großausstellungen, das Sichgegenseitige-Erschlagen durch Statistiken und die Einnahmenhöhepunkte werden sich totlaufen. Das Publikum wird die Kopien, die Imitationen nicht mehr erwerben wollen, denn es wird erkennen müssen, daß es Schund und Tand erworben hat. Schtonk! Dennoch sind die Museen – gezwungen auch durch politische Diktionen – auf dem besten Wege ins goldene Disneyland. Die Museen werden zum Goldenen Kalb, das man anbetet, das man braucht, um Ernsthaftigkeiten zu vergessen, um sich zu verlustieren. In der Tat waren Museen immer Orte auch der De-

system has in actual fact been going on for a long time. There is only one concept which is always used to justify this: money. Culture under the dictates of the Macdonald principle. Fast consumption, fast succession, constantly fresh goods. Humboldt wastes away in the cerebellum. At that moment in which society places the museum in the stocks of its financeability, the museum itself is in jeopardy. Achievements dating back to the French Revolution, such as that citizens have a right to culture without compulsory state favours, are once again being purged, this time by financial means. The museum is devoted to populism, it no longer establishes theories, no longer communicates theories, it follows the post-modern thesis that "theory is terrorism" (J.-F. Lyotard). The question is, how long the public will accept such a new trend from the museum. It is foreseeable that this lightness of being, which increasingly pervades our museums too, will at some point meet with rejection. The museum is not a place of 'events culture'; that should be left to the theatre, the opera, the operetta, the musical and to experimental theatres.

The modernist museum still reflects that beautiful sentence by the founder of the Museum of Modern Art, Mr. Barr jun.: "The museum is a laboratory, and the public is invited to take part in the experiments."

But experiments are no longer possible when populism is being practised. The obsession with big exhibitions which trump each other for statistics and record takings will run its course. The public will no longer want to acquire the copies, the imitations; for it will have to recognise that it has acquired trash and trumpery. Shtonk! And yet the museums are following the best road to Disneyland – forced to do so by political styles. The museums are becoming the golden calf which is worshipped, which is needed in order to forget more serious matters, to amuse oneself. Of course, museums were always also places of delectation, but they were also always places for learning, for collecting one's thoughts, for understanding.

I am not concerned with redeeming the museum as a 'learning situation' (a typical expression of the 70s), by saying that a

lektierung, aber sie waren auch immer Orte des Lernens, des Sich-Sammelns, des Verstehens. Es geht mir nicht darum, das Museum als Lernort, ein typischen Ausdruck der siebziger Jahre, dadurch abzulösen, daß man sagt, das Museum, zum Beispiel das der bildenden Künste, ist ein Ort der reinen Sinne. Doch Museen im kulturellen Bereich dienen vermehrt Ratio und Emotion. Sie müssen die Waage im Gleichgewicht halten, sie dürfen nicht nur das Eine, geschweige denn auch nur das Andere sein. Da sie etwas aufbewahren, das ohne sie unwiderruflich verlorengegangen wäre, da sie dennoch resistent gegen politische Unvernunft bleiben könnten, spricht vieles dafür, das Museum als Museum zu erhalten.

Als fanatischer, leidenschaftlicher Museumsmann glaube ich weniger an das Museum als Institution denn an die Inhalte im Museum. Die Kunstwerke sind es, die Artefakte, die Naturalien, die als Energiespender täglich vitalisierend die Institution tragen. Die Institution darf man in Frage stellen, nicht aber ihre Inhalte. Das heißt aber, daß es Bindungen gibt, die auch bei der Aufbereitung der Inhalte mitverantwortlich sind. Das Museum kann nicht so tun, als ob es eine reine Abendschule oder gar ein Forum der Ablenkung sei. Wenn der Adorno-Satz stimmt, daß in Zeiten von vermehrter Freizeit es darum gehe, »diese Freizeit in Freiheit« umspringen zu lassen, dann ist das Museum als Institution ein viel zu wichtiger Ort. Er ist jene kulturelle Option, in der ohne zusätzliche große Investitionen – der Museumsboom widerspricht dem nicht – kulturelle Funktionen für die Gesellschaft wahrgenommen werden, weil die Museen nicht an Sitzplatz-Kapazitäten, wie zum Beispiel das Theater oder die Oper, gebunden sind.

Dennoch ist davor zu warnen, die Museen wie Theater zu führen. Sie brauchen keine Intendanten! Sie brauchen Wissenschaftler, die die Verantwortung für das Museum übernehmen. Diesen können Manager hinzugesellt werden, die auf Zeit Öffentlichkeitsfunktionen wahrnehmen, die im Bereich der Vermittlung und der Ausstellungen tätig sind.

Es ist in der Tat davon auszugehen, daß Museen Institute sind, in denen ein not-

museum, for example a museum of the fine arts, is a place of pure sensuality. Museums are increasingly coming to serve both reason and emotion in the arts. They have to maintain a state of balance, they are not allowed to do only the one thing – let alone only the other. There is much to be said for keeping the museum as a museum, since museums preserve something which, without them, would have disappeared for ever; yet they have nevertheless managed to continue to resist political irrationality.

As a fanatical, passionate museum man myself, I believe less in the museum as an institution than in the contents of the museum. It is the works of art, the artefacts, the natural objects which are the daily sources of energy that keep the institution alive. The institution may be called into question, but its contents may not. However, this means that there are some responsibilities which also play a role in the work of preparing the contents. The museum cannot act as if it were simply an evening class, or even a forum for diversion. If Adorno was right when he said that in an age of increased leisure time, it is a matter of letting this leisure time leap around "in freedom", then the museum as an institution is far too important a place. It states that cultural option in which, without additional large-scale investment (and the museum boom does not contradict that), cultural functions are recognised as being there for society, because museums are not tied to seating capacities, as are, for example, theatres or opera houses.

Nevertheless, one ought to warn against managing the museums like theatres. They do not need managers. They need scholars who can take over responsibility for the museum. These could be assisted by managers, entrusted with public functions for a period of time, who work in the field of mediation and exhibitions.

In fact, one may assume that museums are institutions in which a necessary change in society's consciousness can be achieved. With all the regionalism dominant in postmodernism, we are learning that man will live a mobile existence and be at home in a large area, that he is part of an international framework; that he must learn to think super-terrestially, i.e. planetarily, in

Paul Outerbridge Jr., *Abstraction*, 1922

wendiger Bewußtseinswandel der Gesellschaft vollzogen werden kann. Bei allem postmodern dominanten Regionalismus lernen wir, daß der Mensch ortsbeweglich und großräumig leben wird, daß er im internationalen Gefüge steht, daß er außerirdisch, also planetarisch denken lernen muß, um dennoch immer wieder zu sehen, daß die Limits und die Enge, die Begrenztheit seines Lebensraumes und die Unentrinnbarkeit auf der Kugeloberfläche unüberwindbar sind.

Wissen, Wollen und Erleben verlangen von jedem Erdenbürger hohe seelische Kräfte, die er für sich und die Gemeinschaft einsetzen muß, wenn ein friedliches Miteinander gewährleistet werden soll, wenn Gerechtigkeit und Toleranz keine hohlen Begriffe bleiben sollen. Bei diesem Prozeß, bei dieser Utopie, können nicht nur analytisch arbeitende Fachinstitute, also Universitätsinstitute mitwirken, vielmehr müssen sich diesen Aufgaben die kulturellen Einrichtungen als das Ganze umfassende und ästhetische Möglichkeit stellen. Museen können Erkenntniswerte mit Erlebniswerten verbinden, sie können den geistigen Hunger ebenso stillen wie sie die seelische Vereinsamung aufheben können.

Das heißt auch, daß das Museum implizit nach außen, zum Besucher hin gerichtet sein muß. Museen haben verschiedene Aufgaben, die sie als wissenschaftliche Institute ebenso ausweisen wie als Zentren der Information, der Dokumentation und Bildungspflege. Nur das kann sinnvoll vermittelt werden, was ich kenne, was ich wissenschaftlich erarbeitet habe. Ein Haas-Haus ersetzt keinen Abteiberg!

Als wissenschaftliche Institute sind die Museen verpflichtet, an einer neuen Bestandsaufnahme der natürlichen Dinge der Welt und der Artefakte auf der Erde in bezug auf Zeit und Raum und in bezug auf den Menschen mitzuwirken. In ihnen besteht eine Bestandsdokumentation, die wissenschaftliche Fragestellungen zu zeitlichen und räumlichen, ökologischen Beziehungen erlaubt. Deshalb sind die Museen als wissenschaftliche Institute wichtig, wenn Planungen in bezug auf Gestaltung unserer Umwelt anstehen. Sind sie wichtig, um rationale und emotionale Erschließungen

order nevertheless to realise time and again the insuperability of the limits, narrowness and restrictedness of his 'living space' and the ineluctability of his life on the surface of the globe.

Knowledge, desire and experience require great spiritual strength of every citizen of the earth; strength which has to be employed for oneself and for the community if peaceful coexistence is to be ensured, if justice and tolerance are not to remain simply empty notions. It is not only specialist institutions working analytically, i.e. university institutes, which have a part to play in this process, in this utopia: cultural institutions, too, have to face these tasks as an aesthetic possibility which encompasses the whole. Museums can combine perceptual values with experiential values, they can satisfy intellectual hunger just as they can also counteract spiritual isolation. This also means that the museum has to be implicitly oriented to the outside world, to the visitor. Museums have a variety of duties which make them scholarly institutions as well as centres of information, documentation and education. Only that which I know, that which I have studied in a scholarly way, can be sensibly mediated. A Haas Haus cannot replace an Abteiberg Museum.

As scholarly institutions, museums are under the obligation to collaborate on a new inventory of natural things in the world and of artefacts on the earth, in relation to time and space and in relation to human beings. They provide a documentary record of what exists, which allows scholarly questions to be asked concerning temporal, spatial and ecological relationships. Which is why museums, as scholarly institutions, are important when we come to consider measures relating to the organisation of our environment. They are important in enabling rational and emotional inferences about society to be made.

On the other hand, they are 'showcases', i.e. places of information, for learning about and understanding the connections between things, places for taking in the pictorial and cultural heritage, places for reliving the past, for experiencing the present and reflecting the future. Museums are places of communication. Museums are places for

der Gesellschaft zu ermöglichen. Andererseits sind sie Schaumuseen, also Orte von Information, des Lernens und Verstehens von Zusammenhängen, Orte der Aufnahme von Bildgut und Bildungsgut, Orte des Erlebnisses des Vergangenen, des Erlebens der Gegenwart und der Reflexion des Zukünftigen. Museen sind Stätten der Kommunikation. Museen sind Orte der »seelischen Gesunderhaltung«. (Wilhelm Schäfer) Museen entsprechen gesellschaftlichen Bedürfnissen. Oder?

Es stellt sich neu die Frage, ob die Museen auch diesen gesellschaftlichen Bedürfnissen entsprechen. Es ist nachzuweisen, daß in den letzten Jahrzehnten Museen sich mehr und mehr dem Informationsdruck gebeugt haben. Desgleichen spiegeln die Präsentationen, die Ankäufe, Erwerbungen, die ganzen infrastrukturellen Setzungen diese neuen Bedürfnisse wider. Ein Museum ohne Museumspädagogik ist heute außerkakanisch kaum denkbar.

Die Museumspädagogik versucht sich seit einigen Jahren aus der schulischen Versklavung herauszuschleichen; wir sprechen lieber von Bildung und Kommunikation. Wir wollen nicht mehr den Menschen, der dem Körper erlaubt, seinen Kopf zu begleiten, Museen sind nicht mehr nur Orte der Ratio, sondern des Erlebnisses. Insofern haben die Museen mit allen Mitteln und Techniken, Medien, Aktivitäten auf die neuen Anforderungen reagiert. Deshalb sind sie nicht unbedingt besucherfreundlicher geworden. Die These würde lauten: Die Museen sind trotzdem vermehrt besucht worden, obwohl sie als relativ konservative Institutionen gar nicht so schnell reagieren konnten. Die jetzigen Umstellungen sind eigentlich Reaktionen auf Forderungen von vor zwanzig Jahren: Forderungen des Publikums.

Das Publikum hat die Museen trotzdem erobert, es hat den Museen die Schläfrigkeit nicht übelgenommen. Die sogenannte Schwellenangst, von der wir immer sprechen, erweist sich im nachhinein als eine Erfindung des Feuilletons. Das Publikum hat keine Angst, es ist neugierig, es will wissen, es will be-greifen, letzteres zum Entsetzen der Aufseher im Museum. Das Publikum will wieder Realität begreifen, der Betrachter will verstehen und lernen.

the "preservation of spiritual health" (Wilhelm Schäfer). Museums correspond to social needs. Or do they?

The question of whether museums do actually correspond to these social needs should be asked again. It can be proved that, in the past few decades, museums have yielded more and more to the pressure of information. And these new needs are also reflected in the presentation, purchasing, acquisitions, in the whole orientation of the infrastructure. A museum without museum pedagogics is today hardly conceivable outside of Kakania (Musil).

For some time now, museum pedagogics has sought to escape from its school-like enslavement; we prefer to speak of education and communication. We no longer want people who simply allow their bodies to accompany their heads; museums are no longer places of reason, but of experience. In this respect the museums have reacted to the new requirements with all the means and technology, media and activities at their disposal. For all that, they have not necessarily become visitor-friendly. The thesis would be: the number of visitors to museums has increased, despite the fact that, as relatively conservative institutions, they are not able to react very quickly at all. The present reorganisation activities are actually reactions to demands dating back twenty years: the demands of the public.

The public has conquered the museums nonetheless; it was not offended by the museums' sluggishness. In retrospect, the so-called *Schwellenangst* or 'entrance phobia', the fear of entering a place, which we are always speaking about, has proved to be an invention of the feuilletons. The public is not afraid, it is inquisitive, it wants to know, it wants to grasp things (much to the horror of museum attendants). The public wants to comprehend reality, the spectator wants to understand and learn. The museum also enjoys high social acceptance. However, it could lose this. It can deliver as many exhibitions as it wishes, but it should never deny its own collections. Shamefully enough, a trend can be discerned in which all the museum's energies are taken up by short-term activities, denying the long-term goals, such as the maintenance and expansion of the collection. It

Roy Lichtenstein, *Vergrößerungsglas*, 1963
Roy Lichtenstein, *Magnifying Glass*, 1963

Das Museum hat also eine hohe gesellschaftliche Akzeptanz. Diese allerdings kann es verlieren. Es kann mehr und mehr Ausstellungen liefern, aber es sollte nie seine Sammlungen negieren. In beschämender Weise ist jener Trend zu erkennen, der aufzeigt, daß alle Energien in kurzfristige Aktivitäten hineingesteigert werden, um die langfristigen Ziele, die Pflege und den Ausbau der Sammlung, zu negieren. Es ist festzustellen, daß viele Museen sich mehr und mehr von sich selbst entfremden. Diese Entfremdung spürt das Publikum, es kommt zu den Vernissagen, die anderen Tage bleibt das Museum leer. Immer dort, wo der Ereignischarakter im Museum forciert wird, muß man sich fragen, ob dieser Ereignischarakter auch den eigentlichen Werten der Sammlung entspricht. Museen sind keine Theater, sondern Ankäufer.

Ein Museum kann keine Ausstellung machen, die wichtiger ist als die Sammlung. Dennoch ist das Museum zunehmend ein Ausstellungsinstitut geworden. Das war es nicht von seinen ursprünglichen Intentionen her. Es sollte deshalb bedenken, daß es primär seiner Sammlung verantwortlich ist. Doch die Kustoden und Direktoren kennen immer weniger ihre Sammlung. Statt dessen schwärmen sie immer mehr von vergangenen Ausstellungen, sie erkennen nicht mehr die präzisen Wertvorstellungen, die die eigene, immer gegenwärtige Sammlung bedeutet. Das heißt, sie können mit dieser Sammlung nicht mehr umgehen; sie können sie nicht mehr ausstellen, sie können sie nicht mehr vermitteln. Das Bleibende im Museum wird in Frage gestellt zugunsten durchreisender Werte, die oft nach zwei bis drei Jahren schon vergessen sind. Hier, in diesem Bereich, müssen die Alarmglocken läuten. Wenn das Museum seine Beziehungen, emotionale wie wissenschaftliche, rationale wie instinktive Bindungen an die Sammlungsinhalte und ihre Werte mehr und mehr reduziert, um schnellen Setzungen den vermehrten Zugriff als eigentliche gesellschaftliche Option zu gewähren, wird das Museum Teil eines Kulturkarussells, das ebenso wie das Theater vom Spielplan lebt, aber nicht mehr von den Sammlungen.

can be established that many museums are becoming increasingly alienated from themselves. The public can sense this alienation: it comes to the openings, but on the other days the museum remains empty. Wherever the 'events-character' of the museum is forced, one has to enquire whether this 'events-character' also corresponds to the actual values of the collection. Museums are not theatres, but purchasers.

A museum cannot put on an exhibition which is more important than its collection. Nevertheless, the museum has increasingly become an institution for staging exhibitions. This was not the original intention. Museums should therefore bear in mind that they are primarily responsible to their own collections. Yet the curators and directors know ever less and less about their collections. Instead, they increasingly enthuse about past exhibitions, no longer realising the precise set of values represented by their own ever-present collections. This means that they are unable to cope with their respective collections; they are unable to exhibit it any more, unable to mediate it. The permanent element of the museum is called into question, in favour of transitory values which are often forgotten two or three years later. Here, in this sphere of activity, the alarm has to be sounded. If the museum is constantly reducing its relationships and commitments – both emotional and scholarly, rational and instinctive – to the contents and values of its collection, solely in order to allow increased scope for quick arrangements as an actual social option, then the museum becomes part of a cultural carousel, living – just like the theatre – from its programme, but not from its collection. On the battlefield of social reception, involving in everyday political policies, the museum behaves increasingly like an market factor, like a business institute. Branch offices are set up, further branches planned, new financial backers sought, museum combines (no, museum trusts) are set up. Art is exhibited, is surrendered using all means available, and a new kind of curiosity appears, quite in the sense of the voyeurism which Duchamp fought so hard against. Art is divested of its secrets, it loses its aura, its fascination is destroyed.

Das Museum auf dem Schlachtfeld der gesellschaftlichen Rezeption, eingebunden in die politische Tagespolitik, verhält sich mehr und mehr wie ein Wirtschaftsfaktor, wie ein Wirtschaftsinstitut. Zweigstellen werden errichtet, Filialen geplant, neue Geldgeber gesucht, Museumskombinate, nein, Museumstrusts entstehen. Kunst wird ausgestellt, wird preisgegeben mit allen Mitteln, eine neue Art von Neugier, ganz im Sinne eines Voyeurismus, den Marcel Duchamp so stark bekämpft hat, stellt sich ein. Die Kunst wird ihrer Geheimnisse entkleidet, die Aura geht verloren, das Faszinosum wird zerstört. Die Konsequenz bedeutet die Aktivierung des Bildes. Wie wäre es mit den Lichthackern einer Diskothek im Bruegel-Saal! Thrilling, isn't it? Echt stark.

Die Kunst kommt in Container, die auf Straßen und Bahnen verschiebbar sind; sie wird Ereignis, kurzfristig den Blicken ausgesetzt, woandershin verschoben, um neue Erregungen zu erzeugen. Die Kunst verliert ihren ernsthaften Charakter, die Museumsinhalte werden ihrer statischen, immanenten und langwährenden Eigenschaften beraubt. Nicht mehr die Qualitäten an sich sind gefragt, nur noch jene, die in der unmittelbaren zeitgebundenen, jetztzeitigen Rezeption gewinnbringend eingesetzt werden können. Die Kunstwerke verlieren ihre ureigensten Optionen, sie können sich nicht mehr entfalten, da sie gesellschaftlich zu nicht stimmberechtigten Partizipationsscheinen degradiert werden. Die Kunst wird nicht ausgestellt, sondern abgestellt, zumeist einfach hingestellt.

Die Frage nach den Kunstwerken im Zeitalter ihrer technischen Reproduzierbarkeit (Walter Benjamin) stellt sich neu. Umberto Eco hat die Frage aufgeworfen, die Frage nach dem offenen Kunstwerk, aber auch jene, was wichtiger sei, die Reproduktion oder das Original.

Im Grunde genommen dienen diese postmodernen Gedankenspiele nicht mehr dem Original, sondern dem Zitat. Der Ersatz, die Replik sind genauso wichtig wie das Original. Erst die Reproduktion schafft durch Bekanntwerden die Bewertung des Originals. Dieses selbst hat gar keine Chance mehr, aus eigener Kraft weiterzu-

The consequence of this is that the picture becomes activated. What about a discothèque lightshow in the Breughel rooms? Thrilling, isn't it? Really great.

Art comes in containers which can be transported by road and rail; it is an event, exposed to view for a short period of time, before being transported elsewhere to produce new excitations. Art is losing its serious character, the contents of museums are being robbed of their static, immanent and lasting qualities. Qualities as such are no longer called for, with the exception of those which can be profitably assured of an immediately fashionable reception here and now. Works of art are losing their most fundamental options, they can no longer develop, having been degraded socially to non-voting participation receipts. Art is not exhibited but deposited, and usually simply set down.

The question of the role of the work of art in an age of technological reproducibility (Walter Benjamin) can be reiterated. Umberto Eco has raised this question, as the question of the open work of art; and also another, which is even more important: the reproduction or the original?

Basically, this post-modern play of ideas no longer serves the original but the paraphrase. The substitute and the replica are just as important as the original. It is the reproduction which first creates valuation of the original by making it known. The latter no longer has any chance at all of continuing to grow by itself, to convince future spectators. It is bound fast, exactly defined, re-dimensioned, robbed of its actual capabilities, e.g. to breathe and to live. It becomes once again a document, a bearer of data. The exhibition tradition is becoming a virus to be identified, one which, in its aesthetic deduction, is at the same time abandoned to its destruction for having been recognised. Everything is neutralised, the tips are snipped off; it is no longer even necessary to sharpen the knives, for the times when the museum was required to be a necessary institution have long since passed.

It is a matter of defending the museum against its adversaries. As a scholarly institution, the museum has not deserved such proceedings, but it must face them.

wachsen, um künftige Betrachter zu überzeugen. Es wird festgebunden, auf den Punkt gebracht, re-dimensioniert, seiner eigentlichen Fähigkeiten, zum Beispiel zu atmen und zu leben, beraubt. Es wird wieder Dokument, Datenträger. Das Ausstellungsgut wird ein zu identifizierender Virus, der in der ästhetischen Deduktion zugleich der Vernichtung preisgegeben wird, weil er erkannt wird. Alles wird entschärft, die Spitzen werden gekappt, das Schleifen der Messer ist schon nicht mehr notwendig, denn das Diktat ist längst nicht mehr das nach dem Museum als einer notwendigen Institution.

Es gilt, das Museum gegen seine Anhänger zu verteidigen. Das Museum als wissenschaftliche Institution hat diese Vorgänge nicht verdient, aber es muß sich ihnen stellen. Es sei noch einmal davor gewarnt, dem Museum die wissenschaftliche Kompetenz zu entziehen. Wenn sie diese aufgibt, gibt es sich selbst auf. Es gibt sich auch deshalb auf, weil auf die Dauer keiner mehr hinkommen möchte, denn die Aussagen des Museums werden genauso belanglos wie die Tagespresse. Vielleicht wird es dann endlich der bequeme Ort als Fortsetzung der Politik mit pseudo-ästhetischen Mitteln. Diese Erkenntnis heißt, daß es darum gehen muß, das Museum vom politischen Geschehen freizuhalten, nicht von den gesellschaftlichen Aufgaben, nicht von den politischen Aussagen. Es geht nicht um die Entschärfung, sondern die Präzisierung. Wir dürfen nicht Aussagen kaschieren, nur weil sie vielleicht unangenehm sind. Wir müssen diese steigern, geradezu immer neu evozieren und provozieren. Das heißt: So wie die Künstler die Gesellschaft fordern, muß diese die Künstler auffordern. Denn fördern heißt auch fordern. Im Museum müssen diese Welten zusammenkommen, müssen die Fragestellungen brisant bleiben, akut werden. Es ist völlig egal, ob sie von einem Museum der zeitgenössischen Kunst, des 20. Jahrhunderts, des Barock, des Mittelalters usw. reden. Es ist gleichgültig, ob wir uns ein Museum der Künste, der Kultur, der Technik oder der Naturwissenschaften anschauen. Überall müssen bohrende Fragen mit immer steter Exaktheit beantwortet werden. Museen können dies,

One should beware of removing the museum from scholarly competence. When it renounces this then it renounces itself. And the reason it renounces itself is because, in the long run, nobody then wants to visit it any more, because the museum's statements become as meaningless as those of the daily papers. Perhaps it would then finally become a comfortable place for the continuation of politics with pseudo-aesthetic means. The import of this realisation is that it is a matter of keeping the museum free from politics, but not from social duties or from political statements. It is not a question of neutralising, but of specifying. We cannot afford to conceal statements simply because they are perhaps uncomfortable. We have to intensify them, evoking and provoking them time and again. This means that just as artists make demands on society, so the latter must also challenge the artists. For to support also means to challenge. These worlds have to come together in the museum; questioning has to remain explosive and become acute. It is completely irrelevant whether they are talking about a museum of contemporary art, of the 20th century, of the Baroque, the Middle Ages etc.. It does not matter whether we are looking at a museum of the fine arts, of culture, of technology or of science. Penetrating questions must be answered with ever more constant exactitude everywhere. Museums can do this, but one also has to let them do it.

My faith in the museum therefore seems to be still unbroken. Yet, as a museum man, I myself question this institution – for which I also share some responsibility – every day. It is, for example, shocking to see the academic arrogance with which employees work against the intentions of the works of art as such, because what they see in them is only this or that document for a certain thesis, because they are not capable – the university denies this possibility – of recognising works of art as living beings. I would seriously plead for a museum of the senses, for a living museum, for a museum which is fit place for debate. Museums are places of tolerance. In them, many things are united which are actually incompatible. In them, different world views are thrown

doch man muß auch die Museen lassen. Mein Glaube an das Museum ist also scheinbar dennoch ungebrochen. Doch als Museumsmann stelle ich diese Institution, die ich mitzuverantworten habe, täglich neu in Frage. Es ist zum Beispiel erschütternd zu sehen, mit welch akademischer Arroganz Mitarbeiter gegen die Intentionen von Kunstwerken an sich arbeiten, weil sie in jenen genau nur jene Dokumente für eine bestimmte These sehen, weil sie nicht in der Lage sind – die Universität verneint diese Möglichkeiten –, in Kunstwerken lebende Wesen zu erkennen. Ich plädiere ernsthaft für ein Museum der Sinne, für ein lebendes Museum, für ein Museum, das als Ort von Auseinandersetzungen tauglich ist. Museen sind Orte der Toleranz. In ihnen vereinigen sich viele Dinge, die eigentlich unvereinbar sind. In ihnen stürzen Weltbilder auf kleinstem Raum aufeinander, in ihnen aber wird auch der Benutzer aufgefordert, da er selbst den Ablauf der Chronologie vorgibt, sich mit diesem Aufeinanderprallen, mit diesen erstaunlichen Ergebnissen auseinanderzusetzen. Deshalb sind Museen anstrengende Orte.

Ich könnte mir vorstellen, aber das wäre eine Utopie, die eigentlich so auch nicht realisierbar ist, daß ich zigarrerauchend durch ein Kunstmuseum gehe, daß alle halbe Stunde ein Servierwagen mit einer freundlichen Bedienung vorbeikommt, die nicht nur Kognak serviert oder Kaffee anbietet, sondern zugleich auch über Rubens informiert. Diese Freiheiten sind uns nicht gegeben – die Fragilität der Kunstwerke ist zu groß. Das heißt, wir tragen große Verantwortungen.

Immer noch nehmen Museen glücklicherweise ihren Auftrag des Bewahrens wahr. Da heißt, sie konservieren die Gemälde, sie setzen sie hinter Glas, sie schützen sie paradoxerweise vor dem Publikum. Und mit Recht: Denn dieses Publikum reagiert immer aggressiver, fast pathologisch. Das ist kein Widerspruch zu früheren Aussagen, sondern nur eine strikte Reaktion auf die fast vorgeschriebenen Verhaltensweisen. Das Bild als Bild wird nicht mehr reflektiert, deswegen gehört es unter reflektierende Glasscheiben. Es wird zum Schutz seiner selbst, zur Sicherheit seiner

together in a very small space. In them, too, the visitor is asked to study this clash of opposites, study these astonishing results, since he determines the sequence of the chronology himself. This is why museums are such strenuous places.

I can imagine – although it would be a utopia which is not actually realisable as such – that I am permitted to walk through a museum of art smoking a cigar, that a friendly service trolley comes along every half-an-hour, not only serving cognac or coffee but also providing me with information about Rubens. These freedoms are not granted to us – the fragility of works of art is too great for that. Which means that we ourselves have a very great responsibility.

Fortunately enough, museums still take their job of preservation seriously. This means that they preserve paintings, they place them behind glass, they protect them – paradoxically enough, from the public. And with justification. For this public reacts ever more aggressively, even pathologically. That does not contradict what was said earlier, it is only a extreme reaction to the almost prescribed ways of behaving. The picture as a picture is no longer reflected upon, and for that reason it belongs behind self-reflecting plates of glass. For its own protection, for the safety of its own physical presence it is increasingly placed in a cage. Actually, that contradicts that important paragraph about the freedom of art in the civil code. I am not now referring to those politicians who judge works of art without having ever seen, experienced or heard them, but that truth which says that art can only arise where extreme freedom rules. For me, it is no coincidence that there was no serious building activity in Austria until Parliament passed a law promoting it in 1986.

That means that the museum must also be in a position to present this freedom, to guarantee it for its works of art.

We know that museums are places of manipulation. Museum people are supposed to agree with these manipulations, for they determine which work hangs next to which, which aesthetic and optical interactions are desirable and which should be avoided. However, the problem

Dorothea Lange, *Die Straße in den Westen*, New Mexico, 1938
Dorothea Lange, *The Road West*, New Mexico, 1938

physischen Präsenz, mehr und mehr in den Käfig gesteckt. Das widerspricht eigentlich jenem wichtigen Paragraphen der Freiheit der Kunst im Grundgesetz. Ich meine jetzt nicht jene Politiker, die die Kunstwerke beurteilen, ohne sie jemals gesehen, erfahren oder gehört zu haben, sondern jene Wahrheit, die besagt, daß Kunst nur dort entstehen kann, wo äußerste Freiheit herrscht.

Das heißt, das Museum müßte in der Lage sein, diese Freiheit auch zu präsentieren, sie den Kunstwerken zu garantieren. Wir wissen, daß Museen Orte der Manipulation sind. Museumsleute sollten ja zu diesen Manipulationen sagen, denn sie bestimmen, welches Werk neben welchem hängt, welche ästhetischen und optischen Interaktionen erwünscht sind oder vermieden werden sollen. Das Problem ist ein anderes. Dort, wo Zerstörung droht, wird Freiheit eingeschränkt. Ich plädiere lebhaft dafür, daß nicht die Freiheit der Kunst eingeschränkt wird, sondern die Freiheit des Publikums. Es könnte die Kunst genauso gut betrachten, wenn die Kunstwerke auf den Rängen der Manege säßen, das Publi-

is a different one. Where destruction threatens, freedom is restricted. I sincerely plead that not the freedom of art should be restricted, but the freedom of the public. The latter could look at art just as well if the works of art were placed in the ringside seating and the public were separated from the works of art like wild animals by bars. The idea of the circus has always impressed me, it really should be extended to serve the cause of art. For in actual fact, the wild animals are the works of art, the contents of the collection, the accusations of history, the visions of the future which lead one astray to aggressiveness. It is the pictures that are aggressive, their originality, the contents of museums; the public should be protected from them. It belongs, paradoxically enough, in the cage.

This idea is not heretical, it has been attempted time and time again. Barriers, video supervision, Big Brother is watching you, his master's voice warning you to keep your distance – all play an ever more important role. Alarm systems, buzzing, piping, shrill sounds characterise the visit to a museum more and more, not however

kum aber wie die wilden Raubtiere durch die Gitter vor den Kunstwerken geschützt wird. Diese Zirkusvorstellung hat mir immer imponiert, sie müßte zugunsten von Kunst erweitert werden. Denn in der Tat sind die wilden Tiere die Kunstwerke, die Sammlungsinhalte, die Vorwürfe der Geschichte, die Visionen für die Zukunft, die zur Aggressivität verleiten. Das Aggressive sind die Bilder, sind die Eigenarten, die Inhalte der Museen, das Publikum muß davor geschützt werden. Es gehört, paradoxerweise, in den Käfig.

Dieser Gedanke ist nicht ketzerisch, sondern immer wieder versucht worden. Barrieren, Video-Überwachung, der große Bruder überwacht dich, his master's voice weist dich zurück, spielen mehr und mehr eine Rolle. Alarmanlagen, summende, piepsende, schrille Töne bestimmen mehr und mehr den Museumsbesuch, nicht aber mehr jene Auseinandersetzung mit dem Museum, die letztlich für den einzelnen Freiheit bedeutet. Die Museen haben die Massen gerufen, die Massen sind gekommen, die Demokratie findet dennoch nicht statt. Museumsinhalte sind merkwürdig diktatorisch, entsprechen nur eigenen Gesetzlichkeiten. Diese Freiheiten sollten wir dem Museum mit seinen Inhalten gewähren, denn sonst wäre es nur die Fortsetzung der Gesellschaft mit ästhetischen Mitteln: Doch dieses in einer Gesellschaft, die weniger und weniger an Ästhetik glaubt. Wenn der Kritiker meint, daß im Museum Tore geschossen werden müssen, daß ein jubelndes Publikum alkoholisiert die Stars feiert, der sollte das Museum nicht mehr betreten. Es sei denn, wir begründen ein Stadion-Museum, jetzt wäre der Platzbedarf noch größer. Tendenz steigend!

the act of coming to terms with the museum, which in the end means freedom for the individual. The museums have invoked the masses, the masses have come, but still there is no democracy. The contents of museums are remarkably dictatorial, corresponding only to their own regulations. We should preserve these freedoms for the museum and its contents, for otherwise it would only be the continuation of society with aesthetic means – and that in a society which believes less and less in aesthetics. If the critic thinks that in the museum goals have to be shot, that a cheering public would celebrate the stars in an alcoholised state, then he should not enter the museum any more. Unless of course, we were to found a stadium museum, where the floor space required would now be even larger. An upward trend!

Der Planet Museum

Herwig Zens

Stellen Sie sich vor, Sie betreten ein Museum nicht durch einen prunkvollen Eingangsraum, der von historistischen oder postmodernen Schnörkeln überladen ist, sondern durch einen Baucontainer. Dort ist die Kasse untergebracht, und es gibt weder Postkarten, Diapositive, T-Shirts noch mit Klimt bedruckte Anstecktücher und auch keine Leinentasche mit der siebenunddreißigsten Verulkung der Mona Lisa. Der Schmerz über diese fehlende Grundausstattung wird jedoch von der Dame an der Kasse dadurch gemildert, daß man Ihnen mitteilt, daß im Eintrittspreis die Benützung des Buffets inkludiert ist. Wird auch schon etwas sein um diesen Preis ...

Es führt keine Prunktreppe hinauf, und keinerlei Pfeile und Beschriftungen weisen zu irgendwelchen Kunstobjekten, obwohl Sie doch genau wissen, daß es derlei hier geben soll.

Sie schreiten also weiter auf diesem Planeten der Unmusealität. Auf der Wiese steht ein einzelnes Gebäude mit zwei Türen. Natürlich führt auch ein Weg herum, und durch die beiden Glastüren sieht man auf der gegenüberliegenden Seite des Ziegelklotzes den Weg weiterführen. Da wird es also nun beginnen. Die Verwunderung ist jedoch groß, wenn Sie in dem von oben belichteten Raum weder Skulpturen noch Bilder oder erklärende Tafeln antreffen. Es befindet sich darin nichts. Rein gar nichts außer Ihnen selbst. Und hier kann man nun die ersten Studien an den Raumfahrern unternehmen. Zornig bis abweisend oder verunsichert lächelnd reagieren die einen. Völlig hilflos der Großteil, und einige beginnen aus den Türen zu schauen, zur Decke zu blicken und in der beklemmenden Stille in sich hineinzuhorchen. Vergleiche mit dem bahnhofähnlichen Trubel des Louvreeingangs oder den oft penetranten Gerüchen im Kuppelbereich des Kunsthistorischen Museums kommen auf und lassen eine verwunderte Gelöstheit und Öffnung entstehen.

Vielleicht haben Sie den Planeten schon erkannt, und ich möchte Sie auch nicht

The Planet Museum

Herwig Zens

Imagine you enter a museum not through a stately entrance hall overcharged with historic or post-modern flourishes, but through a building container. That is where the ticket office is, but there are no postcards, slides, T-shirts or scarves with Klimt prints, nor canvas bags with the thirty-seventh travesty of the Mona Lisa. The anguish at this lack of the most basic facilities is, however, soothed by the lady at the desk, when she says that the price of the ticket includes the use of the buffet. There must be something good at this price ...

No stately stairway leads upstairs and no arrows and signs indicate the whereabouts of any kind of art objects, although you know quite well that they ought to be here. And so you stride forward across this unmuseological planet. On the field there is a single building with two doors. Of course, there is also a path round it, and through the two glass doors one sees that the path continues on the other side of this brick monstrosity. So that is where it will begin. However, your amazement is indeed great when, in the room with overhead lighting, you meet neither sculptures nor pictures, nor explanatory notices. There is nothing inside. Nothing whatsoever except you yourself. And here one can make the first studies of the space travellers. Some react angrily or rejectingly, or smile unsettled. Most are completely helpless, and some begin to look out of the two doors, glance up at the ceiling and listen to the oppressive silence within themselves. Comparisons are made with the station-like bustle at the entrance to the Louvre or the often penetrating smells in the area of the dome of the Kunsthistorische Museum. which allows a bemused mood of relaxedness and openness to arise.

Perhaps you have already recognised this planet, and I really do not want to detain you much longer with a description of this 'topsy-turvy' museum world. But just one more little step.

Across a field with a magnificent oak one reaches a windowless block, consciously

mehr lange mit der Schilderung dieser »verkehrten« Museumswelt aufhalten. Nur einen kleinen Schritt noch.

Über eine Wiese mit prachtvollen Eichen kommt man zu einem bewußt tresorartig gestalteten Klotz ohne Fenster, der nur an seinen vier Ecken unscheinbare Türen aus Metall – vergleichbar einem Garagentor – besitzt. Sie können das Quadrat betreten, wo immer Sie wollen. Es gibt keine Gehrichtung, und es wird Ihnen auch bestimmt keine japanische, italienische oder sonstige Reisegruppe den Weg verstellen, denn Reisegruppen gibt es hier keine. Auch wild herumtobende Kinderscharen habe ich noch nie gesehen. Natürlich gibt es auch hier Kinder, doch bedingt durch das Ambiente und das ungewohnte Schau- und Geherlebnis benehmen sie sich hier plötzlich überhaupt nicht »aufgekratzt«, wie man es sonst in Museen immer wieder beobachten kann.

»Im eigentlichen Museum (Labyrinth) befinden sich persische Kulturen (Amlasch, Luristan) neben Sammlungsbereichen aus dem frühen China der Han-, Tang- und Ming-Zeit.

Khmer-Skulpturen und chinesische Figuren aus der Han-Zeit stehen in Korrespondenz zur Malerei von Gotthard Graubner sowie Plastiken von Jean Fautier und Erwin Heerich ...

Afrika verbindet sich mit Ozeanien und Werken aus dem 20. Jahrhundert, Yves Klein mit Kulturzeichen der Maori.«

So lesen wir auf dem äußerst bescheidenen Faltblatt, das ohne jegliches Glanzpapier und kunsthistorisch überdrehtes Gestammel auskommt.

Dieser Planet ist schwer auf einer Himmelskarte der musealen Eitelkeiten zu finden, ähnlich dem Stern des »Kleinen Prinzen« von Saint-Exupéry. Der Schöpfer dieser realen Unwirklichkeit, ein wohlhabender Immobilienhändler, legt auch absolut keinen Wert auf einen allzugroßen Bekanntheitsgrad, ja es soll schon vorgekommen sein, daß er sein Museum, wenn es allzu populär wird, einfach zusperrt, um es ohne weitere Vorankündigung wieder zu öffnen. Er braucht auch keine Besucherzahlenrekorde, um von irgendwelchen Geldgebern freundliches Schulterklopfen

designed like a safe, with inconspicuous metal doors – like garage doors – at its four corners only. You can enter the square wherever you want to. There is no direction to follow and there are certainly no Japanese, Italian or any other kind of tourists blocking the way, for there are no groups of tourists here. Nor have I ever seen any hordes of wild kids romping here. Of course there are children here too; however, due to the atmosphere of the place and the unusual pedestrian and visual experience it provides, they suddenly behave not at all boisterously, as one can usually observe them behaving in museums.

"In the actual museum (labyrinth), Persian cultures (Amlash, Luristan) are to be found beside areas of the collection devoted to early China of the Han, Tang and Ming periods.

Khmer sculptures and Chinese figures from the Han period are related to the painting of Gotthard Graubner as they are to the sculpture of Jean Fautier and Erwin Heerich ...

Africa is connected with Oceania and works from the 20th century, Yves Klein with the cultural signs of the Maori."

This we read on the extremely modest leaflet, which is not printed on glossy paper and contains no over-excited art historical stammering.

Like the star of Saint Exupéry's *Little Prince*, this planet is difficult to find on a heavenly map of the museological vanities. The creator of this real unreality, a wealthy estate agent, places absolutely no importance whatsoever on too great a degree of fame; indeed, it is even said that he simply closes his museum when it becomes too popular, only to open it again without prior announcement. Nor does he need record numbers of visitors in order to receive friendly pats on the shoulder from this or that sponsor. There is no parking space for buses here and museum tourism would be hard-pressed on this island of Hombroich near Neuss, since there are no labels at all, no guided tours and no stories surrounding the exhibits. The buffet alone, which is, incidentally, excellent in its simplicity, is not enough to attract the education-sated masses.

Museumsinsel Hombroich bei Neuss, BRD, Innenansicht (Photo 1991)
Museumsinsel Hombroich near Neuss, FRG, view of interior (photograph 1991)

Museumsinsel Hombroich bei Neuss, BRD,
(Photo 1991)
Museumsinsel Hombroich near Neuss, FRG,
(photograph 1991)

zu erhalten. Es gibt auch keinen Parkplatz für Busse, und der Museumstourismus täte sich sehr schwer auf dieser Insel Hombroich bei Neuß, da es keinerlei Beschriftungen, keine Führungen und auch keine Stories rund um die Objekte gibt. Nur das Buffet allein, das übrigens in seiner Schlichtheit ganz ausgezeichnet ist, reizt die bildungsübersättigte Masse nicht.

Wie soll's denn auch gehen, wenn man unter anderem in einen runden, verglasten Raum entlassen wird, in dessen Mitte sich ein zylinderartiger Stein befindet. Soll sich Tante Amalie draufstellen, um sich so wie neben der »Venus von Milo« oder dem »David« von Michelangelo photographieren zu lassen?

Aber junge und alte Leute sah ich dort sehr versunken sitzen, um über das Durchwanderte und Erlebte nachzudenken und dann vielleicht noch einmal eine Runde in anderer Erlebnisreihenfolge zu starten.

Neben einigen Besuchen zu den verschiedensten Jahreszeiten habe ich diesen Planeten Museum auch immer wieder mit Studenten besucht, die vorher die glitzernden Tempel der Museumsbauwut gesehen haben. Vom Mönchengladbacher über das neue Wallraff-Richartz-Ludwig Museum bis Stuttgart und Frankfurt. Es gab noch keinen unter den jungen Leuten, der nicht eindeutig dieses völlig zuwiderlaufende Phänomen Hombroich als die überzeugendste Lösung eines zeitgerechten Museums empfunden hätte.

Beim gemeinsamen Nachdenken mit den Studenten über dieses Phänomen fiel mir ein Beispiel aus meiner Lehrertätigkeit ein: Als es modern wurde, die letzten Schultage durch Aktivitäten fächer- oder klassenübergreifender Art zu füllen (denn der Spannungseffekt war durch die bereits feststehenden Noten genommen), überschlugen sich die Lehrerinnen und Lehrer mit den abstrusesten Angeboten. Vom biologischen Kochkurs bis zum Entenzählen und gälischen Volksliedern gab es alles. Der unangefochtene Spitzenreiter in der Beliebtheit der Sechzehn- und Siebzehnjährigen war jedoch zum großen, neidvollen Erstaunen aller Kolleginnen und Kollegen ein älterer Kollege, der in seine Programmzeile eintrug: »Auf der Wiese

But how could it be different when, among other things, one is released into a circular, glazed room, in the middle of which is a stone like a bar-stool. Should Aunt Amalia sit upon it and have herself photographed, as she would beside the Venus de Milo or Michelangelo's David?

However, I saw both young and old people sitting there immersed in thought about what they had wandered through and experienced, perhaps before starting off on yet another round of a different sequence of experiences.

Apart from a few visits at various times of the year, I have also repeatedly visited this planet museum with students who have already witnessed beforehand the glittering temples of the museum-building fury. From Mönchengladbach to the new Wallraff-Richartz-Ludwig Museum, or to Stuttgart and Frankfurt. There was not a single one of these young people who did not feel that the completely contrary phenomenon of Hombroich was the most convincing solution for a museum suited to our age.

When I was reflecting upon this phenomenon together with my students, an example from my experience as a schoolteacher occurred to me. When it became the thing to fill up the last days of the semester with activities involving all pupils regardless of subjects or classes (for the suspense effect had vanished once the final marks had been given out), the teachers would fall over themselves to come up with the most abstruse offer. There was everything from the wholefood cookery course to counting ducks and gaelic folksongs. The undisputed favourite among the sixteen and seventeen-year-olds was – to the great and envious astonishment of all his fellow teachers – that of an old teacher who entered as his programme title: "Lying in a field and reading *one* book". The rules of the game entailed spending three days somewhere in the Waldviertel, intensively studying one single book and then, on the last day, sharing with the other pupils the sum of the resulting perceptions gained from reading it. The throng for collective solitude with one book was overwhelming and only with effort could greater disputes be avoided. The magic was therefore in

liegen und *ein* Buch lesen«. Die Spielregeln sahen vor, daß man sich drei Tage hindurch, die man irgendwo im Waldviertel verbrachte, mit nur einem Buch intensiv auseinandersetzte und die Summe seiner Leseerkenntnisse am letzten Tag den Mitschülern vermittelte. Der Andrang zur kollektiven Einsamkeit mit einem Buch war gewaltig, und nur mit Mühe konnten größere Streitereien vermieden werden. In der völligen Andersartigkeit liegt also der Zauber. Diese Erkenntnis ist keineswegs neu, doch wird immer wieder darauf vergessen und damit die Chance des Planetenerlebnisses kläglich vertan.

Ein altes Wiener Sprichwort, das jedoch nahtlos auf ganz Österreich übertragen werden kann, besagt, daß der Wiener nur zweimal in seinem Leben das Kunsthistorische Museum betritt: Das erstemal an der Hand seines Vaters und das zweitemal, wenn er seinem eigenen Sohn in diesen heiligen Hallen den Schauer des Kulturgutes vermitteln will. Mit der Analyse dieses Witzes könnte man nun ganze Artikel füllen oder sich allein an der Tatsache festkrallen, daß es sich immer um einen Sohn und niemals um eine Tochter handelt usw. usw. Auch das Problem der Schwellenangst wissen gelehrte Museumspädagogen hier abzuhandeln, doch wollen wir damit nicht das Papier verschwenden.

Warum ergeht es dem jungen Mann genauso wie seinem Vorgänger mit der Pullmankappe? Oder stimmt das heute vielleicht gar nicht mehr?
Leider stimmt es zum Großteil immer noch, doch kann man dem Herrn mit der Pullmankappe kaum einen Vorwurf daraus machen. Hatte er denn die Möglichkeit, den Museumsplaneten einmal für sich allein zu entdecken und sich völlig seiner kindlichen Neugierde hinzugeben? Denn hier allein liegt der Schlüssel zum Museumserlebnis. Nicht in auszufüllenden Bögen, Suchspielen, Bilderrallyes, Töpfern im Museum und wie all der gutgemeinte museumspädagogische Zierat heißt. Ein sehr weiser, altgewordener Museumsaufseher sagte mir einmal beim Betrachten einer Studentin, die mit Händen und Füßen einer relativ uninteressierten Klasse die

what was completely different. This perception is by no means new, but it is time and again forgotten – and the chance of a planetary experience thereby lamentably squandered.

An old Viennese proverb, which is, however, perfectly applicable to the whole of Austria as well, says that an inhabitant of Vienna only visits the Kunsthistorische Museum twice in his life: the first time holding his father's hand and the second time when he wants to convey to his own son that shudder of cultural tradition which is to be experienced in these holy halls. One could fill whole articles with analyses of this joke or dig one's nails into the fact that it is always a son and never a daughter etc., etc.. Learned museum pedagogues would here know how to introduce a treatise on the problem of the 'entrance phobia', the fear of entering a place; we, however, do not want to waste paper on that.

Why is it that this young man is in just the same situation as his predecessor with the beret? Or is that perhaps no longer true today?
Unfortunately, it is still largely true, yet one can hardly take this as a reason for accusing the gentleman with the beret. Did he ever once have the chance to discover the museum planets for himself, to surrender completely to his childlike curiosity? For here alone lies the key to the experience of the museum. Not in all the form-filling, search games, picture rallies, pottery-making and whatever other embellishments have been invented by well-intentioned museum educationalists. A very old and wise museum attendant once told me, as we watched a girl student attempting, with the aid of every gesture at her disposal, to explain to a relatively uninterested class the attraction of a picture from the late Middle Ages: "In our museum there is much too much talking, too little looking and hardly any understanding done."

These two inquisitive girls from Guatemala have definitely understood more about the nature of museum objects than the sheltered child who is dragged along to a

Paul Almasy, *Visite chez l'ancêtre*, Guatemala, 1965

Reize eines spätmittelalterlichen Bildes zu erklären versuchte: »In unserem Museum wird viel zu viel geredet, zu wenig geschaut und kaum etwas begriffen.«

Diese beiden neugierigen Mädchen aus Guatemala haben bestimmt viel mehr vom Wesen musealer Güter begriffen als das gutbehütete Kind, das jeden Sonntag in ein anderes Museum geschleppt wird, obwohl es sich doch viel lieber das Gerippe des Dinosauriers oder den kleinen Hund im Porträt der Prinzessin von Velázquez zum zehnten Mal angesehen hätte. Kinder haben ein sehr ernstes Verständnis zu ihren Objekten im Museum, wie ein kleines Beispiel zeigt: Was soll die bestarrangierte Teddybärenausstellung, von einem Bühnenbildner in mystisches Dunkel getaucht; mit Teddys in allen Größen und in allen Ecken des Foyers des Naturhistorischen Museums, wenn dafür das Lieblingsobjekt der ständigen Ausstellung, das Gerippe eines Riesenwalrosses weichen mußte? Die ganze Ausstellung war gestrichen. Sollten sich doch die dummen Erwachsenen mit den Bären herumschlagen, wer das Gerippe eines Riesenwalrosses verrückt, hat keinerlei Verständnis von den wahren Aufgaben eines Museums!

Die Bindung an ein Objekt – später werden es mehrere, und es ändern sich natürlich auch die Schwerpunkte, bis im günstigsten Fall die Liebe einfach einem ganzen Haus und seiner Sammlung gehört – ist das Schlüsselerlebnis für eine positive Einstellung zum Museum. Und dieses Initialerlebnis liegt meist auf einer ganz anderen Ebene, als der Erwachsene glaubt. Was soll der Vierjährige mit den »Kinderspielen« von Bruegel, wo das Bild für ihn noch dazu viel zu hoch hängt? Auch wenn es die Tante oder der Onkel noch so gut meint mit den Erklärungen des »Radschlagenden« oder des »Reifentreibenden«. Der junge Kunstfreund sieht eben nur den unteren Rand und vielleicht noch eventuell zwanzig Zentimeter, alles andere verzerrt sich für ihn derart, daß er einfach nichts mehr sieht. Ein Seehundjunges am unteren Rand eines Snyder-Bildes, dessen Schnauze genau in seiner Nasenhöhe liegt, ist da natürlich wesentlich attraktiver.

Der geniale Farbauftrag eines Vermeer ist

different museum every Sunday, even though she would far rather see – for the tenth time – the skeleton of the dinosaur, or the little dog in Velazquez's portrait of the princess. Children have a very serious understanding of their museum objects, as a little example shows: what is the point of a perfectly arranged exhibition of teddy bears, organised by a stage designer and immersed in mysterious darkness, with teddies of all shapes and sizes in every corner of the entrance hall of the Naturhistorische Museum, if one's favourite object, the skeleton of a giant walrus, has to make way for it? The whole exhibition is ruined. The stupid grown-ups can do what they want with the bears, whoever moves the skeleton of a giant walrus has no understanding of a museum's true responsibility.

The relationship to an object (later it will become several objects – and of course the areas of interest change until, ideally, a whole museum and its collection becomes a passion) is the key experience for a positive attitude to the museum. And this initial experience is usually on quite another level to that imagined by the adult. What is the four-year-old supposed to do with Brueghel's *Children's Games* when the picture still hangs far too high for him or her? Even if auntie or uncle mean do well with their explanations of the children somersaulting or trundling hoops. The young art lover sees only the bottom edge of the picture and perhaps twenty centimetres above it, everything else is so distorted that he or she simply cannot see anything at all. A baby seal at the bottom of a Snyders picture, located exactly at the level of his nose, is naturally far more attractive.

The ingenious application of paint in a Vermeer only becomes a way of relating to his pictures after a certain age, and the general rule is that for the vast majority of visitors the narrative components of a pictorial representation provide a considerably easier approach. As the Viennese say: *"des G'schichtl rundumadum"* ('the little story round-aba-dowm'). After all, it is the stories which one remembers. To whom does the third foot in Brueghel's *Peasant Wedding* belong? Who is the figure

eben erst ab einer gewissen Altersstufe ein Einstieg, wobei es eine allgemein bekannte Weisheit ist, daß für den überwiegenden Teil der Beschauer die narrative Komponente einer bildhaften Darstellung der wesentlich leichtere Einstieg ist. Auf wienerisch: »des G'schichtl rundumadum«. Diese Geschichten sind es ja auch, die man sich merkt. Wem gehört der dritte Fuß in Bruegels »Bauernhochzeit«, wer ist die Figur im Hintergrund bei den »Meñinas« von Velázquez, wieso sieht sich der Buddha von Naim June Paik im Fernseher selbst usw. Mit Studenten wurde hier an der Akademie dieser narrative Charakter einmal direkt beim Wort genommen, und der Erfolg bei Schulklassen und Erwachsenen war durchschlagend: Ein Team von Lehramtskandidaten hat alle Dargestellten auf Herbert Boeckls »Großem Familienporträt« interviewt, das Bild in eine Bühnenbildstaffage zerlegt und von den jeweils betroffenen Figuren Leitungen zu Walkmen gelegt, die der Beschauer oder Miterleber aufsetzen und sich so zwischen Original und Bildstaffage ein »Bild« des Bildes machen konnte.

Zugleich hatten die Studenten, die dieses museumspädagogische Experiment auch sehr liebevoll betreuten, eine kleine Ateliersituation aufgebaut, wo demonstriert wurde, wie Ölfarben angerieben, Leinwände grundiert und gespannt sowie andere technische Hürden gemeistert werden konnten. Es war interessant, mit welchem Ernst sich Schulklassen mit dieser Situation auseinandersetzten, und wie auch immer wieder Erwachsene besonders an den technischen Vorgängen großes Interesse zeigten. Betrat man die nachgebaute Bühne über eine kleine Rampe, so konnte man sich in die Gruppe einfügen, und die Polaroidphotos bewiesen immer wieder, daß jede Veränderung der Situation die sehr locker erscheinende Kompositionsanordnung völlig zerstörte.

Eine Erfahrung am Rande, die jedoch auch sehr symptomatisch war, stellte sich durch das Entsetzen einiger Akademieprofessoren ein, die in dieser räumlichen Situierung eine Entweihung, Kinderspielereien usw. sahen. Ihre Eingesponnenheit

in the background of *Las Meñinas* by Velazquez, why is Naim June Paik's Buddha looking at himself in a television set, etc.? One year, students here at the Academy took this narrative character literally for once, and its success with school classes and adults was amazing: a team of students studying for their Teachers' Certificate interviewed all the characters depicted in Herbert Boeckl's *Large Family Portrait*, divided the picture into stage set staffages and attached cables from the respective figures to walkmen, which the viewer or participant could then listen to and thus, between the original and the staffage, create a 'picture' for himself.

At the same time, the students who conducted this museological experiment in such a delightful way also set up a little studio situation, where it was demonstrated how to grind oil paints, ground and stretch canvasses and overcome other technical hurdles. It was interesting to see the seriousness with which the school classes confronted this situation, as well as the great interest which many adults showed, especially in the technical processes. As soon as as one walked up the little ramp on to the stage that had been constructed, one became part of the group; polaroid photographs prove time and again that every little change in the situation completely destroyed the apparently very fragile arrangement of the composition.

One side-effect of this (although it was, nevertheless, very symptomatic) was the horror which it evoked in some of the professors at the Academy, who saw this spatial situation as a profanation, as children's games etc. Their self-absorption in the process of painting made them take it for granted and prevented them from understanding the need for help in interpretation.
The very thing that the people actively participating in this student experiment were lacking – namely naturalness – is what is talked away by the professional assistants.
At the present time, the museum teaching scene has e.g. a fatal inclination towards a low horizon.

Herbert Boeckl, *Das große Familienbild*, 1942
Herbert Boeckl, *Large Family Portrait*, 1942

Verräumlichtes Bild nach Herbert Boeckls *Das große Familienbild*, 1988
Spatial reconstruction of Herbert Boeckl's *Large Family Portrait*, 1988

in die Selbstverständlichkeit des Malvorganges verbaute jegliches Verständnis für eine Interpretationshilfe.

Was die praktisch Ausführenden an diesem Studentenwerk bemängelten – die Selbstverständlichkeit –, zerreden die Berufshilfesteller.

Die derzeitige museumspädagogische Landschaft hat zum Beispiel einen fatalen Hang zu einem tiefen Horizont.

Was auch immer betrachtet wird, ganz wichtig scheint es, daß man am Boden herumlümmelt.

Es ist durchaus richtig, daß man im Kreis sitzende Kinder wesentlich leichter auf etwas konzentrieren kann und daß durch die Untersicht auch freiere Sicht gegeben ist. Doch hat der Maler sein Bild wirklich für diese Ansicht gemalt? Existiert das Bild im Museum wirklich dafür, daß es von am Boden Liegenden mit irgendwelchen abscheulichen Ölkreiden nachgekritzelt wird?

Es ist nichts gegen eine praktische Arbeit vor dem Original einzuwenden, nur müßte das Museum auch die dafür notwendigen Räume haben. Für manche Altersgruppen und zu bestimmten Lehrzwecken ist auch nicht immer das Original erforderlich. Ganz dümmlich wird die Situation dann, wenn ein Professor mit seinen Studenten am Boden hockt und ein mildtätiger Ordner oder besonders fortschrittlich gesinnter Museumspädagoge die Bilder auf den Boden stellt. So erlebt in …

Wenn die »Museumstante« den Kindern von Calgary (siehe S. 33) die Stammesgewohnheiten der Ureinwohner Kanadas am Boden sitzend erklärt, so ist das in Ordnung. Ein Am-Boden-Hocken vor Dürers »Allerheiligenbild« bringt niemandem etwas.

Die Methode des lebenden Bildes ist für Zehn- bis Dreizehnjährige von außerordentlicher Spannung, wobei sich Kinder auch in einzelne Gegenstände eines Bildes verwandeln können. Bei einer Arbeit in der »Neuen Pinakothek« kam es zum Beispiel immer wieder vor, daß sich Mädchen in die Rolle der Glocke von Pilotys Bild »Seni an der Leiche Wallensteins« verwandeln wollten. Die etwas rauheren bayerischen Landburschen, die mit Autobussen zum Muse-

Regardless of what one is looking at, it seems most important to loll around on the floor.

It is quite true that it is far easier to concentrate when one is seated in a circle with children and that the lower perspective produces a freer view of things. Yet did the painter really paint his picture to be looked at from this angle? Does the picture in the museum really exist so that it can be copied from a prone position on the ground using some horrible oil crayons?

There can be no objection to practical work in front of the original, but the museum must also have the requisite space for it. For some age groups, and for certain teaching purposes, the original is not always necessary. The situation becomes quite ridiculous when a professor is squatting on the floor with his students and a charitable supervisor or especially progressive museum pedagogue takes down the pictures and places them on the floor. As experienced in …

It is all very well when the 'museum Lady' explains the tribal habits of the original inhabitants of Canada to the children from Calgary (see p. 33) while sitting on the floor. But squatting on the floor in front of Dürer's *Adoration of the Trinity* will not get anyone anywhere.

The method of the living picture is extremely exciting for children between the ages of ten and thirteen, enabling them to transform themselves even into the individual objects of a picture. In the case of a project at the Neue Pinakothek it repeatedly happened that girls wanted to transform themselves into the bell in Piloty's picture *Seni beside the Corpse of Wallenstein*. The rather rougher Bavarian country boys, ferried to the museum in coaches and, once there, gladly handed over to the museum pedagogues by their teachers, were of course far more interested in the situation of the stabbing of Wallenstein. For the twelve-year-olds the situation often came precariously close to the 'Pradler knights game': "… can I be stabbed again, Mr. Teacher?" was the frequently quoted question. For such actions it is enough, having viewed the original, to look at the projection of a slide in a room set up for the purpose; and indeed, if one wants to introduce

um gekarrt worden waren und dort von den Lehrern gerne dem Museumspädagogen übergeben wurden, waren natürlich wesentlich mehr an der Situation des Erstechens von Wallenstein interessiert, wobei die Situation bei den Zwölfjährigen oft gefährlich nahe an die »Pradler Ritterspiele« geriet: »... darf ich nochmal erstochen werden, Herr Lehrer?« war die oft gestellte Frage. Zu derlei Aktionen genügt nach Besichtigung des Originals durchaus die Projektion eines Dias in einem dafür eingerichteten Raum, und wenn man sich rechtzeitig um die Heranführung an museale Güter kümmern will, muß man derlei Räume in den Neubauten der Museen berücksichtigen.

»Lebendiges Museum«
The "living museum"

Die Form des lebendigen Museums ist besonders in den Vereinigten Staaten und auch in Kanada sehr beliebt geworden und wird von jung und alt begeistert angenommen. Die Siedlerzeit mit dem leichten Hauch von Wildwest spielt hier eine genauso große Rolle wie der gepflegte europäische Stil in der neuen Heimat.

Mit großem Ernst – und von uns Europäern völlig zu Unrecht verlacht – werden Gesamtsituationen mit wissenschaftlicher Akkuratesse nachgebaut und nachgespielt, wobei jede handelnde Figur in ihrer Biographie genau erfaßt ist. Unterhält man sich mit einem der Akteure oder mit einer der Damen, so bekommt man ganz präzise Antworten, etwa: »Ich bin Miss ..., derzeit dreiunddreißig Jahre und habe fünf Kinder, mein Mann ist derzeit im Krieg und wird nächstes Jahr fallen. Ich werde daraufhin verarmen und mit einundvierzig Jahren in Toronto sterben ...« Das klingt für uns zwar etwas makaber, doch bin ich sicher, daß diese Form der Verlebendigung sehr bald auch in Europa Platz greifen wird, wenn sie nicht in leicht verkleideter Form schon da ist. Man soll sich nur einmal in Osttirol die Erzählungen des Altbauern anhören, wenn er mit den Gästen aus Deutschland spricht. Er verkauft sich genauso als Museumsstück wie der Kanadier. Der feine Unterschied besteht nur darin, daß die Akteure in Louisbourg bezahlte Akteure sind. Doch wir spielen immer, live ...

Der Museumsbesucher, einst ein Relikt des

children in good time to the objects of the museum, then one must ensure that such rooms are included in the new museum buildings.

The form of the living museum has become particularly popular in the United States and in Canada, and is accepted enthusiastically by both young and old alike. Here in the 'new country', the past age of the settlers and a hint of the wild west plays just as important a role as the cultivated European style does.

With great seriousness, which we Europeans scoff at without any justification, whole situations are recreated and acted out with scientific accuracy, whereby the biography of each character involved is exactly described. If one talks to one of the actors or actresses, one receives very precise answers, for example: "I am Miss ...., am at present thirty-three years old and have five children, my husband is at present fighting in the war and will fall next year. After that I shall become poor and die in Toronto at forty-one ..." That sounds somewhat macabre to us, but I am sure that this form of enlivenment will very soon catch on here in Europe – if it has not already arrived here in disguised form. One only has to listen to the stories told by an old farmer in East Tyrol when he talks to his guests from Germany. He sells himself in just the same way as a museum piece, like the Canadians. The subtle difference is, that the actors in Louisbourg are paid actors. Still, we are always acting, acting live ...

Heritage-Museum in Bakersville, Kanada, Photo 1990
Heritage-Museum in Bakersville, Canada, photograph 1990

spätbürgerlichen Snobismus, wurde ab den sechziger Jahren von der Tourismusbranche entdeckt. Durch die Videokassette wäre es ja durchaus möglich, den Pseudobildungshunger im Fauteuil mit der Bierflasche in der Hand und den »Solettis« am Tisch zu befriedigen, so wie das Fußballinteresse. Ein Vergleich zwischen Fußballplatzbesuchern und Museumsbesuchern fällt jedoch mit großem Vorsprung zugunsten der »Museumsinteressierten« aus. Wieso kommt es zu dieser Situation, wenn die Sache mit dem verweigernden Museumsbesucher nach außen hin doch noch stimmen soll? Die Frage ist ganz einfach zu beantworten: Genauso, wie man Millionen dazu bringen kann, plötzlich kilometerweit zu laufen, und das als gesundes Jogging verkauft, bringt man Unmengen – warum, weiß niemand – auf speziellen und daher sehr teuren Fahrrädern auf Berge und, was ja noch viel seriöser wirkt: Millionen in Museen.

Menschen, die während des ganzen Jahres nie auf die Idee kämen, ein Museum zu besuchen, verwandeln sich in der Gestalt

After the 60s, the museum visitor, once a relic of late-bourgeois snobbism, was discovered by the tourist industry. With the video cassette it would be quite feasible to satisfy the hunger for pseudo-education, as is done with the interest in football: in an armchair with a bottle of beer in one hand and a packet of crisps on the table. However, if one compares the number of people who go to football matches with the number of museum visitors, the later win by a wide margin. How does this situation arise, if it is true that museum visitors are 'reluctant'? The question can be answered quite easily: just as one can make millions of people suddenly run for kilometres and sell it as healthy jogging, so one can make crowds – why, no-one knows – ride up mountains on special and very expensive bicycles, and (which indeed sounds even more serious) make millions go to the museums.

People who would never hit upon the idea of visiting a museum at any other time of the year, change into museum fanatics once they adopt the form of city tourists. People who have not seen *David* when in

von Citytouristen zu Museumsfanatikern. Wenn man in Florenz den »David« nicht gesehen hat, nicht bei 35 Grad im August auf der Akropolis herumgestrampelt ist und nicht mindestens drei Stunden für den Besuch des Toulouse-Lautrec-Spektakels in Paris gewartet hat, zählt man ebenso nicht dazu, wie wenn die Farbe des Rackets oder das Modell des Computers nicht stimmt. Und all das soll schnell und umsatzfördernd vor sich gehen ...

Daß neben all diesem Trubel, der durch die Lobby der Fremdenverkehrswirtschaft immer mehr angeheizt wird und wahrscheinlich notgezwungen aus organisatorischen Gründen in einer Welt der Faksimiles enden wird (niemand murrt, wenn er in der Albertina nicht den »Originalhasen« Dürers optisch streicheln kann), daß oft jene unter die Räder kommen, die sich wirklich Mühe geben, Kunstwerke zu begreifen, ist bedauerlich. Und hier sollte man versuchen, gegenzusteuern.

Wer je erlebt hat, mit welcher Intensität Blinde Plastiken (ob nun Original oder Gipsabguß) begreifen können, wird sich nur kopfschüttelnd wundern, daß dafür in diesem Riesenwirtschaftsfaktor kaum Geldmittel vorhanden sind.

Menschen, die wirklich etwas »begreifen«, braucht man auch nichts zerreden. Dann wird eben mit den Händen geschaut, aber es bedarf kaum eines Wortes, wie beim Eintritt in den Planeten Museum.

Es ist sinnlos, sich gegen die wirtschaftlichen Interessen, die unzweifelhaft am Faktor Museum bestehen, zur Wehr setzen zu wollen. Man soll bei Neuanlagen von Museen darauf achten, daß diese neben ihrem wissenschaftlichen, konservatorischen und ökonomischen Wert auch immer wieder ihre Aufgabe zu erfüllen haben, Interesse und Neugierde bei Kindern zu erwecken.

Zur Wiederholung: eine publikumswirksame Teddybärenausstellung rechtfertigt nur sehr schwer das Wegräumen des Gerippes eines »Riesenwalrosses«, denn es gibt schließlich auch ernsthafte Besucher eines Museums.

Die Ernsthaftigkeit eines Museumsbesuchers ist nicht altersbedingt.

Florence, not walked over the Acropolis at 35 degrees centigrade in August and not waited for at least three hours to see the Toulouse Lautrec spectacle in Paris lack something, as when the colour of the racket or the model of the computer is not right. And all that should happen quickly and profitably ...

The fact is, that, quite apart from all the rumpus which is continually being caused by the lobby of the tourist industry, we will finally be left with a world of facsimiles – and probably of necessity, for organisational reasons. (No-one grumbles about not being able to optically stroke the 'original' hare by Dürer in the Albertina). It is most deplorable that those who really do make the effort to understand art are often left by the wayside, and we ought to try to counteract that situation here.

Anyone who has experienced the intensity with which blind people can understand sculpture (whether original or plaster casts) will only shake his head in disbelief that there are hardly any financial means available for their needs, even though this could become a huge market factor.

People who really 'understand' something do not need to have it talked to death. They look with their hands and they do not need a single word, as in the entry to the Planet Museum.

It is pointless to try to struggle against the economic interests which are without doubt also vested in the museum factor. One should bear in mind when constructing new buildings for museums that, in addition to their scholarly, conservational and economic value, they also always have a responsibility to arouse the interest and curiosity of children as well.

To repeat: a publicly successful teddy bear exhibition has difficulty in justifying the act of clearing away the skeleton of a 'giant walrus'. There are, after all, also serious visitors to a museum.

And the seriousness of a museum visitor does not depend upon age.

»Die *Venus von Milo* und andere weltberühmte Skulpturen aus dem Pariser Louvre können Kunden eines Münchner Einkaufszentrums im Wagerl zur Kassa und dann nach Hause führen. Es handelt sich um originalgetreue Kopien, die dort ausgestellt waren und jetzt zu verkaufen sind.« Photo Keystone, 1988

"Shoppers at a Munich shopping centre can fill their trolleys with the *Venus de Milo* and other world-famous sculptures from the Louvre in Paris, wheel them to the cash desk and then take them home. The statues are faithful copies of the original and were formerly on exhibition, but are now up for sale." Photograph Keystone, 1988

Für ein Museum im Kopf mit Ausblick auf Wolken und Länder

Mario Terzic

Grenze Italien-Österreich, Zollamt Brenner,
21. 4. 1992
Italian-Austrian border, Brenner customs,
1992-04-21

Grenze Italien/Österreich, Zollamt Brenner, 21. 4. 1992. Die Ladungen der LKWs von links nach rechts: »Gold der Kelten«, »Henry Moore – Das Spätwerk«, »Metropolitana Berlin–Rom«, »24 der 100 teuersten Künstler 1991«, »Prunkharnische der Gonzaga«, »Streetfurniture des AAD Chicago«, »Weisheit in Stein – Sammlung Conte Pavone«, »Sieben Kopien des Spinetts von W. A. Mozart«, »Joseph Beuys – Arbeiten in Blei«, »Mobil – Die Öko-art collection«, »Nordkunst – Südkunst«.

Als Zwischenlager für den zirkulierenden Strom der Kulturgüter errichten wir Museen.
Sie entstanden als Repräsentationsmaschinen in der großen Zeit der Dampfmaschinen und Weltausstellungen, entwickelten Eigengesetzlichkeit und erleben gerade einen neuerlichen sogenannten Aufschwung. Gilt die Metapher von der »Kunstverpackung«, so ist heute, da Verpackung zu einem Müllproblem der postindustriellen Gesellschaft geworden ist, umso dringlicher die Frage nach Überprüfung von Inhalt, Mitteln, Zielen, ja Visionen zu stellen.
Im 19. Jahrhundert haben humanistische Gelehrte alle ihnen erreichbaren beweglichen Kulturspuren der Vergangenheit mit Objektcharakter (obere Gewichtsgrenze etwa der Parthenonfries), vorerst noch ohne Marktwert, zu sammeln und anzuhäufen begonnen. Ein romanischer Crucifixus, eine Madonna Cimabues ... später ein Pamphlet der Dadaisten mutierten zu Kunstwerken und werden nun von der Wissenschaft immer aufwendiger analysiert, erhalten und in wechselnden Zusammenhängen neu geordnet.
In der Gegenwart, der Epoche der Produkte, definiert sich jede Institution über Umsatzkapazitäten. Museen müssen ihre Angebote nach denselben Methoden von Werbung und Vertrieb transportieren wie

Towards a Museum of the Mind with a View of Clouds and Countries

Mario Terzic

Border Italy/Austria, Brenner customs, 21.4.1992. The loads in the lorries from left to right: *'Gold of the Celts'*, *'Henry Moore – the Late Work'*, *'Metropolitana Berlin–Rome'*, *'24 of the 100 Most Expensive Artists in 1991'*, *'Ceremonial Armour of the Gonzagas'*, *'Street Furniture of the AAD Chicago'*, *'Wisdom in Stone – the Conte Pavone Collection'*, *'Seven Copies of W.A. Mozart's Spinette'*, *'Joseph Beuys – Works in Lead'*, *'Mobil – the Eco-Art Collection'*, *'North Art – South Art'*.

We build museums for the intermediate storage of the circulating stream of cultural goods.
They originated as machines for representation purposes, in the great days of steam-engines and world exhibitions, became autonomous and are at present undergoing a new so-called 'boom'. If the metaphor of 'art packaging' is valid, then the urgency of the question of the examination of contents, means, aims and indeed visions is that much greater today, when packaging has become a problem of refuse disposal in post-industrial society.
In the 19th century, Humanist scholars began to collect and accumulate all the remnants of past culture that they could lay their hands on, in the form of movable objects (upper weight limit approximately that of Parthenon Frieze), these being at first still without market value. A Romanesque Crucifix, a Madonna by Cimabue ... later a pamphlet by the Dadaists ... all mutated into works of art and, from then on – analysed by scholars in ever more extravagant ways – were preserved and reclassified in a variety of contexts.
At the present time, in this age of the manufactured product, every institution defines itself in terms of its turnover capacity. Museums must communicate what they have to offer by the same methods of advertising and distribution as the

die Produzenten von Autos, Unterhaltungselektronik oder Speiseeis. Folglich haben italienische Händler und deutsche Manager auf internationaler Ebene die Lenkung von Museumsketten übernommen, Bernie Ecclestone soll sich für das Projekt einer Weltkulturneuordnung interessieren.

Zahllose lokale Kulturpolitiker sorgen dafür, daß Geld, Energie und Parkplätze bereitgestellt werden.

Siegreiche Architekten bauen immer mehr Museen der Fünfsternkategorie ... und dann stehen sie da – leise summend und dampfend, im Tag- und Nachtbetrieb, klimatisiert, gesichert, versichert und in die Medientermine eingebettet.

Künstler wetteifern im Liefern der Produkte, die die neuen Hallen füllen. Der Bedarf ist gewaltig, und es scheint, als wären wir auf die Maßstäbe Makarts und der Pariser »pompiers« zurückgeworfen.

Doch entgegen den beharrlichen Tendenzen der Kunstprodukte, sich anzuhäufen; der Märkte, Deponien zu schaffen; des Kapitals, Werte zu steigern; der Politik, Triumphbögen zu fordern, haben Künstler seit Beginn des 20. Jahrhunderts Leuchtfeuer einer Freiheit entzündet, die aus den historischen Labyrinthen herausführen könnten!

Es geht nicht um window-shopping am »Kulturkorso«, sondern um Sehen als schöpferischen Akt. Künstler markieren die Spuren ihres Geistes nicht mehr durch den Großverbrauch von Leinwand und Gips.

Avantgardisten entdecken und modellieren die Geschwindigkeit, schleudern die Schatten ihrer Versuche mit Apparaten und Maschinen in die Zukunft – Hundertstelsekundenbildhauer treten auf. Nur wer Augen hat zu folgen, der sieht!

Zeus, Aphrodite, Dionysos und die ganze olympische Bildungsbürgerverwandtschaft sind nicht mehr aus parischem Marmor, stehen nicht mehr auf Podesten. Die Szenen des erotischen Welttheaters werden für die Kameras gestellt und medial um den Erdball verbreitet. Anstelle der Götter entflammen Divas aus Hollywood und

manufacturers of cars, audio systems or ice-cream. As a result of this, Italian traders and German managers have taken over the management of museum chains at an international level; it is even rumoured that Bernie Ecclestone is interested in a project entitled 'New Cultural World Order'.

Numerous local politicians responsible for the arts ensure that money, energy and parking space is made available.

Winning architects build ever more museums of the five-star category ... and there they stand – quietly humming and steaming, running day and night, air-conditioned, safeguarded, insured and bogged down in dates with the media.

Artists compete with one another to deliver the products which fill the new halls. The demand is enormous, and it seems as if we have been thrown back on the standards of Makart and the Parisian "pompiers".

Yet despite the persistent tendency of art products to accumulate, of the market to create waste disposal sites, of capital to increase the value of things, of politics to demand triumphal arches, artists have, ever since the beginning of the 20th century, been lighting the flares of a freedom which could lead us out of the historical labyrinth. It is not a case of window-shopping on the 'cultural corso', but of seeing as a creative act. Artists no longer mark the tracks of their spirit with a great consumption of canvas and gypsum.

Avantgarde artists discover and shape speed itself, propelling the shadow of their experiments with apparatuses and machines into the future – hundredths-of-a-second sculptors appear. Only he who has eyes to follow, sees!

Zeus, Aphrodite, Dionysos and all the relatives of the Olympian educated classes are no longer made of Paros marble, they no longer stand on pedestals. The scenes of the erotic world theatre are set up for the cameras and disseminated around the globe by the media. In place of the gods it is divas from Hollywood and Cinecittà, models from advertising who excite our senses, and we are abducted by the embrace of Mr. and Mrs. Woodman under

Man Ray, *Mr. and Mrs. Woodman*, 1927

Man Ray, *A Francis Picabia en grande vitesse*, Cannes, 1924

Marcel Duchamp, *Schachfiguren*, 1918/19
Marcel Duchamp, *Chess Pieces*, 1918/19

Yves Klein, *Verkauf von immateriellen,
malerischen Sensibilitätszonen*, Paris, 10. 2. 1962
Yves Klein, *Sale of Immaterial, Painterly Zones
of Sensibility*, Paris, 1962-02-10

Cinecittà, Models aus der Werbung unsere Sinne, und die Umarmung von Mr. und Mrs. Woodman entführt uns unter Sterne, die vielleicht ebenso hell leuchten wie einst die von Kythera.

Für die nicht endenwollenden Feldzüge der Strategen ersinnt ein scharfer Geist Spielfiguren, die Fläche von einigen Quadratzentimetern genügt – auf ins Schlachtgetümmel! Frauen und Lorbeer warten auf den Sieger.

Mit einer Geste, einer einzigen Handbewegung gelingt einem Helden der visuellen Künste die Schöpfung immaterieller, malerischer Sensibilitätszonen. Museen welken zu Lagerhallen historischen Gerümpels. Aufforderung an alle: Bauen Sie Ihre eigenen Sensibilitätszonen! Stecken Sie sich prächtige Balzkreise ab, setzen Sie Duftmarken Ihrer Phantasie!

Hin und wieder wird die alte Kulturmaschine verwendet wie auch ein Atelier oder eine Werkstatt, um demonstrativ »seherische« Notwendigkeit herzustellen – so zum Beispiel mit einem Blick ins schwarze Ofenloch. Doch selbst diese Tat gilt mehr den Medien als den scheuen Musen.

Die magischen Felder der Großstadt sind Museum der Gegenwart geworden, Tourismus eine seiner Erfahrungsmöglichkeiten. Also bietet ein Künstler Sehwerkzeuge an und entwickelt komplexe Szenarien: Es entsteht der »Sehwerkzeugkasten«. Inhalt: Stadtplan mit Führer, Arbeitsbögen aus Papier und Karton mit Anleitung, Aufkleber sowie diverse Objekte. Der moderne Stadtwanderer bringt seine Erfahrung, Sensibilität, Kunstwissen, Architekturfühlen, Bewegungslust mit und schafft sich mittels der Sehwerkzeuge seine eigenen Bilder.

Projekt für ein Museum im Flugzeug – Bausteine für noch nie gesehene Ausstellungen

Muße für freischwebende Saltos im Kopf und für Kunstbetrachtung ist auf der Erde knapp geworden. In den Pionierzeiten des Fliegens, die nur wenige Reiche als Passa-

stars which perhaps shine just as brightly as those of Cythera once did.

A keen-witted man invents the board pieces for the strategists' never-ending campaigns; all that he needs is a few square centimetres – off to the fray! Women and laurel await the victor.

With one gesture, one single movement of the hand, a hero of the visual arts succeeds in creating immaterial painterly zones of sensibility. Museums are fading away into warehouses of historic junk. An invitation to everyone: build your own zones of sensibility! Stake out splendid mating circles, leave behind the scent marks of your imagination!

Now and again the old cultural machine is used like a studio or a workshop, in order to deliberately produce 'visionary' necessity – for example, with a glance into the black hole of the stove-pipe. Yet even this act is performed more for the media than for the shy muses.

The magical fields of the city have become the museum of the present, tourism one of its experiential possibilities. Thus an artist offers 'looking-tools' and develops complex scenarios: 'looking-toolboxes' are made. Contents: map of the city, work folder of paper and cardboard with instructions, stickers and various other objects. The modern city wanderer brings with him his experience, sensibility, knowledge of art, feeling for architecture and desire for movement; and he uses his 'looking-tools' in order to create his own pictures.

Project for a museum in an aeroplane – building blocks for an exhibition never seen before

On the earth there is a shortage of leisure time both for free-floating mental acrobatics and for contemplating art. In the pioneer days of flight, which only the wealthy few could experience as passengers, luxury was provided in the form of exquisite meals. Today, millions of travellers fly every day. All that remains of

giere erleben konnten, wurde mit erlesenen Speisen Luxus geboten. Heute sind täglich Millionen Reisende im Flugzeug unterwegs. Vom Erlesenen ist nur eine Fastfood-Erinnerung geblieben. Verzichten Sie gleich ganz auf Ihre Mahlzeit mit Farbstoff und Benzoesäure! Bestellen Sie bei der Stewardeß wahren Sinnen- und Geistesluxus, Ihr Museum: »Would you kindly bring me the museum, please?« Hoch über den Kulturmaschinen der alten Welt, fern vom Gedränge der Besuchermassen, den Eröffnungsreden der Kuratoren, didaktischen Hinweisen und freundlichen Aufmerksamkeiten von Sponsoren schöpfen Sie die universellen Möglichkeiten der servierten Bausteine aus! Mit dem erregenden Blick über Wolken und Länder, mit pochendem Herzen folgen Sie den Menüvorschlägen, oder komponieren Sie selbst –

the exquisite meals is a memory of fast-food. Forget your meal with its artificial colourings and benzoic acids once and for all! Order from the stewardess real luxury for your senses and mind – your museum: "Would you kindly bring me the museum, please?"
High above the cultural machines of the old world, far from the throng of visitors, from curators' opening speeches, from didactic instructions and the friendly attentions of sponsors, you can take advantage of the universal possibilities of the building blocks which you are served! With an exciting view over clouds and countries, with a palpitating heart, you can either follow our meal suggestions or else compose your own:

Joseph Beuys, *Ofenloch*, Düsseldorf, 1981
Joseph Beuys, *Stovepipe*, Düsseldorf, 1981

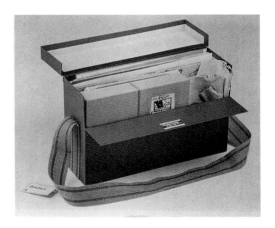

Mario Terzic, *Sehwerkzeugkasten – Paris*, 1990
Mario Terzic, *Looking-Tool-Box – Paris*, 1990

MENÜ *I*

JOIE DE VIVRE

Einige Schnitte und Löcher Fontana.

Morgenrötliche Schrittfolgen im Garten der Villa Gamberaia, unter Fontänen und Wasserschleiern Jean Tinguely.

Heiße Abgase Bugatti Royale, 12 Zylinder, 12.763 ccm Hubraum an Altweibersommer aus Elsässer Weinbergen.

2 oder 3 federnde Pirouetten à la Ballets Russes. Schweißduft Meret Oppenheim. Anemonen, Ginster.

Kandinsky »little accents«. Panflöten.

Ballspiel mit Photomodellen von Man Ray auf Lichtungen im Wald von Barbizon. Himmel von Théodore Rousseau.

Augenrast in Mobile Calder mit hymnischen Zeilen Prévert.

Windgleiten mit Prunkepauletten – links Balenciaga, rechts Fortuny.

Flüchtige Begegnung mit Aristide Maillol.

Addio metafisico.

MENÜ *I*

JOIE DE VIVRE

A few slices and holes of Fontana.

Sunrise-coloured sequence of steps in the garden of the Villa Gamberaia, beneath Jean Tinguely fountains and waterfalls.

Hot exhaust fumes of Bugatti Royale, 12 cylinder, 12.763 cc with Indian summer from Alsatian vineyards.

2 oder 3 springy pirouettes aux Ballets Russes. Meret Oppenheim scent of sweat. Anemones, broom.
Kandinsky's *Little accents*. Pipes of Pan.

Ball game with photographic models by Man Ray in the groves of the Forest at Barbizon. Sky by Théodore Rousseau.

Rest for the eyes in a Calder mobile with hymnic lines by Prévert.

Wind-gliding with ceremonial epaulettes – left Balenciaga, right Fortuny.

Fleeting encounter with Aristide Maillol.

Addio metafisico.

MENÜ II

PLASTISCHE KONSTRUKTION MIT MOTORENGERÄUSCH

Esprit Corbusier

Lissitzky	Gabo	Krupp	Tatlin	Fuller	Prouvé
Gabo	Krupp	Tatlin	Fuller	Prouvé	Lissitzky
Krupp	Tatlin	Fuller	Prouvé	Lissitzky	Gabo
Tatlin	Fuller	Prouvé	Lissitzky	Gabo	Krupp
Fuller	Prouvé	Lissitzky	Gabo	Krupp	Tatlin
Prouvé	Lissitzky	Gabo	Krupp	Tatlin	Fuller
	Gabo	Krupp	Tatlin	Fuller	
		Tatlin	Fuller		

Olivetti   Sottsass   Pirelli

Rietveld   Zig Zag Zig

Taifuntest von Norman Foster

Wroom Wroom Wroooom / Kawasaki 500

MENÜ III

OHNE TITEL

Menu II

PLASTIC CONSTRUCTION WITH DIN OF AN ENGINE.

Esprit Corbusier

Lissitzky	Gabo	Krupp	Tatlin	Fuller	Prouvé
Gabo	Krupp	Tatlin	Fuller	Prouvé	Lissitzky
Krupp	Tatlin	Fuller	Prouvé	Lissitzky	Gabo
Tatlin	Fuller	Prouvé	Lissitzky	Gabo	Krupp
Fuller	Prouvé	Lissitzky	Gabo	Krupp	Tatlin
Prouvé	Lissitzky	Gabo	Krupp	Tatlin	Fuller
	Gabo	Krupp	Tatlin	Fuller	
		Tatlin	Fuller		

Olivetti   Sottsass   Pirelli

Rietveld   Zig Zag Zig

Typhoon test by Norman Foster

Vroom vroom vrooom / Kawasaki 500

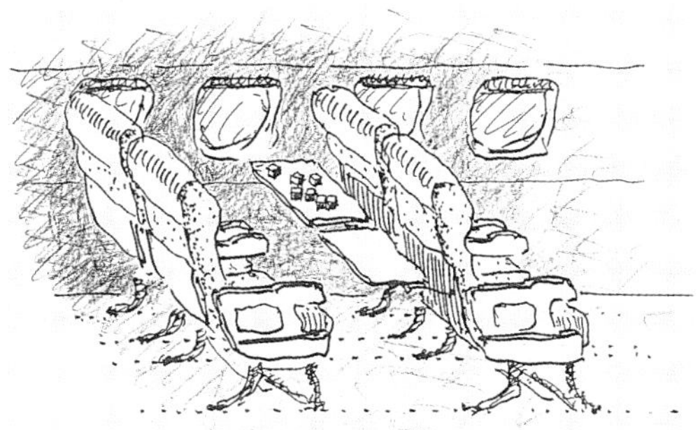

Flugzeug, *Kunst-Menüs*
Aeroplane, *Art-Menus*

Menu III

UNTITLED

Mario Terzic, *Menü I*
Mario Terzic, *Menu I*

Mario Terzic, *Menü II*
Mario Terzic, *Menu II*

Mario Terzic, *Menü III*
Mario Terzic, *Menu III*

Die Architektur des Museums der Gegenwart Betrachtungen aus der Frankfurter Perspektive

Vittorio Magnago Lampugnani

Als im März 1945 die Dritte U. S.-Armee in Frankfurt am Main einmarschierte, lagen 17 Millionen Tonnen Schutt auf den Trümmern einer historischen Stadt, die einst zu den schönsten Deutschlands gezählt hatte und von welcher fast nichts übriggeblieben war. Der Wiederaufbau geriet eher zum Neubau: was in Jahrhunderten sorgfältig und liebevoll übereinandergeschichtet, komplettiert, modifiziert und verschönert worden war, wurde nun endgültig abgeräumt und eiligst mit Bruchstücken einer abstrakten »Neuen Stadt« ersetzt. Um den »Römer« im Herzen der Stadt entstand schon Anfang der fünfziger Jahre eine gut gemeinte, aber naiv gedachte und auf jeden Fall völlig displazierte vorstädtische Idylle mit niedrigen Wohnhäusern und heimeligen Spielstraßen. In den sechziger und siebziger Jahren, während am Stadtrand gewalttätige Siedlungen emporwuchsen und vermittels brutal trassierter Stadtautobahnen mit dem Zentrum verbunden wurden, verwandelte man, gleichsam als verschämte Kompensation, die fahrig zusammengeflickte Innenstadt teilweise in eine Fußgängerzone und möblierte sie grobschlächtig. Unmittelbar nebenan sprossen eine Handvoll kaum erstklassiger Bürohäuser wie geometrisch glitzernde Pilze aus dem Boden und schickten sich an, die noch halbwegs intakte alte Bausubstanz des Westends anzufressen. Um diese Zeit begann man, von Frankfurt am Main als von der häßlichsten Stadt Deutschlands zu munkeln.

Um diese Zeit begann man aber auch, sich gegen die fortschreitende Zerstörung der Architektur (und der Identität) der Stadt zu wehren. Bürgerinitiativen bekämpften den Vormarsch der kommerziellen Umwidmung des urbanen Gewebes und seine physische Auflösung. Der Zuspruch, der ihnen zuteil wurde, veranlaßte die Stadtregierung, sich deren Ziele zu eigen zu

The Architecture of the Contemporary Museum: Reflections from a Frankfurt Perspective

Vittorio Magnago Lampugnani

When, in March 1945, the 3rd U.S. Army marched into Frankfurt am Main, 17 tons of rubble were lying on top of the ruins of a historical city which had once been regarded as one of the most beautiful in Germany, yet of which almost nothing now survived. Reconstruction developed into new construction: what had been carefully and lovingly built up layer upon layer, perfected, modified and beautified was now cleared away once and for all, to be hurriedly replaced by the fragments of an abstract 'new city'. At the beginning of the fifties, there developed around the Römer, in the heart of the city, a well-intended but naively thought-out and, at all events, completely misplaced 'idyllic' suburban landscape, with low residential buildings and homely play-streets. During the sixties and seventies, when violent housing estates shot up on the outskirts of the city, linked to the centre by means of brutally mapped-out city motorways, the carelessly pieced-together city centre was partly transformed (more or less by way of modest compensation) into a pedestrian area, and roughly furnished as such. Right next door, a handful of rather poor-quality office blocks sprouted from the ground like glittering geometrical mushrooms and set about eating away at the old architectural substance of the Westend, which was still half-intact. It was around this time that people began to whisper about Frankfurt am Main being the ugliest city in Germany. However, it was also around this time that people began to offer resistance to the progressive destruction of the architecture (and identity) of their city. Pressure groups fought the advance of commercial reallocation of the urban structure and its physical disintegration. The encouragement which they received caused the city council to adopt their aims as its own and come out in its turn against the devaluation

machen und nun ihrerseits gegen die Entwertung der Stadt anzutreten.

Die Stadtregierung tat indessen noch mehr: sie schrieb die Architektur als Politikum auf ihre Fahnen, und zwar nicht nur defensiv, um das gute Vorhandene zu erhalten, sondern offensiv, um hochwertiges Neues zu realisieren. Die baukünstlerische *Tabula rasa* von Frankfurt am Main legte eine solche Strategie nahe, die besondere Situation der Stadt forderte sie. Denn die hochbezahlten und anspruchsvollen Mitarbeiter der Banken und großen Konzerne waren nur zu halten, wenn man ihnen eine entsprechende urbane Umgebung anbot.

Das erste große Projekt, das im Rahmen dieser Strategie lanciert wurde, war jenes des Museumsufers. Zwischen 1980 und 1990 sind in Frankfurt am Main zwölf neue Museen entstanden. Teilweise handelt es sich um Neubauten, teilweise um Restrukturierungen oder Ergänzungen. Sie sind fast ausnahmslos von hochbegabten und prominenten Architekten entworfen und zeigen so etwas wie einen Querschnitt durch die Geschichte der internationalen Baukunst des vergangenen Jahrzehnts auf. Zu erstaunlich reinen Materialisierungen der jeweiligen »Handschrift« ihrer Autoren geraten, stellen sie sich allerdings nicht selten mit ihren störrischen Raumkonstruktionen und ihrer künstlerischen Autonomie der praktischen Nutzung, für welche sie bestimmt sind, selbstvergessen entgegen. Das Vorhaben erregte jedenfalls Aufsehen, fand in der Presse weltweit ein breites Echo und trug der Stadt den Ruf eines Mekka der zeitgenössischen Architektur ein.

Weniger vermerkt wurde indessen das, was das größte Verdienst des Projekts Museumsufer ist. Denn die Realisierung einer zusammenhängenden Folge von belehrenden und unterhaltenden Institutionen hatte nicht nur das Ziel, ein vielfältiges Panorama von spektakulären Schauplätzen bildnerischer Formen zu schaffen. In erster Linie ging es darum, eine Sequenz von Bürgervillen, die das »Gesicht« der Stadt zum Fluß hin bestimmten, vor dem drohenden Abriß zu retten. Die Altbauten wurden sorgfältig erhalten und mit mehr oder minder Geschick dem neuen Zweck

of the city. Nevertheless, the city council did even more: it took up the cause of architecture as a political matter; and, moreover, not only defensively, in order to preserve the good buildings that already existed, but also offensively, so as to realise new projects of high quality. Although such a strategy was indeed suggested by the *tabula rasa* of Frankfurt am Main, the city's special situation positively demanded it. For one could only hold on to the highly paid and fastidious employees of the banks and large companies if one offered them a suitable urban environment in which to live.

The first big project to be launched within the framework of this strategy was that of the riverbank museum complex. Between 1980 and 1990, twelve new museums were built in Frankfurt am Main. In part, these were new buildings; in part, conversions or extensions. Almost without exception they were designed by highly talented and prominent architects, and display something resembling a cross-section through the history of international architecture over the past decade. Turning out to be astonishingly pure materialisations of their authors' respective 'signatures', they not infrequently offer absent-minded resistance (in their obstinate spatial constructions and artistic autonomy) to the practical use for which they were intended. At all events, the project attracted attention, met with a wide response from the world's press, and gained the city the reputation of being the mecca of contemporary architecture.

Meanwhile, the great service performed by the riverbank museum project had received rather less attention. In realising a coherent series of institutions for educational and entertainment purposes, the aim was not only to create a variegated panorama of spectacular showplaces with artistic forms; it was, in the first place, also a matter of saving from threatened demolition a row of middle-class villas which dominated the city's riverside 'face'. The old buildings were carefully preserved and more or less skilfully adapted to their new purpose (and to new architectural intentions). That applies to the *Deutsche Architectur Museum* by Oswald Matthias

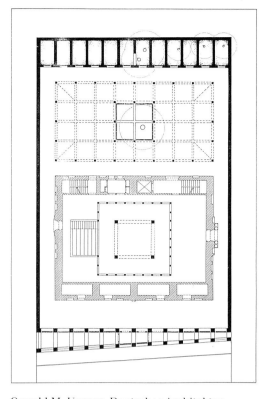

Oswald M. Ungers, Deutsches Architekturmuseum Frankfurt, Grundriß Erdgeschoß, 1981–84
Oswald M. Ungers, German Museum of Architecture in Frankfurt, ground floor plan, 1981–84

Ante Josip von Kostelac, Jüdisches Museum
Frankfurt, Schnittperspektive, 1985–89
Ante Josip von Kostelac, Jewish Museum,
Frankfurt, section, 1985–89

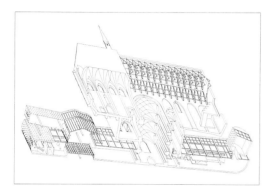

Josef P. Kleihues, Museum für Vor- und Frühgeschichte, Frankfurt, Isometrische Gebäudeuntersicht, 1985–89
Josef P. Kleihues, Museum for Ancient and
Prehistory, Frankfurt, isometric projection from
underneath the building, 1985–89

(und den neuen architektonischen Absichten) gefügig gemacht. Das trifft für das *Deutsche Architektur-Museum* von Oswald Matthias Ungers zu, für das *Deutsche Filmmuseum* von Helge Bofinger, für das *Museum für Kunsthandwerk* von Richard Meier, für das *Jüdische Museum* von Ante Josip von Kostelac sowie für das *Deutsche Postmuseum* von Behnisch und Partner. Das trifft aber auch zu für Josef Paul Kleihues' *Museum für Vor- und Frühgeschichte* (obwohl dort nicht eine Villa, sondern eine Kirche erhalten wurde) und für Marie-Theres Deutschs und Klaus Dreißigackers *Portikus* (er schiebt sich keck hinter eine klassizistische Ruine). Das *Ikonenmuseum* (Oswald Matthias Ungers) ist ohnehin ein umgebautes Interieur, die Erweiterungsbauten des *Städels* (Gustav Peichl) und des *Liebieghauses* (Ernst Ulrich Scheffler und Thomas Warschauer) eben Annexe. Lediglich die *Kunsthalle Schirn* von Dietrich Bangert, Bernd Jansen, Stefan Scholz und Axel Schultes, das *Museum für Moderne Kunst* von Hans Hollein und das *Museum für Völkerkunde* (wiederum von Richard Meier geplant) sind reine Neubauten, fügen sich jedoch bewußt in ihre städtische Umgebung ein. Alle diese Architekturen stellen, wenngleich auf freilich unterschiedliche Art und Weise, eine ernsthaft betriebene Stadterhaltung und Stadtreparatur dar, die den leichtfertigen Umgang mit der historischen Stadt demonstrativ abgelöst hat. Als Galionsfigur eines veränderten Verständnisses von Urbanität hat das Projekt an den beiden Ufern des Mains nicht nur den Frankfurter Bürgern erneut ein Gefühl für urbanes Leben vermittelt, sondern auch andere Städte zum Nachdenken und Nachahmen gebracht.

Überdies kann es, jenseits der spezifischen Frankfurter Belange, zu einer Klärung dessen beitragen, was heute die Bauaufgabe Museum bedeutet und bedeuten muß. Denn in kaum einer anderen Stadt wurde sie von allen Seiten so ernst genommen und so intensiv betrieben.
Bereits auf den ersten, noch vergleichsweise flüchtigen Blick läßt sich feststellen: Die Bauaufgabe Museum stellt nicht die Spielwiese für Architekten dar, die mancher Baumeister zu Beginn des europäischen

Ungers, to the *Deutsche Filmmuseum* by Helge Bofinger, to the *Museum für Kunsthandwerk* ('Museum of the Decorative Arts') by Richard Meier, to the *Jüdische Museum* by Ante Josip von Kostelac, as well as to the *Deutsche Postmuseum* by Benisch and partners. However, it also applies to Josef Paul Kleihues' *Museum für Vor- und Frühgeschichte* ('Museum of Prehistory and Ancient History'), although in this case it was not a villa but rather a church which was preserved, and to the Portikus by Marie-Therés Deutsch and Klaus Dreißigacker, which they audaciously slid in behind a classicistic ruin. The *Ikonenmuseum* (by Oswald Matthias Ungers) is a renovated interior anyway, while the extension buildings of the *Städel* (Gustav Peichl) and the *Liebieghaus* (Ernst Ulrich Scheffler and Thomas Warschauer) are - obviously enough - annexes. The only completely new buildings are the *Kunsthalle Schirn* by Dietrich Bangert, Bernd Jansen, Stefan Scholz and Axel Scholtes, the *Museum für Moderne Kunst* by Hans Hollein and the *Museum für Völkerkunde* ('Museum of Anthropology'; another of Meier's designs); each of them has been consciously designed to fit in with the urban environment.

Of course, all these buildings represent, in different ways, a serious approach to urban preservation and urban repair, which has demonstratively replaced the thoughtless treatment accorded to the historical city. As the figurehead of a changed understanding of urbanity, this project along the banks of the Main has not only given the citizens of Frankfurt a new feeling for urban living, but also made other cities reflect upon and imitate its example.

Furthermore, beyond the specific requirements of Frankfurt, it can help to contribute to a clarification of what the architectural task of the museum signifies today, what it must signify. In hardly any other city has this been taken so seriously and pursued so intensively by all sides.
At even the first (still comparatively fleeting) glance, it can be established that the architectural problem of the museum does not constitute a playground for architects,

Museumsbooms, also Anfang der siebziger Jahre, zu gewärtigen meinte. Was zunächst vielerorts euphorisch als die Gelegenheit für die große neue Freiheit der Architektur begrüßt wurde, hat sich bei genauerer Betrachtung und vor allem in der konkreten Anwendung als fester Bestandteil der Disziplin des Bauerns entpuppt, der als solcher auch ihren Regeln zu folgen hat. Es sind die Regeln der Architektur der Stadt, der Aufgabe und der Form.

Vor allem in Frankfurt am Main hat sich gezeigt, daß Museen mitnichten singuläre bauliche und funktionale Episoden in einem städtischen Gefüge sein können, zu welchem sie sich indifferent verhalten. Im Gegenteil dazu müssen sie als integraler Bestandteil einer Stadt verstanden werden, die sie ergänzen, vervollständigen und verbessern sollen. Das muß keineswegs dogmatisch im Sinn des Kontextualismus aufgefaßt werden. Die Frankfurter Museen sind für die Stadt deswegen so wertvoll und bereichernd, weil sie entscheidend zu deren Erhaltung und Reparatur beigetragen haben. Das ist für Frankfurt am Main, der doppelt zerstörten und zutiefst verunstalteten Stadt, angemessen: sie vermag dadurch etwas von der verlorenen Identität wieder zurückzugewinnen.

Für andere Städte, die eine andere Geschichte geprägt hat und die entsprechend andere Situationen aufweisen, mögen andere Strategien richtig sein. Konkret gesagt: in anderen urbanen Situationen, etwa in intakten städtischen Gefügen, kann sich die öffentliche Funktion Museum durchaus auch mit monumentalen Solitärbauten repräsentieren, deren Platz durch sinnvolle Abrisse geschaffen wird, wie es etwa beim Pariser Centre Georges Pompidou der Fall gewesen ist. Und in wieder anderen Situationen, die etwa durch die Gruppierung von Einzelbauten gekennzeichnet sind, sollte ein Museum sich als weiterer Einzelbau behaupten, wie es etwa Peter Zumthor bei der neuen Landesgalerie Vorarlberg in Bregenz zu tun beabsichtigt. Es geht weder um Einseitigkeit noch um Orthodoxie, sondern darum, ein Museum immer als Teil seines Kontextes zu betrachten und entsprechend zu konzipieren.

as some of them expected it would at the beginning of the European museum boom, i.e. at the beginning of the seventies. What received a euphoric welcome in many places as the opportunity for a great new freedom in architecture, has, after closer examination and, more particularly, in concrete application, turned out to be a fixed component of the discipline of architecture, which, as such, also has its rules to follow. These are the rules of the architecture of the city, of the challenge it presents, of its form.

Above all in Frankfurt am Main it has been shown that museums can in no way be unique architectural and functional episodes in an urban structure to which they behave indifferently. On the contrary, they must be understood as integral components of a city which they should complement, complete and improve. This must by no means be understood in a dogmatic way, in the sense of contextualism. The reason why the Frankfurt museums are so valuable and beneficial for the city is precisely because they have made a decisive contribution to its conservation and repair. This is quite appropriate for Frankfurt am Main, a city doubly destroyed and profoundly disfigured: in this way it was able once more to regain something of its lost identity. For other cities, which have been shaped by a different history and exhibit of correspondingly different situations, other strategies may be appropriate. To put it in concrete terms: in other urban situations, for example in urban structures which are intact, the public function of the museum might quite possibly also be represented by monumental free-standing buildings whose place is created by useful demolitions, as was the case, for instance, with the Centre Georges Pompidou in Paris. And in still other situations, for instance those characterised by grouping together isolated buildings, a museum should assert itself as yet another isolated building, as Peter Zumthor, for example, intends to do with the new Landesgalerie Vorarlberg in Bregenz. It is a question neither of one-sidedness nor of orthodoxy, but one of always regarding a museum as part of its own wider context and of designing it accordingly.

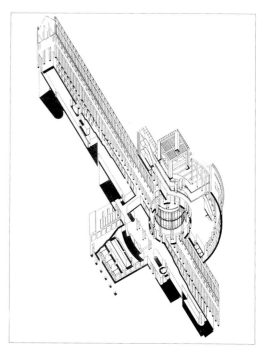

Bangert, Jansen, Scholz und Schultes, Kunsthalle Schirn, Frankfurt, Isometrische Gebäudeuntersicht, 1983–85
Bangert, Jansen, Scholz and Schultes, Kunsthalle Schirn, Frankfurt, isometric projection from underneath the building, 1983–85

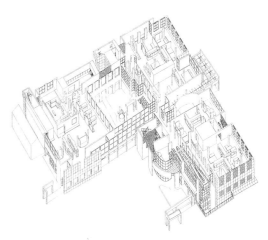

Richard Meier, Museum für Kunsthandwerk, Frankfurt, Isometrie Ausstellungsräume 1. Obergeschoß, 1982–85
Richard Meier, Museum of Arts and Crafts, Frankfurt, isometric projection of the exhibition rooms, first floor plan, 1982–85

47

Gustav Peichl, Zubau Städel Museum,
Frankfurt, 1987–90
Gustav Peichl, Extension of the Städel Museum,
Frankfurt, 1987–90

Ebensowenig wie über seine urbanistischen Maßgaben kann sich ein Museum über jene seiner Aufgabe hinwegsetzen. Ein Museum ist zunächst ein Ort für Kunstwerke, die dort aufbewahrt und ausgestellt werden. Ein Museum ist aber auch ein Ort für die Menschen, die diese Kunstwerke möglichst konzentriert und ungestört betrachten wollen. Daraus ergeben sich keine beliebigen Raumprogramme, sondern vielmehr genaue Vorgaben, die in Architektur umgesetzt zu werden haben. Nur in ganz besonderen Räumen können Kunstwerke heimisch werden. Ihnen gemeinsam ist notwendigerweise jene Zurückhaltung, die den Ausstellungsstücken bescheiden den Vortritt läßt und lediglich deren schützenden Hintergrund bildet. Doch die extreme Neutralität, die sich aus dieser ersten Anforderung ableitet, kollidiert mit dem Identifikationsbedürfnis, das sich aus der zweiten ergibt. Die Besucher eines Museums geben sich nicht damit zufrieden, die Kunstwerke störungsfrei studieren und genießen zu können, sondern verlangen auch nach Elementen der Aneignung und der Orientierung. Der Widerspruch ist real, aber mitnichten unauflösbar. Er verlangt allerdings, daß sich der Architekt mit ihm (und mit seiner Spezifik) intensiv auseinandersetzt, und daß er diese Auseinandersetzung in den Dienst architektonischer Qualität stellt.

Hinzu kommt, daß die Institution des Museums seit ihrer Etablierung im 19. Jahrhundert einen tiefen Wandel durchgemacht hat. Was zunächst lediglich ein Ort der Betrachtung, Instruktion und Kontemplation für ein ausgewähltes bürgerliches Publikum war, ist heute ein Element der Massenausbildung und Massenunterhaltung. Dies kann man gutheißen oder ablehnen; ignorieren kann man es nicht. Zum großen Museum des 20. Jahrhunderts gehören neben den konventionellen Ausstellungssälen, denen die ebenso konventionellen Kabinette beigestellt sein müssen, Räume für Wechselausstellungen, Auditorien, Buchläden und Büchereien, Mediatheken, Cafés und Restaurants sowie ein Museumsladen. Dazu selbstverständlich ein großes öffentliches Foyer, das eine ähnliche Funktion wie das Foyer eines Theaters zu erfüllen hat: die Menschen

A museum can disregard the stipulations of its role as little as it can the urban stipulations. A museum is, first and foremost, a place where works of art are kept and exhibited. But a museum is also a place for people, who want to look at these works of art with as much concentration and as little distraction as possible. Instead of arbitrary spatial programmes, this entails exact specifications, which have to be translated into architecture. Works of art can only be at home in quite special spaces. Common to them all is, of necessity, that restraint which modestly allows the exhibits to come to the fore, and solely provides the protective backdrop. However, the extreme neutrality which can result from this first requirement tends to collide with the need for identification which results from a second requirement: for the visitor to a museum is not satisfied with simply being able to study and enjoy the works of art undisturbed, but also demands some elements of identification and orientation. The contradiction is a genuine one, but by no means insoluble. However, it is necessary for the architect to confront it (and its specific characteristics) and to use this confrontation to achieve architectural quality.

There is also the additional fact that the institution of the museum has undergone a profound transformation since its establishment in the 19th century. What was at first a place of contemplation, instruction and reflection for a select middle-class public is today an element of mass education and mass entertainment. This may be welcomed or rejected, but it cannot be ignored. Beside conventional exhibition rooms (to which must be added the equally conventional museum galleries), the large 20th century museum also includes rooms for temporary exhibitions, an auditorium, a bookshop and library, a mediatheque, a cafe and a restaurant, as well as a museum shop. And, of course, it also includes a large public entrance hall, which has similar functions to those of the foyer in a theatre: namely, to receive the people as they stream into the building, and to provide them with the opportunity for socialisation and communication while they orient themselves to what the institution has to

aufnehmen, die in das Gebäude hineinströmen, und ihnen in der Zeit, in welcher sie sich über das institutionelle Angebot orientieren und für das eine oder das andere entscheiden, die Gelegenheit zur Geselligkeit und zur Kommunikation bieten. Daraus ergibt sich ein außerordentlich differenziertes funktionales und räumliches Programm, das sich in ganz neue architektonische Gebilde niederschlagen wird. Erste Beispiele dafür existieren bereits: so das bereits erwähnte Centre Pompidou auf dem Pariser Plateau Beaubourg von Renzo Piano und Richard Rogers, aber auch, in einem ganz anderen architektursprachlichen Duktus, das Sainsbury Wing von Robert Venturi und Denise Scott Brown, die erlesen historisierende, elegant angepaßte Erweiterung der Londoner National Gallery.

Die beiden gerade erwähnten Beispiele könnten den Eindruck vermitteln, als sei die Architektursprache des zeitgenössischen Museums ebenso beliebig, wie der zeitgenössische architektonische Eklektizismus es suggeriert. Dem ist nicht so. Bleiben wir der Einfachheit halber bei den zwei Beispielen des Beaubourg und des Sainsbury Wing. Die High-Tech-Architektur des ersten ist kein vom Inhalt losgelöster Formalismus, der einer Laune der Architekten entspringt, sondern Zeichen, ja Manifest einer Aufbruchsstimmung, die auch das inhaltliche Programm des Museums vermittelt und verkörpert. Was mitten im Herzen von Paris in den siebziger Jahren entstand, war auch gar kein Museum im eigentlichen Sinn, sondern eine gewaltige Kulturmaschine, die sich nicht nur architektonisch auf eine Reihe von Experimenten einließ. Diese Experimente ermöglicht und repräsentiert die bunte und freche Architektur aus Stahl, Gußeisen, Glas und Plexiglas. Anders die vor einem Jahr fertiggestellte Erweiterung der National Gallery. Hier ging es in jeder Beziehung um eine Erweiterung: um die Fortsetzung des ehrwürdigen, international etablierten Museums am Trafalgar Square und um die Schaffung eines Ortes, in welchem die historischen Gemälde, die im Altbau keinen Raum mehr hatten, optimal ausgestellt werden sollten. Im Grunde sollte das Gebäude des 19. Jahrhunderts vergrößert

offer and decide in favour of one thing or another. This results in an exceptionally varied functional and spatial programme, and this will be reflected in quite new architectural structures. The first examples of this already exist: the aforementioned Centre Pompidou, designed by Renzo Piano and Richard Rogers, on the Plateau Beaubourg in Paris, for instance; or, alternatively, in the ductus of a quite different architectural language, that of the Sainsbury Wing by Robert Venturi and Denise Scott-Brown, the exquisitely historicising, elegantly converted extension of the National Gallery in London.

The two previously mentioned examples might give the impression that the architectural language of the contemporary museum is just as arbitrary as the contemporary architectural eclecticism might seem to suggest. But it is not so. Let us, for simplicity's sake, stay with the two examples of the Beaubourg and the Sainsbury Wing. The high-tech architecture of the former is in no way formalism divorced from content, simply deriving from an architect's whim, but a sign, a manifesto proclaiming a mood of new departure, which also conveys and embodies the programme of the museum's activities. Nor was what developed in the heart of Paris in the seventies a museum at all in the usual sense, but a powerful cultural machine which entered into a series of experiments, not only in architecture. These experiments facilitated and represented the colourful and audacious architecture of steel, cast iron, glass and plexiglass. Not so with the extension to the National Gallery, which was completed a year ago. In all respects, this was an extension: the continuation of the honourable, internationally established museum in Trafalgar Square; the creation of a place in which those historical paintings for which there was no longer enough room in the old building could be displayed to the best advantage. Basically, the building was supposed to be enlarged and nothing else. The architects submitted to this stipulation with a modesty as rare as it is admirable. However, the mimesis was not taken to such lengths that the extension could not be recognised for what it was. It was built in the 1980s, and even if it does

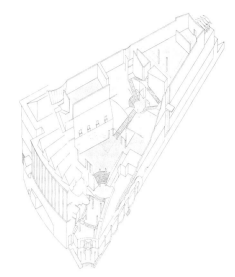

Hans Hollein, Museum für Moderne Kunst, Frankfurt, 1987–90
Hans Hollein, Museum of Modern Art, Frankfurt, 1987–90

Hans Hollein, Museum für Moderne Kunst,
Frankfurt, 1987–90
Hans Hollein, Museum of Modern Art,
Frankfurt, 1987–90

werden und sonst nichts. Dieser Maßgabe haben sich die Architekten mit ebenso seltener wie bewundernswerter Bescheidenheit unterworfen. Dennoch ist die Mimesis nicht so weit gegangen, daß man die Erweiterung nicht als solche erkennen könnte. Sie ist in den achtziger Jahren des 20. Jahrhunderts entstanden, und wenn sie sich auch den institutionellen und architektonischen Regeln des 19. Jahrhunderts beugt, so verrät sie dennoch unmißverständlich ihr Entstehungsdatum.

Das Museum also war und ist kein Ort, in welchem sich Architektenwillkür frei zu entfalten vermag. Das Museum ist aber auch kein Ort, in dem der Architekt von städtebaulichen, funktionalen und repräsentativen Bedingungen (und, müßte man hinzufügen, ökonomischen und juristischen Zwängen) geknebelt wird. Das Museum ist eine Bauaufgabe wie jede andere auch, mit Zwängen und Freiheiten, vielleicht sogar eine besonders günstige Aufgabe, weil die Zwänge nicht sonderlich ausgeprägt und die Freiheiten beachtlich sind. Mithin ist sie so etwas wie ein seismographisches Instrument, welches die Oszillationen und Erschütterungen der architektonischen Kultur frühzeitig und feinfühlig registriert. Vor allem aber ist sie die nahezu ideale Gelegenheit für den Architekten, seine ureigene Aufgabe zu erfüllen: aus einer Vielzahl von Bedingungen etwas zu schaffen, was diese Bedingungen in eine Poesie des Raumes sublimiert.

pay its dues to the institutional and architectural rules of the 19th century, it nevertheless betrays unmistakeably the date of its construction.

Thus the museum was not and is not a place in which the capriciousness of architects is able to develop freely. However, nor is the museum a place in which the architect is simply gagged by the conditions of urban planning, function and representation (and, one must add, also by economical and legal constraints). The museum presents an architectural task like any other, with constraints and liberties; perhaps it is even an especially favourable task, since the constraints are not overly pronounced and the liberties are considerable. It is therefore something like a seismographic instrument, which registers the oscillations and convulsions of architectural culture at an early stage and with great sensitivity. However, above all, it presents the architect with the almost ideal opportunity to fulfil the task peculiar to him alone: that of creating from a multitude of conditions and constraints something which sublimates those conditions and constraints and turns them into a poetry of space.

Hans Hollein, Museum für Moderne Kunst, Frankfurt, 1987–90
Hans Hollein, Museum of Modern Art, Frankfurt, 1987–90

Museums-Positionen in Österreich

Schnittstellen: das Objekt, die Form, die Verpackung und der Architekt

August Sarnitz

Museum Positions in Austria

Interfaces: the Object, the Form, the ' Packaging and the Architect

August Sarnitz

Gottfried Semper, Kunsthistorisches Museum, Wien, Blick in das Stiegenhaus, Photo 1891
Gottfried Semper, Museum of Fine Arts, Vienna, view of the great stairs, photograph 1891

Gottfried Semper, Erster Entwurf für das Wiener Forum mit den beiden Hofmuseen im Vordergrund, Federzeichnung, 1869
Gottfried Semper, first sketch for the Vienna Forum, with the two Imperial museums at the front, ink drawing, 1869

In seinem als Komödie bezeichneten Prosawerk »Alte Meister« reflektiert Thomas Bernhard über Kunst, Kunstbetrachtung, Musik, Philosophie, Literatur und das Leben. Im Mittelpunkt steht der 82jährige Musikphilosoph Reger, der seit sechsunddreißig Jahren in einem Zweitagerhythmus das Kunsthistorische Museum am Vormittag besucht, um anschließend seine Reflexion im Café des Hotels Ambassador fortzusetzen. Zwei Wiener Institutionen verbinden sich dialektisch in dieser Betrachtung zu einer Einheit; das Museum einerseits und das Kaffeehaus andererseits verdichten sich als Symbole für zwei Aspekte des Lebens: die auratische und die reale Welt des Menschen, die Welt des Geistes und die Welt der Gedanken. Das Kunsthistorische Museum als eine Stätte des »Geistes«, als eine Stätte der künstlerischen Ideale – weltentrückt in einer scheinbar zeitlosen Raumsymphonie –, wo der Dialog und die Frage nach den Dingen des Seins und des Lebens als kultische Handlung im Museumsbesuch gipfelt. Museum als Gralshüter menschlicher Geheimnisse, Museum als Ort menschlicher Perfektion in Sachen Kunst.

Im Gegensatz dazu steht das Kaffeehaus als eine Stätte der »Gedanken« – rational, weltlich und alltäglich –, wo das Leben sich reflektierend manifestiert.

Das Museum mit seinen Inhalten ist somit eine Aufforderung zum Dialog, nicht jedoch eine Antwort. Das Museum ist Weg, Diskussion, Agora oder Aktion – ein auratisiertes Medium des Gedankenaustausches. In diesem Sinn ist auch jedes Museum subjektiv, als es auratisch verklärt, was objektiv als Information betrachtet werden kann: das Museum als Mega-Chip authentischer Künstlichkeiten. Der Weg durch diese Künstlichkeiten macht neugierig und weckt den Geist. Somit sind wir dort angelangt, wo seit Beginn der Aufklärung

In his novel *Old Masters,* Thomas Bernhard reflects upon art and the appreciation of art, upon music, philosophy, literature and life. At the centre of the novel is Reger, the 82-year-old philosopher of music. Every other day for thirty-six years he has spent the mornings visiting the Kunsthistorische Museum and then continued his reflections in the cafe of Hotel Ambassador afterwards. In his contemplations, two Viennese institutions are combined dialectically to form a unity; the museum on the one hand and the coffee-house on the other become increasingly concentrated symbols for two different aspects of life: the world of auras and the real world of human beings; the world of the spirit and the world of thought. The Kunsthistorische Museum as a place of the "spirit", as a place of artistic ideals, existing at a remove from the world in a seemingly timeless spatial symphony; the dialogue and questions concerning Being and Life culminate in the ritual act of visiting the museum. The museum as the guardian of human secrets, the museum as a place of human perfection in matters of art.

In contrast to this, the coffee-house is for Reger a place of "thoughts" – rational, worldly and mundane – where life manifests as action.

The museum and its contents thus present a challenge to enter into a dialogue, yet do not provide an answer. The museum is a way, a discussion, an agora or an action – an auric medium for the exchange of opinion. In this sense every museum is also subjective when it transfigures into an aura what can objectively be regarded as information; the museum as a mega-chip of authentic artificiality. The way through this artificiality makes one inquisitive and arouses the mind. And thus we arrive at that element which every museum has used to legitimise at least part of its existence ever

jedes Museum einen Teil seiner Existenz legitimiert, nämlich in der Vermittlung von Inhalten und Gedanken.

Daß sich das Museum des Bildungsbürgertums im 19. Jahrhundert zu einer Informationsschnittstelle unserer Zeit entwickelt hat, ist durch das Centre Pompidou in Paris, das Museum of Modern Art in New York oder das Air and Space Museum in Washington D. C. dokumentiert. Der Wandel des Museums ist aber nicht nur ein Wandel seiner Inhalte, sondern auch ein Wandel seiner Verpackungsformen. Das Ausstellen im Museumsbereich ist nicht mehr beschränkt auf eine einmalige Hängung von Bildern oder Objekten, sondern ein Perpetuum neuer Verpackungen.

Ausstellungen sind – in einer möglichen Interpretation – Vorbilder für zukünftige Konventionen. Eine Ausstellung stellt aus, indem sie eine Position oder Positionen dar-stellt und öffentlich zugänglich macht. »Ausgestellt sein« hat nicht nur den Charakter des medial vermarkteten, sondern hat auch den Nimbus des schutzlosen Allgegenwärtigen. Die ausgestellten Objekte und Gegenstände können sich einer Vereinnahmung durch das Publikum nicht verwehren, gleichzeitig bedrängen sie durch die öffentliche Diskussion die konventionelle Meinung. Somit fungiert die Ausstellung als ein Vermittler zwischen dem Gegenwärtigen und dem Zukünftigen. Den Protagonisten der Moderne war die mediale Wirkung der Ausstellung bekannt, und sie wurde gekonnt und zielgerichtet eingesetzt. In den Ausstellungen wurden labormäßig alle jene Ideen und Vorstellungen exemplarisch aufgezeigt, die als zukünftige Realität anzusehen waren. Der theoretische Unterbau, den die wichtigen Ausstellungen vermitteln wollten, war gedacht als Plattform für die individuelle und spezifische Interpretation im einzelnen. Der normative Charakter der klassischen Modernen manifestierte sich beispielsweise in jeder ihrer Ausstellungen.

In Wien trägt die Secession, das Vorbild eines Ausstellungstempels per se, nicht nur eine sakrale Symbolik in der Dreischiffigkeit der Innenraumanlage, sondern auch durch den vergoldeten kuppelartigen Dachaufsatz aus vegetabilem Metallge-

since the time of the Enlightenment, namely the communication of contents and thoughts.

The fact that the 19th century museum of the educated classes has today developed into an information interface has already been demonstrated by the Centre Pompidou in Paris, the Museum of Modern Art in New York and the Air and Space Museum in Washington DC. However, the transformation of the museum is not only a transformation of its contents but also a transformation of its packaging. Exhibiting in the museums sector is no longer limited to the single act of hanging pictures or installing objects, but involves a perpetuum of new kinds of packaging.

Exhibitions are – in one possible interpretation – models for future conventions. An exhibition exhibits by 're-presenting' a position or several positions and making them publicly accessible. 'To be exhibited' not only means to have the character of something marketed by the media, but also to wear the nimbus of unprotected ubiquity. The exhibited objects cannot defend themselves from being collected by the public, and yet at the same time they put the pressure on conventional opinion by means of public discussion. The exhibition thus serves as a mediator between the present and the future. The protagonists of Modernism knew about the medial effects of exhibitions and employed them skilfully and purposively. All those ideas and imaginations which were regarded as constituting future reality were displayed in an exemplary way at exhibitions, as if they were laboratories. The theoretical basis which important exhibitions wanted to communicate was conceived as a platform for detailed individual and specific interpretations. The normative character of classical Modernism is manifest, for example, in every single one of its exhibitions. In Vienna, the Secession, which is the model of an exhibition temple *per se*, displays a sacral symbolism not only in the three aisles of its interior layout, but also in the gilded dome-like skylight turret, made of gilded wire netting, and the entrance, decorated with the motto *Der Zeit ihre Kunst. Der Kunst ihre Freiheit* ('To the Age its Art. To Art its Freedom'). Few exhibition

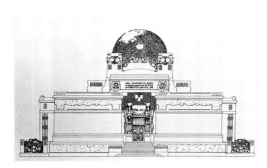

Joseph Maria Olbrich, Secession, Wien, 1898
Joseph Maria Olbrich, Secession, Vienna, 1898

flecht sowie den mit dem Motto »Der Zeit ihre Kunst. Der Kunst ihre Freiheit« geschmückten Eingang. Wenige Ausstellungshäuser sind direkter, unverblümter in ihrem Anspruch des künstlerischen *hic et nunc:* die Aufforderung zum künstlerischen Ungehorsam ist hier gewissermaßen in Stein gehauen.

Was sich in Wien um die Jahrhundertwende durch den Bau der Secession ereignete, ist ein gelungenes Beispiel für eine neue Museums-Position: die Unzufriedenheit mit dem Status quo führte die Secessionisten zum Bau einer eigenen Ausstellungshalle, deren mediale Wirkung als Bauwerk gleichzusetzen war mit den Wirkungen der dort stattfindenden Ausstellungen. So gesehen kann die Secession – in ihrer Entstehungszeit betrachtet – als ein gelungenes Beispiel einer Positionierung gelten.

Positionen und Inhalte

Unterschiedliche Positionen reflektieren nicht nur unterschiedliche Inhalte, sondern fordern auch besondere, spezifische Darstellungen. Die »Verpackung« wird hier im doppelten Sinn bedeutungsvoll: einmal als Gestaltung des Gebäudes und einmal als Gestaltung der Ausstellung selbst.

In den letzten zehn Jahren hat sich in Österreich eine neue Entwicklung der Museen und Ausstellungen manifestiert. Ausgehend von einer größeren Anzahl vielbeachteter Großausstellungen, die in Österreich und im Ausland präsentiert wurden, entwickelte sich eine neue Haltung gegenüber dem Museum beziehungsweise dem Museumsbesuch. Die große Publikumswirkung von Großausstellungen wie »Die Türken vor Wien« (1983), »Traum und Wirklichkeit« (1985), »Zauber der Medusa« (1987), »Bürgersinn und Aufbegehren« (1988) und »Wunderblock« (1989), um nur einige zu nennen, haben eine im Ausland erprobte Praxis der »Temporary Exhibitions« auch in Österreich bestätigt: das Ereignis Großausstellung als Idealverpackung eines Sonderthemas. In Ergänzung zu den bestehenden Museumsräumen wurde deshalb die Forderung nach flexiblen Räumen für Wechselausstellungen immer nachhaltiger. Das Mu-

halls are more straightforward, more outspoken in their demands for the artistic *hic et nunc;* the call to artistic disobedience is likewise chiselled in stone here.

What occurred in Vienna at the turn of the century with the construction of the Secession is a perfect example of a new 'museum position': the dissatisfaction with the status quo led the Secessionists to build their own exhibition hall, one whose medial effect as architecture was comparable to the effects of the exhibitions which were shown there. Seen in this way, the Secession can be regarded – at least in its original stages – as a successful example of positioning.

Positions and Contents

Different positions reflect not only different contents but also require their own particular, specific presentation. The 'packaging' is here important in two senses: on the one hand as the design of a building, and on the other as the design of the exhibition itself.

Over the past ten years, a new trend has become evident with regard to museums and exhibitions in Austria. Initiated by a number of highly praised large-scale exhibitions which were presented in Austria and abroad, a new attitude developed towards the museum and the museum visitor. The great public effect of big exhibitions such as *Die Türken vor Wien* ('The Turks before the Gates of Vienna') (1983), *Traum und Wirklichkeit* ('Dream and Reality') (1985), *Zauber der Medusa* ('The Magic of the Medusa') (1987), *Bürgersinn und Aufbegehren* ('The Public Spirit and Revolt') (1988) and *Wunderblock* (1989) – to name but a few – confirmed the value for Austria of a practice which was already well-established abroad: that of staging temporary exhibitions, i. e. large-scale exhibition events involving ideal packaging of a special theme. As a result, there was an increasingly vigorous demand for more flexible spatial accommodation for temporary exhibitions in museums, over and above the space that was already available. The museum differentiated between temporary exhibitions and permanent exhibitions, whereby the differences were

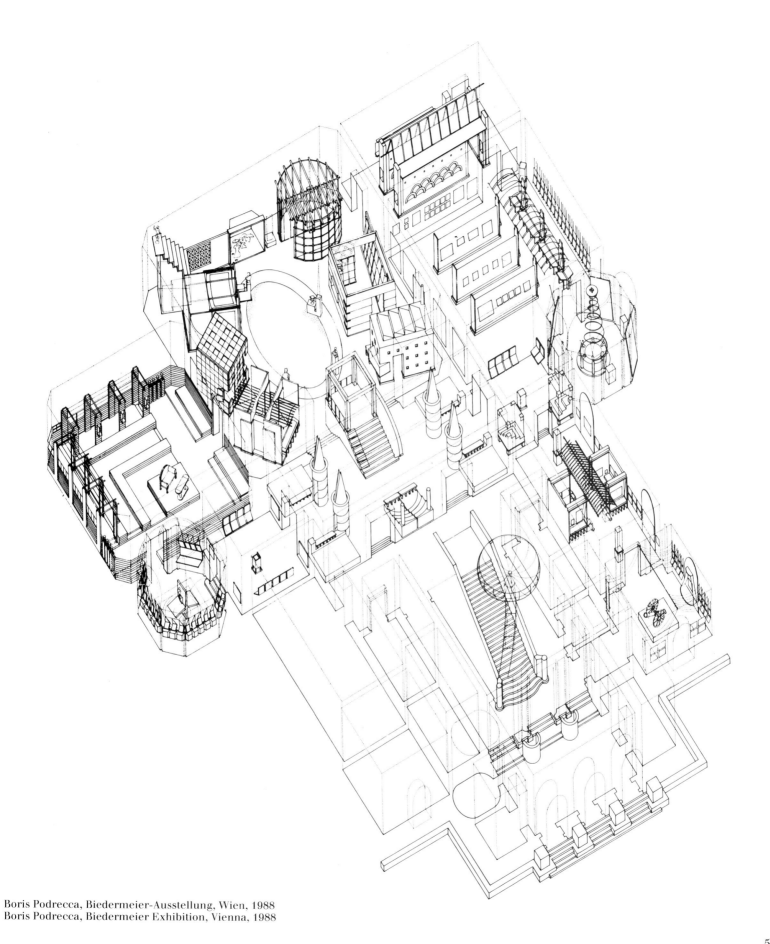

Boris Podrecca, Biedermeier-Ausstellung, Wien, 1988
Boris Podrecca, Biedermeier Exhibition, Vienna, 1988

Boris Podrecca, Biedermeier-Ausstellung,
Detail, Wien, 1988
Boris Podrecca, Biedermeier Exhibition, detail,
Vienna, 1988

seum differenziert zunehmend zwischen Wechselausstellung und permanenter Ausstellung, wobei sich die Anforderungen auch in den Flächenproportionen eindeutig niederschlagen: Alle neuen Museen haben Wechselausstellungsmöglichkeiten, der Typus der Kunsthalle ohne permanente Ausstellung wird immer relevanter. Die »Bespielbarkeit« von Museen wird in ähnlicher Weise diskutiert wie die Bespielbarkeit von Opernhäusern und Theaterbauten. In diesem Sinn haben die Museen – zumindest teilweise – den Höhepunkt des besucherorientierten Interface erreicht: Ausstellung als Ereigniswelt.

Der Bau der Wiener Museen während der Gründerzeit mit den öffentlichen Ringstraßenbauten orientierte sich an den Beispielen anderer europäischer Großstädte, wie etwa Paris. Im Programm der Wiener Stadterweiterung von 1857 gehörte der Neubau für die kaiserlichen Kunstsammlungen zu den großen Ringstraßenprojekten. Die Festlegung der »Positionen« an der Ringstraße erfolgte erst 1864 – wobei man eine Zeitlang auch die Bestände des 1863 gegründeten Kunstgewerbemuseums sowie jene der Schatzkammer mit den übrigen Sammlungen in einem einzigen Komplex vereinigen wollte. Somit ist die »Position« auch als Positionierung zu verstehen, nämlich in bezug auf die städtebauliche Lage und die inhaltliche Zuschreibung des Museumsinhaltes selbst. Die beiden Ringstraßenbauten für das Kunsthistorische Museum und das Naturhistorische Museum wurden in der Architektenerläuterung von Semper und Hasenauer künstlerisch begründet, indem die Anlage als eine »Agora« von Museen beschrieben wurde, bestehend aus den zwei ausgeführten Baukörpern und einem dritten, projektierten, der den Museumsbereich abgeschlossen und ihm eine U-Form verliehen hätte. Die gegenwärtige Planung für das Museumsquartier (Architekten Ortner und Ortner) kommentiert nicht zuletzt eine städtebauliche Planung aus dem 19. Jahrhundert im Sinne eines architektonischen Dialoges.

Auch ein weiteres wichtiges Museum geht in seiner urbanen Positionierung auf die Ringstraßenplanung zurück: das Museum für angewandte Kunst, damals als *Kunst-*

also clearly reflected in the area requirements. All new museums have facilities for temporary exhibitions, and the type of the exhibition hall which does not have a permanent exhibition is becoming increasingly relevant. The 'playableness' of museums is being discussed in a way similar to that of the 'playableness' of opera houses and theatres. In this sense the museums have – at least partially – reached the peak of the visitor-oriented interface: the exhibition as an event.

During the construction phase of the *Gründerzeit*, when the public buildings on the Ringstrasse were built, the design of Vienna's museums was influenced by the example of other European capitals, such as Paris. In the programme for the urban expansion of Vienna in 1857, the new building for the Imperial art collections was one of the largest of the Ringstrasse projects. The 'positions' on the Ringstrasse were first established in 1864, although it was for some time planned to combine the collections of the Kunstgewerbemuseum ('Museum of Arts and Crafts', founded in 1863, and the Treasury with the other collections in a single complex. Thus a 'position' should also be understood as 'positioning', namely with regard to the urban planning situation and the attribution of the actual contents of the museum collection. The two museums on the Ringstrasse (built for the Kunsthistorische Museum and the Naturhistorische Museum respectively) were justified on artistic grounds by the architects Semper and Hasenauer in their explanatory report, where the site is described as an "agora" of museums, consisting of the two aforementioned buildings and a projected third edifice, which would have enclosed the museum area in a U-shape. The present planning of the Museum Quarter (architect: Ortner and Ortner) is not least a comment on the urban planning of the 19th century, in the sense of architectural dialogue.

Another important museum also traces its urban 'positioning' to the Ringstrasse: the Museum for Applied Art, at that time still called the Kunstgewerbemuseum and based upon the model of the Victoria and Albert Museum in London. It reflects the

gewerbemuseum bezeichnet, reflektiert das Selbstverständnis der kaiserlichen Sammeltätigkeit auf dem Gebiet der angewandten Kunst, welches das Kunstgewerbe einer ursprünglich wissenschaftlichen Institution zuwies, die den Kontakt zwischen Industrie und Kunst herstellen sollte. Das Österreichische Museum für Kunst und Industrie, 1866–1871 nach Plänen von Heinrich von Ferstel gebaut, war als Backsteinbau im Stil der strengen Neurenaissance ausgeführt, der seinerzeit ebenso für Bahnhöfe und Schulbauten verwendet wurde. Die Bestände des Museums waren auch nicht durch habsburgische Sammeltätigkeit zusammengetragen worden, sondern wurden planmäßig als *Vorbildmaterial* herbeigeschafft und gekauft. Nicht nur die gesammelten Gegenstände, auch das Gebäude selbst sollte als Vorbild und Muster dienen, und zwar in der stilistischen Übereinstimmung zwischen Architektur und angewandten Künsten. Im Vergleich mit dieser ursprünglichen Intention des Kunstgewerbemuseums kann man auch die geplanten und in Ausführung befindlichen baulichen Eingriffe verstehen, die Peter Noever als Direktor des Museums im Zuge der Renovierung durchführen ließ.

Neben den notwendigen baulichen Adaptierungen verstehen sich diese architektonischen und künstlerischen Interventionen als beispielhafte Ausformulierungen architekturtypologischer Einheiten: das Tor (Walter Pichler), das Stiegenhaus (Sepp Müller), das Freilufttheater (Peter Noever), das Schau-Fenster (SITE) und das Café (Hermann Czech). Somit wird der Kreis der ursprünglichen Intention, das Museum als Vorbild und Muster zu proklamieren, durch diese neuen architektonischen Interventionen von 1988 bis 1992 geschlossen.

Das Museum als bestimmter Ort innerhalb des Stadtgefüges ist als Ausdruck des kulturellen kollektiven Gedächtnisses als städtebauliche Ikone zu verstehen, wo sich Momente der Geschichte verdichten, um als Konzentrat die Zeiten zu durchdringen. Museums-Positionen verstehen sich deshalb auch immer als eine Position der Permanenz innerhalb des urbanen Kontextes,

way in which the Imperial collection of fine art, together with that of the decorative arts, was originally regarded as being a scientific institution which was supposed to produce a connection between industry and art. As a brick construction, the Viennese Kunstgewerbemuseum, which was designed by Heinrich von Ferstel in 1866-1871, was built in strict Neo-Renaissance style, which at the time was also used for stations and schools. Furthermore, the museum's collections had not been built up through the collecting activities of princes but had been obtained and procured according to a plan, as "material to serve as models". Not only the collected objects, but also the building itself was supposed to serve as a model and example; namely of the stylistic correspondence between architecture and the applied arts. Compared with these original intentions of the Kunstgewerbemuseum one can understand the systematic interventions that Peter Noever commissioned in the course of the renovation of the museum.

Besides the necessary constructional adaptations, its architectural interventions by architects and artists can be understood as an exemplary formulation of architecturally typological units: the gate (Walter Pichler), the staircase (Sepp Müller), the open-air theatre (Peter Noever) and the shop-window (SITE), and the cafeteria (Hermann Czech). Thus the circle of the original intention comes to a close by proclaiming the museum as a model and example through the new architectural interventions of 1988-1992.

The museum as a place within the framework of the city is an expression of the collective cultural memory as an icon of urban planning, where moments of history coalesce to permeate time in concentrated form. Museum positions are therefore always to be understood as positions of permanence within the urban context, as places where supra-temporal dialogue should be possible.

This cultural intensification in connection with urban planning was largely ignored in Austria during the sixties and seventies, when the museum discussion came to be regarded as secondary not only *in puncto*

Heinrich von Ferstel, Österreichisches Museum für Kunst und Industrie, Wien, Stubenring, Photo vor 1906
Heinrich von Ferstel, Austrian Museum for Art and Industry, Vienna, Stubenring, photograph from before 1906

57

wo zeitüberschreitender Dialog möglich sein soll.

Diese kulturelle Verdichtung im Zusammenhang mit Stadtplanung wurde in den sechziger und siebziger Jahren in Österreich weitgehend ignoriert, wodurch nicht nur die Museumsdiskussion in puncto Ausstellung, sondern auch in puncto Verortung stiefmütterlich behandelt wurde. So war in Wien das Museum des 20. Jahrhunderts (Architekt Karl Schwanzer, 1958) lieblos in eine Parkfläche gesetzt worden – wie ein unfreiwillig gelandetes UFO –, jedoch ohne Bezug zum tatsächlichen kulturellen Leben. Dieser Museumsbau war ursprünglich als österreichischer Pavillon auf der Weltausstellung in Brüssel gezeigt worden, bevor er in Wien mit kleinen Veränderungen als Museum genutzt wurde. Die Position dieses Museums war eine Metapher für das im Wien der sechziger Jahre herrschende Un-Verständnis der modernen Kunst gegenüber.

Als in den achtziger Jahren die thematischen Großausstellungen auch in Wien und Österreich aktuell wurden – nach dem Beispiel der großartigen Ausstellungen Paris – Berlin, Paris – Moskau, Paris – New York im Centre Pompidou in Paris –, entwickelte sich dadurch auch ein neues Selbstverständnis der betreffenden Institutionen, nämlich der Museen, was deren Anstrengungen, das kulturelle Erbe in Österreich entsprechend zu dokumentieren, verstärkte.

Das Gesicht der Zeit

Die österreichische Nachkriegsarchitektur (1945–1960) des Wiederaufbaus hat nicht mit internationalen Horizonten gelebt; schon aus geschichtlichen Gründen waren entsprechende Werke und Offenheit nicht möglich: sie hat ein durch und durch begrenztes Leben erfahren – und nicht den Dialog mit der eigenen Geschichte. Der neue Weg der österreichischen Architektur manifestierte sich ikonenhaft in den achtziger Jahren durch drei Architekturausstellungen von unterschiedlicher Genealogie. Die im Jahr 1982 gezeigte Ausstellung »New Wave of Austrian Architecture«, präsentiert im »Institute for Archi-

exhibitions, but also *in puncto* location. Thus, in Vienna, the Museum des 20. Jahrhunderts ('Museum of the 20th Century') (architect Karl Schwanzer, 1958) was set down unfeelingly in a park – like an UFO that has landed unwillingly – without any connection to actual cultural life. This museum building was originally shown as the Austrian pavilion at the World Exhibition in Brussels, before being afterwards used, following minor alterations, as a museum in Vienna. The position of the museum was a metaphor for the lack of understanding for modern art in Vienna during the 60s.

When, in the 80s, thematic large-scale exhibitions were also realised in Vienna and Austria (after the example of the splendid exhibitions Paris – Berlin, Paris – Moscow and Paris – New York at the Centre Pompidou in Paris) the institutions concerned (namely the museums) began to develop a new image of themselves and view their efforts to appropriately document Austria's cultural heritage in a new light.

The Face of the Age

Post-war Austrian architecture did not have an international horizon; even from the historical point of view, international work and openness to it had not been possible. It lived a thoroughly restricted life – that of the homogeneity of western Modernism – and was unable to participate in a dialogue with its own history. In the 80s, the new path which Austrian architecture was to follow appeared like an icon, through architectural exhibitions of varying genealogy. The exhibition *New Wave of Austrian Architecture,* which was shown in 1982, presented at the Institute for Architecture and Urban Studies in New York, showed the works of the youngest generation of architects in Austria, such as Hermann Czech, Rob Krier, Missing Link (Adolf Krischanitz and Otto Kapfinger), Heinz Tesar, Heinz Frank and the team Appelt-Kneissl-Prochazka, who are all still actively present in the architectural scene ten years later. At almost the same time an exhibition entitled *Versuche zur Baukunst*

tecture and Urban Studies« in New York, zeigte Arbeiten der jüngsten Architektengeneration in Österreich, der etwa Hermann Czech, Rob Krier, Missing Link (Adolf Krischanitz und Otto Kapfinger), Heinz Tesar, Heinz Frank sowie das Team Appelt-Kneissl-Prochazka angehörten, und die eine Dekade später ihre aktive Präsenz in Sachen Architektur erhielt. Fast gleichzeitig zeigte eine Ausstellung »Versuche zur Baukunst« eine Reihe von jüngeren Architekten, deren Namen im Wiener Umfeld heute eine »veröffentlichte« Position darstellen: Alessandro Alvera, Luigi Blau, Roland Hagmüller, Otto Häuselmayer, Dimitri Manikas und Boris Podrecca.

Diesen beiden Ausstellungen war eine Präsentation vorangegangen, die sich »Sechs Architekten vom Schillerplatz« nannte und das Selbstverständnis einer Architektengeneration darstellte, welche die ersten internationalen Erfahrungen in die österreichische Architektur einbrachte. Architekten wie Johann Georg Gsteu, Hans Hollein, Wilhelm Holzbauer, Josef Lackner, Gustav Peichl und Johannes Spalt entwickelten den Dialog mit der internationalen Architektur und machten mit ausgeführten Bauten auch im Ausland auf die Qualität der österreichischen Architektur aufmerksam. Eines der besten Beispiele im Bereich der Museumsarchitektur ist Hans Holleins Museumsbau in Mönchengladbach, der mit einem Schlag den Architekten, die Stadt und das Museum weltberühmt machte. Das seit 1972 geplante und 1982 fertiggestellte Museum hat den herkömmlichen Begriff eines Museumsbaus gesprengt. Das gilt sowohl hinsichtlich der Bautypologie als auch hinsichtlich der Museumsatmosphäre. »Während bisher ein Museum als ein *Gebäude* angesehen wurde, das mehr oder minder stark untergliedert werden konnte, so erscheint im Falle von Holleins Museum Mönchengladbach der Gebäudebegriff fehl am Platze. Vielmehr müssen wir von einer Gebäudelandschaft sprechen.«[1]

Der Museumsboom mit seinen Großausstellungen und Museumsplanungen hat in Österreich vielfältige Spuren hinterlassen. Auf der Spurensuche für die neuen Museums-Positionen gibt es eine Vielzahl von

('Attempts at Architecture') showed a number of younger architects whose names today represent a 'public' position in the Viennese milieu: Alessandro Alvera, Luigi Blau, Roland Hagmüller, Otto Häuselmayer, Dimitri Manikas and Boris Podrecca.

These two exhibitions had been preceded by a presentation entitled *Sechs Architekten vom Schillerplatz* ('Six Architects from Schillerplatz'), representing a generation of architects' own conception of itself, a generation which contributed the first international experiences to Austrian architecture. Architects like Johann Georg Gsteu, Hans Hollein, Wilhelm Holzbauer, Josef Lackner, Gustav Peichl and Johannes Spalt all helped to develop an international architectural dialogue and their buildings (including those abroad) focused attention on the quality of Austrian architecture. One of the best examples of this in the field of museum architecture is Hans Hollein's museum building in Mönchengladbach, which made the architect, the city and the museum world-famous overnight. Planned since 1972 and completed in 1982, it went beyond the traditional notions of a museum building. That goes both for the typology and the atmosphere of the museum. "Whereas up until now a museum has been seen as a building which could be more or less strictly subdivided, in the case of Hollein's Museum Mönchengladbach the notion of a building is inappropriate. We must speak instead of an architectural landscape."[1]

The museum boom, with its large-scale exhibitions and museum planning, has left a variety of traces in Austria. In the search for traces of new 'museum positions' there are many examples which combine individuality and quality in their architectural efforts.

The whole spectrum of the museums discussion which took place in Austria in the 80s was characterised by an optimism resulting from the success of the large-scale exhibitions, and this continued in an imaginative project for the Guggenheim Museum, excavated from solid rock, in Salzburg. It was the reshaping of the Austrian museum scene, interpreted as medi-

Hans Hollein, Städtisches Museum, Abteiberg Mönchengladbach, 1972–82
Hans Hollein, Municipal Museum, Abteiberg Mönchengladbach, 1972–82

Beispielen, bei denen Ernsthaftigkeit im gestalterischen Bemühen mit Eigenständigkeit und Qualität vereint ist.

Das Spektrum der Museumsdiskussion in Österreich in den achtziger Jahren war durch einen Optimismus gekennzeichnet, der aus den Erfolgen der Großausstellungen resultierte und in einem phantasievollen Projekt für das Guggenheim Museum im Fels des Salzburger Mönchsbergs sich fortsetzte: die Neugestaltung der österreichischen Museumslandschaft fungiert als Vermittler zwischen »alter« und »neuer« Welt. Hans Hollein, Architekt des Museums in Mönchengladbach und des neuen Museums für moderne Kunst in Frankfurt, hat durch eine Vielzahl von Beiträgen den Dialog zwischen Architektur und Museum interpretiert. Seine Museumsräume sind auratische Raumkompositionen, welche einen direkten Bezug zum ausgestellten Kunstobjekt herstellen und in situ eine Kunsttransformation im Sinne einer Nobilitierung durchführen. Die Einmaligkeit des Kunstwerkes wird durch die Besonderheit des Raumes kompatibel ergänzt. Das Frankfurter Museum für moderne Kunst kommentiert Michael Mönninger wie folgt: »Dennoch sind die Ausdrucksqualitäten dieses Baus nicht übersetzbar. Trotz seiner peniblen Einpassung bleibt das Museum ein Fremdkörper, der in seiner Abstraktion und Kälte fast an die konstruktivistischen Geometrien der frühen Russen erinnert. Fast kommt einem wieder das Wort von der ›absoluten Architektur‹ ins Gedächtnis, jene Entwurfshaltung, die Hollein und andere ›Progressive‹ in den sechziger Jahren propagiert hatten. Um dem Diktat der Zweckgebundenheit und der seriellen Ästhetik zu entfliehen, predigte damals eine noch junge Architektengeneration den Aufbruch ins Universum der grenzenlosen Gefühle, Sensualismus und Psychologismus, Megamaschinen und mobile Städte, pneumatische Architekturen und psychedelische Raumwirkungen – all diese Konzepte sollten Architektur zu einer Erweiterung der Sinnesorgane machen: ›Architektur ist die menschlichste Kunst. Sie ist elementar, sinnlich, primitiv, brutal und archaisch und zugleich Ausdruck der subtilsten Gefühle des Menschen, Materiali-

ator between the 'old' and the 'new' world. Hans Hollein, the architect of the museum in Mönchengladbach and the new Museum for Modern Art in Frankfurt, has made a variety of contributions to the interpretation of the dialogue between architecture and the museum. His museum rooms are auric spatial compositions, which create a direct connection to the art object exhibited, and *in situ* carry out a transformation of art in the sense of an ennoblement. The uniqueness of the work of art is complemented by the peculiarity of the room. Michael Monninger commented on the Frankfurt Museum for Modern Art as follows: „However, the expressive qualities of this building are not translatable. Despite his meticulous adjustments, the museum remains a foreign body which, in its abstraction and coldness, almost reminds one of the Constructivist geometries of the early Russians. That term 'absolute architecture' almost springs to mind again, that attitude to the design which Hollein and other 'progressives' propagated during the sixties. In order to escape from the dictates of purposiveness and serial aesthetics, a generation of architects, all of them at that time still young, preached the start of a journey into a universe of boundless feeling, sensualism and psychologism, megamachines and mobile cities, pneumatic architecture and psychedelic spatial effects – all these concepts were to make architecture an extension of the senses: 'Architecture is the most human of all the arts. It is elementary, sensual, primitive, brutal and archaic and yet at the same time the expression of the most subtle feelings of man, the materialisation of his spirit. It is both flesh and spirit, and erotic in the truest sense of the word.' Thus Hans Hollein in a lecture in 1962."[2]

As a "museum in the rock", the Guggenheim Museum in Salzburg would be a complete novelty, architecturally, structurally, conservationally and museologically. "In contrast to conventional additive tectonic forms of construction, subtractive 'building into the rock' allows more freedom, a more plastic, more complex spatial conception and expansion – a genuine three-dimensionality. No longer is

Hans Hollein, Guggenheim Museum, Salzburg, 1988, Modell
Hans Hollein, Guggenheim Museum, Salzburg, 1988, model

Hans Hollein, Guggenheim Museum, Salzburg, 1988, Modell, Blick in die obere Hauptebene
Hans Hollein, Guggenheim Museum, Salzburg, 1988, model, view of the upper level galleries

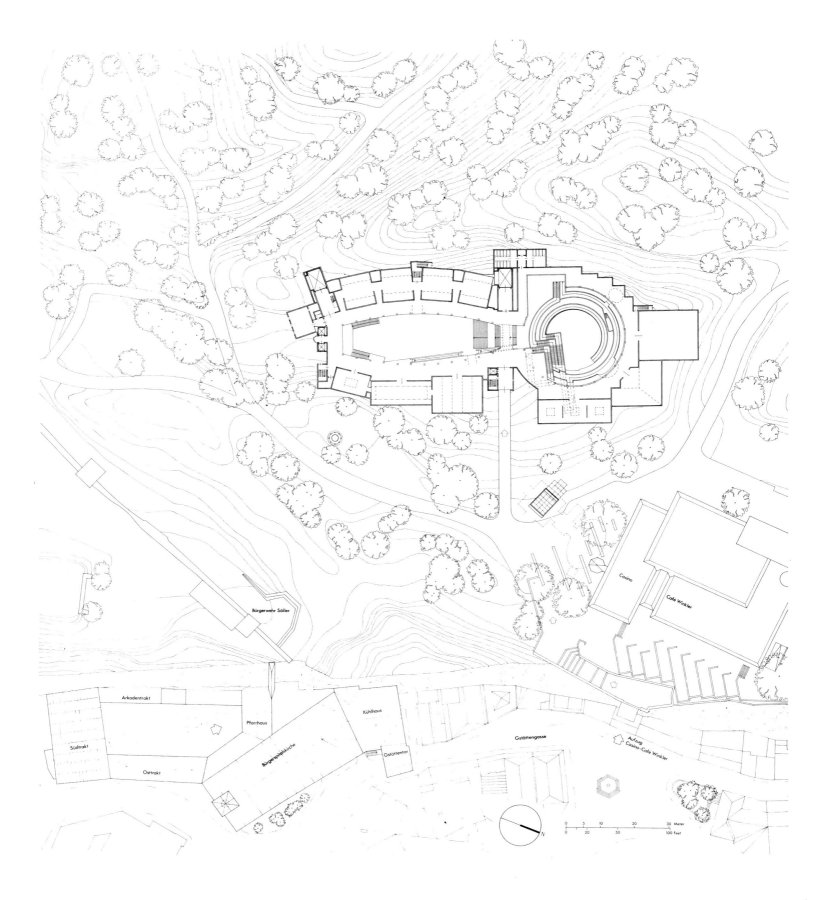

Hans Hollein, Guggenheim Museum, Salzburg, 1988, Obere Hauptebene mit Eingang vom Mönchsbergplateau
Hans Hollein, Guggenheim Museum, Salzburg, 1988, upper level plan showing the entrance from the top of the Mönchsberg plateau

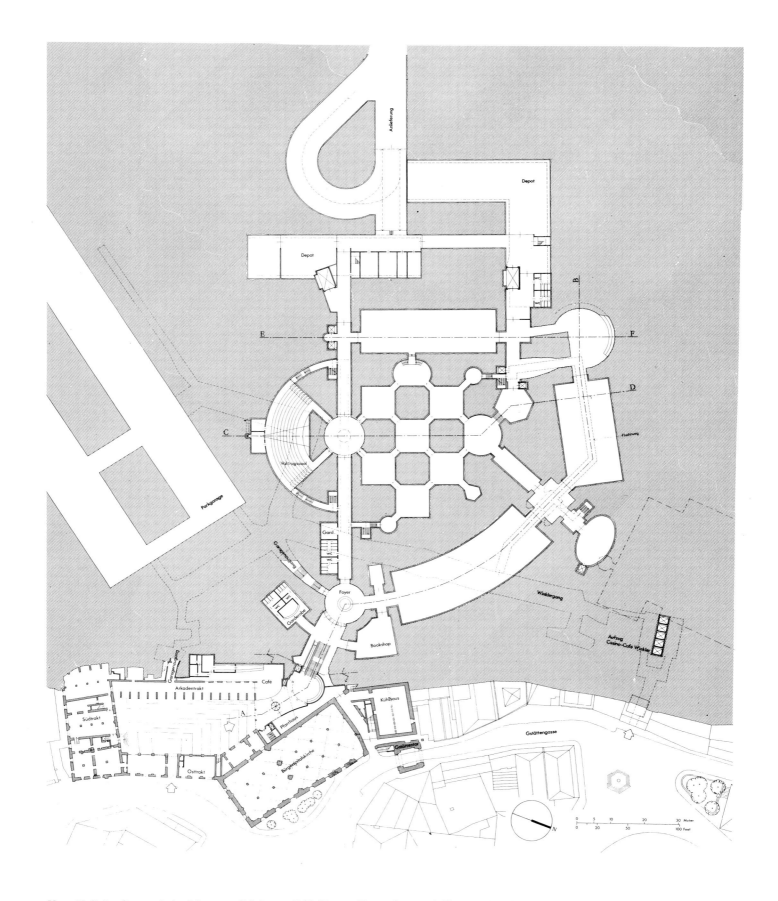

Hans Hollein, Guggenheim Museum, Salzburg, 1988, Untere Hauptebene mit Eingang durch das Bürgerspital
Hans Hollein, Guggenheim Museum, Salzburg, 1988, lower level plan showing the entrance from the Bürgerspital

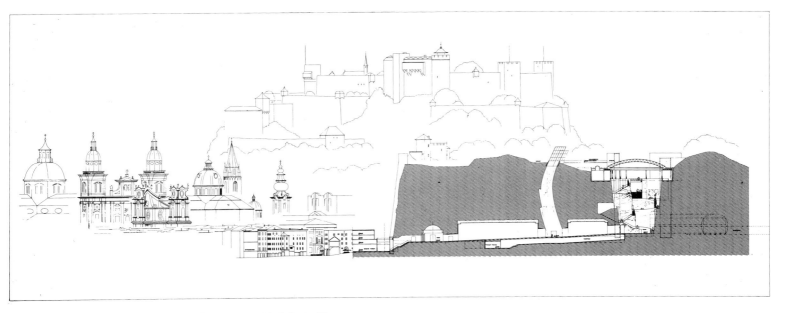

Hans Hollein, Guggenheim Museum, Salzburg, 1988, Schnitt Eingang
Hans Hollein, Guggenheim Museum, Salzburg, 1988, section through the entrance

Der Besucher des eigentlichen Museums im Fels hat die Möglichkeit sowohl kurzer, rascher als auch ausgedehnter und umfassender Wege. Ein direkter, schneller, linearer Durchgang, an den die wesentlichen Sammlungsteile angeschlossen sind, führt zum Sunk, eine matrixartig ineinanderfließende Raumgruppierung ermöglicht ausführliche Betrachtung und Inbezugsetzung. Die Konfiguration der Bereiche und der Einzelräume bestimmt sich sowohl vom museologischen Konzept her als auch von den statisch-konstruktiven Bedingungen der Felsmechanik (des Bauens von Kavernen im Fels) sowie von den Wege- und Lichtführungen.

Es ist die Intention dieses Entwurfes, die Sonderausstellungsbereiche in den Gesamtkomplex zu integrieren, sie jedoch auch vollkommen getrennt betreiben zu können. Die Konzeption ist so angelegt, daß Erweiterungsmöglichkeiten an verschiedenen Punkten gegeben sind. Sie ist weiters so angelegt, daß auch ganz andere Sammlungskonstellationen und Abfolgen möglich sind, bewußte Flexibilität des Systems mit Hinsicht auf mögliche ganz andere oder zusätzliche Inhalte.

Auch im eigentlichen Sammlungsbereich sind an unterschiedlichen Orten und Höhenlagen Museums-Shops, gastronomische Bereiche und Lounges mit vielfältigen Ausblicken angesiedelt.

(Hans Hollein)

The visitor to the museum can choose between short, more direct routes and more extensive circuits. The direct, linear route, which passes through the central parts of the exhibition spaces, leads to the Sunk, while the matrix-like configuration of additional exhibition rooms permits in-depth study and invites contemplation. The arrangement of the individual areas and exhibition spaces is determined by the museological concept pursued, the engineering requirements imposed by rock mechanics – as well as by routing considerations and lighting conditions.

It is the intention of this project to integrate the special exhibitions areas into the overall complex while at the same time allowing them to be used independently from the rest of the museum. The arrangement of rooms permits display areas to be combined in various ways to suit entirely different purposes – a flexible system designed for the most diverse objectives.

Also in the exhibition area proper, various shops, cafeterias, restaurants and lounges have been envisaged in different locations and at various levels, providing attractive vistas.

(Hans Hollein)

Hans Hollein, Guggenheim Museum, Salzburg, 1988, Modell, Blick in das Innere des Museums
Hans Hollein, Guggenheim Museum, Salzburg, 1988, model, interior view of the museum

sation seines Geistes. Sie ist Fleisch und Geist zugleich und im wahrsten Sinne erotisch‹, so formulierte Hans Hollein in einem Vortrag 1962.«[2]

Das Guggenheim Museum in Salzburg wäre als »Museum im Fels« (Hans Hollein) ein grundsätzliches Novum, architektonisch, konstruktiv, konservatorisch und museologisch. »Im Unterschied zum konventionellen additiv-tektonischen Hochbau erlaubt ein – subtraktives – Bauen im Fels eine plastisch viel freiere und komplexere räumliche Konzeption und Expansion – eine echte Dreidimensionalität. Die Unterschiede von Grundriß und Schnitt sind aufgehoben. Raum entwickelt sich in alle Richtungen.

Das Verweilen im Museum – im Inneren des Berges – soll ähnliche Erlebnisse bieten wie die Stadt selbst. Zum Unterschied etwa von Aufführungen der Festspiele kann hier eine viel größere Zahl von Personen zeitlich gestreuter partizipieren, Kultur in höchster Qualität ist nicht nur für einige Auserwählte, für einige wenige Abende, sondern für jeden, das Jahr hindurch, zugänglich.

Licht, Tageslicht, wird intensiv, bisweilen auch dramatisch wahrgenommen. Licht in bezug zum Raum von manchmal monumentalen Dimensionen provoziert ein Bewußtsein des Potentials archetypischer und atavistischer Situationen. Der Weg führt hinauf zum Licht. Raum wird erobert, in Besitz genommen, plastischer Raum, den ich besteige und betrachte. Der Austritt ins Freie, ins Grüne, am Ende des Rundganges oben am Berg bietet einen Blick zurück in die Tiefe des Felsens und einen Ausblick auf die Stadt.« (Hans Hollein, Erläuterungsbericht)

Der Erfolg österreichischer Museumsarchitektur wird im Ausland neben Hans Hollein durch Gustav Peichl bestätigt. Der Zubau zum Städel-Museum in Frankfurt (1987–1990) und die Kunsthalle in Bonn, offiziell als »Ausstellungshalle der Bundesrepublik Deutschland« bezeichnet, sind zwei bemerkenswerte Bauwerke. Die im Juni 1992 eröffnete Kunsthalle Bonn wurde als quadratischer Solitärbaukörper mit den gigantischen Maßen von 100 Meter auf 100 Meter Seitenlänge ausschließlich für Wechselausstellungen – die Konzeption

there a difference between plan and section, space is free to develop in all directions."

"The museum inside the mountain is to confront the visitors with an experience not dissimilar to that offered by the city itself. But, unlike the Festival performances, it is open to a much larger audience, which can come and go as it pleases. Outstanding cultural experiences are made accessible not only to the chosen few on just a few nights of the year but rather all the year round to the general public."

"Light, indeed broad daylight, is experienced intensely, even dramatically. Light, related to space, to a space of – at times – monumental dimensions, evokes an awareness of the potential inherent in archetypical and atavistic situations. The path leads up to the light, space is conquered, taken into possession, space that becomes something tangible as I progress upwards and look. And at the end of the tour, as I step forth into the open at the top of the mountain, into the lush green spaces outside, I look back into the depth of the rock and out over the city." (Hans Hollein, explanatory report)

The success of Austrian museum architecture abroad is confirmed not only by Hans Hollein but also by Gustav Peichl. The extension to the Städel Museum in Frankfurt (1987-1990) and the Kunsthalle in Bonn, officially described as the "Exhibition Hall of the Federal Republic of Germany", are two remarkable buildings. Opened in June 1992, the Bonn Kunsthalle was planned as one single square building unit with the gigantic dimensions of 100 metres by 100 metres, to be devoted solely to temporary exhibitions (designed for the "exhibition" and "communication" purposes) without a collection of its own.

"There is no doubt that Peichl has succeeded in mediating between these extremes – a purely functional museum on the one hand and an architectural monument on the other. What distinguishes him in this is that he has not had to accept any limitations. Function and architectural development are not in each other's way here, exhibition designers and architect are in harmony. Peichl demonstrates that the often invoked conflict between the two

zielt auf die Funktionen »Ausstellung« und »Kommunikation« – ohne eigene Sammlung geplant.

»Peichl ist es zweifelsohne gelungen, zwischen diesen Extremen – reines Zweckmuseum einerseits, architektonisches Monument andererseits – zu vermitteln. Was ihn dabei auszeichnet, ist die Tatsache, daß er keinerlei Einschränkungen in Kauf hat nehmen müssen. Zweck und architektonische Ausgestaltung stehen sich hier nicht im Wege, Ausstellungsmacher und Architekt finden sich in Harmonie. Peichl demonstriert, daß der öfters beschworene Konflikt zwischen den ›beiden Parteien‹ durchaus vermieden werden kann, daß eine Synthese möglich ist. Wenn die Bonner Kunst- und Ausstellungshalle in der Abfolge bedeutender Museumsbauten bewertet werden soll, dann wird man diesem Umstand in besonderem Maße Rechnung tragen müssen. Der Ausgleich zwischen Form und Funktion ist erreicht. Das Rezept ist denkbar einfach. Der Architekt geht davon aus, daß der Ausstellungstätigkeit im Inneren eine maximale Entfaltung gesichert werden soll. Er schafft somit in erster Linie Raum, der großzügig dimensioniert und nicht durch voreilige architektonische Maßnahmen eingeschränkt ist.«[3]

Der Zubau zum Städel-Museum Frankfurt hingegen beherbergt die großartige Sammlung der klassischen Moderne in einer Abfolge von Kabinetten mit Seitenlicht und größeren Ausstellungsräumen mit traditionellem Oberlicht. Das architektonische Ergebnis ist ein Bauwerk mit viel Understatement, das von Falk Jaeger positiv gegen die omnipräsente Postmoderne gestellt und subtil umschrieben wurde mit »nichts weiter als Wand, Raum und Licht«. Innerhalb der funktionsgerechten Anordnung und Aufteilung der Räume wurde eine zentrale Halle mit Verteilerfunktion im organisatorischen Schwerpunkt situiert. Der natursteinverkleidete Baukörper mit den wohlgesetzten Fensteranordnungen im Anklang an die bestehende Baustruktur ergibt ein ruhiges Erscheinungsbild.

In Österreich hat Gustav Peichl ein kleines Kunstforum geplant, das in einem Bankgebäude der Wiener Innenstadt untergebracht wurde. Das Kunstforum besteht aus

sides can indeed be avoided, that synthesis is possible. If the Bonner Kunst- und Ausstellungshalle is to be assessed in relation to other important museum buildings, then particular account must be taken of this point. A balance between form and function has been reached. The recipe is extremely simple. The architect's starting point is that maximum development should be secured for exhibition activity inside the building. Consequently he is first concerned to create space that is generous in its dimensions and not restricted by over-hasty architectural measures."[5]

By way of comparison, the extension to the Stadel Museum houses its magnificent collection of classical Modernism in a succession of small rooms with side lighting and larger exhibition rooms with traditional overhead lighting. The architectural result is a building containing a great deal of understatement, which Falk Jaeger has favourably compared to the omnipresent Post-Modernism and subtly described as "nothing other than wall, space and light."

Within the functionally-oriented arrangement and division of the rooms, a main hall with a dividing function served as the organisational focus. The building units, panelled in natural stone, with a well-spaced arrangement of the windows in accordance with the existing architectural structure, results in an appearance which is restful and built according to scale.

In Austria, Gustav Peichl designed a small art forum housed in a bank building in Vienna's city centre. The Kunstforum consists of two large exhibition rooms which are solely used for temporary exhibitions. Conceptually, the Kunstforum is an attempt to assume the position of an overture, to provide art information. The design of the rooms shows parallels to both the Städel Museum in Frankfurt and the Kunsthalle in Bonn.

Also connected to the subject of exhibition halls which do not possess the specific character of a museum are two other interesting projects: the Traisen Pavilion in St. Pölten (1988) by Adolf Krischanitz and the temporary hall for the Technical Museum in Vienna (1989) by Boris Podrecca. The cheerful atmosphere of the Traisen

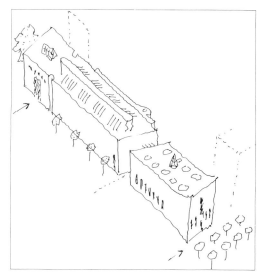

Gustav Peichl, Zubau Städel Museum, Frankfurt, 1987–90
Gustav Peichl, Extension of the Städel Museum, Frankfurt, 1987–90

Gustav Peichl, Bundeskunsthalle, Bonn, Ansicht, 1992
Gustav Peichl, Bundeskunsthalle, Bonn, general view, 1992

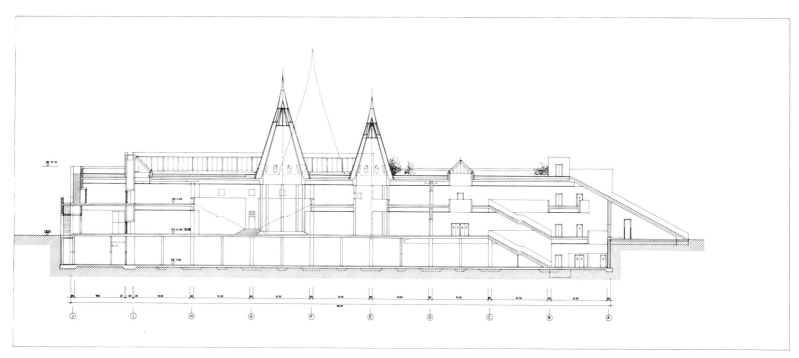

Gustav Peichl, Bundeskunsthalle, Bonn, Schnitt, 1986–92
Gustav Peichl, Bundeskunsthalle, Bonn, section, 1986–92

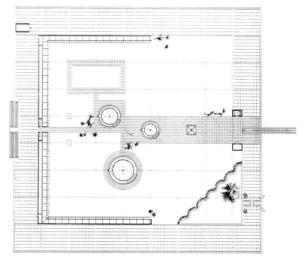

Gustav Peichl, Bundeskunsthalle, Bonn,
Plan Dachgarten, 1986–92
Gustav Peichl, Bundeskunsthalle, Bonn,
roof top plan, 1986–92

Gustav Peichl, Bundeskunsthalle, Bonn, Ansicht Dachgarten, 1992
Gustav Peichl, Bundeskunsthalle, Bonn, view of the roof garden, 1992

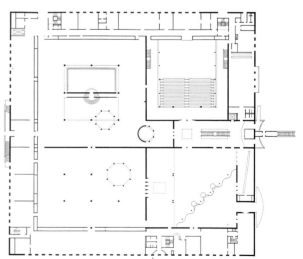

Gustav Peichl, Bundeskunsthalle, Bonn,
Plan Erdgeschoß, 1986–92
Gustav Peichl, Bundeskunsthalle, Bonn,
ground floor plan, 1986–92

Gustav Peichl, Bundeskunsthalle, Bonn, Eingang, 1992
Gustav Peichl, Bundeskunsthalle, Bonn, entrance, 1992

Gustav Peichl, Städel Museum, Frankfurt,
Gartenansicht, 1990
Gustav Peichl, Städel Museum, Frankfurt,
view from the garden, 1990

Gustav Peichl, Städel Museum, Frankfurt, Eingangshalle, 1990
Gustav Peichl, Städel Museum, Frankfurt, entrance hall, 1990

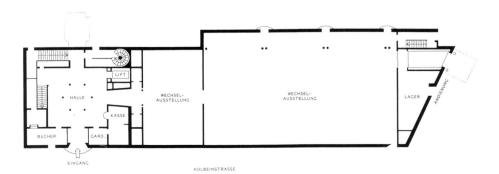

Gustav Peichl, Städel Museum, Frankfurt,
Plan Erdgeschoß, 1987–90
Gustav Peichl, Städel Museum, Frankfurt,
ground floor plan, 1987–90

zwei größeren Ausstellungsräumen, die ausschließlich für Wechselausstellungen verwendet werden. Konzeptionell versucht das Kunstforum die Position einer »Ouvertüre« zu übernehmen, als Kunstinformation. Die Gestaltung der Räume zeigt Parallelen sowohl zum Städel-Museum in Frankfurt als auch zur Kunsthalle Bonn.

Im weiteren Zusammenhang zum Thema Ausstellungshallen ohne spezifischen Museumscharakter stehen zwei interessante Projekte, der Traisen-Pavillon in St. Pölten (1988) von Adolf Krischanitz und die temporäre Halle für das Technische Museum Wien (1989) von Boris Podrecca. Der von heiterer Atmosphäre geprägte Traisen-Pavillon zeigt Anklänge an ein Gestell im Semperschen Sinn, gebaut als zylinderförmige Stahlstruktur mit diagonalen Verstrebungen und semi-transparenten Wänden. Assoziationen zu von Nomadenvölkern entwickelten Zeltkonstruktionen drängen sich auf, wenn die Beleuchtung des Innenraums die Wände als weiße Zeltplanen erscheinen läßt.

Im Gegensatz dazu impliziert die konvexe Dachform der temporären Halle für das Technische Museum von Boris Podrecca den Begriff des schützenden Daches, das gesamte Bauwerk wirkt als strukturale Großform. Diese Halle wurde als ein Provisorium für die Ausstellung »Phantasie und Industrie« konzipiert. Der ursprüngliche Wunsch war – bedingt durch den beschränkten finanziellen Grundrahmen von zwei Millionen Schilling –, eine aufblasbare Halle für das einmalige Ereignis der Ausstellung zu bauen. Von seiten des Museums blieb aber die Wahl einer anderen Halle – immer im Rahmen des Budgets – offen, die sich auch für weitere Veranstaltungen eignen könnte. In der nachfolgenden Untersuchung erwies sich ein einfacher und nackter Zimmermannsbau (Doppelnagelbinder, einseitig auf dem Boden ruhend, mit dem Auflager auf einer mittigen Säulenreihe und einfacher Verschalung mit Trapezblecheindeckung) kostengleich mit der ursprünglich gedachten, anonymen Traglufthalle samt thermischen und baupolizeilichen Zwängen.

Die heterogene Begriffswelt der Museumsdiskussion inkludiert in besonderer Weise

Pavilion is evident in the Semper-like framework, built as a cylinder-shaped steel structure with diagonal strutting and semi-transparent walls. It evokes associations with the tent-like structures of nomadic peoples, the illuminated interior reminding one of the walls of white tent canvas. In contrast to this, the convex form of the roof of Boris Podrecca's temporary hall for the Technical Museum involves the notion of the protective roof, and the whole building creates the effect of a large-scale structural form. This hall was conceived as provisional accommodation for the exhibition *Phantasie und Industrie*. The original intention was to build an inflatable hall for this one-off exhibition. However, the Museum retained the option of another hall – always keeping within the scope of the budget – which could also be used for other events. In the subsequent investigation a bare and simple wooden building (double nailed roof frame, one side resting on the ground, with the support resting on an axial series of columns and simple covering boards with trapezoidal aluminium roofing) proved to cost the same amount of money as the originally planned, anonymous air-inflated structure which was subject to numerous thermal constraints and building regulations.

The heterogeneous conceptual world of the museums debate includes special kinds of attempts at experimental and avantgarde design. A most promising concept in this respect is the new cultural area in St. Pölten. The core of this is a museum complex which houses a regional gallery, a natural history collection, a collection of contemporary history and a museum laboratory.

The transformation or adaptation of existing rooms led Hermann Czech to a series of convincing exhibition designs. For the exhibition *Von Hier Aus* ('From Here') in Düsseldorf, the architectural task involved a question of synoptic differentiation: to organise and to structure the existing interior of a hall. By means of a new sequence of articulated rooms within the existing spatial enclosures, Hermann Czech was able to achieve an urban situation. Another example of spatial

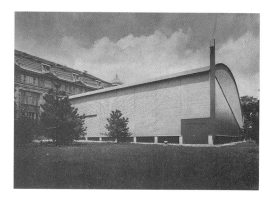

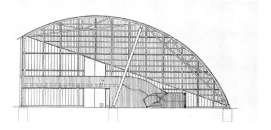

Boris Podrecca, Temporäre Ausstellungshalle, Technisches Museum, Wien, Ansicht, Seitenansicht und Schnitt, 1989
Boris Podrecca, temporary exhibition hall, Technical Museum of Vienna, elevation, side-elevation and section, 1989

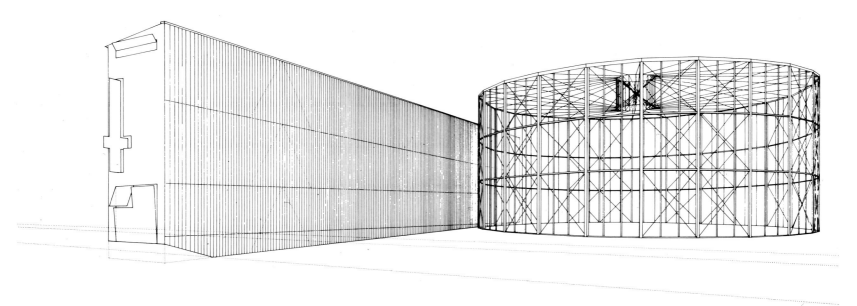

Adolf Krischanitz, Traisen-Pavillon, St. Pölten, Perspektive, 1989
Adolf Krischanitz, Traisen Pavilion, St. Pölten, perspective drawing, 1989

Versuche zum avantgardistischen Experiment. Ein vielversprechendes Konzept wird hierzu für den neuen Kulturbezirk in St. Pölten vorbereitet. Das Kernstück bildet ein Museumskomplex, in dem eine Landesgalerie, eine Naturwissenschaftliche Sammlung, eine Sammlung für Zeitgeschichte sowie ein Museumslabor untergebracht sind.

Im Rahmen von Ausstellungsgestaltungen im In- und Ausland kam Hermann Czech durch die Transformation oder Adaption von bestehenden Räumen zu einer Reihe von überzeugenden Ergebnissen. Bei der Ausstellung »Von hier aus« in Düsseldorf war die architektonische Aufgabe eine Frage der synoptischen Differenzierung: einen bestehenden Halleninnenraum zu organisieren und zu strukturieren. Durch eine neue Abfolge von artikulierten Räumen innerhalb der bestehenden Raumhüllen ermöglichte Hermann Czech eine urbane Situation. Ein anderes Beispiel von Raumtransformation war Czechs Gestaltung der Ausstellung »Wunderblock« im alten Messepalast in Wien. Dort wurde eine bestehende Halle durch verschiedene

transformation was Czech's design for the exhibition *Wunderblock* in Vienna's old Messepalast. There, an existing hall was made spatially explorable by means of various new levels and a new route direction: movement as metaphor and as function.

Adaptation and transformation were also the themes dealt with by Elsa Prochazka in her design and museological reconstruction of the Jewish Museum in Hohenems (1991). The location of this 'museum-intervention' is the Villa Heimann-Rosenthal, an upper-class villa dating from 1864, built by the architect from St. Gall, Felix Wilhelm Kubly. Its use as a Jewish Museum requires both cultural-historical as well as spatial mediation. The spatial mediation acquires an informal, almost homely character by preserving the existing rooms of the villa, while the cultural-historical mediation is provided by various polychrome elements within the framework of complex 'wall facing' and 'wall lining'. Both the materials and the quality of the craftsmanship create an aura of the extra-

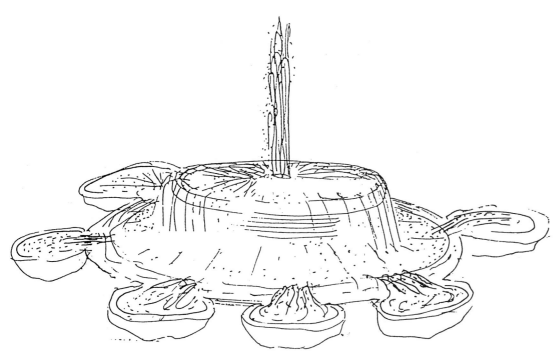

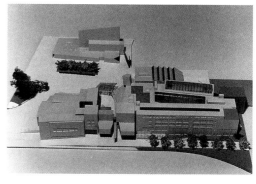

Wettbewerb Kulturbezirk St. Pölten,
Preisträger Hans Hollein, Museum, 1992
Competition for the Cultural Precinct, St. Pölten,
prize-winner Hans Hollein, Museum, 1992

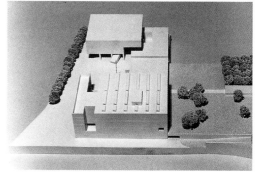

Wettbewerb Kulturbezirk St. Pölten,
Preisträger Paul Katzberger, 1992
Competition for the Cultural Precinct, St. Pölten,
prize-winner Paul Katzberger, 1992

János Kárász, Schemaskizze Museumslabor St. Pölten, 1991
János Kárász, schematic drawing of the Museum Laboratory, St. Pölten, 1991

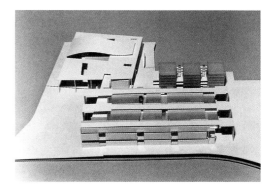

Wettbewerb Kulturbezirk St. Pölten,
Preisträger Klaus Kada, 1992
Competition for the Cultural Precinct, St. Pölten,
prize-winner Klaus Kada, 1992

neue Ebenen und durch eine neue Wege-
führung räumlich erlebbar gemacht: Bewegung als Metapher und als Funktion.
Adaption und Transformation waren auch
für Elsa Prochazka die grundlegenden
Themen bei der Gestaltung und museologischen Bearbeitung des Jüdischen Museums in Hohenems (1991). Ort der Muse-
ums-Intervention war eine großbürger-
liche Villa aus dem Jahr 1864, die Villa
Heimann-Rosenthal, gebaut von dem St.
Gallener Architekten Felix Wilhelm Kubly.
Die Verwendung als Jüdisches Museum
bedurfte sowohl einer kulturell-histori-
schen als auch räumlichen Vermittlung:
räumlich geschah dies durch einen informellen, beinahe wohnlichen Charakter,
indem die bestehenden Räume der Villa
erhalten blieben, während die kulturell-
historische Vermittlung durch verschiedene polychrome Elemente innerhalb
einer komplexen »Wandbekleidung« und
»Wandverkleidung« stattfindet. Sowohl die
Materialien als auch die handwerkliche
Qualität der Ausführung schaffen eine Aura
des Besonderen, aber auch der Distanz. So
vereint das Jüdische Museum Hohenems

ordinary, although it is also one of distance:
in this way the Jewish Museum of Hohenems combines a awareness of history with
an interpretation of history.
Within the context of historically established and concentrated structures, architectural interventions are only feasible in
the form of subtle reinterpretations – if they
are not to destroy the torso of a building's
architectural history in the process. An
example of such architectural reinter-
pretation in recent years was provided by
the investigations into the possibility of
adapting the architectural substance of
the Graphische Sammlung Albertina in
Vienna. The planning process has not yet
been completed, due to the complex and
varied requirements of this important
depot and museum for graphic art. The
architectural study by John Sailer and
Rudolf F. Weber (1991) demonstrates the
possibility of re-using the inner courtyards,
the main entrance and also the old ramps,
thereby transforming the architectural
substance in an intelligent way. Such
attempts should be regarded as charac-
teristic of many projects in Austria from

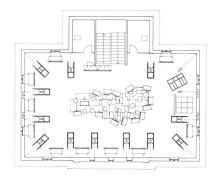

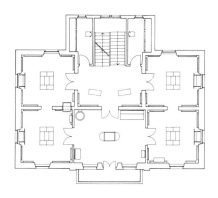

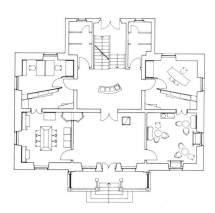

Elsa Prochazka, Jüdisches Museum,
Hohenems, Grundrisse, 1991
Elsa Prochazka, Jewish Museum,
Hohenems, floor plans, 1991

Geschichtsbewußtsein und Geschichts-
interpretation.
Im Umfeld historisch gewachsener und
verdichteter Strukturen sind architektonische Eingriffe nur als subtile Umdeutungen möglich, welche die an der Bausubstanz ablesbaren Zeugnisse der Baugeschichte nicht zerstören. Ein Beispiel für
solche baulichen Umdeutungen waren in
den letzten Jahren die Untersuchungen,
die Bausubstanz der Graphischen Sammlung Albertina in Wien zu adaptieren.
Wegen der komplexen und differenzierten
Anforderungen dieses bedeutenden De-
potmuseums für graphische Kunst ist der
konzeptuelle Prozeß noch nicht abgeschlossen. Die architektonische Studie von
John Sailer und Rudolf F. Weber (1991)
zeigt die Möglichkeiten auf, sowohl die
Innenhöfe und den Hauptzugang als auch
die alten Rampen neu zu nutzen und somit
die Bausubstanz auf intelligente Weise zu
transformieren. Die genannten Ansätze
sollen stellvertretend für viele Projekte in
Österreich verstanden werden, aus denen
für die vorliegende Ausstellung ausgewählt wurde.

Die Ausstellung »Museums-Positionen«
versteht sich als »work in progress«, als
Zeitschnitt innerhalb einer Entwicklung.
Die Auswahl ist, wie schon in der Einlei-
tung gesagt, als »pars pro toto« zu verstehen
– die nicht genannten Museen werden in
ihrer Qualität und Bedeutung in keiner
Weise in Frage gestellt.
Bisher noch nicht vorgestellt wurden die
Museen als Sinnbild für das kulturelle
Erbe. Das Museum als kulturelle Schnitt-
stelle, als intellektueller Brennpunkt der
Gegenwart und der Geschichte, präsentiert sich als das neue Spiegelbild einer
postindustriellen Gesellschaft, in dem sich
die wirtschaftliche Leistung mit kulturel-
lem Selbstverständnis neu verknüpft.
Die Ausstellung »Museums-Positionen«
will dazu beitragen, ein Defizit abzubauen,
das darin besteht, Österreich fast ausschließlich als ein Land des kulturellen
Erbes zu betrachten. Die Wirkung dieser
Ausstellung könnte eine dreifache sein: sie
könnte, erstens, eine *Öffnung* der österreichischen Aktivitäten über die eigenen
Grenzen hinaus einleiten, zweitens eine

whose ranks those for the present exhibition were chosen.

The exhibition Museum Positions can be
regarded as 'work in progress', as a temporal cross-section through a process of
development. The selective criteria for
choosing the museums in Austria were
based, on the one hand, on the quality of the
individual museum and, on the other hand,
on its relevance and exemplariness for the
museums scene. In order to create an
objective temporal framework, special
selective criteria were applied such as the
museums' planned or recently completed
rebuilding activities, or new building situations. The method of selection involved
evaluation of the individual museum's
variety and independence, combined with
the principle of quality as the final criterion.
The task of making a representative selection from the great number of museums
proved to be not only difficult but almost
impossible: the choice should therefore
primarily be understood as *pars pro toto* –
those museums which have not received
mention have in no way been called into
question as far as their quality and importance are concerned. The institution of the
museum as a metaphor for the cultural
heritage has not yet been introduced. The
museum as a cultural interface, as an
intellectual metaphor for the present and
for history, emerges as the new reflection
of a post-industrial society in which economic performance is linked in a new way
to the cultural self-image.
An exhibition like Museum Positions will
help to reduce a deficit, one which consists
of the fact that Austria can be regarded as
a country with a cultural heritage and
almost nothing else. This exhibition could
have a threefold effect: firstly, as an *opening*
for Austrian activities beyond the country's
borders; secondly, as a *presentation* of new
museum buildings from an architectural
point of view, set against the background
of the visual arts; and thirdly, as a *discussion*
of new conceptions of the museum, new
museum structures and the kind of
museology which is relevant to the *debut de
millénaire.*

Präsentation neuer Museumsbauten unter architektonischen Gesichtspunkten im Umfeld der bildenden Künste initiieren und drittens eine *Diskussion* über neue Museumskonzeptionen, neue Museumsstrukturen und relevante Museologie für den Beginn des neuen Jahrtausends in Gang setzen.

Architektonische Konzepte

Die ausgewählten Museumsprojekte lassen sich grundsätzlich in drei Bereiche unterteilen, entsprechend dem Umgang mit ihrem »Bestand«, wobei Bestand einerseits als der Sammlungsbestand des Museums, andererseits als der bauliche Bestand zu sehen ist. Der erste Bereich enthält Museumsneubauten und Museumsanbauten, bei denen der Bestand sowohl in baulicher als auch in inhaltlicher Sicht komplett oder größtenteils neu strukturiert wird. Der zweite Bereich betrifft die Museumsumbauten in bestehender Bausubstanz (»Bestand«), wobei ausstellungstechnische und konservatorische Aspekte im Vordergrund stehen. Der dritte Bereich schließlich behandelt Kunst- und Ausstellungshallen am Beispiel der neuen, temporären Ausstellungshalle der Stadt Wien am Karlsplatz als flexible Raumhülle für wechselnde Ausstellungen, aber ohne eigenen Sammlungsbestand.

Museen definieren sich baulich entweder durch *Raumhüllen* oder durch *Raumformen*. Die flexible Raumhülle will Inhalte ermöglichen, die vorher nicht – oder noch nicht – festgelegt wurden. Die Raumhüllen von Mies van der Rohe oder die Raumtragwerke von Buckminster Fuller sind Beispiele für solche potentielle Nutzung, die Raumabfolgen von Louis Kahn hingegen sind Beispiele für Raumhierarchien (dienende und bediente Räume), deren Nutzung eine spezifische Qualität erfordert. Überlegungen bezüglich Raumform versus Raumhülle sind im Museumsbereich begleitet von der Frage nach der Art der ausgestellten Objekte – verlangen sie den Schrein oder den Supermarkt? Der Schrein kennzeichnet nicht nur das Besondere, sondern auch das Transzendente – dem Leben entrückte Dinge –, während der

Architectural Concepts

The museum projects which have been selected can be divided into three basic groups, according to their differing approaches to their 'possessions'. Possessions seen on the one hand as the collections of the museum, on the other as architectural possessions. The first kind of possessions include new museum buildings and museum extensions, with the collection completely or predominantly restructured from both an architectural point of view and that of the collection. The second area involves alterations to the existing architectural substance of the museum (the 'building stock'), whereby the aspects of exhibition technology and conservation remain in the foreground; and the third area concerns art and exhibition halls, for example, the *Kunsthalle,* the City of Vienna's new, temporary exhibition hall at Karlsplatz, which has a flexible spatial enclosure for temporary exhibitions, but does not possess a collection of its own.

Museums are architecturally defined either by *spatial enclosures (Raumhüllen)* or by *spatial form (Raumformen).* A flexible spatial enclosure makes it possible to present things which have not – or have not yet – been decided upon beforehand. The spatial enclosures of Mies van der Rohe or the spatial frames of Buckminster Fuller are examples of this potential utilisation; the spatial sequences by Louis Kahn, on the other hand, are examples of spatial hierarchies (serving and served rooms), whose utilisation demands a specific quality. In the museum sector, the question of spatial form versus spatial enclosure is accompanied by that of the authenticity of the objects exhibited: whether in a shrine or supermarket. The shrine symbolises not only what is special, but also what is transcendental – things at a remove from life – while the supermarket is a symbol not only for self-service and the availability of all things, but also for everyday necessities. Within this field of tension, it emerges that the discussion about spatial form and spatial enclosure belongs to the fundamental self-image of every museum-position. Spatial forms tend to personalise the

Graphische Sammlung Albertina, Wien, Historisches Photo.
Graphische Sammlung Albertina, Vienna, historic photograph

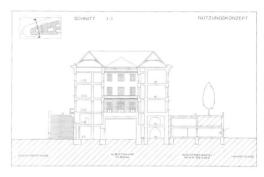

Rudolf Weber, John Sailer, Gutachten Renovierung Graphische Sammlung Albertina, Wien, 1991
Rudolf Weber, John Sailer, report on the renovation of the Graphische Sammlung Albertina, Vienna, 1991

Elsa Prochazka, Jüdisches Museum, Hohenems, 1991
Elsa Prochazka, Jewish Museum, Hohenems, 1991

Supermarkt sinnbildlich nicht nur für Selbstbedienung und Verfügbarkeit aller Dinge steht, sondern auch für Alltäglich-Notwendiges. In diesem Spannungsfeld zeigt sich, daß die Diskussion über *Raumform* und *Raumhülle* zum grundsätzlichen Selbstverständnis jeder Museums-Position gehört. Raumformen tendieren dazu, den Dialog zwischen Besucher und Kunst-Objekt zu personalisieren, die Aura der Kunst-Objekte wirkt institutionalisiert. Raumhüllen hingegen bieten eine allgemeine Zugangsmöglichkeit, bei der Kunstwerke im wahrsten Sinne des Wortes exponiert sind – nackt und unbedeckt in Relation zur allgegenwärtigen Öffentlichkeit.

Es wäre durchaus möglich und denkbar, neue bauliche Rahmenbedingungen für temporäre Kunstbetrachtung zu schaffen, wo *aktive Ausstellungsräume* eine verkürzte Umschlagzeit der Werke aus und in die Depots ermöglichen würden. Dieser aktive Ausstellungsraum wäre eine Mischung aus Depotraum und Ausstellungsraum, bei dem man durch mechanisch verschiebbare Wände die Hängefläche ein und desselben Raumes vervielfachen könnte. Diese Aspekte sollen aber in diesem Zusammenhang nur erwähnt und nicht näher ausgeführt werden.

Der Stand der Dinge

Das Museum ist ein öffentlicher Bau. Seine Signifikanz ist im öffentlichen Bewußtsein dadurch charakterisiert, daß es der Stadt *öffentliche Innenräume* (enclosed public space) zurückgibt und dadurch die Dichte der urbanen Masse relativiert. Jedes Museum führt diesen Dialog mit der Stadt auf eine jeweils sehr »persönliche« und differenzierte Art. In den folgenden Museums-Positionen sollen diese Ansätze kurz skizziert werden, jede einzelne Position wird im Anhang ausführlich geschildert.

Als bauliche Intervention von größtem Umfang präsentiert sich das neue Museumsquartier in Wien, dessen Konzept an der ursprünglichen Idee eines Museumsforums von Semper und Hasenauer am Ende des 19. Jahrhunderts anknüpft. Es ist derzeit das bedeutendste Kulturprojekt der Republik Österreich.

dialogue between the visitor and the art object, and the aura of the art object exerts an institutionalising influence. In comparison, spatial enclosures offer general accessibility, in which the work of art is exhibited in the truest sense of the word – naked and uncovered in relation to the omnipresent public.

It would be both possible and conceivable to create new architectural conditions for temporary art viewing, where active exhibition rooms would ensure a brief transfer time from the depot areas. This *active exhibition room* would be a mixture of depot and exhibition hall, in which one could multiply the hanging area of one and the same space by means of movable walls. However, this aspect is only noteworthy in the present context; it is not a proposal to be realised in practice.

The State of Things

The museum is a public building. Its significance for public consciousness is characterised by the fact that it returns *enclosed public space* to the city, therefore relativising the urban mass. Every museum conducts this dialogue in its own, very individual and idiosyncratic way. The following museum-positions are intended to give a brief sketch of such approaches. Every single position will be described in detail in the appendix. As an architectural intervention on the largest scale, we can present the new Museum Quarter in Vienna, the concept of which develops the original idea of a museum forum proposed by Semper and Hasenauer at the end of the 19th century. The Museum Quarter is Austria's most important cultural project. In the spring of 1990 the decision was taken to transform the area of the Imperial Court Stables built by Fischer von Erlach in the 18th century – later the exhibition halls of the Wiener Messe AG (Vienna Trade Fairs Company) at the Messepalast – in accordance with the plans of the architects Laurids and Manfred Ortner, into a multifunctional cultural centre primarily devoted to the contemporary art scene. The construction of a new Museum moderner Kunst ('Museum of Modern Art) there signals the end of a period of almost thirty

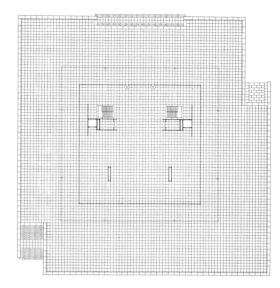

Ludwig Mies van der Rohe,
Neue Nationalgalerie, Berlin, 1963–68
Ludwig Mies van der Rohe,
New National Gallery, Berlin, 1963–68

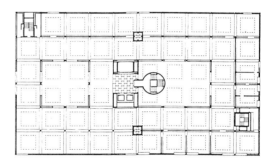

Louis Kahn, Yale Center für Britische Kunst,
New Haven, 1972–77
Louis Kahn, Yale Center for British Art,
New Haven, 1972–77

Im Frühjahr 1990 wurde der Beschluß gefaßt, das Areal der von Johann Bernhard Fischer von Erlach im 18. Jahrhundert errichteten kaiserlichen Hofstallungen und späteren Ausstellungshallen der Wiener Messe AG (»Messepalast«) nach den Plänen der Architekten Laurids und Manfred Ortner in ein multifunktionales, in erster Linie dem zeitgenössischen Kunstgeschehen gewidmetes Kulturzentrum zu transformieren. Durch den damit verbundenen Bau eines neuen Museums moderner Kunst wird ein fast drei Jahrzehnte dauerndes Provisorium – Museum des 20. Jahrhunderts im österreichischen Expo-Pavillon von 1958 und im barocken Palais Liechtenstein – beendet.

Ergänzt wird dieser Gegenwartsbezug des »Museumsquartiers« durch ein Zentrum für Neue Medien (»Informations- und Leseturm«), das es dem Besucher ermöglichen wird, sich in direktem interaktivem Zugriff produktiv und kritisch mit den neuesten Entwicklungen auf dem Mediensektor auseinanderzusetzen. Produktionseinrichtungen für Medienkünstler sind dort ebenso vorgesehen wie ein Kinozentrum, ein Filmmuseum, ein Photoarchiv und eine Videothek sowie ein experimenteller »Kunst- und Museumsfunk«.

Das Österreichische Museum für angewandte Kunst, heute kurz »MAK« genannt, wurde auf kaiserliche Anordnung nach dem Vorbild des Victoria & Albert Museums in London als erstes Kunstgewerbemuseum auf dem Kontinent gegründet und am 12. Mai 1864 zunächst im Ballhaus der Hofburg eröffnet. 1871 wurden das Museum und die ihm angeschlossene, 1868 eröffnete Kunstgewerbeschule in dem repräsentativen Neubau von Heinrich Ritter von Ferstel am Stubenring vereint. Bereits 1877 übersiedelte die Schule aus Raumnot in einen ebenfalls von Ferstel errichteten eigenen Bau. 1909 wurde das Museum mit der Errichtung eines von Ludwig Baumann entworfenen Ausstellungstraktes in der Weiskirchnerstraße erweitert.

Nach der seit 1986 eingeleiteten inhaltlichen und organisatorischen Neustrukturierung wird das Österreichische Museum für angewandte Kunst seit 1989 general-

years' temporary accommodation (as the Museum of the 20th Century in the Austrian Expo pavilion dating from 1958 and the Museum of Modern Art in the Baroque Palais Liechtenstein).

The relationship of the Museum Quarter to the present-day will be enhanced by a centre for new media (the 'Media Tower'). This will give visitors direct interactive access to the latest developments in the media sector. Production equipment for media artists will also be provided, as will a cinema centre, a film museum, a film archive, a videotheque and an experimental 'Art and Museum Radio'.

The Österreichische Museum für Angewandte Kunst ('Austrian Museum for Applied Art'), today known as the MAK, and originally called the K.K. Österreichisches Museum für Kunst und Industrie ('Austrian Museum for Art and Industry'), was founded by Imperial decree, taking as its model the Victoria & Albert Museum in London. It was the first museum of the decorative arts on the continent and was opened on 12th May 1864, being housed at first in the Ballhaus of the Hofburg. In 1871 the Museum and the School of Applied Arts (which had been founded in 1868 and added to the museum) were combined in the representative new building by Heinrich Ritter von Ferstel on the Stubenring. In 1877 the School moved, due to lack of space, to its own building, also designed by Ferstel. In 1909 the Museum was extended by the construction of an exhibition tract, designed by Ludwig Baumann, in Weiskirchnerstrasse.

Besides restructuring its collections and internal organisation, the Austrian Museum for Applied Art has been undergoing general redevelopment and alteration work since 1989. Individual artists and architects have been engaged for the extension work (Walter Pichler, Sepp Müller, Peter Noever, Hermann Czech, the artists' group SITE and others).

Also part of the new open space for exhibitions and events is the terrace plateau designed for the museum garden by Peter Noever. The stairway, which is oriented towards the garden, on the one hand represents a division and breakdown of the

saniert und umgebaut. Für den Ausbau wurden einzelne Künstler und Architekten verpflichtet (Walter Pichler, Sepp Müller, Peter Noever, Hermann Czech, Künstlergruppe SITE u. a.).

Miteinbezogen in den neuen offenen Raum für Ausstellungen und Veranstaltungen ist auch das für den Museumsgarten von Peter Noever entworfene Terrassenplateau. Die zum Garten hin orientierte Treppenanlage stellt einerseits eine Gliederung und Auflösung der Grundstücksgrenze dar und lädt andererseits den Besucher ein, diese Treppen zu begehen: Aus verschiedenen Höhen ergeben sich so unterschiedliche Blickwinkel und Perspektiven auf möglicherweise im Museumsgarten ausgestellte Exponate und Objekte. Von der Stubenbrücke und der Vorderen Zollamtsstraße her gesehen ist das Plateau ein Signal für den Zugang zum Museumsgarten; als Aussichtsterrasse zum Stadtpark bildet es eine städtebauliche Bereicherung. Die komplexen statischen Aufgaben löste Wolfdietrich Ziesel, wobei die Auskragung des Terrassenplateaus konstruktiv mit dem neuerrichteten unterirdischen Tiefspeicher verbunden wurde. In seiner reduzierten Geometrie erinnert das Plateau an Arbeiten russischer Konstruktivisten wie Ladowski oder Korshew.

Die primäre Funktion des Kunsthauses Bregenz, Vorarlberger Landesgalerie, ist die einer Kunsthalle für österreichische und internationale Gegenwartskunst. Aufgebaut werden eine österreichische Sammlung und eine internationale Spezialsammlung von Arbeiten im Spannungsfeld von Kunst und Architektur.

In einem Wettbewerb fiel die Entscheidung zugunsten des Entwurfs des Schweizer Architekten Peter Zumthor. Im Stadtbild stellt sich der Neubau als eigenständiges Glied in die Reihe der bestehenden Solitärbauten an der Uferlinie der Bregenzer Bucht dar. Auch bei diesem Museumsneubau ist an eine Zusammenarbeit des Architekten mit einem Künstler, nämlich Donald Judd aus den USA, gedacht.

Ebenfalls durch einen Wettbewerb wurde die Entscheidung für das Trigon-Museum in Graz getroffen, wo die Architektengrup-

property line, and on the other hand simply invites the visitor to walk up the stairs: at the various levels there are different perspectives and angles of vision, revealing possible exhibits and objects in the Museum garden. Seen from the Stubenbrücke and the Vordere Zollamtsstrasse, it indicates the entrance to the museum garden, and as a terrace with a view of the Stadtpark it is an urban planning improvement. The complex structural requirements are solved in a masterly way by Wolfdietrich Ziesel, whereby the cantilever of the terrace plateau has been structurally connected to the newly built underground car park. In its reduced geometry, the plateau reminds one of the work of Russian Constructivists such as Ladowski or Korshev.

The primary function of the Kunsthaus Bregenz, the Regional Gallery of Vorarlberg, is that of an exhibition hall for contemporary national and international art. A collection of contemporary Austrian art will be started there as well as a special international collection of works related to both art and architecture.

After a competition it was decided to adopt the design of the Swiss architect Peter Zumthor. The new building will become part of the cityscape in its own right, as a new member of the row of existing freestanding buildings along the shores of Lake Constance. A collaboration between the architect and an artist, Donald Judd, from the USA, is also being considered in the case of this new museum building.

The contract for the Trigon Museum in Graz was also decided by competition, the first prize being awarded to the Schöffauer-Schrom-Tschapeller group of architects. Not far from the centre of Graz, the Provincial Government of Styria is planning to build a Kunsthaus, which will be devoted to current artistic work. The purpose of constructing it is to provide a place where contact can be openly established and artistic utilisation mediated; or, alternatively, to quote the architect: "... not a place of views and panoramas, but a place of insights."

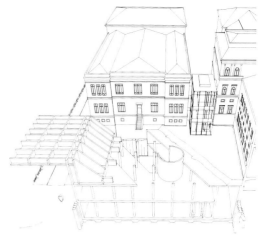

Österreichisches Museum für angewandte Kunst, Wien, Peter Noever, Wolfdietrich Ziesel, Konstruktives Konzept, Terrassenplateau, 1990
Austrian Museum for Applied Art, Vienna, Peter Noever, Wolfdietrich Ziesel, structural concept for the terrace, 1990

pe Schöffauer – Schrom – Tschapeller den ersten Preis erhielt. Das Land Steiermark plant am Rand des Zentrums von Graz ein Kunsthaus, das der Auseinandersetzung mit dem aktuellen künstlerischen Schaffen gewidmet sein wird. Mit der Errichtung soll ein Ort offener Kontaktaufnahme und Vermittlung künstlerischer Benützung entstehen beziehungsweise, um die Architekten zu zitieren, »… kein Ort von Ansichten oder Aussichten, sondern ein Ort von Einsichten.«

Das Technische Museum Wien bietet in seiner ständigen Schausammlung vor allem einen reichhaltigen Überblick über die Geschichte der österreichischen Technik und Industrie. Das erklärt sich auch aus der Absicht der Gründer nach der Jahrhundertwende, die eine repräsentative Darstellung des Fortschritts in der Habsburgermonarchie auf diesen Gebieten anstrebten. Denn es war ein Österreicher, Josef Ressel, der die Schiffsschraube erfand, Josef Madersperger und Peter Mitterhofer entwickelten die Näh- beziehungsweise die Schreibmaschine, und es war ein in Wien lebender gebürtiger Mecklenburger, Siegfried Marcus, der die ersten Versuche mit einem benzinbetriebenen Automobil unternahm.
Technik als sozio-kultureller und ökonomischer Motor im 19. und 20. Jahrhundert soll innerhalb des Kontextes als didaktisch erfahrbare Einheit gezeigt werden. Die Verbindung von alt und neu soll sowohl in baulicher Art durch den Zubau dokumentiert werden als auch inhaltlich durch die Ausstellungsobjekte.

Die Stadt Wien hat mit der Entscheidung für eine temporäre Ausstellungshalle in Wien ihr Interesse dokumentiert, auf die unterschiedlichen Anforderungen von Großausstellungen flexibel zu reagieren. Der zentrale Standort der temporären Kunst- und Veranstaltungshalle am Karlsplatz ergibt einen »Kulturkorso« zwischen Secession, Akademie, Künstlerhaus, Historischem Museum der Stadt Wien und Technischer Universität genau an der Grenze zwischen dem ersten und dem vierten Wiener Gemeindebezirk. Die Ausrichtung der Halle parallel zur verlängerten Wienzeile

The permanent collection of the Technical Museum of Vienna presents above all a varied history of Austrian technology and industry. This can also be said to have been its founders' intention just after the turn of the century; they sought to convey for representation purposes a picture of the progress that had been made in these fields under the Habsburg monarchy. For it was the Austrian Josef Ressel who invented the ship's screw, the Austrians Josef Madersperger and Peter Mitterhofer who developed the sewing machine and the typewriter, and a native of Mecklenburg resident in Vienna, Siegfried Marcus, who made the first experiments with a petrol-driven car. Technology as the socio-cultural and economic motor of the 19th and 20th centuries is shown to be an integrated whole which can be apprehended didactically within its context. It is intended to document the connection between the old and the new both from the architectural aspect (in the form of the extension), and in terms of the collections (in the form of exhibited objects).

With its decision to build a temporary exhibition hall in Vienna, the municipal council has recorded its interest in responding in a flexible way to the various requirements of large-scale exhibitions. The central location of the temporary exhibition and events hall, the Kunsthalle, at Karlsplatz produces a 'cultural corso' between the Secession, the Academy of Fine Arts, the Künstlerhaus and the Technical University, exactly on the border between the 1st and the 4th Municipal Districts of Vienna. The orientation of the hall parallel to the extension of the Wienzeile has various historical precedents and produces a most interesting protected area at the rear of the site. It was designed by the Viennese architect, Adolf Krischanitz.

Two of the other selected 'museum positions' are intensively concerned with questions of architectural adaptation and conservation: those of the Kunsthistorische Museum and the Theatermuseum.

The Kunsthistorische Museum ('Art History Museum') not only contains the

weist auf verschiedene historische Vorbilder hin und ergibt einen sehr interessanten geschützten Raum an der Rückseite der Anlage. Der Entwurf stammt vom Wiener Architekten Adolf Krischanitz.

Zwei andere der ausgewählten Museums-Positionen beschäftigen sich intensiv mit Fragen der baulichen Adaptierung und der konservatorischen Aspekte: Kunsthistorisches Museum und Theatermuseum. Das Kunsthistorische Museum enthält nicht nur die berühmte Gemäldesammlung, sondern birgt vielmehr einen »Kosmos«, der noch weit vielschichtiger ist, als es selbst eine der größten Sammlungen alter Meister je sein kann. Seine Schätze sind – wie fast alle bedeutenden Wiener Sammlungen – ein Erbstück aus der Habsburgermonarchie. Josef II. hatte den habsburgischen Kunstbesitz – 1776 bis 1778 ins Belvedere übersiedelt – schon 1781 der Öffentlichkeit zugänglich gemacht. Das Haus am Ring wurde als Pendant zum Naturhistorischen Museum 1891 eröffnet, beherbergt jedoch heute nur noch einen Teil des riesigen Besitzstandes: andere Teile sind in der Hofburg, in Schloß Schönbrunn sowie in Schloß Ambras bei Innsbruck untergebracht. In der Gemäldegalerie des Kunsthistorischen Museums begegnet der Besucher Meisterwerken der deutschen, der niederländischen, der italienischen und spanischen Malerei, Künstlern wie Dürer und Cranach, Bruegel und Rubens, van Dyck und Rembrandt, Tizian und Raffael beziehungsweise Velázquez, um nur einige der Fixsterne zu nennen. Bei den Plänen für das Kunsthistorische Museum handelt es sich um ein Beispiel für eine komplexe und diffizile Adaptierung hinsichtlich höchster konservatorischer Anforderungen der Bausubstanz, verbunden mit einer möglichen neuen Verbindung zum künftigen Museumsquartier.

Die Theatersammlung, Grundstock des österreichischen Theatermuseums, besteht seit 1922, als die Sammlung aus dem Kaiserhaus und die Privatsammlung des Burgtheaterdirektors Hugo Thimig zusammengefaßt wurden. Sie war damals schon führende Dokumentationsstätte auf dem Gebiet des Barocktheaters; Josef Gregor,

famous collection of paintings; it conceals, in addition, a whole cosmos which is vastly more complex than even one of the great collections of old masters could be. Like almost all the important Viennese collections, its treasures were inherited from the Habsburg monarchy. Josef II made the dynastic art possessions – which were at that time still in Belvedere – accessible to the public as early as 1781. The museum on the Ring was opened as the 'companion piece' to the Naturhistorische Museum ('Natural History Museum') in 1891 and today houses only part of the vast collection; other parts are accommodated in the Hofburg, in Schönbrunn Palace as well as at Castle Ambras near Innsbruck. In the aforementioned Picture Gallery the visitor encounters masterpieces of German, Netherlandish, Italian and Spanish painting, artists such as Dürer and Cranach, Breughel and Rubens, van Dyck and Rembrandt, Titian and Raphael and Velasquez, to name but a few of the fixed stars. The building work here provides an example of a complex and difficult adaptation, involving the strictest conservational requirements for the architectural building substance, combined with a possible new connection to the future Museum Quarter.

The Theatre Collection, the basic stock of the Austrian Theatre Museum, has been in existence since 1922, when it was put together as such from the Imperial collection and the private collection of the Burgtheater director Hugo Thimig. Even at that time it was the leading documentation centre for the field of the Baroque theatre; Josef Gregor, the founder of the Theatre Collection, also turned his attention to 20th century theatre, so that today Austria possesses one of the largest collections of Americana in the world, as well as exhibits documenting Russian avantgarde theatre. In addition to a great variety of photographs, stage designs and written documents, the Theatre Museum also possesses three-dimensional objects such as theatre models or costumes. The architectural adaptation involves work on an important Baroque palace containing the famous Eroica Room, so named because it was here

der Gründer der Theatersammlung, richtete sein Augenmerk aber auch auf das Theater des 20. Jahrhunderts, so daß Österreich heute neben Belegen zum russischen Avantgardetheater auch eine der größten Amerikana-Sammlungen besitzt. Neben Photos, Bühnenbildentwürfen und Schriftstücken der verschiedensten Art umfaßt das Theatermuseum im Palais Lobkowitz auch dreidimensionale Objekte, wie Theatermodelle oder Kostüme. Bei der baulichen Adaptierung handelt es sich um ein bedeutendes Barockpalais mit dem berühmten Eroica-Saal, benannt nach der an dieser Stelle stattgefundenen Uraufführung von Beethovens gleichnamiger Symphonie.

Die Absicht und die ersten Konzepte für den Bau eines neuen jüdischen Museums in Wien wurden im Frühjahr 1991 vorgestellt. Im politischen und historischen Zusammenhang ist der Bau eines jüdischen Museums in Wien eine besondere Entscheidung. Bereits im März 1990 wurde das jüdische Museum eröffnet – zunächst allerdings nur im Rahmen eines Provisoriums. Im ersten Stock des Hauses Seitenstettengasse 4, im ehemaligen Festsaal der Israelitischen Kultusgemeinde, hat das Museum bis zum Umzug in ein eigenes Haus eine vorübergehende Bleibe gefunden. Die Architektur des neuen Museums wird durch einen internationalen Wettbewerb für den neuen Standort am Judenplatz in Wien gefunden werden.

Die völlig unterschiedlichen Charaktere der hier vorgestellten Museums-Positionen sind Ausdruck der vielfältigen Museumslandschaft in Österreich, die einen Einblick in die unterschiedlichen Strukturen und Entwicklungen erlauben.
Architektur ist eine öffentliche Sache, ohne daß ihr Anforderungsprofil in Sachen Gestalt von der breiten Öffentlichkeit sachlich verifiziert werden kann. Die Gestaltung des öffentlichen Raumes verlangt den Konsens und liefert Beweise dafür, daß inhaltliche Verständigung in kulturellen Angelegenheiten auch einen gebauten Ausdruck, eine *Baugestalt* finden muß. Ohne den Mut der öffentlichen Hand zur *Baugestalt* fehlt die Identität des öffentlichen Stadtraumes. Die vorgestellten Projekte zu

that the premiere of Beethoven's eponymous symphony was held.

The proposal and the preliminary plans for building a new Jewish Museum in Vienna were presented in the spring of 1991. The decision to create a Jewish Museum in Vienna was an important one, considering the political and historical context, and a museum has now been open to the public since March 1990, though it is only housed in provisional quarters. It will remain there (on the second floor of Vienna's main synagogue, Seitenstettengasse 4) until the new building in Judenplatz has been completed. The archictectural design of the new museum at the new site will be decided upon by means of an international competition.

The heterogeneous character of the museum positions presented here reflects the variety of the museum scene in Austria and allow an insight into some of the different structures and developments.
Architecture is a public matter – a *res publica* – although its list of requirements in the matter of form cannot be publicly verified. The design of public space is a matter of agreement, and provides proof of the fact that the communication of content in cultural matters also has to be given expression in buildings, as architectural form. If the public authorities do not have the courage to support architectural form then the public space lacks identity. The projects presented in Museum Positions can be regarded as positive examples of an improved attitude, as places of cultural concentration, as examples of architectural culture. However, the future can only promise what is thought about in the present.
A new era has dawned, an era of change, when positions are shifting or being modified, and institutions reflecting upon their past reservedness and isolation. A new era has also dawned for visitors to places of cultural interest, since they are now being invited to enter into a new dialogue with the arts.
Concerning the museum positions themselves in their critical role, Goethe's definition of critical reflection provides the

den Museums-Positionen sind positive Beispiele für eine Haltung, die bereit ist, Orte der kulturellen Verdichtung auch als Beispiele von Baukultur anzusehen. Die Zukunft kann aber nur das versprechen, was in der Gegenwart gedacht wird.

Eine Wendezeit ist angebrochen, eine Zeit der Wende, in der sich Positionen ändern und verändern und die für Institutionen Verantwortlichen nachdenken über die Zurückhaltung und die Isolation in der Vergangenheit. Eine Wendezeit ist auch angebrochen für die Besucher der Kulturstätten, mit der Aufforderung, den neuen Dialog mit der Kultur aufzunehmen.

Was die kritische Aufgabe der Museums-Positionen selbst betrifft, so gibt Goethes Hinweis über die kritische Reflexion folgenden Anhalt: Kritik, so meint er, hat sich an drei Fragen zu halten: »Was hat sich der Autor (›das Museum‹) vorgesetzt? Ist dieser Vorsatz vernünftig und verständig? Und inwiefern ist es gelungen, ihn auszuführen?«

Anmerkungen

1 Heinrich Klotz, Waltraud Krase: *New Museums in the Federal Republic of Germany.* Academy Editions, London 1986, S. 17
2 Michael Mönninger in: Vittorio M. Lampugnani (Hrsg.): Museumsarchitektur in Frankfurt 1980–1990. Prestel, München 1990, S. 86
3 Werner Oechslin: Gustav Peichl, Die Kunst- und Ausstellungshalle in Bonn. In: Katalog »Die Kunst- und Ausstellungshalle der Bundesrepublik Deutschland«, Hatje 1992, S. 17

Alessandro Alvera, Karl Stronsky, Neugestaltung des Bundesmobiliendepots, Wien, 1991
Alessandro Alvera, Karl Stronsky, new design for the State Collection of Furniture, Vienna, 1991

following hint: criticism, he says, should always bear in mind three questions: "What did the author (the museum) resolve to do? Is the resolution rational and intelligent? And to what extent has he succeeded in carrying it out?"

Notes

1 Heinrich Klotz, Waltraud Krase: *New Museums in the Federal Republic of Germany.* Academy Editions, London 1986, p. 17
2 Michael Mönninger in: Vittorio M. Lampugnani (ed.): Museumsarchitektur in Frankfurt 1980–1990. Prestel, München 1990, p. 86
3 Werner Oechslin: Gustav Peichl, Die Kunst- und Ausstellungshalle in Bonn. In: Katalog »Die Kunst- und Ausstellungshalle der Bundesrepublik Deutschland«, Hatje 1992, p. 17

ADOLF KRISCHANITZ	Kunsthalle Karlsplatz, Wien, 1991–1992 *Exhibition and Events Hall, Vienna, 1991–1992*
DANIELLA LUXEMBOURG	Jüdisches Museum, Wien, 1991 Architektur-Konzepte *Jewish Museum, Vienna, 1991* *Architectural Concepts*
RUDOLF LAMPRECHT	Kunsthistorisches Museum, Wien, 1989–1992 Tageslicht und Kunstlicht *Kunsthistorisches Museum, Vienna, 1989–1992* *Daylighting and Artificial Lighting*
PETER ZUMTHOR	Kunsthaus Bregenz, 1990–1995 *Kunsthaus Bregenz, 1990–1995*
ORTNER & ORTNER	Das Museumsquartier Wien, 1986–1996 *The Museum Quarter in Vienna, 1986–1996*
HANS HOLLEIN	Niederösterreichisches Landes-museum St. Pölten, 1992–1998 *Lower Austrian Provincial Museum, 1992–1998*
PETER NOEVER, SEPP MÜLLER, WALTER PICHLER, HERMANN CZECH, SITE U. A.	Österreichisches Museum für angewandte Kunst, Wien, 1989–1993 *Austrian Museum for Applied Art, Vienna, 1989–1993*
KARL UND EVA MANG	Das Österreichische Theater-museum, Wien, 1985–1991 *The Austrian Theatre Museum, Vienna, 1985–1991*
ATELIER SCHÖNBRUNNER STRASSE	Zubau Technisches Museum, Wien, 1990– *Addition Technical Museum, Vienna, 1990–*
SCHÖFFAUER, SCHROM, TSCHAPELLER	Trigon Museum, Graz, 1988–1996 *Trigon Museum Graz, 1988–1996*

Kunst- und Veranstaltungshalle Karlsplatz Baubeschreibung eines temporären Gebäudes

Adolf Krischanitz

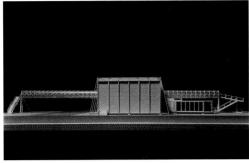

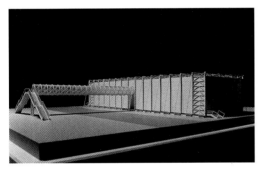

Adolf Krischanitz, Kunsthalle Karlsplatz, Wien, Modell, 1991
Adolf Krischanitz, Kunsthalle Karlsplatz, Vienna, model, 1991

Städtebauliche Situation

Die Prüfung mehrerer Standortvarianten ergab zweifelsfrei den Standort Karlsplatz im Bereich der Verlängerung Wienzeile als den interessantesten. Mit dieser zentralen Standortwahl ergibt sich ein »Kulturkorso« zwischen Secession, Akademie, Künstlerhaus und Technischer Universität genau an der Grenze zwischen dem ersten und dem vierten Wiener Gemeindebezirk. Die Ausrichtung der Halle parallel zur verlängerten Wienzeile weist auf verschiedene historische Vorbilder (Verlängerung des Naschmarktes etc.) hin, ergibt einen sehr interessanten geschützten Raum an der Rückseite der Anlage und geht keine »unverhältnismäßigen« und sinnlosen Parallelitäten mit den mächtigen Platzwänden des Karlsplatzes ein. Eine begehbare Röhre ermöglicht eine verkehrsfreie Überquerung der Straße (verlängerte Wienzeile) in 5,5 m Höhe.
Die Verwendung der Grundkonstruktion (Kunsthalle in der Reithalle) und mehrerer technischer Equipments, wie Klimaanlage etc., ermöglichte auf einem neuen Standort und durch entsprechende Ergänzung und Adaption eine kostengünstige Konzeption einer neuen/alten Kunsthalle.

Nutzung

Die Gebäudeanlage besteht aus zwei Hallen, die mit unterschiedlichen Höhen hintereinander angeordnet sind. Die große Halle (54,0/17,6/9,1 m) ist geeignet, Veranstaltungen wie Theater- und Filmaufführungen und vor allem Ausstellungen der bildenden Kunst aufzunehmen. Über diese Nutzungen hinaus ist es denkbar, auch Veranstaltungen des Bezirkes oder der Technischen Universität zu beherbergen. Die angrenzende kleinere Halle (32,4/10,6/3,3 m) beinhaltet ein klimati-

Karlsplatz Exhibition and Events Hall Specifications for a Temporary Building

Adolf Krischanitz

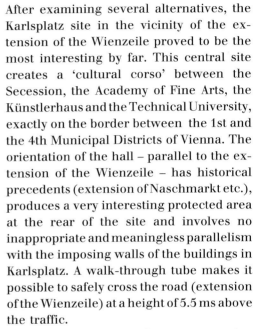

City Planning Situation

After examining several alternatives, the Karlsplatz site in the vicinity of the extension of the Wienzeile proved to be the most interesting by far. This central site creates a 'cultural corso' between the Secession, the Academy of Fine Arts, the Künstlerhaus and the Technical University, exactly on the border between the 1st and the 4th Municipal Districts of Vienna. The orientation of the hall – parallel to the extension of the Wienzeile – has historical precedents (extension of Naschmarkt etc.), produces a very interesting protected area at the rear of the site and involves no inappropriate and meaningless parallelism with the imposing walls of the buildings in Karlsplatz. A walk-through tube makes it possible to safely cross the road (extension of the Wienzeile) at a height of 5.5 ms above the traffic.
By utilising an existing basic construction (the exhibition hall in the former Riding Arena), as well as several of its original technical facilities, such as a air-conditioning etc., it became possible to design a cost-effective new/old exhibition hall on a new site by making the appropriate extensions and conversions.

Utilisation

The construction consists of two halls, arranged at different heights, one behind the other. The large hall (54.0 / 17.6 / 9.1 ms) is suitable for staging events such as theatre or film performances, above all exhibitions of the visual arts, but also for hosting events organised by the local community or the Technical University. The smaller adjacent hall (32.4 / 10.6 / 3.3 ms) contains an air-conditioned depot, several office units, an entrance hall and, in particular, a small coffeehouse with a

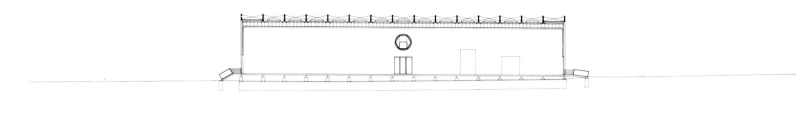

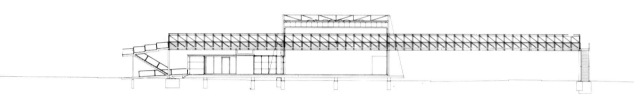

Adolf Krischanitz, Kunsthalle Karlsplatz, Wien, Längsschnitt und Querschnitt, 1991/92
Adolf Krischanitz, Kunsthalle Karlsplatz, Vienna, longitudinal and lateral section, 1991/92

siertes Depot, einige Büroeinheiten, die Eingangshalle und vor allem ein kleines Kaffeehaus mit Küche und Nebenräumen. Beide Hallen sind für eine temporäre Nutzung gedacht und in kürzester Zeit auf- und abbaubar. Die Fundamente sind Betonfertigteile, die die Gebäude nur punktuell abstützen und nachher wieder ohne Probleme entfernbar sind.

Die Heizung und Vollklimatisierung der Halle erfolgt mittels Klimaaggregaten, einer Kältemaschine und Gebläsekonvektoren durch Anschluß an das Fernwärmenetz.

Die Belichtung der Ausstellungshalle ist über das Dach (39 Lichtkuppeln) und über eine abgehängte Decke gewährleistet. Dieser Zwischenraum wird auch zur Unterbringung der Beleuchtung genutzt. Die »bezirksüberspannende« Rohrbrücke dient neben der Führung des Fußgängerverkehrs auch der Anbringung der Veranstaltungsankündigungen und ist als Symbol der Anlage von entscheidender Bedeutung.

kitchen and adjoining rooms. Both halls are designed for temporary use and can be assembled and dismantled in the shortest possible time. The precast-concrete foundations provide only pointwise support for the building and can be removed afterwards without difficulty.

The hall is heated and fully air-conditioned by means of air-conditioning units, a refrigeration unit and fan convectors, connected to the district heating network.

The exhibition hall is illuminated from the roof (39 domelights) and a suspended ceiling. The intermediate space is also used for accommodating the lighting. The 'trans-district' tubular bridge, besides serving as a pedestrian passageway, can also be useful for posters advertising exhibitions and is of decisive importance as a symbol of the building.

Adolf Krischanitz, Kunsthalle Karlsplatz, Wien, Lageplan
Adolf Krischanitz, Kunsthalle Karlsplatz, Vienna, site plan

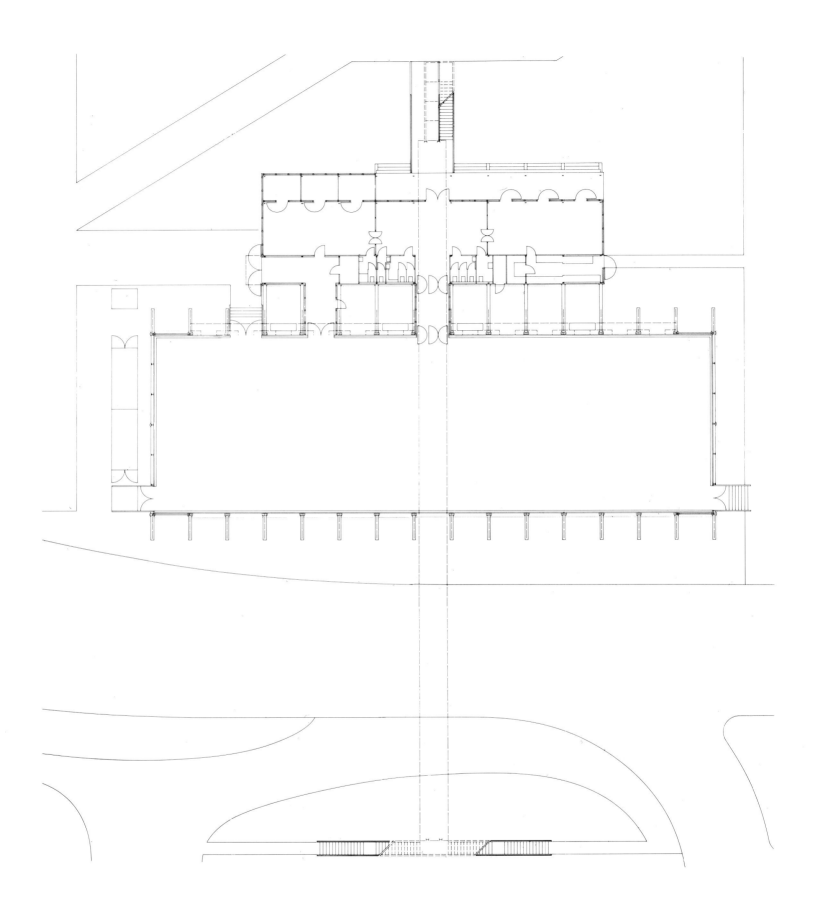

Adolf Krischanitz, Kunsthalle Karlsplatz, Wien, Grundriß
Adolf Krischanitz, Kunsthalle Karlsplatz, Vienna, floor plan

88

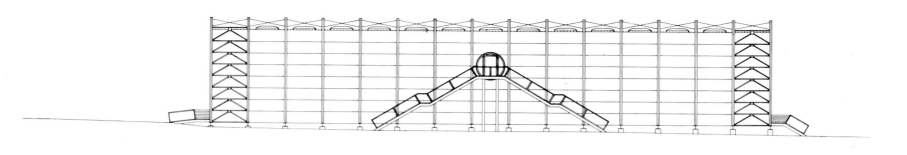

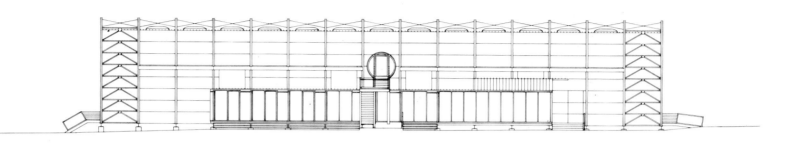

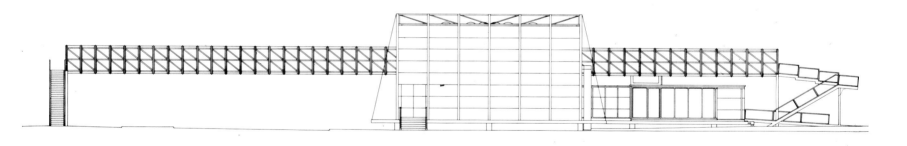

Adolf Krischanitz, Kunsthalle Karlsplatz, Wien, Straßenansicht, Ansicht zum Park mit Eingang, Seitenansicht mit Sky-walk
Adolf Krischanitz, Kunsthalle Karlsplatz, Vienna, street elevation, view from the park with entrance, side elevation with sky-walk

Adolf Krischanitz, Kunsthalle Karlsplatz, Wien, Konstruktionsphotos der Röhre, Sommer 1992
Adolf Krischanitz, Kunsthalle Karlsplatz, Vienna, construction photographs of the tube, summer 1992

Kunsthalle Karlsplatz, Wien, Ansicht von der Straße
Kunsthalle Karlsplatz, Vienna, view from the street

Ansicht von der Straße, Detail
View from the street, detail

Detail der Röhre (Sky-walk)
Detail of the tube (sky-walk)

Detail vom Eingang (unten) und Sky-walk
Detail of the entrance (below) and the sky-walk

Kunsthalle mit Cafeteria
Kunsthalle with cafeteria

Eingangshalle mit Blick in die Cafeteria
Entrance hall with view of the cafeteria

Detail Cafeteria
Detail of the cafeteria

Ansicht Kunsthalle mit technischen Einrichtungen
View of the Kunsthalle with technical equipment

Abgang des Sky-walk und Eingangssituation
End of the sky-walk and entrance to the hall

Gedanken zum geplanten Jüdischen Museum der Stadt Wien

Daniella Luxembourg

Thoramantel, Wien 1906
Torah mantle, Vienna 1906

Das Jüdische Museum Wien wird die kulturellen Beiträge und die reichhaltige Geschichte der Juden in der Monarchie, in Österreich und in Wien hervorheben. Es ist unmöglich, die Auswirkungen der Wiener Jüdischen Gemeinde auf die gesamte westliche Kultur in Abrede zu stellen. Sowohl Juden als auch Nichtjuden werden weiterhin von den kulturellen, akademischen und künstlerischen Beiträgen der Wiener Juden beeinflußt, von denen es viele aus ihrer Heimat in Osteuropa in dieses kulturell reiche Zentrum gezogen hat.

Das Jüdische Museum in Wien wird am Ende des 20. Jahrhunderts von der ersten Nachkriegsgeneration geschaffen und steht somit unter der Erfahrung des Holocaust. Was auch immer aus der Vergangenheit gezeigt wird – vom Mittelalter bis zu den Anfängen des Naziregimes –, es wird aus dem Blickwinkel der Augenzeugen dieses in der Geschichte einmaligen Ereignisses dargestellt. Wie auch immer, dieses Museum ist kein Holocaust-Museum. Es ist ein Museum, das auf starken historischen Grundlagen aufbauend neue Verbindungen zwischen der Vergangenheit und der Gegenwart suchen und diese durch verschiedene Aktivitäten aufzeigen wird.

Das Jüdische Museum ist eine Weiterführung jener Jüdischen Gemeinde, die im Jahre 1895 das erste Jüdische Museum der Welt schuf, von dem kürzlich Objekte gefunden wurden, die im neuen Museum gezeigt werden. Darüber hinaus werden die mittelalterlichen Wurzeln der Gemeinde durch die Errichtung des Museums am Judenplatz in der Inneren Stadt aufgezeigt, am Ort der ersten Wiener Judenstadt.

Die Möglichkeit der archäologischen Dokumentation des Lebens in der Wiener Judenstadt des Mittelalters durch Aufgraben des Platzes stellt eine greifbare Verbindung von Vergangenheit und Gegenwart dar.

Das Museum wird sich mit drei Hauptthemen befassen. Das erste ist eine große

Ideas about the Project of a Jewish Museum in Vienna

Daniella Luxembourg

The Jewish Museum in Vienna will emphasize the cultural contributions and the rich history of the Jews in the Austrian Empire, Austria and Vienna. It is impossible to deny the effect that the Jewish community of Vienna has had upon the entire sphere of Western culture. Both Jews and non-Jews continue to be influenced by the cultural, academic and artistic contributions of the Viennese Jews, many of whom were drawn to this rich cultural center from their homelands in Eastern Europe.

The Jewish Museum in Vienna is created at the end of the 20th Century and thus conceived from the absolute experience of the Holocaust by the first generation after. Whatever is shown from the past, from the Middle Ages, up to the beginning of the Nazi regime, is shown through the eyes that witnessed this absolute event in history. The museum, however, is not a museum about the Holocaust. It is a museum that on the basis of a strong historical framework will seek for possible new connections between the past and the present, and will demonstrate it through various activities.

The Jewish Museum in Vienna is a continuation of the vibrant Jewish community which created in 1895 the first Jewish Museum in the world, parts of which were discovered recently and will appear in the new museum.

A further continuation of the Jewish community's roots, from as far back as the medieval period, will be demonstrated by creating the museum on the Judenplatz, the site where the Jews lived in the Middle Ages. This major square in the first district of Vienna, still bears the medieval name. The possibilities of incorporating a real archeological documentation of the life of the Jewish community in Vienna during the middle ages by digging into the "Judenplatz" is an obvious physical connection between the past and the present.

Dauerausstellung, die sich auf die kulturellen Aspekte der Wiener Jüdischen Gemeinde bezieht.

Die zweite Kategorie wird sich mit Judaica und dem Holocaust befassen. Die Judaica werden durch die Sammlung Max Berger im Inneren einer rekonstruierten Synagoge repräsentiert. Das Ausstellen von Judaica in ihrer »natürlichen Umgebung« wird die Rolle jedes einzelnen Objektes veranschaulichen und den Besucher, der diesen Stücken noch nicht begegnet ist und wenig Ahnung von jüdischen Gebräuchen hat, darüber informieren. Das rekonstruierte Interieur einer Synagoge als Teil einer Dauerausstellung will die außergewöhnlichen architektonischen Leistungen des Wiener Synagogenbaus im späten 19. und frühen 20. Jahrhundert veranschaulichen. Im Besitz der Israelitischen Kultusgemeinde Wien sind Ritualgegenstände und Bücher, die nach dem Zweiten Weltkrieg noch nie gezeigt wurden. Diese Objekte wurden während der Nazizeit zusammengetragen, und ein Teil von ihnen steht im Museum als Mahnmal für den Holocaust. Die Objekte selbst werden stumme Zeugen für das »Verschwinden« ihrer Besitzer sein. Auf allen Seiten des Ausstellungsraumes werden eigene kleine Studienbereiche eingerichtet sein, in denen sich der Besucher mittels audiovisueller Medien über den Zweiten Weltkrieg informieren kann.

Das dritte Hauptthema ist gegenwartsbezogen und wird Wechselausstellungen und Kunstinstallationen aufnehmen. Zusätzlich wird ein Auditorium die Vorführung von Filmen, literarische Abende, Theateraufführungen, Lesungen und Diskussionen ermöglichen.

Die Möglichkeit der Schaffung von Museumsräumen unterhalb des Judenplatzes, einschließlich der eventuellen archäologischen Funde, sowie die Verbindung mit einem bereits bestehenden Haus werden das Potential des Museums noch besser zur Geltung bringen.

Die gesamtarchitektonische Einbindung in das Erscheinungsbild des Judenplatzes wird in einem internationalen Wettbewerb unter der Teilnahme von österreichischen und internationalen Architekten sowie unter Beiziehung einer internationalen Jury zur Diskussion gestellt.

The museum will deal with three main categories. The first will be a large exhibition which concentrates on the cultural aspects of the Viennese Jewish community.

The second category will deal with Judaica and the Holocaust, the Judaica exhibit showcasing the Max Berger Collection within a reconstructed synagogue. Exhibiting Judaica in their "natural environment" will depict the role of each item and educate visitors who have not encountered the objects and have little knowledge of Jewish customs. The use of the reconstructed interior of a synagogue as part of the permanent exhibit will highlight the tremendous architectural efforts that were in the building of synagogues during the late 19th & 20th Centuries in Vienna.

In the possession of the Viennese Jewish community are Jewish ritual objects and books in held storage. These items were gathered during the Second World War and some of them will be stored in the museum as a permanent reminder of the Holocaust. The objects themselves will provide a silent testimonial to the disappearance of their owners. On each side of the storeroom will be a small personal study area where visitors can learn about the Second World War through audio-visual means.

The third category is a contemporary one and will house temporary exhibitions and installations. In addition, an auditorium will allow for the programming of films, literary evenings, theatrical performances, lectures and dialogues on subjects of interest.

The possibility of creating a museum space under the Judenplatz, including a possible archeological excavation and connecting it to an existing building on the square, will enhance the museum's potential.

The whole architectural approach to the Judenplatz will be discussed in an international competition with the participation of Austrian and international architects and will be judged by an international jury.

Thoraschild, Wien 1806
Torah shield, Vienna 1806

Besaminbüchse, Österreich 1854
Spice box, Austria 1854

Das Wiener Jüdische Museum

Daniella Luxembourg

Jewish Museum of Vienna

Daniella Luxembourg

Wien, Judenplatz
Vienna, Judenplatz

Im politischen und historischen Rahmen des heutigen Wien ein Jüdisches Museum zu errichten, ist eine bedeutende kulturhistorische Absichtserklärung. Die folgenden Ausführungen nennen grundsätzliche Anhaltspunkte, um sich ein Bild über das Museum machen zu können:

A. Die Notwendigkeit eines eigenen Gebäudes – eine klar umrissene Darstellung des Themas, ein tatsächliches kulturhistorisches Bekenntnis.

B. Ein zentraler Standort des Gebäudes als Teil dieses Bekenntnisses.

C. Zentrierte Unterbringung vorhandener privater und öffentlicher jüdischer Sammlungen und einer bereits existierenden Bibliothek. Als Brennpunkt, um in Zukunft weitere Stiftungen und Sammlungen anzuziehen, wird die Einrichtung zum Zeugnis des blühenden jüdischen Lebens in der Vergangenheit werden.

D. Ein Veranstaltungszentrum, in dem es ganzjährig Aktivitäten mittels Audio-Vision, Film, Theater, Musik, Lesungen, Studios, eine Judaika-Buchhandlung und ein Kaffeehaus geben soll.

E. Die Notwendigkeit, auf das jüdische Phänomen in Wien einen zeitgenössischen und prüfenden Blick zu werfen, was bisher prinzipiell nur in Ländern außerhalb Österreichs geschehen ist. Das wird nach und nach zeitgenössische Ausstellungen und Installationen fördern, welche Vergangenheit und Gegenwart miteinander verbinden.

Forschungsarbeit für dieses Vorhaben:

Seit August 1991 arbeitet eine Forschergruppe unter meiner Anleitung. Gezielt verfolgen sechs Kunsthistoriker und Historiker spezifische Richtlinien, sie prüfen, registrieren und erforschen alles verfügbare Material in öffentlichen und privaten Sammlungen in Österreich und in Israel. Die Ergebnisse dieser Forschung und permanente Beratungen mit Historikern und

Creating a Jewish museum in Vienna is an important cultural-historical statement in the political and historical framework of Vienna today. Enclosed are basic points for conceiving the museum:

A. The need for a separate building – a defined entity for the subject, a definite historical-cultural statement.

B. A central location for the building as part of that statement.

C. Housing of Jewish collections that until now are scattered in private collections and in some museums in a central place. A focus to attract more donations and collections in the future, the structure will make a statement about the richness of Jewish life in the past.

D. An activity center with year-round activities in the field using audio-visual equipment, films, theatre, music, lectures, study areas, Judaica book store, and a coffee shop.

E. The need of a contemporary look and examination of the Jewish phenomena in Vienna that until now was basically done in countries outside Austria. This will eventually encourage and sponsor contemporary exhibitions and installations, creating links between the past and the present.

Research for the proposal:

Since August 1991, a research team has been working under my supervision. Six art historians are following a specific guideline, examing, registering, and researching all available material in public and private collections in Austria and Israel.

The outcome of the research together with permanent consultations with historians and philosophers entered the script for the museum and serves as a measure for the space needed.

As for the activities, auditorium, and other facilities – similar examples were taken into consideration.

Philosophen ermöglichten dieses Manuskript über das Museum und dienen als Parameter für den benötigten Raum.

Die Museums-Struktur:

Das Museum ist ein Komplex mit folgenden Bereichen:
Eingangshalle, Raum für die permanente Ausstellung, Auditorium, zwei Hallen für Wechselausstellungen und -Installationen sowie Nebenräume für Lagerräume, Büros, Werkstätten, Archive und Forschungsbibliothek.

Die Eingangshalle:

Der Eingang in das Museum soll attraktiver Mittelpunkt, Endpunkt bei Verlassen der Ausstellungen sowie Ort des Wieder-Zurückkommens sein. Dieser Bereich sollte öffentlich zugänglich sein und einige Dienste offerieren, wie beispielsweise einen Erfrischungs- und einen Bücherstand, und den direkten Zugang zu sämtlichen Aktivitäten, die das Museum anbietet.

Permanente Ausstellungen:

Der Bereich der permanenten Ausstellungen sollte, bezugnehmend auf die Themen 1–10, in Zuwanderung, Holocaust, Synagoge und Ritual, intellektuelle und kulturelle Phänomene gegliedert sein und den angegebenen Größenordnungen entsprechen. Dieser Bereich sollte als »Ausstellungs-Schleife« angelegt sein, die dem Besucher eine bestimmte Geschichte erzählt. Ausgangs- und Endpunkt dieser historischen Schleife sollte durch den Holocaust-Bereich führen. Somit bekäme der Holocaust, obwohl räumlich vergleichsweise klein, eine geschichtlich starke Aussage.
Die Schleife sollte beginnen mit:
1. Zuwanderung. Ein Bereich, der Wien als Zentrum der österreichisch-ungarischen Monarchie und als »Zentrum Europas« darstellt, das Einwanderer aus allen Teilen des Habsburger-Reiches aufnimmt.
2. Holocaust. Hier soll eine Gedenkausstellung der zerstörten Ritualgegenstände untergebracht sein, die der Jüdischen Gemeinde Wiens gehörten.
Dazu sollten hier etwa zehn kleine Studios

The space needed is basically the core area for the function described.

The museum structure:

The museum is a complex including areas such as: entrance, permanent exhibition space, auditorium, two exhibition halls for temporary exhibitions and installations, as well as a background area of storage, offices, workshops, archives and research library.

Entrance:

The entrance to the museum should be the central point of attraction and the point of departure from exhibitions as well as a point of return. This area should be open to the public and offer services such as a kiosk, book shop, and direct access to all of the activities the museum offers.

Permanent exhibitions:

The permanent exhibition area should be divided with regard to subject matter 1–10: migration, Holocaust, synagogue and ritual, intellectual an cultural phenomena and will follow the size indicated. The area should be arranged as a loop that tells a certain story to the visitor. The point of departure and return in that historical loop should pass through the Holocaust area. Thus the Holocaust, being quite small in size compared to the other areas, becomes a strong historical point.
The loop should start with:
1. Migration. An area that will expose Vienna as the center of the Austro-Hungarian empire and the center of Europe absorbing immigrants from all over the Empire.
2. Holocaust. This will include a storage exhibition of the burnt ritual objects that belonged to the Jewish community of Vienna.
Accompanying this, there should be a study area divided into 10 booths enabling individuals to see videos, films, and other documentation of the Holocaust.
3. Reconstructed 1920's small synagogue that will house parts from the Berger collection and will show ritual objects in

zur Verfügung stehen, die es kleinen Gruppen ermöglichen, Videos, Filme und andere Dokumentationen zum Thema »Holocaust« zu sehen.

3. Rekonstruierte kleine Wintersynagoge, in Wien 16., Hubergasse, von Ignaz Reiser ab 1926 in expressiv-modernistischem Stil errichtet, in der Teile der Berger-Sammlung untergebracht und Ritualgegenstände in ihrer ganzen Schönheit zu sehen sein werden. (Informationen über Synagogen und jüdische Institutionen werden das Programm begleiten.)

4.–10. Wien, das kulturelle und intellektuelle Phänomen, das die ganze Welt beeinflußt hat, soll hier, unterteilt in sechs Hauptgruppen, als Fortsetzung in der Ausstellungs-Schleife präsentiert werden: Musik und Theater, Kunst und Design, Psychologie und Medizin, Literatur und Journalismus, Philosophie und Politik, Industrialismus und internationale Verbindungen. Jedes Fachgebiet soll in flexibler Ausstellungsform geschichtliche Hintergrundinformation sowie Kunstgegenstände aus der jeweiligen Periode und zeitgenössische Darstellungsformen bieten.

Auditorium für Konzerte, Lesungen, Symposien:

Für etwa 450 Besucher (so angelegt, daß es in zwei Hälften unterteilt werden kann).

Zwei Räume für Wechsel-Ausstellungen:

1. Geschichtliche Ausstellungen
Dieser Bereich wird sich auf jüdische und historische Themen konzentrieren. Man sollte anstreben, dreimal jährlich größere Ausstellungen – wie z. B. »Freud und seine Zeit« oder »Die Geschichte des Unterbewußten« etc. – zu veranstalten.

2. Gegenwartskunst und Installationen
Der Dialog zwischen Vergangenheit und Gegenwart ist mit ein Wesensgrundzug des Jüdischen Museums in Wien. Dieser Dialog sollte durch die Vorstellung von Kunstwerken und Installationen zeitgenössischer (jüdischer und nichtjüdischer) Künstler gefördert werden.

Lagerräume, Büros, Werkstätten, Archive, Forschungsbibliothek und Leseraum

their splendor. (Information on the synagogue will accompany the program.)

4.–10. Vienna, the cultural and intellectual phenomenon which influenced the entire world, will be exhibited as continuation in the loop exhibition and will be divided into six main issues: music and theatre, design and art, psychology and medicine, literature and journalism, philosophy and politics, industrialism and international connections. Each subject will combine historic background information with artifacts of the period and contemporary expression of our time.

Concert, lecture, and symposium auditorium:

For approximately 450 people (with partition into half size) cultural events in the auditorium combined with the temporary exhibitions should be a permanent activity center.

Two areas for temporary exhibitions:

1. Historical Exhibitions
This area will concentrate on Jewish and historical subject matter.
One should aim to have three times a year major exhibitions such as: "Freud and His Time", "The Story of the Subconscious", etc.

2. Contemporary Art and Installation Room
A conversation between the past and the present is basically at the "raison d'etre" of the museum in Vienna. One should encourage this contemporary conversation by commissioning works of art and installations by artists (Jewish and non-Jewish).

Storage, offices, workshop areas, archives, research library, and reading room

Photoprojekt Judenplatz mit historischen Gedanken

Maria Theresia Litschauer

Ausgehend von der Idee eines Jüdischen Museums unter dem Judenplatz habe ich die Architektur des Platzes in drei Ebenen photographiert.

Den Platz abschreitend (ca. 90:42 Schritte) postierte ich die Kamera in den Mittelpunkt, das Objektiv auf meiner Augenhöhe. Von diesem fixierten Standpunkt schwenkte ich in der Waagrechten in 30-Grad-Abständen auf drei Ebenen (Straßenniveau, Mittelteil der Häuser, Giebel) einen vollen Kreis. Das sind pro Ebene 12 Kamerapositionen.

Aufgrund des ungefähren rechteckigen Grundrisses ergeben sich zwischen den Hauptachsenpositionen Verzerrungen, Verschiebungen, Überlagerungen, die die heutige Architektur des Platzes aufbrechen und auf die Geschichte des Ortes verweisen sollen.

In einer größeren Ausdehnung befand sich hier bis zu Beginn des 15. Jahrhunderts die sogenannte Judenstadt. 1421 wurde die Gemeinde vertrieben und die mittelalterliche Synagoge geschleift, das Baumaterial bei der Errichtung der Universität verwendet. Der ursprünglich als Schulhof bezeichnete Platz wurde daraufhin in Neuer Platz und ab 1434 in Judenplatz umbenannt.

Für die Präsentation meiner Arbeit habe ich die Form des Tableaus gewählt. Die kreisförmig gesetzten Architekturschnitte sind linear geordnet in drei Ebenen. Als vierte und unterste Ebene setzte ich leere Rahmen als Repräsentation der Grundmauern der ausgelöschten Judenstadt einerseits und des zukünftigen Museums andererseits.

Photo project Judenplatz with associated historic ideas

Maria Theresia Litschauer

Learning about the idea of the Jewish Museum underneath Judenplatz I started to develop a concept on the architecture of the place.

Measuring the place by steps (90 by 42) I placed the camera in the center, the objective (80 mm lens/approximately normal eyes-angle) on the height of my eyes. From this fixed point I turned the camera horizontally in 30 degree-steps finishing the circle on three levels (streetlevel, middle part of the houses, gables).

The nearly rectangular ground-plan of the place in combination with my working in a circle makes the architecture distorted, displaced, overlapped and stands as reference to the history of the site.

Till the beginning of the 15th century here the socalled Judenstadt was located. 1421 the Jewish community was driven away and the medieval synagogue demolished. The building-stones were used for the construction of the university. The originally as Schulhof characterized place was then called Neuer Platz and 1434 changed into Judenplatz.

As form of presentation I have chosen a tableau with 4 series: the circular produced cuts of architecture in linear order in 3 series. Under the three picture-series I place a fourth consisting of empty frames: the representation of the under-streetlevel existing foundation-walls of the former Judenstadt as well as the Jewish Museum to be founded.

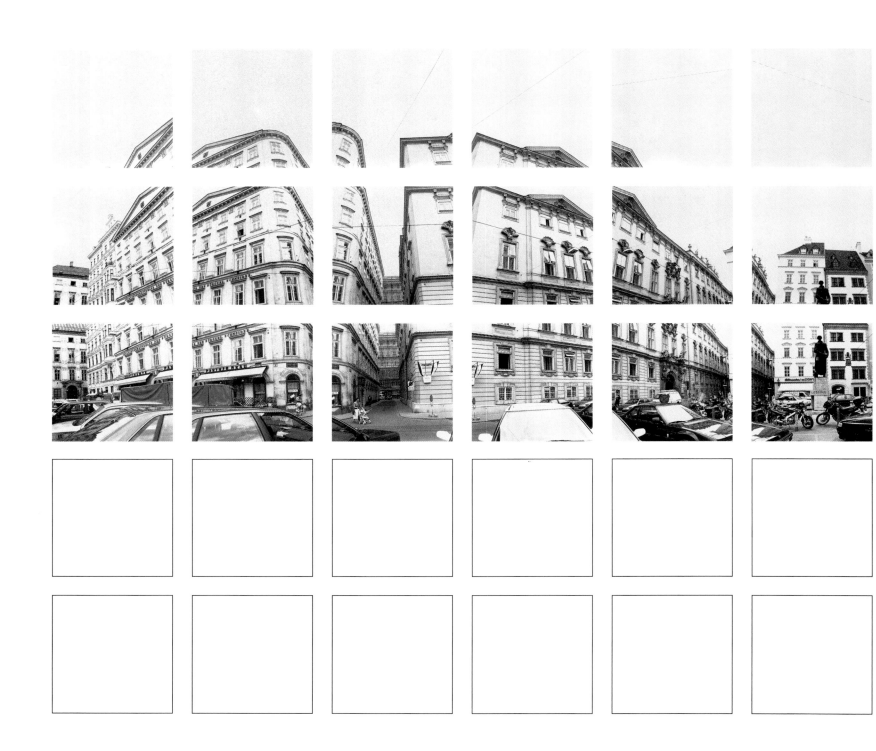

Maria Theresia Litschauer, Photo-Installation *Judenplatz Wien*, 1992
Maria Theresia Litschauer, Photo-Installation *Judenplatz Vienna*, 1992

Persönliche Anmerkung

Daniella Luxembourg

Wien – die Stadt der Aufklärung und die Hauptstadt des Kaiserreiches, mit ihren Universitäten, Museen, Theatern, Konzertsälen und Kaffeehäusern, war gewissermaßen der Traum des emanzipierten Judentums.

Juden siedelten sich nicht um ihrer selbst willen in Wien an, sondern um ihren Kindern eine bessere Ausbildung und Lebensgrundlage zu ermöglichen. Diese Energie einer Minderheit, die ihre Aussichten verbessern wollte, basierte auf einem starken Glauben an die umfassende Kultur der deutschen Sprache.

Der Ausbruch des Zweiten Weltkrieges machte dieses universale Wissen und den Glauben an die deutsche Sprache nicht mehr länger möglich, und ihre Befürworter blieben beschämt und erniedrigt zurück. Das Konzept des Museums, die architektonische Ausformung und der Standort sowie seine gegenwärtigen Aktivitäten stehen für die Bemühung um einen Dialog mit der Vergangenheit zugunsten einer besseren Zukunft.

(Übersetzung: Arthur Koncar)

Personal note

Daniella Luxembourg

Vienna – the city of enlightenment and the capital of an empire with its university, museums, theaters, concerts, cafes was, in a way, the dream of the emancipated Jew. Jews migrated to Vienna, not for themselves but for their children, to enable them a better education and standing in their lives. This energy of a minority who wanted to ameliorate their own prospects was based on a strong belief of the universal culture of the German language.

With the onslaught of the Second World War that universal knowledge and belief in the German language was no longer possible and its bearers were left ashamed and humiliated.

The museum's concept, architectural statement and location as well as its contemporary activities, are an attempt for a dialogue with the past for a better future.

Zeitgenössischer Dialog

DIE EIGENTLICHE FORMUNG DER ERINNERUNG DURCH DEN KÜNSTLER UND UNS – DAS PUBLIKUM – IST EINES DER INTERESSANTESTEN KULTURELLEN GEHEIMNISSE. JEGLICHER DIALOG MIT DER VERGANGENHEIT, SOWEIT ER JÜDISCHES LEBEN IN WIEN BETRIFFT, IST DAS HAUPTANLIEGEN DES MUSEUMS.

Contemporary Dialogue

THE ACTUAL FORMATION OF A MEMORY BY THE ARTIST AND BY US, THE AUDIENCE, IS ONE OF THE MOST INTERESTING CULTURAL MYSTERIES. ANY DIALOGUE WITH THE PAST CONCERNING JEWISH EXISTENCE IN VIENNA IS THE MAIN INTEREST OF THE MUSEUM.

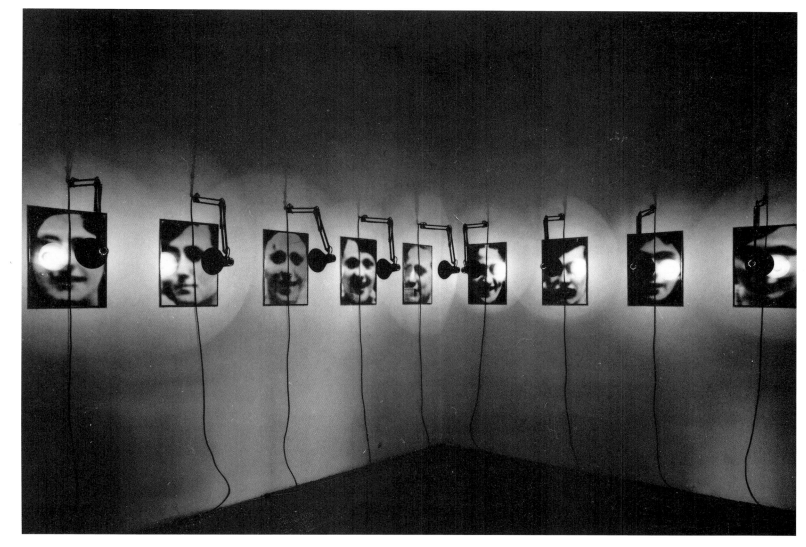

Christian Boltanski, Das Umbauen des Chajes-Gymnasiums (Autel Chajes), 1987, Installation
Christian Boltanski, *The Renovation of Chajes High School (Autel-Chajes)*, 1987, Installation

Die Arbeit basiert auf einem Photo der Abschlußklasse des Jüdischen Gymnasiums »Peretz Chaut« in Wien, Jahrgang 1931. Boltanski photographierte die einzelnen Gesichter nochmals und vergrößerte sie derart, daß sie ihre Eigenständigkeit verloren und zu Symbolen von Erinnerung und Zeit wurden. Die Verwendung von Photographien von Absolventen eines berühmten jüdischen Gymnasiums verdeutlicht den Drang nach Wissen und Studium, der für die jüdische Gemeinde in Wien charakteristisch war; das eigentliche Schicksal der einzelnen Personen wird durch die Erinnerung in einen Ausdruck der Gegenwart umgeformt.

This work is based upon a photograph of the 1931 graduation class of the Peretz Chauth Jewish High School *(Gymnasium)* in Vienna. Boltanski rephotographed the individual faces and enlarged them in such a way that they lose their individuality and turn into symbols of remembrance and time. The use of photographs of graduate students from a famous Jewish *Gymnasium* illustrates the thirst for knowledge and study which characterized Vienna's Jewish community, while the actual fate of the individuals is translated into contemporary terms through the act of remembrance.

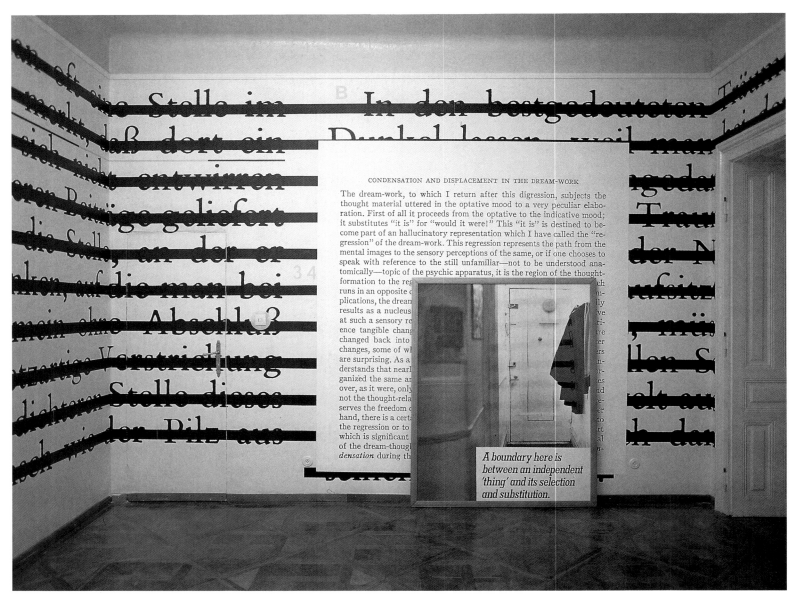

The dream-work, to which I return after this digression, subjects the thought material uttered in the optative mood to a very peculiar elaboration. First of all it proceeds from the optative to the indicative mood; it substitutes "it is" for "would it were!" This "it is" is destined to become part of an hallucinatory representation which I have called the "regression" of the dream-work. This regression represents the path from the mental images to the sensory perceptions of the same, or if one chooses to speak with reference to the still unfamiliar—not to be understood anatomically—topic of the psychic apparatus, it is the region of the thought-

A boundary here is between an independent 'thing' and its selection and substitution.

Joseph Kosuth, *O. & A/F! D! (TO I. K. AND G. F.)'*, Installation in der Sigmund-Freud-Wohnung, Wien, 1987
Joseph Kosuth, *O. & A/F! D! (TO I. K. AND G. F.)'*, Installation in the Sigmund Freud appartment, Vienna, 1987

Jannis Kounellis, *Projekt Synagoge Stommeln*, Installation 1991/92
Jannis Kounellis, *Stommeln Synagogue Project*, Installation 1991/92

Installation in einer der wenigen noch erhaltenen Synagogen Deutschlands nach dem Novemberpogrom 1938 (»Reichskristallnacht«). Drei Holzstelen mit Steinen tragen den Plafond und die Frauenempore der Synagoge.

Installation in one of the few synagogues in Germany to have survived the pogrom of November 1938 (the *'Reichskristallnacht'*). Three wooden columns and stones support the synagogue ceiling and the women's gallery.

Kunst-Mosaik

Wilfried Seipel

Kunsthistorisches Museum, Wien, Saal XIX der Gemäldegalerie (Rubens-Saal), Photo um 1892
Kunsthistorisches Museum (Museum of Fine Arts), Vienna, Room XIX of the Picture Gallery (Rubens), photograph ca. 1892

Als am 17. Oktober 1891 das Kunsthistorische Museum von Kaiser Franz Joseph eröffnet wurde, war es erstmals möglich geworden, die »Kunsthistorischen Sammlungen des allerhöchsten Kaiserhauses« in geschlossener Form einer breiten Öffentlichkeit zugänglich zu machen. Mit dem »Haus am Ring« war nicht nur ein »Gesamtkunstwerk« der Ringstraßenarchitektur beziehungsweise des Historismus entstanden, sondern gleichzeitig auch der jahrhundertelange Sammlungstätigkeit der habsburgischen Herrscherdynastie zu einem für alle sichtbaren äußeren Höhepunkt gelangt. Die dadurch definierte Position des Kunsthistorischen Museums am Schnittpunkt individuell geprägten Sammlungsinteresses, dynastischen Selbstverständnisses und publikumswirksamer Selbstdarstellung in Gestalt einer formalen und ausstattungsmäßigen Prachtarchitektur bestimmte von nun an das Selbstverständnis des Museums und seine Verankerung im gesellschaftlichen Bewußtsein. So sehr auch frühzeitig die räumlichen und strukturellen Defizite des Gebäudes spürbar wurden und zur Verlagerung wichtiger Sammlungsbestände in die Hofburg zwangen, so wenig wurde das Museumskonzept an sich in Frage gestellt. Anders als die zum Teil beträchtlich älteren Nationalmuseen konnte und wollte das Kunsthistorische Museum niemals den Anspruch nationaler Selbstdarstellung erfüllen. Die meist aufgrund persönlicher Vorlieben geprägten Sammlungsschwerpunkte beziehungsweise Sammlungslükken sind bis heute das besondere Merkmal dieses Museums, das den privaten Charakter seiner Sammlungsgeschichte nie verleugnen kann und will.

Nach den ersten hundert Jahren seines Bestehens hat sich an der Wertschätzung und der Stellung des Kunsthistorischen Museums innerhalb der europäischen Museumslandschaft kaum Grundsätzliches geändert. Anerkannt als besonderer Sammlungsort und wissenschaftliche Pflegestätte eines bedeutenden Teils der künst-

Art Mosaic

Wilfried Seipel

When, on 17th October 1891, the Kunsthistorische Museum was opened by Emperor Franz Josef, it became possible to make the "art historical collections of the Supreme Imperial house" accessible to a broad public in a unified form for the first time ever. Yet it was not only a *Gesamtkunstwerk* of Ringstrasse architecture, or historicism, that was achieved with the 'house on the Ring'; it also made it plain for all to see that the collecting process which had been going on for centuries in the ruling Habsburg dynasty had outwardly attained a peak in its development. Thus defined, the Kunsthistorische Museum's position at the convergence of individually determined collecting interests, dynastic self-conception and popular self-representation, in the shape of an architecture which was magnificent in both its form and decoration, from now on came to dominate the museum's view of its role, as well as establishing it in the consciousness of Austrian society. Although the spatial and structural deficiencies of the building became evident at quite an early stage, making it necessary to transfer important parts of the collection to the Hofburg, the concept of the museum itself was hardly called into question at all. In contrast to the national museums, some of which were considerably older, the Kunsthistorische Museum never served the purposes of national self-representation. Most of the collection's typical strengths and weaknesses, which developed as a result of personal preferences, are still special features of the museum even today; indeed, the museum is neither able nor willing to hide the private character of its collection's history.

After its first hundred years of existence, the status and esteem which the Kunsthistorische Museum enjoys within the European museum landscape remains basically unchanged. Acknowledged as being the home of a special collection, and as the patron of scholarly work relating to a important part of Europe's artistic and cultural heritage, covering a period which

lerisch-kulturellen Hinterlassenschaft Europas bis zum Ende der Monarchie waren das Kunsthistorische Museum und die ihm angeschlossenen Sammlungsbereiche – die Geistliche und Weltliche Schatzkammer, die Sammlungen in der Neuen Burg, die Wagenburg in Schönbrunn und Schloß Ambras – stets ein ruhender Pol im immer schneller sich drehenden Karussell des internationalen Museumswesens. Freilich war diese scheinbare Zurückhaltung angesichts europaweiter Entwicklungen im Museumsbereich nicht nur auf dieses Haus allein beschränkt und auch keineswegs »hausgemacht«. So war es sicher nicht das Kunsthistorische Museum allein, das sich in der Mitte der achtziger Jahre plötzlich einer Herausforderung ausgesetzt sah, der es nicht mehr entsprechen konnte. Wie viele andere Museen in Wien konnte es weder dem sensibilisierten Bewußtsein bezüglich einer auch nach konservatorischen und museologischen Gesichtspunkten befriedigenden Präsentation der anvertrauten Kunstwerke entsprechen, noch war es in der Lage, auf das gestiegene kulturelle Bedürfnis einer erstaunlich breiten Öffentlichkeit in entsprechender Weise zu reagieren. Erst das seit Mitte der achtziger Jahre auch in Wien nachweisbare politische Interesse an einer grundlegenden Sanierung führte zur Bereitstellung entsprechender finanzieller Mittel und leitete eine positive Entwicklung ein, die zu einer neuen »Museumsposition« dieses Hauses führte. So konnte Ende 1992 die gesamte Gemäldegalerie in renoviertem Zustand der Öffentlichkeit übergeben werden. Die klimatische, sicherheitstechnische und beleuchtungsmäßige Sanierung dieses bedeutendsten Sammlungsbereiches des Kunsthistorischen Museums setzte nicht nur für Österreich neue Standards auf dem Gebiet der Museumstechnik, so schwierig es auch ist, die historische Bausubstanz, die den strengen denkmalpflegerischen Schutzbestimmungen unterworfen sein muß, den modernen technischen Anforderungen entsprechend zu adaptieren. Daß daneben auch das allgemeine Erscheinungsbild und die museumsdidaktische Vermittlung verbessert wurden, versteht sich von selbst.

Die infrastrukturellen Verbesserungen

lasts until the end of the monarchy, the Kunsthistorische Museum and its associated collections – the Ecclesiastical and Secular Treasury, the collections in the Neue Burg, and those in the Wagenburg at Schönbrunn and at Castle Ambras – have always acted as a steadying influence in the ever-faster carousel of the international museum scene. The apparent reservedness towards larger European developments in the museum sector was, of course, not limited solely to our institution, and was by no means 'homemade'. The Kunsthistorische Museum was therefore certainly not alone in suddenly finding itself confronted, in the mid-eighties, by a challenge which it was no longer capable of meeting. Like many other museums in Vienna, it could neither measure up to the sensibilised consciousness of presentation (which also set great store by conservational and museological concerns), nor was it in a position to react to the increased cultural needs of an astonishingly wide public. It was only with the emergence in Vienna, in the second half of the eighties, of an ascertainable political interest in fundamental renovation work, that the requisite financial means were made available, initiating a positive development which established a new 'museum position' for this house. Thus, by the end of 1992, it was possible to open the whole Picture Gallery to the public in a renovated state. The renovation set new technological standards for Austrian museums as far as the air-conditioning, security and illumination of this most important part of the Kunsthistorische Museum were concerned; yet it also involved the adaptation of the historical building fabric in accordance with modern technical requirements (difficult as that is, since, as a historical monument, the building must, of necessity, meet the strictest standards of preservation). It goes without saying that this also helped to improve both the museum's general image and the mediation of its didactic role.

The improvements in the museum's infrastructure, brought about by the spatial reorganisation, redesign and extension of the restoration workshops, administration offices and depots of the individual collections, as well as of the library and the

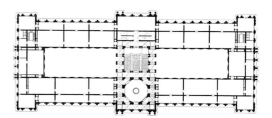

Kunsthistorisches Museum, Wien, Grundriß
Kunsthistorisches Museum (Museum of Fine Arts), Vienna, floor plan

Kunsthistorisches Museum, Wien, Blick in die
sanierten Säle der Gemäldegalerie
Kunsthistorisches Museum (Museum of Fine
Arts), Vienna, view of the restored Picture
Gallery

durch die räumliche Neuordnung, die Umgestaltung und Erweiterung der Restaurierungswerkstätten, Verwaltungsräume und Depots der einzelnen Sammlungen, der Bibliothek und der Reproduktionsabteilung führten nicht nur zu besseren Arbeitsbedingungen und ökonomischeren Arbeitsabläufen, sondern auch zur Erweiterung des Schausammlungsbereiches der Antikensammlung sowie der Ägyptisch-orientalischen Sammlung. Diese auf alle Sammlungsbereiche zutreffende prekäre Raumsituation, die bis in die Zeit vor der Eröffnung dieses Hauses zurückreicht, die bis heute ungelöste Frage der Unterbringung des Heroons von Trysa, das trotz seiner archäologischen Bedeutung nun über hundert Jahre ein unverdientes Schattendasein führt, das Fehlen entsprechend ausgestatteter Depots, vor allem aber von Ausstellungsräumen sowohl für die Tapisseriensammlung als auch für Sonderausstellungen, eines Vortragssaales sowie von Unterrichtsräumen etwa für Einführungsvorträge für Schulklassen, von entsprechenden Räumlichkeiten für Restaurants und Museums-Shops, all dies stellte große Anforderungen an ein zukünftiges Raumprogramm.

Die Veränderung der Besucherstruktur und der unerwartete Zustrom neuer Besucherschichten aus dem Osten Europas sowie die Einschätzung des Museumsbesuchs als Bestandteil der eigenen, stärker als je zuvor kulturell bestimmten Lebensqualität bedeuten heute eine Herausforderung, vor die sich das Kunsthistorische Museum mit seinen gewachsenen und zum Teil festgefahrenen Traditionen bisher noch nie gestellt sah. Um also einer gesamteuropäischen Entwicklung des Museumswesens nicht nachzuhinken und die Versäumnisse der Vergangenheit aufzuholen sowie den politischen Veränderungen im Osten Europas mit den daraus resultierenden neuen Besucherschichten gerecht zu werden, bedurfte es für die neunziger Jahre und darüber hinaus grundsätzlich neuer struktureller, rechtlicher, finanzieller und räumlicher Voraussetzungen: Ob das Museum seinem Stellenwert entsprechend diese besonderen Herausforderungen in der Zukunft erfüllen wird können, hängt nicht zuletzt von einer

reproduction department, led not only to better working conditions and more economical work processes, but also to an increase in the range of exhibits which could be shown from the Collection of Greek and Roman Antiquities and from the Egyptian and Near Eastern Collection. The precarious spatial situation which affects all areas of the collection, and which dates back to the time before the museum was first opened, presents a great challenge to any future spatial programme. So, too, does the question of the accomodation of the *Hieron of Trysa*, which, despite its archaeological significance, has now been leading an undeserved shadow existence for over a century. The problem extends to the lack of properly equipped depots, and, above all, of exhibition rooms for the tapestry collection and for special exhibitions; also, to the lack of a lecture theatre, teaching rooms (e.g. for introductory classes for schoolchildren) and the requisite space for restaurants and museum shops.

The change of visitor patterns and the unexpected stream of new classes of visitor from eastern Europe, the view that a visit to a museum contributes to the quality of life in a world where the influence of the arts is stronger today than ever before, has come to represent a challenge with which the Kunsthistorische Museum, with its well-established and, in part, inflexible traditions, has never previously been confronted. Thus, in order not to lag behind developments taking place in the museum sector in Europe as a whole, in order to make up for past omissions and to be able to cope with the political changes in eastern Europe and the new classes of visitor they are producing, there is a need for fundamentally new structural, legal, financial and spatial conditions for the nineties and beyond. Whether or not the museum will, in future, be competent to face this particular challenge in a manner commensurate with its status depends not least on the large-scale conceptual and architectural integration of the museum into the adjacent area of Maria-Theresien-Platz. This square provides an ideal junction point, surrounded as it is by the Museum Quarter, which is now also about to be developed in the former Imperial stables designed by

großräumigen konzeptionellen und architektonischen Einbindung dieses Museums in den angrenzenden Bereich des Maria-Theresien-Platzes ab. Umgrenzt von dem ebenfalls im Entstehen begriffenen Museumsquartier, den früheren Hofstallungen Fischers von Erlach, sowie vom Naturhistorischen Museum beziehungsweise den jenseits des Rings gelegenen Gebäudefluchten der Neuen Burg mit der Sammlung alter Musikinstrumente, der Hofjagd- und Rüstkammer, dem Ephesosmuseum und vor allem der in den letzten Jahren ebenfalls neugestalteten Geistlichen und Weltlichen Schatzkammer bietet dieser Platz eine ideale Verbindungsfläche.

Auch traditionelle Museen können sich der Verwirklichung ganzheitlicher Denkmodelle und Konzeptionen nicht länger entziehen. Sosehr das Kunsthistorische Museum aufgrund der besonderen Qualität seiner Sammlungen ein in dieser Zusammensetzung einmaliges Konglomerat bildet, das auch im streng historischen Sinn nach wie vor als Kunst- und Wunderkammer bezeichnet werden kann, muß es doch seinen neuen besonderen Stellenwert dadurch erlangen, daß es im konzeptionellen Verbund der angeführten übrigen musealen Institutionen um den Maria-Theresien-Platz seine insulare Situation aufbricht und in einer konzeptionell begründbaren, dem ganzheitlichen Denken unserer Zeit entsprechenden Art und Weise mit seinen Nachbarn in einen Dialog eintritt. Die auf unterirdischem Weg realisierbare architektonische Anbindung dieses Hauses an das Naturhistorische Museum und das Museumsquartier über großzügige Treppen und Korridore mit Schaudepots und Sonderausstellungsräumen, Museums-Shops und Vortragssälen ist in dieser Form in den USA, etwa in Washington, oder zuletzt im Louvre in Paris mit großem Erfolg und öffentlicher Akzeptanz realisiert worden. So wird das seit langem ungelöste Problem der Unterbringung des Heroons von Trysa an diesem unterirdischen Ort ebenso endlich eine faszinierende Lösung finden, wie es auch möglich ist, den längst überfälligen Sonderausstellungsraum für die Tapisseriensammlung, eine der bedeutendsten der Welt, hier un-

Fischer von Erlach, the Naturhistorische Museum and, on the other side of the Ring, the suite of buildings of the Neue Burg, housing the Kunsthistorische Museum's collections of Ancient Musical Instruments and Arms and Armour, the Ephesus Museum and, above all, the reorganised Ecclesiastical and Secular Treasury.

Traditional museums, too, have been unable to avoid developing holistic patterns of thought and ideas. However much the Kunsthistorische Museum forms, in its composition, a unique conglomeration which, on account of the special quality of its collections, can still, in a strictly historical sense, be described as a *Wunderkammer,* or 'chamber of curiosities', it nevertheless still has to attain its new special status by breaking out of its insularity and collaborating with the other museums mentioned above, thus entering into a dialogue with its neighbours in a way which corresponds to the conceptually justifiable holistic thinking of our times. Such an architectural connection as that which could be realised underground between our house and the Museum Quarter, by means of spacious staircases and corridors with exhibition depots and rooms for special exhibitions, museum shops and lecture halls, has already been realised in a similar form in the USA, for example in Washington, or most recently at the Louvre in Paris, with great success and wide public acceptance. This underground location will likewise provide a fascinating solution to the long-insoluble problem of where to accomodate the *Hieron of Trysa*, just as it will also make it possible to provide the special exhibition room so long overdue for the tapestry collection. Yet depots do not have to be solely depots! The quality and variety of, for example, our depot for the Collection of Antiquities, or of the Egyptian and Near Eastern Collection, will also be improved, so that they can be viewed here by the public. Thus the underground extension of the spatial facilities - work upon which is due to start in the coming years - presents a fascinating perspective both for the collections of the Kunsthistorische Museum and, above all, for jointly organised exhibition ventures which could be undertaken in collaboration with, for example,

Kunsthistorisches Museum, Wien; die nach der Generalsanierung 1991 neu gestalteten Säle der Gemäldegalerie
Kunsthistorisches Museum (Museum of Fine Arts), Vienna; the rooms of the Picture Gallery were completely restored in 1991

terzubringen. Depots müssen nicht Depots sein! Qualität und Vielfalt etwa unserer Antikendepots oder der Ägyptisch-orientalischen Sammlung werden hier ebenfalls zu einer für die Öffentlichkeit einzusehenden Neuaufstellung kommen. So ist die in den nächsten Jahren in Angriff zu nehmende unterirdische Erweiterung des Raumangebots sowohl für die Sammlungen des Kunsthistorischen Museums, aber vor allem auch die verbindende und gemeinsam konzipierte Ausstellungstätigkeit zum Beispiel mit dem Naturhistorischen Museum und dem entstehenden Museum moderner Kunst im Museumsquartier eine faszinierende Zukunftsperspektive. Die im Kunsthistorischen Museum zusammengeführten Kunstwerke als materialisierter Ausdruck der Historie auf höchstem künstlerischem und ästhetischem Niveau, die im Naturhistorischen Museum versammelten Naturalia jenseits aller regionalen und zeitlichen Begrenzung und die Herausforderung der Aktualität der Moderne und ihrer Vorläufer, wie sie im Museum moderner Kunst zu finden sein werden, ergeben zusammen jenes faszinierende Mosaik einer ganzheitlich gesehenen Welt, die den Museen insgesamt eine neue Strahlkraft zu verleihen imstande ist. Daß auf diese Weise die einst von Gottfried Semper gedanklich ausformulierte Idee des Kaiserforums eine verdichtete, in neue architektonische Formen gegossene Belebung als Museumsforum erfährt, unterstützt diese Konzeption und unterstreicht ihre städtebauliche Dimension.

the Naturhistorische Museum and the new Museum moderner Kunst which is to be established in the Museum Quarter. Taken together, the works of art which represent a tangible expression of history at its highest artistic and aesthetic level, and which constitute the collections of the Kunsthistorische Museum, the naturalia which transcend all regional and temporal limits and which are collected in the Naturhistorische Museum, and the challenge of the relevance of Modernism and its predecessors, which it will be possible to encounter in the Museum moderner Kunst, produce the fascinating mosaic of a world perceived from a holistic point of view; and that is what these museums are capable of imparting with the help of their new power of attraction. The fact that, in this way, the idea of an Imperial forum, which was once formulated in theory by Gottfried von Semper, has been resurrected and cast in a new and compressed architectural form as a 'museum forum', only serves to support the present concept and underline its urban dimension.

Kunsthistorisches Museum Wien – Tageslicht und Kunstlicht

Rudolf Lamprecht

Das im Zuge der Errichtung der Ringstraße am Ende des 19. Jahrhunderts erbaute Gebäude zur Aufnahme der Kunstsammlungen des Kaiserhauses war wie fast alle großen Museen dieser Zeit ausschließlich für Tageslicht geplant.

In den sechziger Jahren wurden die Gemäldegalerie und die Kunstkammer (damals Sammlung für Plastik und Kunstgewerbe) erstmals künstlich beleuchtet.

Im Zuge der 1990 begonnenen Generalsanierung des Hauses sollte neben der Beseitigung der gravierenden Baumängel und dem Einbau moderner haus- und sicherheitstechnischer Einrichtungen auch eine den konservatorischen und energietechnischen Erfordernissen adäquate Beleuchtung installiert werden.

Für den Lichtplaner ist die Beleuchtung eines denkmalgeschützten, nicht für Kunstlicht konzipierten Gebäudes eine große Herausforderung. Anders als bei der Entwicklung einer Lichtvision für ein neues Gebäude hemmen hier oftmals bestehende Raumproportionen, Deckenmalereien und Stuckelemente die Anordnung einfacher Beleuchtungssysteme, ja sogar der Verkabelung.

Trotzdem ist es hier gelungen, hochtechnische Leuchten zu entwickeln und so einzubauen, daß sie sich in das alte Ambiente des Hauses einfügen und sich gleichzeitig doch als Elemente des ausgehenden 20. Jahrhunderts darstellen.

Tageslichtmuseum?

Bestimmte Freiheiten des »Erlebnis-Konsums« beginnen sich dem Ende zuzuneigen. Die Auseinandersetzung des Besuchers mit einem Gemälde von Giorgione in einem fast leeren Saal an einem sonnigen Frühlingstag (bei 800 Lux vertikaler Beleuchtungsstärke) und wechselnden Lichtstimmungen durch vorbeiziehende Wolken, ist ebenso nicht mehr möglich (= erlaubt) wie das Beobachten von Walfischen

Kunsthistorisches Museum Wien – Daylighting and Artificial Lighting

Rudolf Lamprecht

Built to house the art collections of the Imperial dynasty, the museum was erected in the course of the construction of the Ringstrasse at the end of the 19th century. It was, like almost all large museums dating from this period, solely designed for daylight use.

The Gemäldegalerie (Picture Gallery) and the Kunstkammer (at that time the Sammlung für Plastik and Kunstgewerbe, the 'Collection of the Decorative Arts') first received artificial illumination in the 1960s. Besides remedying the museum's grave constructional deficiencies and installing modern services and security technology, the general renovation which began in 1990 was to include the installation of a lighting system which would adequately meet the requirements of museum conservation and energy technology.

The illumination of a building which is protected as a historical monument, and which was not originally designed for artificial light, presents a great challenge for the light designer. Unlike the development of a lighting scheme for a new building, the installation of simple lighting systems, and even the wiring, was often hampered here by the existing spatial proportions, ceiling frescoes and stucco elements.

Nevertheless, we succeeded in developing high-technology illumination and installing it in such a way that it fitted in with the old atmosphere of the building, while at the same time still being representative of the late 20th century.

Daylight Museum?

Some of the liberties of 'experiential consumerism' are beginning to disappear. It is no longer possible (= permitted) for a visitor to study a painting by Giorgione in an almost empty room on a sunny spring day, with a vertical light intensity of 800 lux and alternating light moods caused by passing

Giorgione, *Der Knabe mit dem Pfeil*
Giorgione, *The Boy with an Arrow*

Kunsthistorisches Museum, Wien, Oberlichtsaal
VI der Gemäldegalerie, Hängung um 1910
Kunsthistorisches Museum (Museum of Fine
Arts), Vienna, roof-lit room (No. VI) in the
Picture Gallery, arrangement of the paintings
ca. 1910

im offenen Meer oder – wie wahrscheinlich in nicht zu ferner Zukunft – das ungehinderte Besteigen des Matterhorns.

Unsere Zivilisation hat beschlossen, dort, wo es ihr paßt, durch drastische Einschränkungen die vorhandenen Naturressourcen und Kunstwerke in die Nachwelt hinüberzuretten. Dabei muß das Abenteuer »Original« domestiziert werden, um dem Surrogat nicht noch mehr Bedeutung zu verleihen.

Bei Ölgemälden besteht zum Beispiel der Kompromiß zwischen Konsum und Erhaltung in der Festsetzung bestimmter Maßnahmen der Schaustellung (unter anderen der Festsetzung einer maximalen Beleuchtungsstärke von 150 Lux auf Ölgemälden). Für den Lichtplaner bedarf es einiger Anstrengungen, einen Raum, der bei einer derartigen Abdunklung kaum mehr Tageslichtwirkung hat, dennoch nicht unangenehm erscheinen zu lassen. Im übrigen taucht diese Problematik bei fast allen Projekten – insbesondere auch bei von uns betreuten Neuplanungen wie zum Beispiel dem Museumsquartier – auf.

Bei der Neukonzeption der Beleuchtung für das Kunsthistorische Museum gingen wir davon aus, dem Tageslicht seine psychologische Dominanz im Raum zu erhalten und die künstliche Beleuchtung, die zum großen Teil auch die Aufgabe der Tageslichtergänzung hat, auf jene Stellen zu konzentrieren, wo es funktionell erforderlich ist – auf die Wände und Objekte.

Gemäldegalerie – Oberlichtsäle

Die alte Hinterleuchtung der Glasoberlichten war aufgrund des schlechten Wirkungsgrades äußerst unwirtschaftlich und erbrachte an den Wänden in Augenhöhe nur eine Beleuchtungsstärke von 85 Lux. Nun werden die Ausstellungswände gezielt durch in die Lichtdecke integrierte Wandfluter beleuchtet. Da für die überdurchschnittlich große Raumhöhe (13,7 m) äußerst präzise Reflektoren erforderlich sind, wurden eigene Leuchten entwickelt.

Bei Reduktion des Energieverbrauchs um ein Drittel konnte eine Erhöhung der Beleuchtungsstärken um ein Drittel erzielt werden.

clouds; just as it is no longer possible to observe whales in the open sea, or – as seems probable in the not-too-distant future – to make an unobstructed ascent of the Matterhorn.

Our civilisation has decided to save existing natural resources and works of art for posterity (in those places where it suits our purposes to do so) by means of drastic restrictions. To this end, the adventurous nature of the 'original' has to be 'domesticated', so as not to increase the surrogate's importance still further.

In the case of oil paintings, the compromise between consumption and preservation is made, for instance, by stipulating certain measures which are to be taken when placing works on display (among others, the stipulation of a maximum light intensity of 150 lux for oil paintings).

It is the task of the light designer to ensure that, even though there is hardly any daylight at all, the fact of darkening a room does not make it seem uncomfortable. Incidentally, this problem arises in almost all projects – and especially in the newer projects in our charge, such as that of the Museum Quarter.

In designing the new lighting system for the Kunsthistorische Museum, we took as our starting point the idea of preserving the psychological dominance of daylight in the room, and of concentrating the artificial lighting (which, to a large extent, was intended to complement the daylight) in those places where it is functionally required: namely, on the walls and objects.

Picture Gallery –
Rooms with Roof Lighting

The old back-lighting by means of glass rooflights was extremely uneconomical due to its low degree of efficiency, (a light intensity of no more than 85 lux at eye level on the walls). The exhibition walls are now directly illuminated by wall spotlights integrated into the luminous ceiling. Since the exceptional height of the rooms (13.7 ms) necessitates the use of extremely exact reflectors, special lights were developed for this purpose.

By reducing energy consumption by a third

Gemäldegalerie – Seitenlichtkabinette

Auch in den Seitenlichtkabinetten sollte eine direkte, möglichst gleichmäßige Beleuchtung der Bildwände durch Leuchtstofflampen-Wandfluter erfolgen. Wegen der Stuckgewölbe mußten in diesem Fall jedoch die parallel zu den Wänden verlaufenden Leuchten abgependelt werden, wobei sich in den einzelnen Konchen U-förmige Leuchtenelemente ergaben. Dabei wurde ein für Leuchtstofflampen extrem kleines, direkt/indirekt wirkendes Reflektorsystem entwickelt.

Kunstkammer

Im Gegensatz zur Gemäldegalerie ist die Aufgabenstellung in den großen Hochparterreräumen eine völlig andere. In den Räumen mit bemalten Gewölben werden eine große Zahl einzelner Objekte frei und in alten, nicht beleuchteten Vitrinen aufgestellt.

Da die Abpendelung jeglicher Trag- oder Beleuchtungselemente für die Erscheinung dieser Räume nicht akzeptabel ist, wurden kleine Niedervoltstrahler in Gruppen an genau definierten Punkten der Gesimse angeordnet. Durch Einsatz verschiedener Strahlertypen und Lampen kann leicht auf unterschiedliche Situationen und konservatorische Erfordernisse eingegangen werden.

Die Deckenfelder werden schwach durch indirekt wirkende Halogenstrahler aufgehellt.

Diese Art der Beleuchtung bewirkt zwar eine leichte Dramatisierung der einzelnen Objekte, ergänzt aber in angenehmer Weise die Tageslichtwirkung und zeigt bei vielen Objekten andere Facetten.

we were able to increase light intensity by a third.

Picture Gallery – Galleries with Side Lighting

In the galleries with side lighting, too, the idea was to make the direct illumination of walls with pictures as uniform as possible by means of fluorescent wall spotlights. However, in this case, the lights which ran parallel to the walls had to be pendant, due to the stuccoed vaulting, which resulted in U-shaped lighting elements in the individual semi-cupolas. For this, an extremely small reflector system with a direct/indirect action was developed for the fluorescent lamps.

Kunstkammer

In contrast to the Picture Gallery, the task in the large rooms on the first floor was a completely different one. In the rooms with painted vaults, a large number of the individual objects on exhibition stand freely or are kept in old, unlit display cases. Since it was not acceptable to have any pendant support fixtures or lighting elements in this room, small low-voltage lamps were installed in groups, at exactly defined points on the cornices. A variety of situations and conservational requirements can be easily catered for by using different types of lamps.

The ceiling areas receive minimal illumination from indirect halogen lamps.

Although this form of illumination causes a slight dramatisation of the individual objects, it complements daylight in a pleasant way and also brings out new facets in many of the objects.

Kunsthistorisches Museum, Wien, Kunstkammer-Räume mit neuer Lichttechnik, Rudolf Lamprecht
Kunsthistorisches Museum (Museum of Fine Arts), Vienna, the rooms of the Kunstkammer with new lighting systems, Rudolf Lamprecht

Kunsthistorisches Museum, Wien, Großer Oberlichtsaal (Saal VI)
Kunsthistorisches Museum (Museum of Fine Arts), Vienna, large roof-lit room (Room VI)

Kunsthistorisches Museum Wien, Kunstkammer-Räume mit neuer Lichttechnik, Rudolf Lamprecht
Kunsthistorisches Museum (Museum of Fine Arts), Vienna, Kunstkammer rooms with new lighting systems, Rudolf Lamprecht

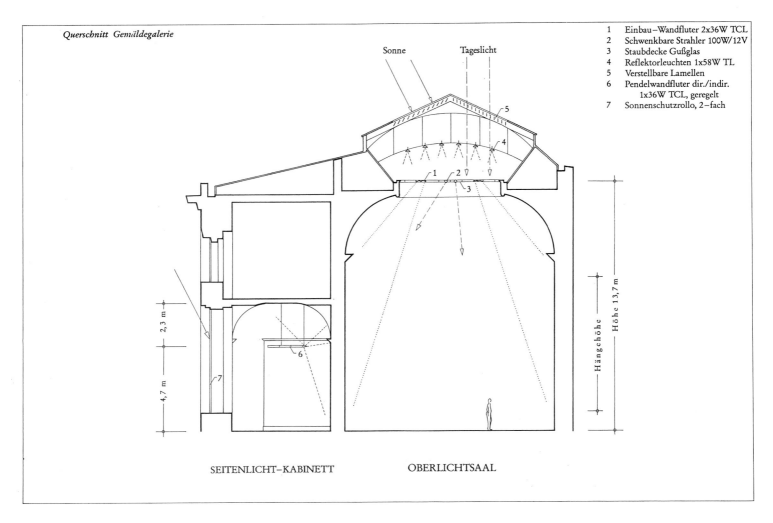

Sonne   Tageslicht

1   Einbau–Wandfluter 2x36W TCL
2   Schwenkbare Strahler 100W/12V
3   Staubdecke Gußglas
4   Reflektorleuchten 1x58W TL
5   Verstellbare Lamellen
6   Pendelwandfluter dir./indir.
    1x36W TCL, geregelt
7   Sonnenschutzrollo, 2–fach

2,3 m

4,7 m

Hängehöhe   Höhe 13,7 m

SEITENLICHT–KABINETT   OBERLICHTSAAL

Schemaschnitt Oberlicht-Seitenlicht,
Rudolf Lamprecht.
Das Tageslicht fällt in den großen Sälen durch
das Oberlicht ein. In die Staubdecke sind zwei-
flammige Wandfluter mit extrem engstrah-
lender Lichtverteilung eingebaut. In den
Seitenlichtkabinetten sind die Wandfluter abgependelt und erleuchten zugleich die Decke.

Detail of the roof lighting/side lighting scheme,
designed by Rudolf Lamprecht.
Daylight enters the large rooms through the
roof-light. 2-rayed wall floodlights with
extremely narrow-beamed light distribution
are installed in the dust-proof ceiling. The
wall floodlights are pendant in the galleries
with side-lighting, yet at the same time
illuminate the ceiling.

Deckenuntersicht Oberlichtsaal
View of the ceiling in the room with roof-
lighting

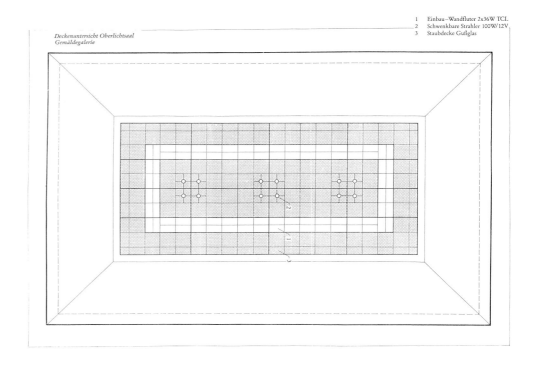

1   Einbau–Wandfluter 2x36W TCL
2   Schwenkbare Strahler 100W/12V
3   Staubdecke Gußglas

Deckenuntersicht Oberlichtsaal
Gemäldegalerie

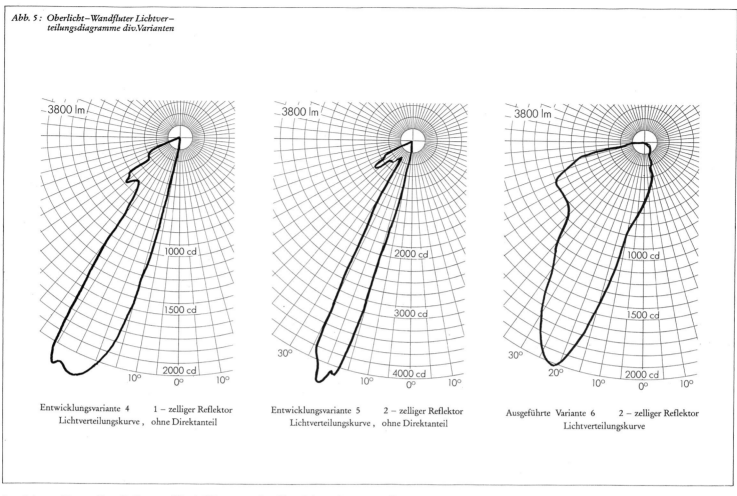

~ 3800 lm

1000 cd
1500 cd
2000 cd
10° 0° 10°

Entwicklungsvariante 4   1 – zelliger Reflektor
Lichtverteilungskurve ,   ohne Direktanteil

~ 3800 lm

2000 cd
3000 cd
30°
4000 cd
10° 0° 10°

Entwicklungsvariante 5   2 – zelliger Reflektor
Lichtverteilungskurve ,   ohne Direktanteil

~ 3800 lm

1000 cd
1500 cd
30°
20°
2000 cd
10° 0° 10°

Ausgeführte Variante 6   2 – zelliger Reflektor
Lichtverteilungskurve

Pendelwandfluter-Detail, Entwurf Rudolf Lamprecht. Die einlampigen, regelbaren Leuchten bewirken sowohl die gleichmäßige Ausleuchtung der Wände bis ca. 4,5 m als auch über einen oberen Schlitz eine Aufhellung der Decke.

Detail of the pendant wall floodlights, designed by Rudolf Lamprecht. The single-lamp, adjustable lights achieve uniform illumination of the walls up to approx. 4,5 ms, brightening the ceiling via an overhead slit.

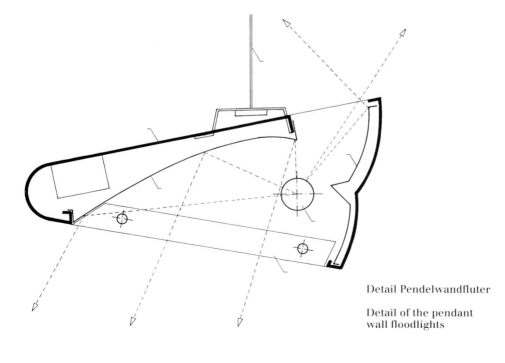

Detail Pendelwandfluter

Detail of the pendant
wall floodlights

121

Kunsthaus Bregenz

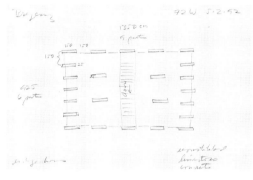

Kunsthaus Bregenz, Donald Judd, Verwaltungsbau und Kommunikationseinrichtungen,
Grundriß und Ansicht Proportionsstudien,
1991–95
Kunsthaus Bregenz, Donald Judd,
Administration building with communication
facilities, floor plan and elevation, proportional
studies, 1991–95

Edelbert Köb

Das Kunsthaus Bregenz ist als Ausstel-
lungshaus und Museum zeitgenössischer
Kunst konzipiert, darüber hinaus als Ort
permanenter Auseinandersetzung mit
Kunst und Gestaltungsfragen. Ergänzend,
im Sinne eines erweiterten Begriffs von
bildender Kunst, werden auch Literatur,
Tanz und Musik, etwa in Form von
Performances oder Medienkunst, in das
Programm miteinbezogen. Ein wichtiger
thematischer Schwerpunkt wird in den
Zwischenbereichen/Verbindungsstellen
zeitgenössischer Kunst zu Architektur und
Design gesetzt.

Die Sammlungs- und Ausstellungstätigkeit

Eine Sammlung österreichischer Kunst
befindet sich im Aufbau. Beginnend in den
siebziger beziehungsweise in den achtziger Jahren wird sie die in diesen Jahrzehnten verstärkt einsetzende internationale Orientierung der mittleren und jüngeren Generation österreichischer Künstler, vor allem in den Bereichen Skulptur
und Malerei, dokumentieren.
Die Sammlung ist nicht enzyklopädisch
konzipiert, sondern wird Schwerpunkte
mit größeren Werkgruppen der wichtigsten Künstler setzen. Ihre museale Präsentation ist erst in einigen Jahren vorgesehen. Sie soll in wechselnden Zusammen-
stellungen jeweils einen aktuellen Einblick
in das österreichische Kunstschaffen geben, ein »Schaufenster« österreichischer
Kunst an einem exponierten Punkt gegen
Westen (Schweiz, Deutschland, Frank-
reich) darstellen.
Bis diese Sammlung aber präsentablen
Umfang und Qualität erreicht haben wird,
wird der museale Teil des Hauses den
Künstlern Rudolf Wacker, Edmund Kalb
und Albert Bechtold gewidmet. Ihre Werke
werden in Zusammenarbeit mit dem Vorarlberger Landesmuseum, Nachlaßver-
waltern und privaten Sammlern entsprechend ihrer Bedeutung für die Anfänge der
Moderne in Vorarlberg, aber auch in Hin-
blick auf die überregionale Bedeutung

Kunsthaus Bregenz

Edelbert Köb

The Kunsthaus Bregenz has been conceived as an exhibition hall and museum, and
furthermore as a place for the continuous
study of art and design. The supplementary
programme attempts to extend the definition of the visual arts, by including literature, dance and music, for instance in the
form of performances or media art. An
important thematic feature will be the
intermediate area / points of connection
between contemporary art, architecture
and design.

Collecting and Exhibiting Activities

At present, a collection of Austrian art is
gradually being established. It will document the increasingly international orientation of the middle and younger generations of Austrian artists from the 1970s
and 1980s onwards, above all in the fields
of sculpture and painting.
The collection is not intended to be ency-
lopaedic, but will focus instead on larger
bodies of work by the most important
artists. It should be ready for presentation
in the museum in a few years time. By
constantly changing the composition of the
collection it is hoped to provide a current
view of the Austrian art scene, a 'display
window' of Austrian art, prominently located in a westward position (Switzerland,
Germany, France).
However, until this collection attains sufficient size and quality for exhibition, the
museum section of the building will be
dedicated to the artists Rudolf Wacker,
Edmund Kalb and Albert Bechtold. Organised in collaboration with the Vorarlberger Landesmuseum, the adminis-
trators of the artists' estates and private
collectors, this will be the first time that
their work has been presented in a large
and representative setting which does
justice to their significance not only for the
beginnings of Modernism in Vorarlberg,
but also in a supraregional significance.
The exhibition programme has two main
functions. Namely, to provide up-to-date

erstmals in größerem und repräsentativem Rahmen vorgestellt.

Das Ausstellungsprogramm stellt sich zwei Aufgaben. Es sind das die aktuelle Information über nationales und internationales Kunstgeschehen und die Konzeption thematischer Ausstellungen. Schwerpunkte werden hier jeweils im Bereich von Einzelausstellungen und Installationen beziehungsweise im Spezialgebiet des Kunsthauses dem Bereich Kunst – Architektur – Design gesetzt werden.

Vermittlungs- und Veranstaltungsschwerpunkte

Die soziologische Struktur, die kulturellen Traditionen und die geringe Verwurzelung moderner bildender Kunst im Lande erfordern neben einer intensiven Öffentlichkeitsarbeit vor allem eine umfassende und zielgruppenorientierte Vermittlungstätigkeit. Museumspädagogische Konzepte sollen vor allem die Zusammenarbeit mit Schulen und Einrichtungen der Volksbildung im Land unterstützen, die didaktische Seite wird bei der Konzeption von Ausstellungen vorrangige Beachtung finden.

Im Rahmen der geplanten Aktivitäten zur Vermittlungsarbeit kommt der Durchführung von Vorträgen, Diskussionen, Filmvorführungen, aber auch Fachtagungen große Bedeutung zu. Das Kunsthaus will damit sowohl ein Fachpublikum wie auch interessierte Laien ansprechen.

Gesellschaftliche Veranstaltungen, etwa in Zusammenhang mit Sponsoring, die Einrichtung eines Cafés sowie eines Book- und Design-Shops sollen ein Zielpublikum von kunstinteressierten Schülern, Künstlern und Studenten ansprechen.

Das Museums- und Ausstellungsgebäude

Das Gebäude ist mehr als Kunsthalle denn als Museum konzipiert. Vier aufeinander gestapelte Großräume, die sich mit Ausnahme des Erdgeschosses nur durch verschiedene Raumhöhen unterscheiden, bilden ein offenes Angebot und eine permanente Herausforderung für die Ausstellungsgestalter, die sich kleinteiligere beziehungsweise differenziertere

information about the national and international art scene, and to design exhibitions which focus on central themes. The latter activity will concentrate either on individual exhibitions and installations, or on that area in which the Kunsthaus specialises: the intermediate sphere of art, architecture and design.

Main Focus of Mediation and Events

Besides intensive public relations work, the sociological structure, cultural tradition and lack of precedent for modern visual art in this area primarily demand comprehensive mediation activity oriented towards a target group. Concepts for museum pedagogics should above all assist collaboration with schools and state education institutions; the didactic side will be given high priority when planning exhibitions. Within the context of the activities planned for mediation work, the organisation of lectures, discussions, film shows and also specialist conferences are all of great importance. The Kunsthaus wants in this way to address both a specialist public and an interested lay public.

Social events (in combination with, for example, sponsoring), the construction of a café, as well as a bookshop and a design shop are all intended to appeal to a target public of art lovers, school pupils, artists and students.

The Museum and Exhibition Building

The architecture of the Kunsthaus, based as it is on formal consistency, largely corresponds to its intended contents. There is a progressive increase in the heights of the rooms, from the ground floor to the skylight room at the top of the building, with a corresponding increase in brightness (daylight) from floor to floor. This is combined with progressive uniformity in the spatial arrangement of the floors, from the lower to the upper, i.e. from the division of the lower floors into various sections, to a hall which covers more than one storey. This obviously corresponds to their respective functions: the more differentiated rooms, which receive less daylight, are for the areas devoted to the museum, while the

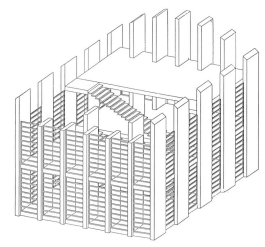

Axonometrie
Axonometric drawing

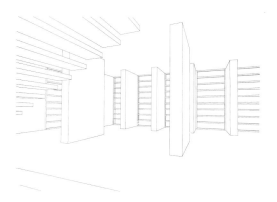

Perspektive Innenraum
Interior perspective

123

Modell Schnittansicht
Model, section

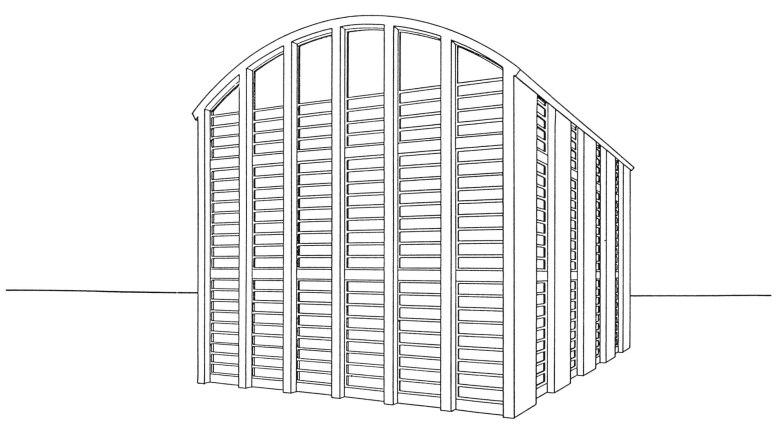

Perspektivische Ansicht
Perspective view

Modell Schnittansicht
Model, section

Situationen jeweils selbst schaffen müssen. Diese rigide räumliche Konzeption entspricht aber den Vorstellungen der Kunsthausleitung von der Präsentation sowohl aktueller zeitgenössischer Kunst als auch der eigenen Sammlung, die nur in wechselnden Ausschnitten und nach wechselnden Gesichtspunkten vorgestellt, mehr Ausstellungs- als Museumscharakter haben wird. Die Möglichkeit des freien Umganges mit Raum – für Kuratoren und Künstler – ist das Charakteristikum und die Qualität dieser Architektur aus der Sicht des Nutzers.

Im ersten Untergeschoß (mit Tageslicht) sind Lager und Werkstättenräume sowie Bereiche für die Museumspädagogik und das Personal vorgesehen.

Veranstaltungen in den Bereichen Performance, Literatur, Musik etc. sollen in den Museums- beziehungsweise Ausstellungsräumen im Kontext mit der bildenden Kunst stattfinden.

Verwaltungsbau mit Kommunikationseinrichtungen

Statt der anfänglich vorgesehenen Adaptierung eines Altbaues auf dem Areal des Kunsthauses für die Verwaltung kam es in der zweiten Planungsphase doch zum Entschluß für einen Neubau. Dadurch wurde es möglich, die gewünschten Kommunikationseinrichtungen, wie Café und Shop, aus dem Kunsthaus in den Verwaltungsbau zu transferieren und die ursprüngliche Idee des geschlossenen Schreins/Depots für den Museums-/Ausstellungsbau zu erhalten. Der mit seinen Kommunikationseinrichtungen im Erdgeschoß auf den Eingang des Kunsthauses orientierte Verwaltungsbau enthält neben den Büroräumen noch eine Handbibliothek und ein Archiv. Mit der zusätzlichen Errichtung eines eigenen Lagerbaues in guter Erreichbarkeit wird der Depotbedarf des Kunsthauses auf lange Sicht abgedeckt.

Archiv Kunst–Architektur als Sammlungs- und Forschungsschwerpunkt des Kunsthauses Bregenz

Das im folgenden kurz AKA genannte Archiv ist geplant als *Dokumentationszen-*

larger and brighter rooms in the two upper storeys are for the exhibition areas.

On the first basement floor (with daylight) are the storage and workshop rooms, as well as the areas for museum pedagogics and personnel.

It is intended that events in the fields of performance, literature, music etc. should take place in the museum or exhibition rooms, against the background of the visual arts.

Administration Building with Communication Facilities

In the second planning phase, it was decided in favour of a new building for the administration, instead of converting an old building on another part of the Kunsthaus site, as had originally been foreseen. In this way it became possible to transfer the desired facilities such as the café and shop from the Kunsthaus itself to the administration building and to retain the original idea of the self-contained shrine/ depot for the museum/exhibition building. The administration building, which needed to be on the ground floor on account of its communications equipment, was thus oriented towards the entrance of the Kunsthaus, and received, besides offices, also a reference library and an archive. With the construction of a separate, easily accessible storage building the long-term needs of the depot are more than catered for.

The Archive for Art and Architecture as a Major Component of Collecting and Research Activities at the Kunsthaus Bregenz

The archive, hereafter named 'the AKA', is planned as a documentation centre for works involving both the visual arts and architecture. It is intended to be an international establishment for study and research, consisting of:

– a collection of projects (drawings, plans, models, documents, bibliography)
– a specialist library
– a photograph and video collection
– realisation of projects 1:1 in the urban or natural surroundings of Bregenz and its environs.

trum für Werke im Spannungsfeld von bildender Kunst und Architektur. Es soll eine internationale *Studien- und Forschungseinrichtung* werden, bestehend aus:

- einer Sammlung von Projekten (Zeichnungen, Plänen, Modellen, Dokumenten, Bibliographien)
- einer Fachbibliothek
- einer Photo-/Videothek
- Realisationen von Projekten 1:1 im Stadt- oder Naturraum von Bregenz und Umgebung.

Die Entscheidung für einen architekturbezogenen Sammlungs- und Forschungsschwerpunkt des Kunsthauses Bregenz ist unter anderem dadurch begründet, daß der Museumsbau von Architekt Zumthor nach seiner Vollendung (1994) der erste größere Neubau für zeitgenössische Kunst seit fast hundert Jahren in Österreich sein wird und im kulturellen Spektrum der kleinen Region Vorarlberg die Architektur einen besonderen Stellenwert besitzt. Historisch durch die traditionelle Vorarlberger Holzarchitektur und die Industriebauten der Gründerzeit, in der Gegenwart durch die hohe Qualität des Bauens in Vorarlberg. Ihre Eigenart ist nicht von einer Tradition der Formen, sondern einer der Gesinnung und des Denkens geprägt. Es kann hier von einem der seltenen positiven Beispiele eines zeitgenössischen Regionalstils gesprochen werden.

Mit der Realisierung eines bereits vorliegenden Entwurfs des renommierten amerikanischen Bildhauers Donald Judd für das Dokumentationszentrum wird dieses eine für seine Funktion geradezu programmatische Architektur von hohem Symbol- und Prestigewert erhalten. Von Bedeutung ist in diesem Zusammenhang auch der Umstand, daß die Bauten von Architekt Zumthor (Ausstellungs- beziehungsweise Museumsbau und Verwaltungsgebäude) und den Entwurf des Künstlers Judd für das Archiv und die regionale Architektur eine gemeinsame geistige Haltung verbindet, die auch für das Programm des Kunsthauses bestimmend sein wird.

Unabhängig von diesen lokalen Bedingungen stehen aber Überlegungen zur Entwicklung der bildenden Künste in den letzten dreißig Jahren, insbesondere die Erweiterung des Skulpturbegriffes, für dieses

The decision to make architecture the central focus of collection and research activities at the Kunsthaus Bregenz was made not least because, with its completion (1994), the museum building, designed by the architect, Peter Zumthor, will be the first large new building devoted to contemporary art to have been constructed in Austria for almost a hundred years; even though, in the cultural spectrum of the small region of Vorarlberg, architecture occupies a position of special importance. Historically, through the traditional Vorarlberg timber architecture and the industrial buildings of the *Gründerzeit;* in modern times through the high quality of architecture in Vorarlberg. What constitutes their uniqueness is not a tradition of form, but rather one of a fundamental attitude and way of thinking. We can here speak of one of the few positive examples of a contemporary regional style.

As the realisation of an already completed design by the renowned American sculptor, Donald Judd, the documentation centre will be provided with architecture of an almost programmatic nature as far as function is concerned, but which also has great symbolic and prestige value. Significant in this connection is also the circumstance that the buildings by the architect Peter Zumthor (exhibition, museum and administration buildings) share with the designs for the archive by the artist Judd (and with the regional architecture), a common intellectual position which will also have a determining influence on the programme of the Kunsthaus.

However, independently of these local conditions, reflections on the development of the visual arts over the past thirty years are also at the forefront of this concept, especially concerning the extension of the idea of sculpture. Significant here is the increasing interest that artists are showing in space as such, in interior and exterior space and in the formative construct – not only as a location, covering and vehicle for art, but also as a subject of art. This is especially true of present-day conceptual painting and sculpture.

The close and fruitful relationship and interaction between art and architecture runs through the whole history of art. The

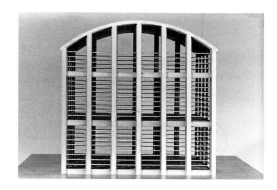
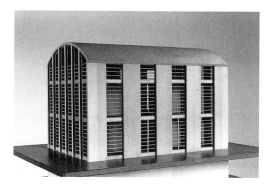

Modellansichten
Views of the model

Konzept im Vordergrund. Signifikant ist hier das zunehmende Interesse der Künstler für den Raum an sich, den Innen- und Außenraum, und für das ihn bildende Konstrukt – nicht nur als Ort, Hülle, Träger von Kunst, sondern als Thema der Kunst. Das gilt im besonderen Maß für die konzeptionelle Malerei und Skulptur der Gegenwart.

Die enge und befruchtende Verbindung beziehungsweise Wechselwirkung zwischen Kunst und Architektur durchzieht die ganze Kunstgeschichte. Das Spektrum der Möglichkeiten reicht vom bildenden Künstler als Architekt oder dem Architekten als Maler/Bildhauer unter Erhaltung der klassischen Disziplinen (etwa bei Michelangelo, Tatlin, Bill, Judd), bis zur Integration von Architektur in gesamtkunstwerkliche Vorstellungen oder einfach Umsetzung von im engeren oder weiteren Sinn architekturbezogener Themen in Malerei, Skulptur, Objektkunst, Environment, Land art etc.

Eine spezielle Beachtung, Betreuung und Bearbeitung aller dieser Aspekte ist als ein Beitrag des Kunsthauses zur wissenschaftlichen Forschung in den Bereichen Kunst-Architektur-Geschichte und Kunst-/Architektur-Theorie gedacht.

Die Sammlung und die Forschungstätigkeit des AKA wird ergänzt werden durch einen dementsprechenden Ausstellungsschwerpunkt und durch eine gleichnamige Publikationsreihe. Die gesamten Aktivitäten in diesem Bereich sollen die Eigenart des Kunsthauses im Sammlungs- und Ausstellungswesen, in einer stetig wachsenden Museumslandschaft von oft zu gleichartigen und miteinander konkurrierenden Häusern, ausmachen.

spectrum of possibilities ranges from the visual artist working as an architect or the architect working as painter/sculptor, and thus preserving the classical disciplines (for example Michelangelo, Tatlin, Bill, Judd), to the integration of architecture in the concept of a *Gesamtkunstwerk,* or the simple translation of themes closely or more distantly related to architecture in painting, sculpture, object art, Environment, Land Art etc.

Despite the wealth and topicality of its selected subjects, there is no other collection or research centre in the world with which the concept of the AAA can be compared. In giving this area such special consideration and treatment, an important and unique contribution is thus being made to scholarly research in the fields of the history and theory of art and architecture. The collection and research activities of the AKA will be extended through exhibitions concentrating on related themes and a series of publications named after it. The AKA constitutes an essential component of the concept of the museum as a whole. In a constantly changing museum scene, where the museums are often far too similar and locked in competition with one another, it forms the distinctive contribution made by the Kunsthaus to the field of collecting and exhibiting.

Kunsthaus Bregenz

Peter Zumthor

Mit unserem Projekt für das Kunsthaus Bregenz versuchen wir, uns auf die eigentliche Aufgabe eines Museums zu besinnen. Nach unserer Auffassung hat ein Museumsgebäude vor allem ein Ort zu sein für die Kunstwerke und ein Ort für den Menschen, der diesen Kunstwerken ungestört und in Ruhe begegnen möchte. Diesem Grundgedanken ist der Entwurf verpflichtet. Wir waren deshalb bestrebt, den Gehalt der Architektur aus der spezifischen Funktion des Gebäudes und dem besonderen Ort, für den es gedacht ist, zu gewinnen.

I. Das Bauwerk im Stadtbild

Im Stadtbild stellt sich der Neubau als eigenständiges Glied in die Reihe der bestehenden Solitärbauten, die die Uferlinie der Bucht von Bregenz vor dem Hintergrund der Altstadt punktartig besetzen. Die Ausbildung des Baukörpers als freistehender Solitär in der Uferlinie gewährt eine selbstbewußte, aber auch »selbstverständliche und nicht überformte Einbindung«. (Zitat Jurybericht)
Das auf der Seeseite des Grundstückes konzentrierte Bauvolumen läßt das dahinterliegende Altstadtgefüge unberührt und einen großen Teil der Bauparzelle unbebaut. Anstelle des abgebrochenen »Forsterhauses« wird an der Kornmarktgasse ein Neubau erstellt, der im Erdgeschoß das Museumscafé und einen Buchladen, in den zwei Obergeschossen die Räume der Museumsverwaltung mit der Bibliothek enthält. Dieser neue Baukörper besetzt den Ostteil der Parzelle an der Kornmarktgasse und formuliert gegenüber dem Kornmarkttheater einen Platzraum, der zum Eingang des neuen Kunsthauses hinführt. Die Freifläche ist als großzügiger Eingangsplatz gestaltet, der für Ausstellungen und Aktionen im Freien genutzt werden kann. Der Platzbelag soll auf die Oberfläche des Gehsteiges an der Kornmarktgasse abgestimmt werden (ruhige und einheitliche Wirkung; Kunsthausplatz nicht als »Belagsinsel«, sondern Teil öffentlicher Gehflächen).

Kunsthaus Bregenz

Peter Zumthor

In our project for the Kunsthaus Bregenz we are attempting to consider the actual purpose of a museum. According to our way of thinking, a museum building primarily has to be a place for works of art, and for the people who wish to encounter those works of art without being disturbed and at their leisure. The design is committed to this basic idea. We have therefore striven to arrive at the architectural content via the specific function of the building and the particular location for which it is intended.

I The Building as Part of the Cityscape

Within the cityscape, the new building constitutes an independent element in the row of existing single buildings which occupy the shoreline of Lake Constance and punctuate the background of the old city. Construction of the building as a free-standing single unit on the shoreline ensures a poised but also "natural and not over-developed integration" (quote from the ajudicators' report).
The construction volume, which is largely concentrated on the lake side of the property, leaves the old city structure at the rear untouched and a large part of the plot of land undeveloped. In place of the demolished 'forester's house', a new building will be constructed in Kornmarktgasse, containing the museum café and a bookshop on the ground floor, and the offices of the museum administration and the library on the two upper floors. This new building occupies the eastern part of the plot in Kornmarktgasse, creating between itself and the Kornmarkttheater opposite an open space which leads to the entrance of the new Kunsthaus. This free area is intended as a spacious entrance area which can also be used for outdoor exhibitions and actions. The surface covering of the open space should match that of the pavement in Kornmarktgasse (producing a simple, relaxing and uniform effect; the Kunsthausplatz is not a 'surface island', but part of the public walking area).

Peter Zumthor, Kunsthaus Bregenz, Wettbewerbsmodell, 1991
Peter Zumthor, Kunsthaus Bregenz, competition model, 1991

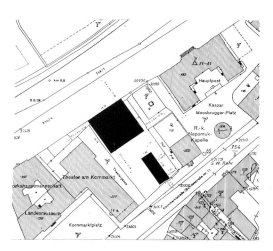

Peter Zumthor, Kunsthaus Bregenz, Lageplan
Peter Zumthor, Kunsthaus Bregenz, site plan

Innenraumansicht, Arbeitsmodell
Interior view, working model

II. Der innere Aufbau des Gebäudes

Der Aufbau des Baukörpers mit quadratischem Grundriß entspricht der spezifischen Nutzung der Geschosse als Ausstellungsräume. Drei Mauerscheiben tragen die drei Obergeschosse und das seitlich mit Schnitt freigelegte, das heißt von einem Belichtungsgraben für die Untergeschosse (hinter der Glashülle der Fassade verborgen) umgebene Erdgeschoß, das auf der Höhe des Kunsthausplatzes liegt. Die drei ungleich gesetzten Mauerscheiben umschließen die Säle mit einer raumhaltigen Schicht und trennen die Vertikalerschließungen (Treppe, Personenlift, Steigzone der Haustechnik, Warenlift) vom eigentlichen Ausstellungsraum ab. Ihre Lage im Raum entspricht dem Verlauf des Rundganges durch alle Geschosse, verweist auf Ein- und Ausgänge und formuliert mit der gebotenen Zurückhaltung entsprechende Raumzonen. Nach oben leicht zunehmende Raumhöhen und ein Aussichtsfenster auf den Bodensee im obersten Geschoß stiften unterschiedliche räumliche Identität.

Alle Obergeschosse und das Erdgeschoß sind als in sich stimmige Ausstellungssäle konzipiert, die bei Bedarf zusätzlich frei unterteilt werden können. Das Erdgeschoß, das von seiner Lage als Eingangsgeschoß her auch Sondernutzungen (Foyerausstellungen, Vorträgen usw.) dienen kann, konnte als dritter Ausstellungssaal freigespielt werden, indem Verwaltung, Cafeteria, Buchladen und Museumsbibliothek in den separaten Neubau am Platzeingang ausgelagert werden.

Im ersten Untergeschoß liegen die öffentlichen Toiletten, der Unterrichts- und Werkraum für die Museumspädagogik, Personalräume und Pack- und Lagerzonen, im zweiten Untergeschoß die Räume der Haustechnik, die Werkstätten, ein Reproraum mit Originalarchiv sowie die Lager.

III. Belichtung der Ausstellungsräume

Über den Sälen der Obergeschosse, oberhalb der Staubdecke aus Glaspaneelen, liegt ein durchgehend freier Lichtraum, in den das Tageslicht seitlich rundum einfällt.

II The Inner Structure of the Building

In its square layout, the structure of the building corresponds to the specific utilisation of the floors as exhibition rooms. Three wall panels bear the three upper floors and the ground floor. The profile of the latter, which is situated at the level of the open space in front of the Kunsthaus, is exposed, i.e. surrounded by a light-ditch for the lower floors (hidden behind the glass fabric of the facade). The three irregularly placed wall panels enclose the halls with a spacious layer and separate the vertical openings (staircase, passenger lift, zone for service installations, goods lift) from the actual exhibition rooms. Their spatial location follows the course of the circular corridor on each floor, provides direction to the entrances and exits, and creates, with the requisite reserve, the appropriate spatial areas. Room heights which increase slightly towards the upper floors, as well as a top-floor picture-window with a view of Lake Constance, help to create variety in the building's spatial identity.

All the upper floors, and the ground floor, are concieved as unified exhibition rooms which can, in addition, be freely divided up as desired. Since the ground floor is at the same time the entrance floor, it can also be used for special purposes (foyer exhibitions, lectures etc.) and could even be turned into a third exhibition space by transferring the administration, cafeteria, bookshop and museum library to the separate new building located in the area outside the entrance.

On the first floor are the public toilets, the classrooms and workrooms for museum teaching, the personnel rooms and the packing and storing zones; on the second floor, the rooms for service installations, workshops, a repro-room with an archive of originals, and a storeroom for hall chairs, audio-visual equipment and exhibition construction material.

III Illumination of the Exhibition Rooms

In the rooms on the upper floors, above the glass-panelled dust-proof ceiling, is a completely free space where daylight enters

Die Menge an Tageslicht, zum Teil reflektiert durch die weiße Massivdecke und diffus gemacht durch die Lichtdiffusionshaut der vorgesetzten Fassade und die ebenfalls lichtstreuende Staubdecke, reicht aus, um die Ausstellungsräume natürlich zu belichten. Leichte Verschattungen, verursacht durch die tragenden Mauerscheiben, wirken als willkommene räumliche Differenzierungen im Innern im Sinne einer lebendigen und nicht allzu abstrakten Raumwirkung.

Das Kunstlicht ist in den Hohlraum über der Staubdecke integriert. Es ersetzt das Tageslicht bei Bedarf, ohne daß die künstlichen Lichtquellen als solche sichtbar werden.

Im Erdgeschoß stehen die tragenden Wandscheiben vor dem Hintergrund der transluzenten Umfassungswand aus Glasbausteinen, womit dieses Geschoß seine besondere Identität als Eingangs- und Mehrzweckgeschoß enthält. Hier fehlt auch die Staubdecke. Tragende Geschoßdecke und Beleuchtungskörper sind offen sichtbar.

IV. Das Äußere

Das Äußere des Gebäudes ist geprägt von einer Lichtdiffusionshaut aus nichtglänzenden Glaspaneelen, geformt in der Art von überschuppten »Glasschindeln«. Diese Haut nimmt dem Tageslicht die Blendwirkung durch die aufgerauhte Oberfläche (milchglasähnlich) und sorgt für eine optimale Steuerung und Umlenkung des Tageslichtes in die Deckenlichträume der Ausstellungsgeschosse. Sie umschließt das feste, isolierte Gebäude als luftdurchspülte Schicht mit einem Meter Abstand. Im Zwischenraum zwischen Glashaut und Gebäude, integriert in die filigrane Aufhängung, befinden sich fest montierte Reinigungsstege und der feuerpolizeilich erforderliche Fluchtweg.

Von außen betrachtet wirkt die Lichtdiffusionshaut der Fassaden als lichthaltige Hülle, die sich je nach Sonnenstand und Belichtungssituation im Charakter verändert. Nachts dringt das Kunstlicht aus dem Gebäudeinneren nach außen und verfängt sich als Indirektlicht in den Glasschuppen der Hülle.

on all sides. The amount of daylight, which is partly reflected by the white fireproof floor and diffused both by the light-diffusion skin of the facade in front of it and by the dust-proof ceiling, is sufficient to illuminate the exhibition rooms naturally. Slight shadows, caused by the load-bearing wall panels, produce welcome spatial differentiation inside, producing a lively but not too abstract spatial effect.

The artificial lighting is integrated into the empty space above the dust-proof ceiling. It replaces daylight when necessary, without rendering the source of the artificial light visible as such. (One exception is the spotlight system which can also be lowered if required).

On the ground floor, the load-bearing wall panels are situated in front of the translucent exterior wall in the form of glass blocks, giving this floor its own particular identity as a multi-purpose entrance floor. The dust-proof ceiling is absent here. The load-bearing intermediate floor and the lighting fixtures are openly visible.

IV The Exterior

The exterior of the building is dominated by a light-diffusion skin made of non-reflecting glass panels, fashioned in the manner of imbricated 'glass shingles'. This skin absorbs the glare of daylight by means of its roughened surface (similar to milk-glass) and ensures the optimal direction and diversion of daylight into the clear ceiling spaces of the exhibition floors. It encloses the solid, insulated building with a metre-wide layer of thoroughly 'scavenged' air. Mounted in between the glass skin and the building itself, integrated into the filigree suspension, are fixed cleaning catwalks and the emergency exit (emergency stairs) required by the fire regulations.

From the outside, the light-diffusion skin of the facade produces the effect of a light-filled covering, which changes in character with the position of the sun and the state of the illumination. At night, the artificial light radiates from the inside of the building and is caught as indirect light in the imbrications of the glass.

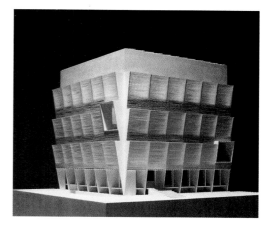

Modellansicht
View of the model

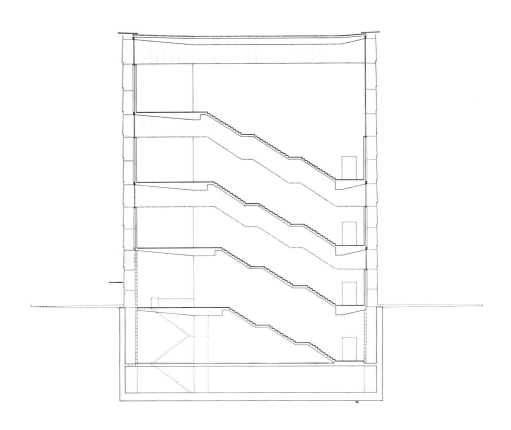

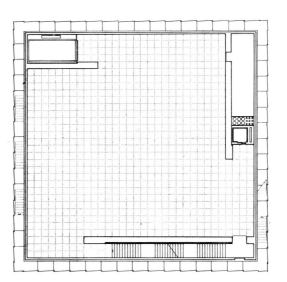

Endgültiges Projekt 1992, Schnitt und
Regelgrundriß
Final project, 1992, section and general floor
plan

132

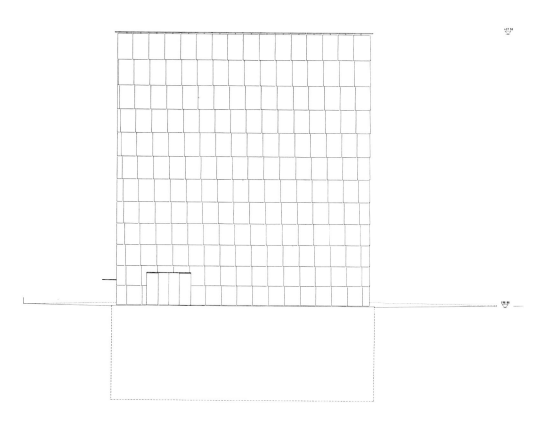

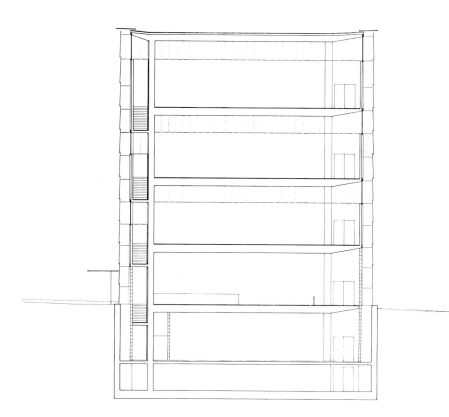

Endgültiges Projekt, 1992, Ansicht und Schnitt
Final project, 1992, elevation and section

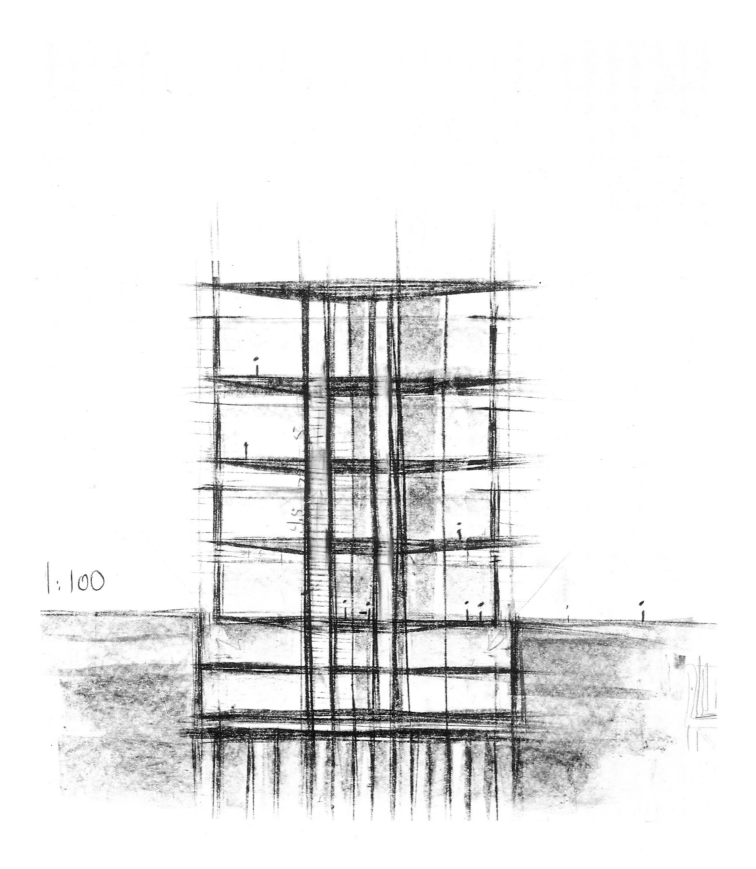

1:100

Skizze des endgültigen Projektes
Sketch of the final project

134

Ansicht von der Hauptpost (Modell)
View from the main post office (model)

Ansicht von der Kornmarktstraße (Modell)
View from Kornmarktstraße (model)

Museumsquartier Wien

Dieter Bogner

Im historischen Kulturzentrum Wiens, im Areal der ehemaligen kaiserlichen Hofstallungen, errichtet die Republik Österreich gemeinsam mit der Stadt Wien in den nächsten Jahren nach den Plänen der Architekten Ortner & Ortner das *Museumsquartier.* Es handelt sich dabei um das größte Kulturprojekt, das in Österreich seit der Errichtung des Kunst- und des Naturhistorischen Museums vor hundert Jahren in Angriff genommen wurde.

Der inhaltliche Schwerpunkt des Museumsquartiers liegt im Bereich interdisziplinärer zeitgenössischer Kunst- und Kulturphänomene. Die im angrenzenden Bereich der Wiener Hofburg beheimateten kunst-, kultur- und naturgeschichtlichen Sammlungen des habsburgischen Kaiserhauses (Kunsthistorisches und Naturhistorisches Museum, Völkerkundemuseum, Antiken- und Musikinstrumentensammlung u. a. m.) erfahren damit eine Erweiterung in die Gegenwart und Zukunft.

Im Zentrum des 44.000 m² großen vielgliedrigen Komplexes stehen das *Museum moderner Kunst,* eine große *Kunsthalle* für temporäre kunst- und kulturgeschichtliche Ausstellungen sowie eine multifunktionelle *Veranstaltungshalle* für Musik, Tanz und Theater. Die im Mittelpunkt gelegene, aus dem 19. Jahrhundert stammende repräsentative Winterreithalle wird in ein großes Foyer verwandelt, das die drei Hauptgebäude des Museumsquartiers besucherfreundlich miteinander verbinden wird. Ein 67 m hoher *Informations- und Leseturm* überragt als wichtiges architektonisches und stadträumliches Zeichen das Areal und wird eine auf Kunst und Kultur spezialisierte Freihandbibliothek sowie ein EDV-Informationszentrum enthalten.

Die von Johann Bernhard Fischer von Erlach im 18. Jahrhundert errichteten barocken Hofstallungsgebäude und die erhaltenen Teile der historischen Bausubstanz werden eine *Architekturgalerie,* zeitgenössische *Kunstgalerien* sowie eine *Mediathek,* ein *Film- und Videozentrum,*

Vienna's Museum Quarter

Dieter Bogner

Over the next few years, the Republic of Austria, together with the City of Vienna, will be constructing in the historic cultural centre of the city, in the area enclosing the former Imperial Court Stables, a Museum Quarter, designed by the architects Ortner & Ortner. This is the largest cultural project to be undertaken in Austria since the construction of the Art History and Natural History Museums a hundred years ago.

The main area of activity of the Museum Quarter lies in the interdisciplinary field of contemporary artistic and cultural phenomena. The collections of fine art, cultural history and natural history deriving from the Imperial House of Habsburg, which are housed in the adjacent area of the Vienna Hofburg (Kunsthistorisches and Naturhistorisches Museum, Völkerkundemuseum, Antiken- und Musikinstrumentensammlung etc.) will thereby be extended to include the present and the future.

In the centre of the 44,000 m² multiform complex will be the Museum moderner Kunst ('Museum of Modern Art'), the Kunsthalle (a large exhibition hall for temporary exhibitions of art and culture), as well as a multi-purpose hall for music, dance, and theatre events. The Winterreithalle, the former winter riding arena, a building which dates from the 19th century, will be transformed into a large foyer connecting the three main buildings of the Museum Quarter with one another in a visitor-friendly way. Rising above the site will be the 67-m-high Information and Reading Tower, an important symbol for architecture and urban planning, which will contain an open-access library specialising in art and cultural studies, and a computer information centre.

The Baroque buildings of the Court Stables, which were designed by Bernhard Fischer von Erlach in the 18th century, together with what has survived of building stock dating from the period of historicism, will accommodate an Architectural Gallery and contemporary art galleries, as well as a Mediateque, a Centre for Film and Video,

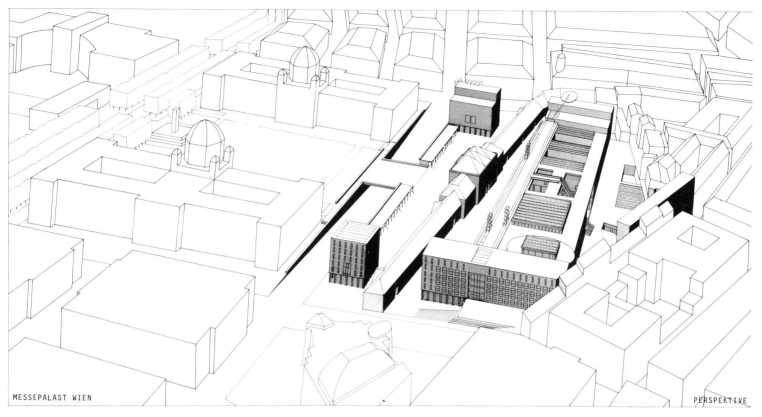

MESSEPALAST WIEN   PERSPEKTIVE

Ortner und Ortner, Museumsquartier Wien, 1986–1996, Perspektive Wettbewerb
Ortner and Ortner, Museum Quarter, Vienna, 1986–1996, perspective view, competition entry

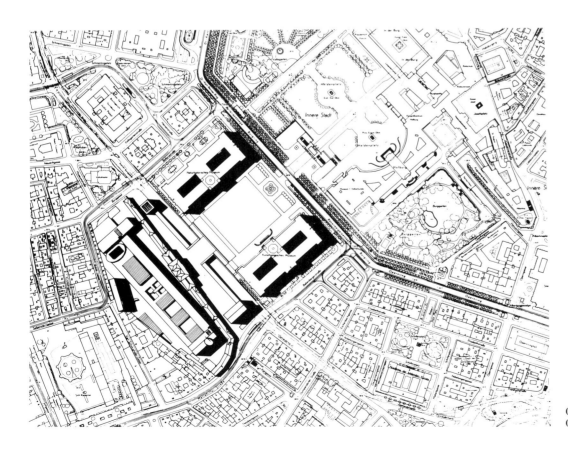

Ortner und Ortner, Lageplan Wettbewerb
Ortner and Ortner, site plan, competition entry

137

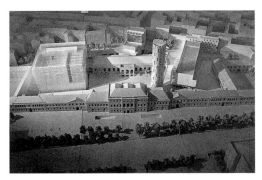

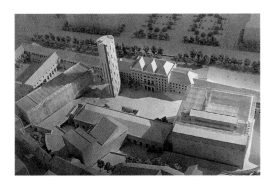

Ortner und Ortner, Großes Arbeitsmodell, 1992
Ortner and Ortner, large working model, 1992

eine *Photogalerie* und andere Einrichtungen der Medienwelt aufnehmen. Ein *Kindermuseum* sowie *Künstlerateliers, Wohnungen* und *Geschäfte* ergänzen das vielfältige kulturelle Angebot des Museumsquartiers.

Durch die Verknüpfung großer kultureller Einrichtungen mit einer Vielfalt mittlerer und kleinerer Institutionen und die Ausstattung des Areals mit einer reichhaltigen Infrastruktur und großzügigen Freiräumen entsteht etwas mehr als hundert Jahre nach der Eröffnung des Kunsthistorischen Museums, am Ende des 20. Jahrhunderts, im Herzen Wiens ein durch Interdisziplinarität und Offenheit geprägtes Kulturzentrum internationalen Maßstabs.

Das Ortner-Projekt entspricht in hervorragender Weise den Anforderungen der Wettbewerbsausschreibung. Durch eine differenzierte Gebäudetypologie in Verbindung mit der am Umraum orientierten Anordnung der Teileinheiten werden das symmetrisch angelegte ehemalige Kaiserforum und das verwinkelte Wohnviertel am Spittelberg gelenkartig miteinander verknüpft. Die Neubauten erheben sich hinter der langgestreckten, niedrigen Barockfassade des palastähnlichen Hauptgebäudes der kaiserlichen Hofstallungen. Stadträumlich beziehen sie sich auf die großen historistischen Museumsbauten sowie auf die Dachlandschaft des 7. Bezirks und ergreifen damit eine klare Position in dem vor mehr als hundert Jahren durch Gottfried Semper aus einem ländlichen Freiraum vor den Stadtmauern in eine monumentale großstädtische Anlage verwandelten Areal.

Zur Planung und Errichtung des Projekts wurde im Winter 1990 von der Republik Österreich und der Gemeinde Wien die Museumsquartier Errichtungs- und Betriebsgesellschaft mbH. gegründet. Als Baubeginn ist nach Abschluß des aufwendigen Planungs- und Genehmigungsverfahrens der Sommer 1993 vorgesehen. Die Hauptgebäude sollen 1996 eröffnet werden.

Museum moderner Kunst

Im Neubau des Museums moderner Kunst wird es erstmals möglich sein, die seit den frühen sechziger Jahren von der Republik

a Photography Gallery and other facilities from the world of media technology. The diversity of the Museum Quarter's cultural range is completed by a Children's Museum, studios for artists, apartments and shops.

The Museum Quarter combines large-scale cultural facilities with a variety of medium-sized and smaller institutions, and is equipped with an extensive infrastructure and a large amount of free space. At the end of the 20th century, slightly more than a hundred years after the opening of the Kunsthistorisches Museum, a cultural centre of international standard, characterised by its interdisciplinary nature and openness, is at last to be built in the heart of Vienna.

The Ortner project fulfils the competition requirements in an excellent fashion. Through a differentiated typology of buildings, combined with an arrangement of the individual units which is oriented to the surrounding area, the symmetrical layout of what used to be the Imperial forum is linked in an articulated way with the winding streets of the residential area of Spittelberg. The new buildings rise from behind the low, elongated Baroque facades of the palatial main building of the Imperial Court Stables. From the point of view of the neighbouring area, they are related to both the great museum buildings of historicism and the skyline of 7th District, thus assuming a clear position on a site which Gottfried Semper transformed from a rural open space into a monumental urban complex more than a hundred years ago.

For the planning and construction of the project, the *Museumsquartier Errichtungs-und Betriebsgesellschaft mbH* (Museum Quarter Construction and Operation Co. Ltd.) was founded by the Republic of Austria and the City of Vienna in the winter of 1990. It is expected that, once the complicated process of obtaining planning permission has been successfully concluded, construction will begin in summer 1993. The main buildings should be opened in 1996.

The Museum of Modern Art

In the new building of the Museum of Modern Art it will be possible to present to the public for the first time ever the art

Österreich aufgebaute Kunstsammlung übersichtlich und unter besten konservatorischen Bedingungen der Öffentlichkeit zu präsentieren. Seit seiner Gründung am Beginn der sechziger Jahre ist das Museum moderner Kunst in Provisorien untergebracht, in einem nach Wien übersiedelten Weltausstellungspavillon von 1958 und in einem barocken Palais.

Das neue Museum mit einer Nettogeschoßfläche von 21.000 m² verfügt über 8.000 m² Ausstellungsflächen für die Sammlungsbestände sowie über größere und kleinere Wechselausstellungsräume. Für die Arbeit von Künstlern im Museum stehen differenzierte »Freiräume« für Installationen, Aktionen und Projekte zur Verfügung. Die museologische, technische und statische Konzeption des Gebäudes ermöglicht die freie Kombination aller Kunstgattungen, beispielsweise die Plazierung schwerer Skulpturen in den Ausstellungsräumen aller Hauptgeschosse, die Einrichtung eigener AV-Medienräume in allen Bereichen der Sammlung und die Installierung einer Studiengalerie als Gelenkstelle zwischen den ständigen Ausstellungsräumen und dem Hauptdepot. Durch das gesamte Gebäude zieht sich ein differenziertes Angebot an Informations- und Vermittlungsräumen, wobei darauf geachtet wird, daß Werkrezeption und -vermittlung räumlich eng miteinander verbunden sind, ohne sich gegenseitig zu stören.

Kunsthalle Wien
Die Kunsthalle erfüllt einen dringenden kulturpolitischen Bedarf in Wien. Sie ist als Ausstellungsort für die Produktion und Übernahme großer, mittlerer und kleiner kunst- und kulturhistorischer Ausstellungen mit internationalem Anspruch konzipiert, für die es derzeit nur beschränkte Möglichkeiten gibt. Sie weist eine Nettogeschoßfläche von 11.000 m² auf. Zur Verfügung stehen in drei Geschossen drei unterschiedlich große Ausstellungshallen (1.400 m², 900 m² und 600 m²), die bei Bedarf in kleinere Einheiten unterteilt werden können.

Veranstaltungshalle
Im Rahmen des Gesamtkonzepts des Museumsquartiers spielt die Veranstaltungs-

collection built up by the Republic of Austria since the early sixties in a comprehensive way and under the best conservational conditions. Since its foundation at the beginning of the sixties, the Museum of Modern Art has been housed in provisional quarters: partly in a world exhibition pavilion which was moved to Austria in 1958, and partly in a Baroque palace.

The new museum, with a total floor area of 21,000 m², has more than 8,000 m² of space at its disposal for exhibiting its collections, as well as both large and small rooms for temporary exhibitions. "Free spaces" for installations, actions and other projects enable artists to work in the museum itself. The museological, technical and structural conception of the building makes it possible to freely combine all forms of art; for example, to place heavy sculptures in the exhibition rooms on all the main floors, to set up A.V. media spaces in all areas of the collection and to install a study gallery as a point of articulation between the permanent exhibition rooms and the main depot. Throughout the building there are various information and communication rooms, whereby one should note that the reception and the mediation aspects are closely connected spatially, yet do not interfere with each other.

The Kunsthalle – Exhibition Hall
The Exhibition Hall satisfies a pressing need of the arts in Vienna. It is conceived as a place for producing and receiving large, medium and small-scale exhibitions of art and culture of an international standard, for which there are at present only limited possibilities. It has a total floor space of 11,000 m². It comprises three exhibition halls of varying size (1,400 m², 900 m² and 600 m²) on three different floors; the halls can also be subdivided into smaller units if required.

Events Hall
Within the framework of the overall concept of the Museum Quarter, the Events Hall has an important role to play in catering for experimental theatre, dance and music events. Its location between the Museum of Modern Art and the Exhibition Hall allows for the possibility of multiple

Modell, Museum moderner Kunst
Model, Museum of Modern Art

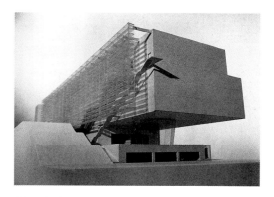

Modell, Kunsthalle
Model, exhibition hall

Modell, Ansicht des Leseturmes
Model, view of the reading tower

halle für experimentelle Theater-, Tanz- und Musikereignisse eine große Rolle. Ihre Lage zwischen dem Museum moderner Kunst und der Kunsthalle ermöglicht ein Zusammenspiel der Nutzungen, sei es für kulturelle Begleitveranstaltungen, Symposien, Eröffnungen, Sponsorenveranstaltungen und anderes mehr.

Informations- und Leseturm

Im Zentrum des Museumsquartiers und als zeichenhaftes Symbol am Abschluß des Museumsforums steht als Konzentrat des aktuellen kulturellen Wissens der Informations- und Leseturm, eine äußerst benutzerfreundlich organisierte Freihandbibliothek. Auf fünf Geschossen werden bis zu 50.000 aktuelle Publikationen zur Verfügung stehen, die alle Gebiete der Gegenwartskunst- und -kultur, sowie Zeitschriften, Schallplatten und andere Tonträger umfassen werden.

Medienzentrum

Im Mittelpunkt steht eine Mediathek, in der der Öffentlichkeit ein leichter Zugang zur Informationsfülle der umfangreichen Wiener Medienarchive geboten wird, aber auch der Zugriff auf die Bestände internationaler Medienzentren erfolgen kann. Weiters ist ein lebendiges und kritisches medienspezifisches Aktionsforum in Verbindung mit einer Ausstellungsplattform für die verschiedensten Phänomene der Medienwelt geplant. Dort soll auf freie, unterhaltsame, kreative und künstlerische Art und Weise die Wirklichkeit und die Wirksamkeit der Medien vermittelt und kritisch durchleuchtet werden. Als weitere Einrichtungen des Medienzentrums sind eine Photogalerie, ein Filmzentrum sowie ein Produktions- und Präsentationsort für Videokunst geplant.

Mit der längst fälligen Umwandlung der heute als kommerzielles Ausstellungsgelände genutzten ehemaligen kaiserlichen Hofstallung im historischen und kulturellen Zentrum Wiens in ein ganzheitlich konzipiertes zeitgenössisches Kunst- und Kulturzentrum wird eine viele Jahrzehnte alte Vision österreichischer Kulturschaffender und Kulturinteressierter zur Realität.

utilisation: for concomitant cultural events, symposia, exhibition openings, sponsors' events and many other uses.

Information and Reading Tower

In the centre of the Museum Quarter, like a symbol at the end of the museum forum, stands a concentration of contemporary knowledge: the Information and Reading Tower, an extremely user-friendly open-access library. Five storeys high, it will stock up to 50,000 current publications covering all fields of contemporary art and culture, as well as periodicals, records and other sound-recording media.

Media Centre

In the centre is a mediatheque, providing the public with easy access not only to the wealth of information in the extensive Viennese media archives, but also to the contents of other international media centres. Furthermore, it is planned to set up a lively and critical action forum specifically concerned with media, combined with an exhibition platform for a great variety of phenomena in the media world. There it should be possible, in an unconstrained, entertaining, creative and artistic way, to communicate and critically examine the reality and the effectiveness of media. Further facilities which are planned for the media centre include a photography gallery, a film centre and a place for the production and presentation of video art. With the long-overdue transformation of the former Imperial Court Stables in Vienna's historic cultural centre from a site at present used for trade fairs into a centre for contemporary art and culture based on a holistic concept, the dream nurtured by Austrian artists and art lovers for so many decades is at last becoming a reality.

Das Museumsquartier Wien

Ortner und Ortner

1

In Gottfried Sempers imperialer Anlage des Wiener Kaiserforums stehen sich die ehemaligen Hofstallungen (erbaut 1720 durch Fischer von Erlach) und die neue Hofburg als Kopfbauten gegenüber. Dazwischen sind axial die beiden Hofmuseen (Naturhistorisches Museum und Kunsthistorisches Museum) mit dem Maria-Theresien-Platz und dem Burgtor angeordnet. Bezogen auf die städtische Gesamtsituation reicht diese Achse bis ins Herz der Innenstadt und bindet formal die dichte Bebauung des siebten Wiener Gemeindebezirks an das Zentrum.

Wenn nun dieses ca. 45.000 m² große Areal der ehemaligen Hofstallungen in ein Museumsquartier gewandelt wird, so handelt es sich dabei sowohl durch den historischen und urbanen Kontext als auch durch die Größe des Vorhabens um eine Aufgabenstellung, wie sie für die alten westlichen Metropolen einzigartig ist.

Der Entwurf für das neue Museumsquartier mißt dem langgestreckten Fischer-von-Erlach-Bau die Rolle einer wertvollen Stadtmauer zu, die nach vorne den Abschluß des Kaiserforums bildet und hinter der sich nun komprimiert eine »Stadt in der Stadt« entwickelt.

Von Bedeutung sind dabei zwei Kraftfelder, die hier aufeinandertreffen. Einmal die imperiale historische Ordnung, die sich von vorne mit den beiden Semper-Museen axial auf den Haupteingang des Fischer-Baues schiebt, und zum anderen das Mietshausquartier des 7. Bezirks, das schräg von rückwärts hereindrängt.

Diese beiden Richtungen werden zu Richtlinien für die Anordnung der Bauten im Museumsquartier. Was dabei entsteht, ist eine sich immer wieder kreuzende Anlage von Baukörpern und Freiflächen, die scheinbar ungeordnet wirkt, der aber tatsächlich als Entstehungsmuster die Kreuzung der monarchischen Monumental-

The Design of the Museum Quarter in Vienna

Ortner and Ortner

1

Gottfried Semper's plan for an Imperial forum in Vienna, which was conceived in the late 19th century, placed the former Imperial stables (built by Fischer von Erlach in 1720) and the Neue Hofburg at either end of the main axis. Between them, the two Imperial museums (Natural History Museum and Museum of Fine Arts), together with the Maria Theresienplatz (Maria Theresa Square) and the Burgtor, are arranged on the transverse axis. The prolongation of the major axis extends all the way to the heart of the city, thus formally linking Vienna's densely built-up seventh district with the city center.

Turning the buildings of the former Imperial stables and the surrounding area – about 45.000 square meters – into a museum quarter is a task that is unique for any of the old western metropolises, both in terms of its historical and urban context and the sheer size of the project.

The design of the new Museum Quarter accords to the long facade of the building by Fischer von Erlach the role of a city wall, the front of which marks the end of the Imperial forum and behind which a compact 'city within the city' is now being developed.

Two significant force fields meet here: on the one hand there is the thrust towards the main entrance of Fischer von Erlach's building, provided by the Imperial historic order together with the transverse axis of Semper's two museums; on the other hand the tenement quarters of the 7th District push in at an angle from behind. Those two directions serve as guidelines for the arrangement of the buildings within the Museum Quarter.

What emerges is a criss-crossing array of buildings and free spaces that at first glance appears random, but is in fact the result of the pattern of the monarchic monumental order intersecting with a democratic one

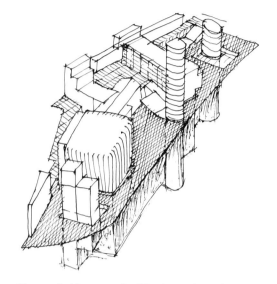

Entwurfsskizze, zweite Wettbewerbsstufe
Conceptual sketch, second phase of the competition

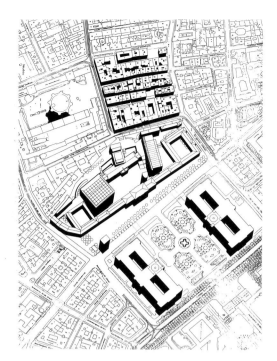

Lageplan, Wettbewerb 2. Stufe
Site plan, competition, 2nd stage

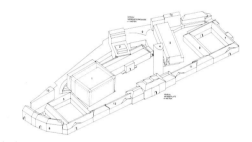

Axonometrie des Gesamtkomplexes
Axonometric view of the overall layout

ordnung mit jener der demokratischen Gewachsenheit zugrunde liegt. So ließe sich in diesem neuen städtischen Zentrum auch eine Form von demokratischem Kulturverständnis finden, das unterschiedliche Bezüge gleichrangig gelten läßt und keine rigorosen Ordnungen mehr herzustellen versucht. Architektonisch kommt diese Haltung der Gesamtanlage zugute, weil nun als Folge der ideellen Verschneidungen zweier Richtungen eine Fülle von Freiräumen mit eigenem Charakter entsteht, die eine lebendige Benützung für unterschiedliche Aktivitäten garantiert. Dem Kaiserforum mit seinen historischen Sammlungen steht so das Museumsquartier mit seiner Gegenwartskultur gegenüber.

2

Von der Funktion her sind im Museumsquartier das Museum moderner Kunst, die Kunsthalle, der Leseturm, eine Veranstaltungshalle für verschiedene Nutzungen, das Museum Ideengeschichte der Österreichischen Moderne und das Medienforum mit Film- und Photographiemuseum untergebracht.
Zentrale Rolle bei der Erschließung kommt der Winterreithalle zu, einem denkmalgeschützten Bau in der Mitte des Areals. Die Halle wird als gemeinsames Foyer für Museum moderner Kunst, Kunsthalle und Veranstaltungshalle zum zentralen Umschlagplatz, der auch außerhalb der Museumszeiten mit seinen Läden und Einrichtungen nutzbar bleibt.
Mit der Winterreithalle eng verknüpft sind auch die so wichtigen Durchwege zur dichtbesiedelten Bebauung des 7. Bezirkes. An dem natürlichen Höhenunterschied von 10 m zwischen dem Niveau des Fischer-Baues und dem höher liegenden Areal der Bezirksbauten sowie der bisherigen Nutzung als Messegelände waren alle Möglichkeiten des Durchgangs gescheitert. Nun aber wird ein vielfältiger Fluß von Rampen und Freitreppen die Verbindungen in Richtung Mariahilfer Straße, Burggasse und Maria-Theresien-Platz herstellen.

that has developed over the course of the centuries. Thus it is also possible to find in this new urban center a kind of democratic understanding of culture which gives weight to different references and no longer attempts to achieve a rigorous order. Architecturally, this approach benefits the overall layout, since the virtual intersection of the two directions creates an abundance of free spaces, each with a character of its own, thus ensuring lively utilization for a variety of activities. The Imperial forum with its historic collections has its counterpart in the Museum Quarter with its contemporary culture.

2

As far as function is concerned, the Museum Quarter will house the Museum of Modern Art (Museum moderner Kunst - MmK), the Art Gallery and a freely usable Multifunctional Hall. In addition there will be a Museum of Modern Austrian Art (The Leopold Collection) and the Media Forum, comprising Museums of Film and Photography, a Media Center and a library.
In terms of access to this complex, the central role will be played by the former Winter Riding Arena, classified as a historical monument and located approximately at the center of this area. As a joint foyer for the Museum of Modern Art, the Art Gallery and the Multifunctional Hall it will become an area whose shops and other facilities may be used even at times when the museum itself is closed.
Upon entering this lobby by the existing outer staircase the visitor will find himself in a room flooded with light and equipped with comfortable seating arrangements and bars, and which provides access to the Museum of Modern Art on the left and the Art Gallery on the right. Like the bow of a ship, the Multifunctional Hall juts into this lobby with its front wall and has its entrance here.
The important passageways through the Museum Quarter to the densely populated 7th District are also closely linked to the Winter Riding Arena. In the past there was no passageway through this area since there is a natural difference of ten meters

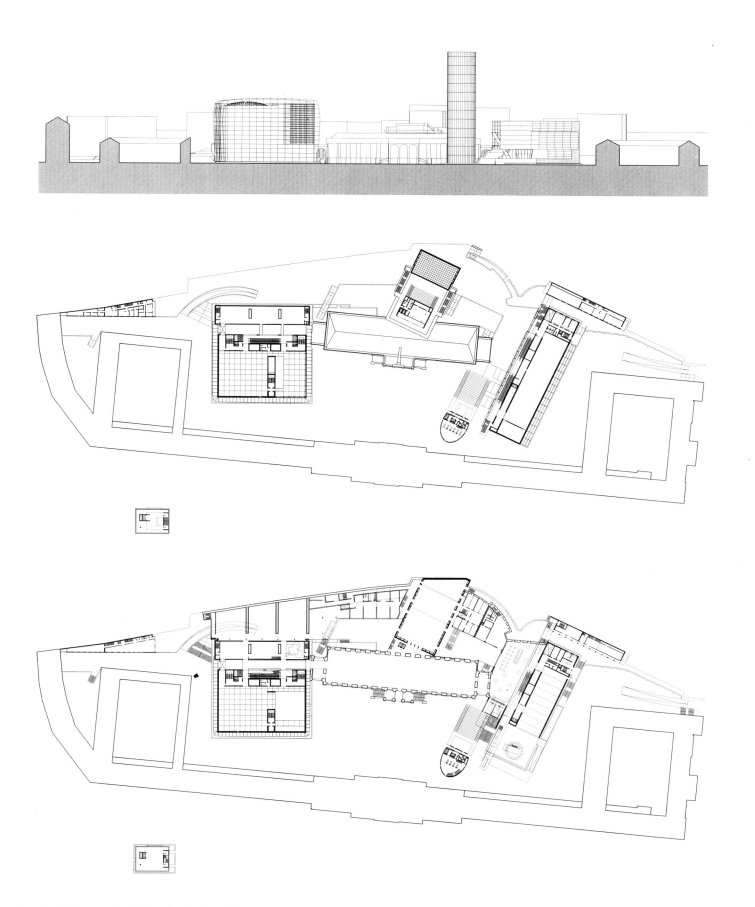

Hauptgeschoß, Obergeschoß, Hauptansicht, 1992
Main floor, second floor and front elevation, 1992

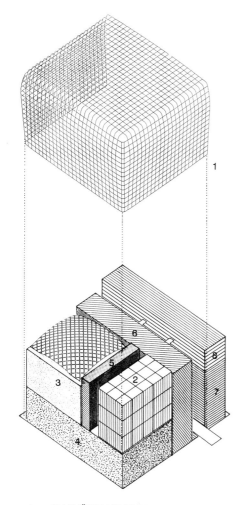

1 GLASHÜLLE MIT FASSADENRAUM
2 TAGESLICHTKUBUS
3 KUNSTLICHTKUBUS MIT KUPPELRAUM
4 WECHSELAUSSTELLUNG MIT SAAL
5 MEDIENRAUM
6 ERSCHLIESSUNG MIT TREPPENHALLE
7 KABINETTE
8 VERWALTUNG

Konzeptskizze des Museums moderner Kunst
Conceptual sketch of the Museum of Modern Art

3

Das Museumsquartier wird kein hehrer Hort für elitäre Hochkultur sein. Es soll vielmehr eine heitere, widersprüchliche, im Grundsatz »unordentliche« Atmosphäre geschaffen werden, die eine lebendige Mischung kultureller Selbstdarstellung unserer Gegenwart ermöglicht.

Mit den neuen Baulichkeiten soll dafür ein urbanes Ensemble entstehen, das durch seine Großzügigkeit und Frische zu einer gediegenen Ungezwungenheit aller Beteiligten verhilft.

Von außen betrachtet wird sich hinter der langgestreckten Hauswand des Fischer-von-Erlach-Baues eine markante Silhouette dieser Stadt abbilden.

Was an diesem »Stadtmodell« aber über seine direkten Funktionen hinaus wichtig wäre, ist, daß es zeigen könnte, wie Stadt nur durch Verdichtung attraktiver gemacht werden kann. Und wie Altes und Neues sich auf engstem Raum zu neuer Gemeinsamkeit mischen lassen. Von seinem urbanen Stellenwert, vom Anspruch der demokratischen Selbstdarstellung und dem eines kulturellen Leitbildes her hat dieses Quartier ein direktes Pendant: die Akropolis.

in height between the level of the Fischer von Erlach building and the higher terrain of the apartment buildings behind it and the complex was utilized for trade fairs. Now, however, a variety of ramps and outer staircases will link the Museum Quarter with the surrounding Mariahilfer Strasse, Burggasse and Maria Theresien-Platz.

3

When erected, the Museum Quarter will not be a lofty repository of elitist high culture; instead, a cheerful, purposefully unorganised atmosphere, full of contradictions, is to be created that will permit a lively mixture of different presentations of our contemporary culture.

The new buildings are intended to provide an urban architectural ensemble which, in its generous dimensions and unconventionality, will promote the dignified casualness of museum organizers and visitors alike.

Viewed from outside the old Baroque building, a striking skyline will be visible behind the long facade of Fischer von Erlach's building. It is hoped, however, that beyond its immediate functions this 'model of a city' will also demonstrate that the only way to make the city more attractive is to make it more compact. And also how the old and the new may be combined to give rise to a new harmony. From the point of view of its urban significance, its claim of democratic self-representation and its function as a cultural model, the Museum Quarter may be viewed as a direct modern counterpart of an ancient Greek acropolis.

(Translation by Maria E. Clay)

Großer Platz vor der Veranstaltungshalle
Large Square in front of the events hall

Detail der Kunsthalle und des Leseturms
Detail of the exhibition hall and the reading tower

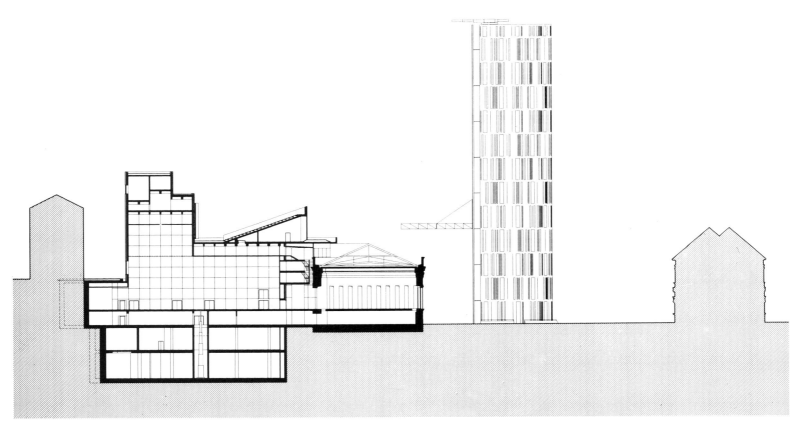

Schnitt durch die Veranstaltungshalle
Section through the main events hall

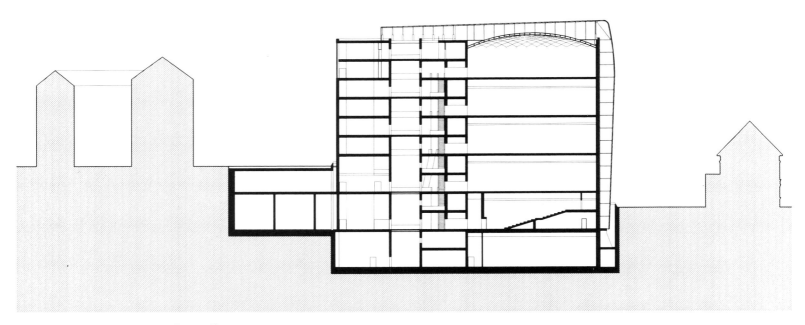

Schnitt durch das Museum moderner Kunst
Section through the Museum of Modern Art

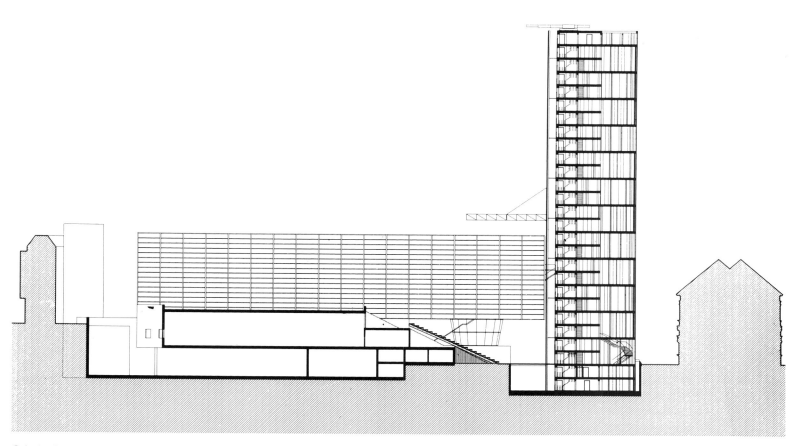

Schnitt durch den Leseturm
Section through the reading tower

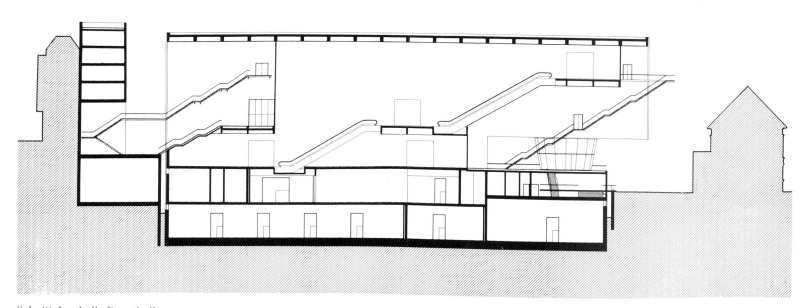

Schnitt durch die Kunsthalle
Section through the exhibition hall

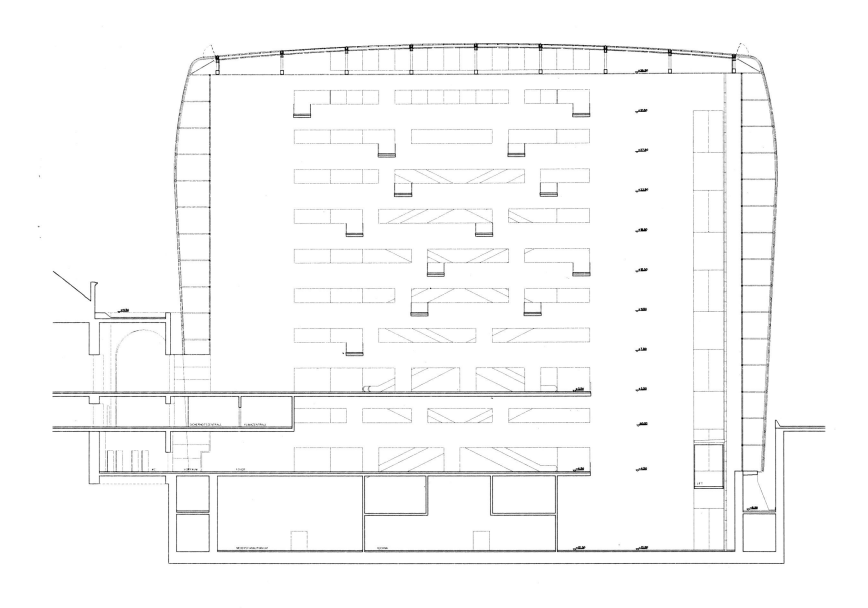

Schnitt durch das Museum moderner Kunst
Section through the Museum of Modern Art

148

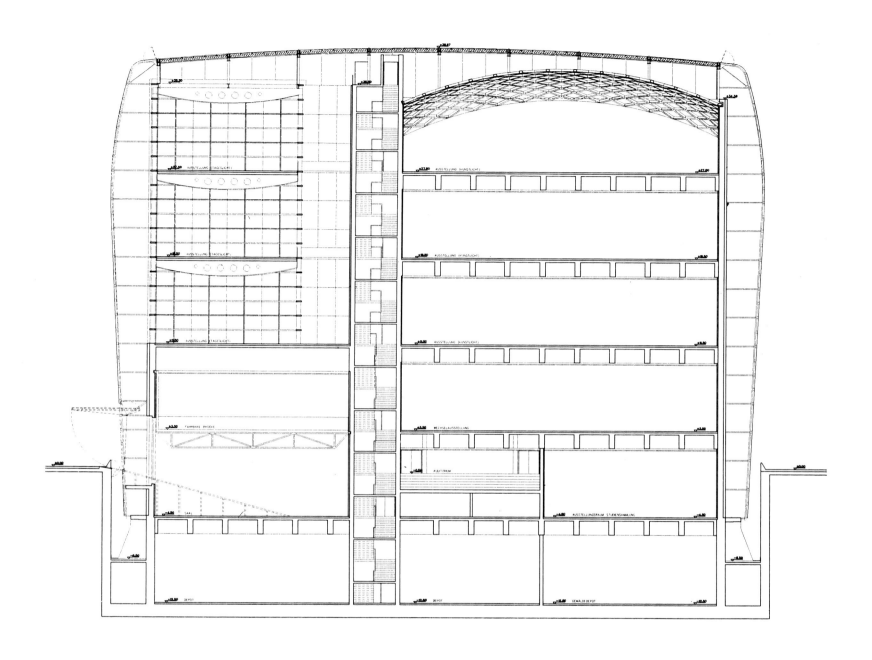

Schnitt durch das Museum moderner Kunst
Section through the Museum of Modern Art

Nachtansicht, Modell, Leseturm und Museum moderner Kunst
Night view, model, reading tower and Museum of Modern Art

Nachtansicht, Modell, Kunsthalle und Detail Leseturm
Night view, model, exhibition hall and detail of the reading tower

Nachtansicht, Modell, Veranstaltungshalle und Museum moderner Kunst
Night view, model, exhibition hall and Museum of Modern Art

Nachtansicht, Modell
Night view, model

Nachtansicht, Modell, Hauptansicht Messepalast
Night view, model, view of the Vienna Museum Quarter

Nachtansicht, Modell, Detail der Kunsthalle
Night view, model, detail of the exhibition hall

Modell, Detail der Kunsthalle und des Leseturms
Model, detail of the exhibition hall and the reading tower

Das Niederösterreichische Landesmuseum

Norbert Steiner

Egon Schiele, Zerfallende Mühle, 1916
Egon Schiele, Decaying Mill, 1916

Am 10. Juli 1987 beschloß der Niederösterreichische Landtag in einer historischen Sitzung die Gründung einer eigenen Landeshauptstadt und wählte dafür St. Pölten aus. Seit damals laufen Planungen und Maßnahmen, um die räumlichen und baulichen Voraussetzungen dafür zu schaffen, daß die derzeit in der Bundeshauptstadt Wien untergebrachten zentralen Einrichtungen des Landes nach St. Pölten übersiedeln können.

Die Planung für diese neue Landeshauptstadt für Niederösterreich war von Anfang an darauf gerichtet, nicht nur einen neuen politischen und wirtschaftlichen Schwerpunkt zwischen Wien und Linz zu entwickeln. Es wird vielmehr versucht, auch einen neuen kulturellen Kristallisationspunkt in der vielfältigen Kulturlandschaft Niederösterreichs zu schaffen. Neben dem Landhaus soll ein Kulturbezirk entstehen, als Bindeglied zwischen dem alten Stadtkern mit seinem vielfältigen städtischen Leben und dem neuen Landhaus-Stadtteil. Die Nachbarschaft und enge Verflechtung mit der Altstadt und anderen städtischen Einrichtungen, zu Schulen und Erholungsgebieten soll vermeiden helfen, daß dieser Kulturbezirk die Aura eines Kulturghettos, eines womöglich den normalen Bürgern entzogenen, verbotenen Bezirks erfährt. In diesem Kulturbezirk wird eine Konzerthalle entstehen, eine umfangreiche Bibliothek, das Landesarchiv und ein ORF-Landesstudio. Größte Einrichtung wird aber das NÖ. Landesmuseum mit einer Ausstellungshalle sein.

Das in Wien seit 1911 vorhandene NÖ. Landesmuseum war und ist trotz mehrfacher Neuaufstellung eher eine landeskundliche Lehrsammlung. Diese Sammlung wurde in den vergangenen Jahrzehnten entsprechend den Gegebenheiten des Landes ohne Hauptstadt zum Teil dezentralisiert.

Sehr schnell wurde allen an der Planung Beteiligten klar, daß es nicht genügt, die in Wien bestehenden Einrichtungen und

The Lower Austrian Provincial Museum

Norbert Steiner

In a historic session on 10th July 1987, the Lower Austrian Provincial Diet resolved to establish its own provincial capital and chose St. Pölten as the site. Since that time planning and implementation measures have been in train to find the space and carry out the construction required to enable the facilities of the province currently accommodated centrally in the federal capital of Vienna to be relocated to St. Pölten.

Right from the outset the planning for this new provincial capital for Lower Austria had a broader objective than just developing a new political and commercial hub between Vienna and Linz. It also endeavoured to create a new seed about which the varied cultural landscape of Lower Austria would crystallise. In the vicinity of the "Landhaus" (diet building) a new cultural district should emerge to form a link between the old centre with its rich panoply of city life and the new "Landhaus" district. This proximity and close-knit relationship with the old part of the city and other municipal facilities, such as schools and recreation areas, are intended to help avoid this district becoming a cultural getto with the aura of a no-go area for the ordinary citizen. The cultural district is to have a concert hall, an extensive library, the provincial archive and an ORF provincial studio. However the largest facility will be the Lower Austrian Provincial Museum with an exhibition hall. Despite repeated restructuring the Lower Austrian Provincial Museum, which has been in Vienna since 1911, remains primarily a local studies collection. And in past decades this collection has been decentralised to an extent reflecting the situation in a province without capital.

It very quickly became clear to all of the planners that it was not enough to just transfer to St. Pölten all of the existing facilities and collections in Vienna. The new museum is not just intended to preserve. It is to become an arena for a lively discussion of contemporary cultural

Sammlungen einfach nach St. Pölten zu transferieren. Das neue Museum soll nicht nur bewahren. Es soll eine Arena für die lebendige Auseinandersetzung mit zeitgenössischen kulturellen Strömungen und Konflikten werden und Freiräume bieten. Die Zielsetzung für das neue Landesmuseum ist, ein zentrales, neuartiges Museum zu schaffen, das über die museale und didaktische Funktion hinaus Innovationen veranlaßt und einen der kulturellen Bedeutung des österreichischen Stammlandes adäquaten Museumsschwerpunkt in Niederösterreich bildet.

Gesucht wird ein neuartiger Museumstypus, der das Museum zu einem lebendigen Ort der Begegnung und des Kulturaustausches werden läßt. Die wesentlichen Aufgaben sind »Sammeln – Bewahren – Ausstellen – Anregen«.

Das Landesmuseum wird sich nach den Vorstellungen und Konzepten der hierzu tätigen Fachleute und Arbeitskreise aus mehreren Bausteinen zusammensetzen:

Baustein Nr. 1 ist die NÖ Landesgalerie. Die bereits vorhandenen Sammlungen dokumentieren Niederösterreich als Kernland des österreichischen Barock mit einer in Europa einzigartigen Kultur- und Klösterlandschaft. Die Sammlungen aus dem 19. und 20. Jahrhundert belegen mit vielen wichtigen Objekten den Weg zur Moderne. Auch der Weg der traditionellen Kunst in Richtung Moderne ist in der Sammlung nachvollziehbar. Das 20. Jahrhundert soll in der Landesgalerie auch mit Photo- und Videokunst vertreten sein.

Baustein Nr. 2 sind die naturwissenschaftlichen Sammlungen des Landes. Die Exponate des Hauses der Natur, das noch in der Wiener Herrengasse untergebracht ist, sollen im neuen Landesmuseum die Vielfalt der niederösterreichischen Naturlandschaften, von den Alpen über die Böhmische Masse, bis hinein nach Pannonien dokumentieren. Mit lebenden Tieren, vor allem Fischen und Reptilien, und mit Parkanlagen rund um die Museumsgebäude im neuen Regierungsviertel sollen Niederösterreichs Tier- und Pflanzenwelt einen nahtlosen Übergang von der Museumsarchitektur in die Landschaft bilden.

Baustein Nr. 3 wird sich mit Kultur- und Zeitgeschichte befassen. Schon jetzt muß

trends and conflicts, offering a wealth of free space.

The objective is for the new provincial museum to provide an original central service that allows innovation over and above its museological and educational functions, and forms a focus for such activities in Lower Austria that adequately reflects the cultural importance of Austria's original province.

What is sought is a new departure that allows the museum to become a bustling meeting place for cultural exchange, whose essential functions are "collection – preservation – exhibition – stimulation".

The specialists and working parties involved in the conceptualisation envisage the provincial museum as consisting of several elements:

The first of these is the Lower Austrian Provincial Gallery. The existing collections document Lower Austria as the nucleus of the Austrian baroque with a cultural and monastic landscape unique in Europe. The collections from the 19th and 20th centuries include many important items that point the way forward to modernism and reflect the shift from traditional to modern art. The 20th century is also to be represented with photographic and video art in this gallery.

The second element is the province's natural science collections. The exhibits still accommodated in the 'House of Nature' in Vienna's Herrengasse are to document in the new provincial museum the variety evident in the Lower Austrian natural landscapes, from the Alps, over the Bohemian massif and into Pannonia. With live animals with the emphasis on fish and reptiles, and parkland around the museum building in the new government quarter, Lower Austria's flora and fauna are to provide a smooth transition between the museum architecture and the landscape.

The third element will be concerned with cultural and general history. An immediate start must be made on building up collections for this new museum complex. The fourth element, a new type of museum laboratory, is to have the umbrella function of integrating activities and promoting innovation throughout the entire provincial museum. The museum laboratory provides

begonnen werden, für diesen neuen Museumskomplex Sammlungen anzulegen.

Baustein Nr. 4, ein neuartiges Museumslabor, soll eine übergeordnete integrative und innovative Funktion im gesamten Landesmuseum enthalten. Das Museumslabor setzt neue Impulse in der Sicht der Dinge, stellt ständig wechselnde Zusammenhänge her und muß die einzelnen Abteilungen zur Konzeption ständig neuer Sonderausstellungen bewegen. Der »Sauerteig« im Museum wird Querverbindungen in kurzfristigen und längeren Ausstellungen (zwei Monate bis zwei Jahre) aufzeigen.

Mit den Bausteinen 3 und 4 greift das NÖ Landesmuseum den ursprünglichen Museumsgedanken wieder auf: Aus der Beschäftigung mit Vergangenheit und Gegenwart soll ein Blick in die Zukunft möglich werden.

Nach der Durchführung eines internationalen Gutachtens wurde vom Beurteilungsgremium einstimmig Arch. Prof. Hans Hollein als Planer des neuen NÖ Landesmuseums vorgeschlagen. Damit wurde ein hervorragender Partner gefunden, dieses anspruchsvolle, komplexe und sicher noch zu präzisierende Konzept gut weiterzuentwickeln und umzusetzen. Das NÖ Landesmuseum soll 1998 eröffnet werden.

the impetus to look at things from new angles, defines constantly changing relations, and has to encourage the individual departments to mount special exhibitions on a regular basis. Its influence will permeate the museum to mace clear the interconnections in short- and medium-term exhibitions (from 2 months to 2 years). With the third and fourth elements the Lower Austrian Provincial Museum will be taking up again the original idea of a museum; namely that it is necessary to take both past and present into account in order to be able to look into the future.

The international committee responsible for the report commissioned were unanimous in proposing the appointment of Professor of Architecture Hans Hollein to plan the new Lower Austrian Provincial Museum. Undoubtedly an excellent choice for effective further development and implementation of this demanding, complex concept, which has of course yet to be defined more closely. The museum is to open in 1998.

(Translation: All Languages)

Das Projekt

Hans Hollein

Das Projekt baut sich auf den Vorgaben der Aufgabenstellung und des Detailprogrammes auf und sieht den zu errichtenden Kulturbezirk sowohl als integralen Bestandteil des neuen Regierungsviertels, jedoch mit eigener Identität und eigenem Charakter, als auch – seine Anlage und seine Gebäude – als Bindeglied zur Stadt und Auftakt und Entree zum Landeshauptstadtquartier. Es wurde daher in der Situierung und der Anlage der Gebäude auf diesen Aspekt des Zugangs ebenso Wert gelegt wie auf die städtebauliche topographische und funktionelle Eingliederung. Der Bedeutungsgehalt des Kulturbezirkes im allgemeinen als auch der einzelnen Gebäude im besonderen hat hier ebenso eine Rolle gespielt wie die individuelle Ausformung der einzelnen Objekte.

Die vier Hauptobjekte – Niederösterreichisches Landesmuseum und Landesgalerie, Ausstellungshalle, Konzert- und Festsaal sowie Bibliothek – wurden als individuelle Einheiten gesehen, die jedoch in ihrem Miteinander und Zueinander ein kompatibles Ensemble darstellen. Der Kulturbezirk wurde in seinem Charakter als unterschiedlich vom Landhausplatz gesehen, und es wurde eine differenzierte Urbanität angestrebt, die jedoch auch auf die grüne, suburbane Umgebung Bezug nimmt.

Von den funktionellen Zusammenhängen her und der Integration in das Umfeld ergeben sich nach ausführlichen Überlegungen bevorzugte Standorte für die einzelnen Hauptobjekte, wobei hier auch die möglichen unterschiedlichen Bauphasen berücksichtigt wurden. Das Museum steht in engem Zusammenhang mit der Kunsthalle, beide haben einen gemeinsamen Eingangsbereich. Am Zugang, zur Stadt hin, ist die Konzerthalle situiert, ihr Haupteingang, wie auch der benachbarte Eingang zum Museum und zur Kunsthalle, befindet sich unter einem gemeinsamen, schützenden, offenen Dach.

Die Jury hat festgelegt, daß diese Disposition Grundlage des Masterplanes des Kulturbezirks wird.

The Project

Hans Hollein

The project was based on the requirements and program of the cultural precinct looking at it as an integral part of the new government quarters, however, with an identity of its own and a specific character. At the same time the lay-out in general and its buildings were planned as connecting element to the city and as entrance to the new government quarters of the capital. Thus a prime concern in location and conception of the buildings was this specific aspect of access together with the urban, topographic and functional integration.

The meaning of the cultural quarters, in general as well as the significance and the specific character of the individual buildings in particular were considered.

The four main buildings – the Provincial Museum of Lower Austria, with the Art Gallery, the Exhibition Hall, the Concert Hall and the Library – were taken as separate independent units, however, in their correlation and interrelation representing a compatible ensemble.

The necessary functional relationships and the integration into the environment result, after careful study, in certain preferred locations for the various main buildings considering also different construction phases. The museum is in close connection with the exhibition hall sharing one entrance area. At the access – oriented towards the city – the concert hall is situated. The entrance to the concert hall, together with the entrance to the museum, are adjacent under a protecting open roof.

The jury has ruled that those dispositions are the basis for the masterplan for the cultural precinct.

The Museum and the Exhibition Hall Complex

According to the requirements those two institutions were coupled by a common lobby, however, they can act as independent units.

Komplex Museum und Ausstellungshalle

Den Vorgaben entsprechend wurde eine Ankoppelung dieser beiden Objekte mit gemeinsamem Eingang erzielt, wobei jedoch die beiden Objekte auch als vollkommen separierte Einheiten gesehen werden können.

Die *Kunsthalle* ist ein eigener Baukörper, der auch unabhängig erstellt werden kann. Das *Museum* spiegelt in seiner baulichen Konzeption und Gliederung die drei Hauptbereiche (Zeitgeschichte, Kunst- und Naturwissenschaften) wider, die hier sowohl organisatorisch als auch räumlich in einen vernetzten Zusammenhang gebracht wurden. Die museale Konzeption beruht nicht auf einer Trennung, sondern auf einer Überlagerung und Inbezugsetzung der Inhalte, die sich in einer bestimmten Dialektik gegenüberstehen bzw. integriert sind. Sowohl ein getrenntes Erfahren als auch ein gesamtheitliches Erleben ist möglich. Ein lineares Vorgehen des Lernens ist ebenso gegeben wie ein dreidimensional matrixartiges Agieren und Reagieren. Ergänzt wird diese Verflechtung noch durch die Studiensammlung (»Lebendiges Depot«) sowie das Museumslabor, was aktives Arbeiten und Projektionen in die Zukunft ermöglicht.

Von einem gemeinsamen Eingang mit gemeinsam zu nutzenden Einrichtungen wird sowohl die Ausstellungshalle erreicht, die temporären Großausstellungen dient, als auch die Zentrale Halle des Museums. In unterschiedlichen Rundgängen können die verschiedenen, über mehrere Geschosse verteilten Bereiche erfahren werden, wobei laufende Querreferenzen sowohl in horizontaler als auch vertikaler Richtung möglich sind. Vortragssaal, Verwaltung, Labor und didaktische Einrichtungen sowie Museums-Shop und Café sind zentral vom Foyer her erschlossen.

Die (1996 zu eröffnende) Ausstellungshalle kann getrennt oder angekoppelt genutzt werden.

Nicht nur im Inneren des Museums, sondern auch durch die Zuordnung der einzelnen Kulturbauten zueinander ist eine komplex vernetzte Nutzung möglich und so auch der Bildungs- und Erlebnisgehalt gesteigert.

The *exhibition hall* represents a singular structure to be erected separately.

The *museum* mirrors in its conception and structure the three major areas – art, natural science, cultural history – that are spatially and organisationally connected in a complex network. The museological conception is not based on separation but on an overlay and relation of contents in a certain dialectic, or integration. Individual learning as well as a total experience is possible. A linear didactic process is considered as well as action and reaction based on a threedimensional matrix. This interface is expanded by the study collection and the provisions of the museums laboratories which allow participation and projections into the future.

A common lobby with common supporting provisions, accesses both the exhibition hall, which will serve larger temporary exhibitions, as well as the central hall of the museum. Following a variety of routes one can experience various topics which are spread out over different levels of the building. Horizontal as well as vertical cross-references are possible.

Lecture room, administration and laboratory and other didactic services as well as the museum shop, support facilities and cafeteria are connected centrally with the foyer.

The exhibition hall (to be opened in 1996) can be used separately or in connection with the museum proper.

The complex relationship, which the network between the different areas and topics provides, is also carried further in an integrated use of the different main cultural facilities, optimizing education and experiences.

(Original translation: Hans Hollein)

Hans Hollein, NÖ. Landesmuseum
Innenperspektive von der Verteilerzone aus
Hans Hollein, Lower Austrian Provincial Museum
Interior perspective seen from distribution zone

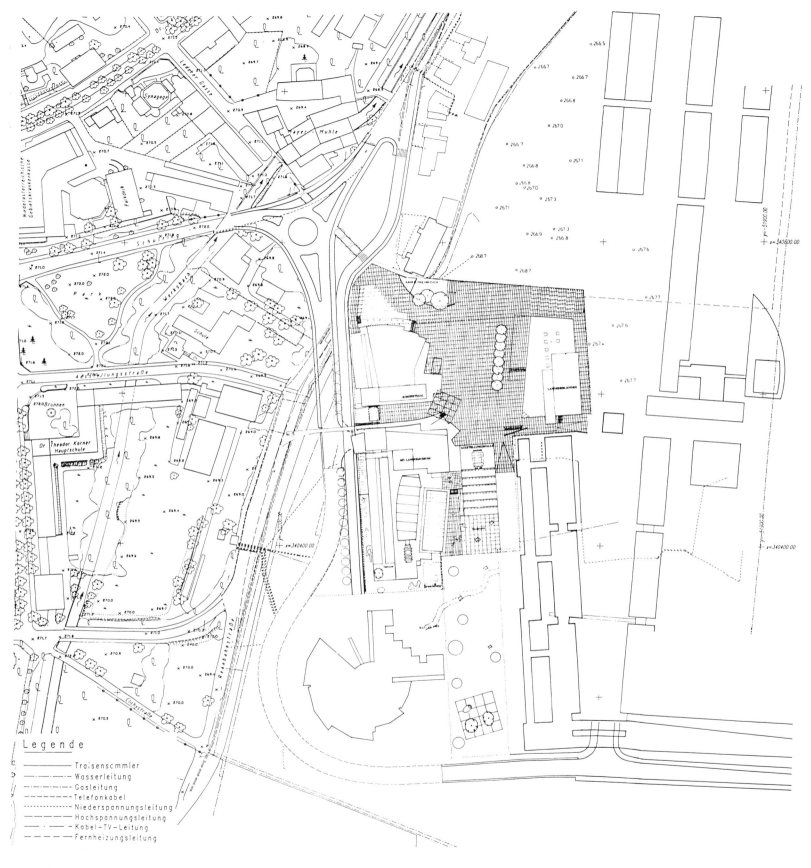

Legende

— Traisensammler
— Wasserleitung
— Gasleitung
— Telefonkabel
— Niederspannungsleitung
— Hochspannungsleitung
— Kabel-TV-Leitung
— Fernheizungsleitung

Lageplan
Siteplan

162

Hans Hollein, Modell Wettbewerb Kulturbezirk
Ansichten von Westen mit Regierungsviertel
Hans Hollein, model competition cultural precinct
West elevation with Government Quarters

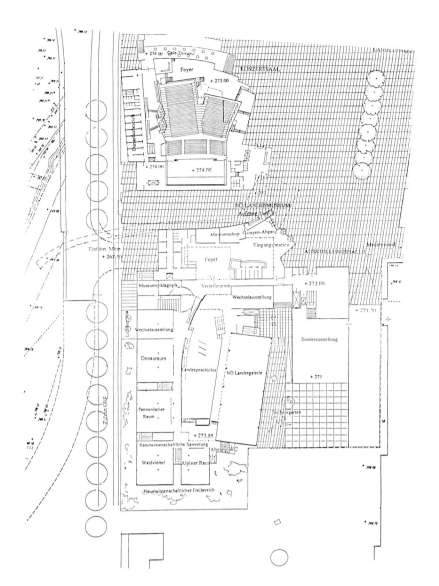

Grundriß Erdgeschoß
1st floor

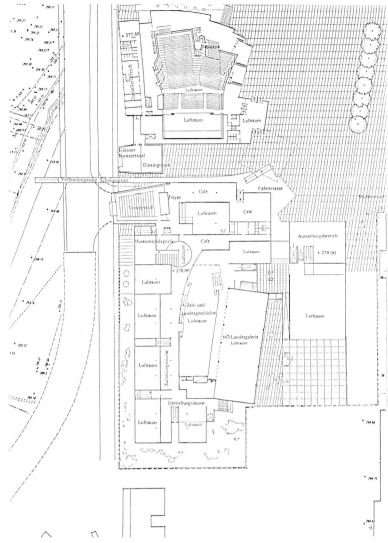

Grundriß 1. Obergeschoß
Mezzanine

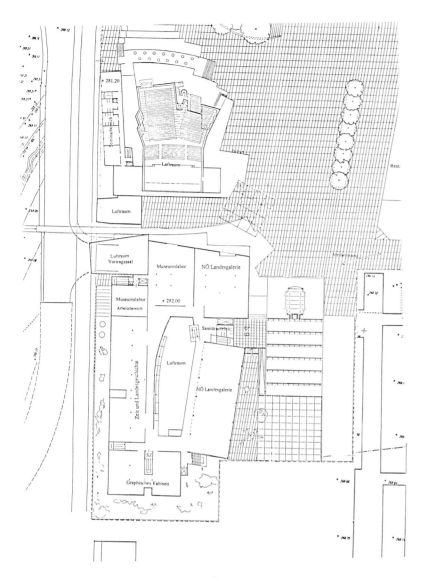

Grundriß 2. Obergeschoß
2nd floor

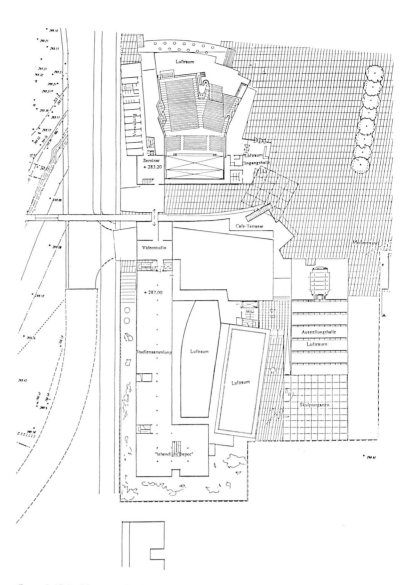

Grundriß 3. Obergeschoß
3rd floor

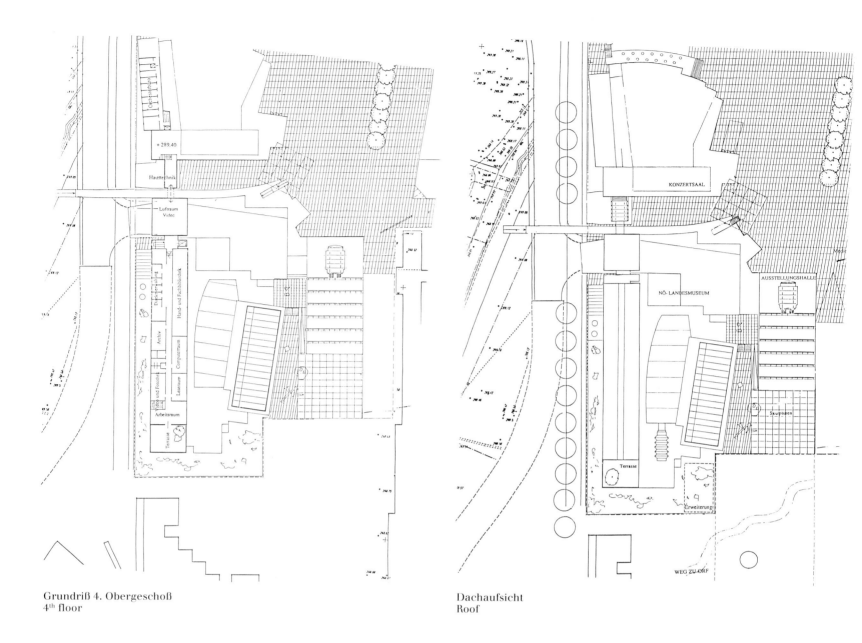

Grundriß 4. Obergeschoß
4th floor

Dachaufsicht
Roof

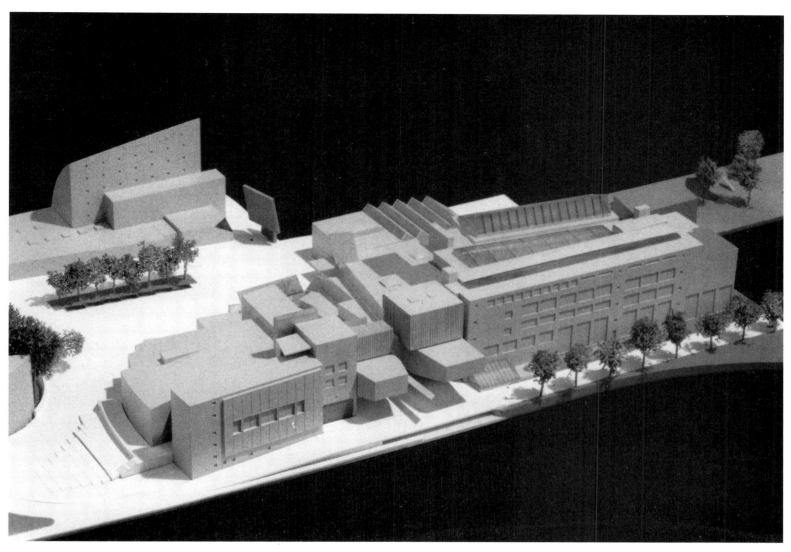

Modell Wettbewerb Kulturbezirk
Ansicht von Nordwesten, Blick von der Stadt
Regierungsviertel im Hintergrund
Model competition cultural precinct
North-west elevation, view from the city
Government Quarters in background

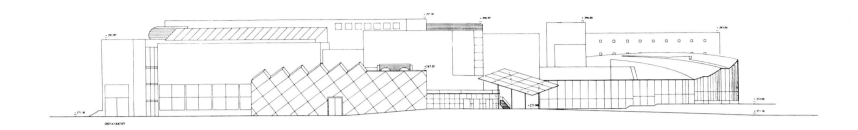

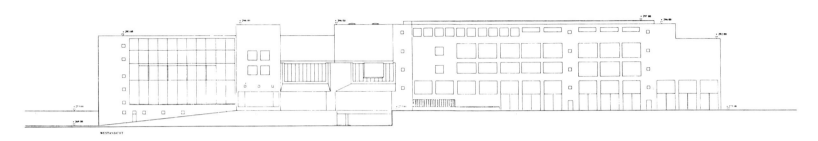

Ost-Ansicht Ausstellungshalle und Museum, Wettbewerbsentwurf
East elevation Exhibition Hall and Museum, competition design

West-Ansicht Museum und Konzerthalle, Wettbewerbsentwurf
West elevation Museum and Concert Hall, competition design

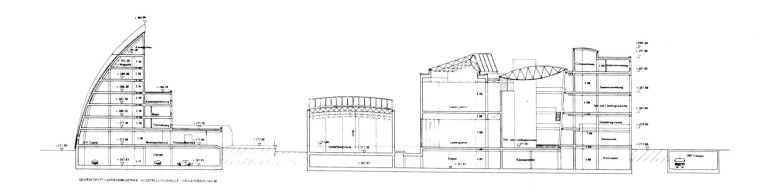

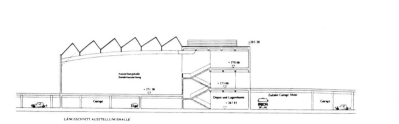

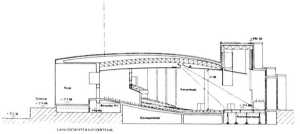

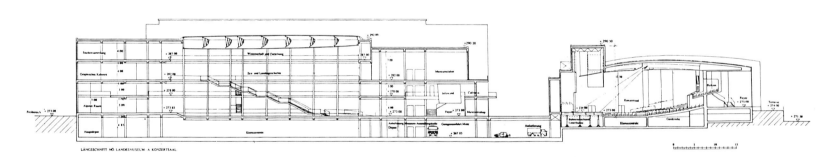

Schnitt Ost-West durch Ausstellungshalle und Museum
Section east-west Exhibition Hall and Museum

Schnitt Süd-Nord durch Ausstellungshalle
Section south-north Exhibition Hall

Schnitt Süd-Nord durch Museum und Konzerthalle
Section south-north Museum and Concert Hall

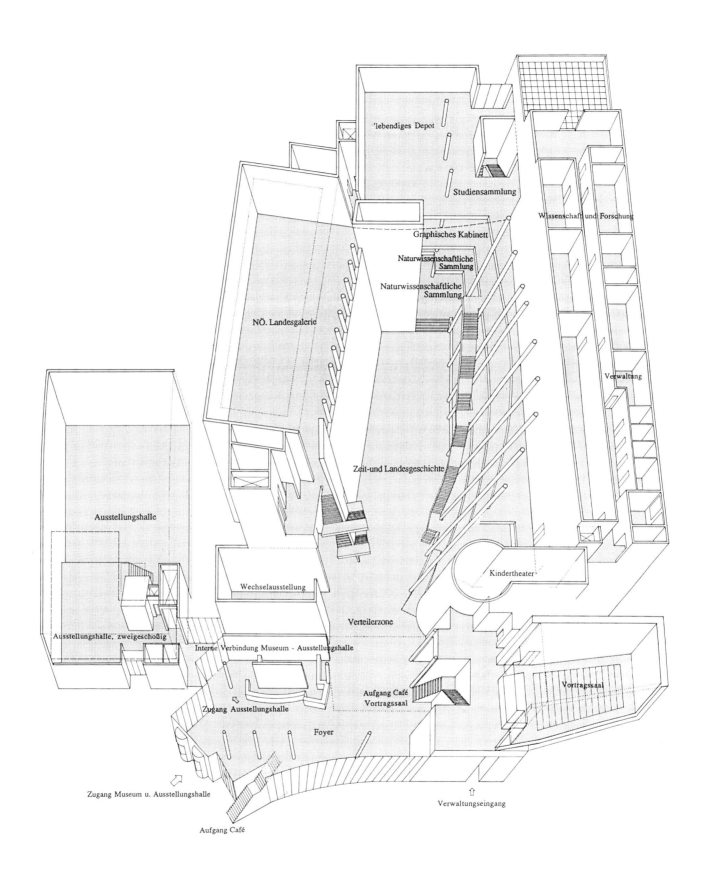

lebendiges Depot

Studiensammlung

Wissenschaft und Forschung

Graphisches Kabinett

Naturwissenschaftliche Sammlung

Naturwissenschaftliche Sammlung

NÖ. Landesgalerie

Verwaltung

Zeit- und Landesgeschichte

Ausstellungshalle

Kindertheater

Wechselausstellung

Verteilerzone

Ausstellungshalle, zweigeschoßig

Interne Verbindung Museum - Ausstellungshalle

Aufgang Café
Vortragssaal

Vortragssaal

Zugang Ausstellungshalle

Foyer

Zugang Museum u. Ausstellungshalle

Verwaltungseingang

Aufgang Café

NÖ. Landesmuseum und Ausstellungshalle
Grundriß Eingangsgeschoß mit Vernetzung der verschiedenen Museumsbereiche
Lower Austrian Provincial Museum and Exhibition Hall
Entrance level with network of various areas of the museum

Modell Wettbewerb Kulturbezirk
Ansicht von Südosten mit Museum und Ausstellungshalle links im Vordergrund
Model competition cultural precinct
South-east elevation with Museum and Exhibition Hall in left foreground

MAK – Österreichisches Museum für angewandte Kunst

Birgit Flos

»Es geht darum, den Raum der Ermattung und Verschleierung einer Probe zu unterziehen, die Kälte der Selbstgefälligkeit, der glänzenden Verschlossenheit mit der gleichzeitigen Durchdringung von Erinnerung und Utopie des Augenblicks zu begegnen, das Museum als geistigen Ort zu begreifen.«
Peter Noever

Das Österreichische Museum für angewandte Kunst in Wien wurde 1864 als »Österreichisches Museum für Kunst und Industrie« gegründet. Es besteht aus zwei Gebäuden, dem 1871 fertiggestellten Museumsbau von Heinrich von Ferstel am Stubenring und einem 1909 dazugekommenen Ausstellungstrakt von Ludwig Baumann in der Weiskirchnerstraße. 1877 war auch der Bau der Kunstgewerbeschule am Stubenring fertiggestellt. In den Statuten für das k. k. Oesterreichische Museum für Kunst und Industrie heißt es unter A, Zweck und Umfang, § 1: »Das k. k. Oesterreichische Museum für Kunst und Industrie hat die Aufgabe, durch Herbeischaffen der Hülfsmittel, welche Kunst und Wissenschaft den Kunstgewerben bieten, und durch Ermöglichung der leichteren Benützung derselben, die kunstgewerbliche Thätigkeit zu fördern und vorzugsweise zur Hebung des Geschmacks in dieser Richtung beizutragen.«
1947 wurde die Institution in »Museum für angewandte Kunst« umbenannt. Seit 1986 ist Peter Noever Direktor des Museums. Er versteht diese Aufgabe als universellen Gestaltungsauftrag aller Funktionsebenen. Das Österreichische Museum für angewandte Kunst (MAK) ist derzeit (Juni 1992) noch eine Baustelle. Hier findet nicht nur ein Museumsumbau statt, sondern die grundsätzliche Neudefinition eines Museums-Ortes. Welche museologischen Vorstellungen der Museumsgründer haben ihre Bedeutung verloren, welche können reaktiviert und neu interpretiert werden? Kann man mit dem Begriff »angewandte Kunst« noch weiter operieren? Wenn man

The Austrian Museum of Applied Art

Birgit Flos

"It is a question of subjecting a space which has become worn out and vague to a test, of confronting and simultaneously permeating its cold complacency and glorious reserve with the recollection and utopia of the moment, of viewing the museum as a place of the intellect."
Peter Noever

The *Österreichische Museum für angewandte Kunst* ('Austrian Museum of Applied Art') in Vienna was founded in 1864 as the Österreichisches Museum für Kunst und Industrie ('Museum of Art and Industry'). It consists of two buildings: the museum building on the Stubenring, designed by Heinrich von Ferstel in 1871, and an exhibition section designed by Ludwig Baumann, dating from 1909. In 1877, construction of the Kunstgewerbeschule ('College of Arts and Crafts') was also completed on the Stubenring. In the statutes for the Imperial-Royal Austrian Museum of Art and Industry it is stated under "A. Use and Extent", para. 1, that "The Imperial-Royal Austrian Museum for Art and Industry has the responsibility of procuring the resources which fine art and science have to offer the arts and crafts, and by facilitating the use of the same, to promote the practise of the arts and crafts and, most importantly, to contribute to the improvement of taste in this direction."
In 1947 the institution was renamed the Museum für angewandte Kunst. Peter Noever has been director of the museum since 1986. He regards his responsibility as comprising the general organisation of the museum on all functional levels.
The Österreichische Museum für angewandte Kunst (MAK) is at present (June 1992) still a building site. What is taking place here is not only the conversion of a museum, but the fundamental redefinition of a museum site. Which of the museological ideas of the museum's founders have lost their original significance; which of them can be reactivated and

die Kategorisierung in bildende und angewandte Kunst weitgehend aufgibt, wie unterscheidet sich ein solches Museum von
anderen Museen moderner Kunst?

Die Neudefinition des MAK ist nicht ein
weiteres, vor allem architektonisches Zeichen für das Zeitphänomen Museum, sondern hier wurde eine in erster Linie inhaltlich bezogene Signalwirkung versucht:
eine Umstrukturierung von Prioritäten.
Keine Museumsneugründung also und
auch keine Übernahme eines eingeführten
Museumstypus, sondern die schwierige
Aufgabe einer Reform von innen: Hier geht
es um die Rückführung von baulichen
Maßnahmen und Museumsaktivitäten auf
eine ursprünglich intendierte Zielsetzung
und den Versuch ihrer zeitgemäßen Über-
tragung und Öffnung.

Die gesetzten Initiativen waren und sind
auch von Infragestellung und Kritik begleitet. Ein Erfolg des Experiments MAK kann
erst nach Jahren überprüft werden, wenn
nicht das Prinzip der Bewegung, der Kon-
frontation, der Infragestellung und des Risikos, das Prozeßhafte der Aktivitäten bereits als Bestätigung dieses Ansatzes gele-
sen werden können.

Die Ausgangssituation: »Unter dem Niveau«[1]

Bei der Übernahme der Direktion Noever
im Februar 1986 war das Haus in einem
desolaten baulichen und einem indiffe-
renten inhaltlichen Zustand. Es gab weder
eine zeitgemäße Museums-Infrastruktur
noch ein eindeutiges programmatisches
Profil: »Als ich das Haus übernommen
habe, waren die Gebäude und die Idee des
Museums selbst in einem Zustand der Ver-
wahrlosung und nicht bespielbar. Eine
grundsätzliche Veränderung war zwin-
gend notwendig. Manche Räume waren so
voll belegt mit Objekten, daß sie für die
Besucher nicht mehr zugänglich waren,
außerdem gab es nicht genug Personal, um
alle Räume geöffnet zu halten.«[2] Eine Renovierung des Hauses war unumgänglich.
Noever nutzte diesen Sachzwang zu einer
Reform auf allen Funktionsebenen. Einem
baulichen Maßnahmenkatalog folgten
Überlegungen zu einer betriebsstrukturellen Neuerung und schließlich ein Über-
denken von Arbeitsstrukturen und Samm-

reinterpreted? Can one still use the concept
of 'applied art'? If one largely renounces
categorisation into fine and applied art,
then how does such a museum differ from
other museums of modern art?

The redefinition of the MAK is not a further,
primarily architectural sign of the temporal
phenomenon of the museum; rather, it is,
in the first place, an attempt to signal
something about its contents: a restructuring of priorities. The museum is thus not
being founded anew, nor is an already
established type of museum being adopted
as a model. The task being undertaken here
is, rather, the difficult one of a reform from
within: it involves a return from architectural measures and museum activities to an
original aim, and an attempt to translate
and expand it in an up-to-date fashion.

The initiatives were – and still are –
subjected to much questioning and
criticism. It will only be possible to examine
the success of the MAK experiment after
several years – unless we regard the
principle of movement, confrontation,
questioning and risk, the developmental
aspect of the activities, as being something
which itself already provides confirmation
of the initiative.

The Initial Situation:
"Not up to Standard"[1]

When Peter Noever took over direction of
the museum in February 1986, the building
was in a desolate state of repair and its
collections indifferently organised. There
was neither an up-to-date museum infrastructure nor a clear programmatic
profile: "When I took over the museum, the
building and the concept of the museum
itself were in a state of neglect and were
unpresentable. A fundamental change was
urgently needed. Some of the rooms were
so full of objects that they were no longer
accessible to the visitor; and, furthermore,
there was not enough personnel to keep all
the rooms open."[2] Renovation of the museum was unavoidable. Noever used this
material pressure for a reform on all
functional levels. A catalogue of architectural measures to be taken was followed
by considerations of how to reorganise the
administrative structure and, finally, by

Österreichisches Museum für angewandte
Kunst, Peter Noevers erstes Pressegespräch als
Direktor im Möbeldepot, 2. 2. 1987
Österreichisches Museum für angewandte
Kunst (Museum of Applied Art), Peter Noever's
first press conference as director (in the
furniture depot), 1987-02-02

Walter Pichler, Detail des Tores
Walter Pichler, detail of the door

lungspolitik. Aus diesen ineinander verzahnten Aktivitäten, deren Aktionskonzept sich Schritt für Schritt herausbildete (»es gab keine kalten Lösungen«), entwickelte sich ein Museumsbild, das in der Museumsdiskussion eine eigenständige Position bezieht.

»Zurück zur Gegenwart«[9]

Eine Neudefinition des Hauses mußte erwartungsgemäß in einen Legitimationsdruck gegenüber dem Gründungsgedanken und der Realität von 125 Jahren Museumsaktivitäten geraten. Wie kann man die Intention der Gründer zeitgemäß übersetzen, ohne sie nur denkmalpflegerisch zu kopieren und weiterzuschreiben? »Die einzige Existenzberechtigung einer solchen Institution ist, daß sie sich selbständig aus der Tradition entwickelt und sich dann von anderen Museumsinstitutionen unterscheidet.« Die ursprüngliche Leitlinie des Museums schrieb vor, die Vorbildhaftigkeit in Geschmack und Ästhetik an älteren Beispielen zu demonstrieren, gleichzeitig war das Museum als eine lebendige Institution mit einem starken Gegenwartsbezug geplant. Der affirmativ pädagogische Ansatz, die Vorbildfunktion der zu sammelnden Objekte zum Kriterium der Weiterführung der Sammlung und deren Präsentation zu machen, entspricht weder der Ambivalenz gefestigten Werten gegenüber noch dem Bedürfnis nach Öffnung, Auseinandersetzung und Widerspruch. »Die Beibehaltung dieser Art von Vorbildhaftigkeit hätte den Erstickungstod des Museums bedeutet. Das Kunsthandwerk kann nach der Industrialisierung des Fertigungsprozesses nicht mehr diese Bedeutung haben, es gehört im schlimmsten Fall eher zur Tourismusgeschichte.« Das MAK sieht auch weiterhin seine Aufgabe in der kontinuierlichen Befassung mit der Entwicklung der Produktkultur (ohne sich zum industriehörigen Design-Center reduzieren zu lassen), es soll aber die zweite Komponente des Gründungsgedankens – der aktive Gegenwartsbezug – im Vordergrund stehen: der Dialog mit zeitgenössischen Künstlern und ihren Werken. »Es geht darum, daß man leblose historische Objekte, die ihre Bedeutung nur durch eine Neubewertung er-

a reconsideration of working structures and collecting policy. From these interrelated activities, out of which a concept of action emerged step by step ("there were no cold solutions"), the picture emerged of a museum which adopts its own independent position in the museum debate.

"Back to the Present"[3]

As expected, redefinition of the museum encountered pressure to legitimise its position with regard to the ideas of the founders and the reality of the museum's 125 years of activity. How can one translate the intentions of the founders in an up-to-date way without simply copying them, in the sense of preserving a historical monument, and then continuing to write from where they left off? "The only justification for the existence of such an institution is that it develops independently from the tradition and then differs from other such institutions." The museum's original guidelines stipulated that it should demonstrate exemplariness in taste and aesthetics, although at the same time it was planned as a living institution with a strong connection to the contemporary world. The affirmative pedagogical initiative of making the objects which are to be collected a criterion for the continuation of the collection and its presentation, corresponds neither to the ambivalence of established values, nor to the need for openness, confrontation and contradiction. "Maintenance of this kind would have meant suffocation of the museum. After the industrialisation of the manufacturing process, crafts can no longer have this meaning; at worst, they belong to the history of tourism." The MAK also continues to see its role as being one of constant involvement with the evolution of the product culture (without allowing itself to be reduced to a design centre in the service of industry), although the second component of the founding idea, that of having an active relation to the present, should be in the foreground. "It is a question of having to examine the strengh and actuality of lifeless historical objects, which maintain their significance only through re-evaluation.

halten, überprüfen muß auf ihre Kraft und Aktualität. Das Museum des 19. Jahrhunderts als Ort der Bewahrung von versteinerten Betrachtungs- und Auffassungsweisen hat sich längst überholt.«

Es geht vor allem um die Schaffung neuer räumlicher Qualitäten. Auch das ist nicht nur architektonisch gemeint: das Museum soll ein geistiger Ort sein, ein Ort der Auseinandersetzung, Forschung und Anschauung, auf jeden Fall aber ein Ort der Gegenwart. Daraus ergibt sich die programmatische Hinwendung zur zeitgenössischen Kunst. »Initialzündungen entstehen in der Kunst und nicht im ›industrial design‹. Es gibt keine angewandte Kunst ohne Kunst.«

Es entsteht ein vermeintlicher Interessenskonflikt zwischen der Tradition (der Betreuung und Weiterführung der kostbaren Sammlungsbestände) und der programmatischen Gegenwartsorientierung (neuer Sammlungsschwerpunkt: Gegenwartskunst, Betonung der Ausstellungsaktivitäten). Die Sammlungen sollen in neuer signifikanter Aufstellung zugänglich gemacht werden. »Aber die Energie soll viel stärker auf die Bereiche Wissenschaft und Forschung gelegt werden. Das heißt: vorhandene Objekte werden bearbeitet, verwendet und nach neuen Gesichtspunkten und Zusammenhängen erforscht.« Es werden also vor allem auch Informationen gesammelt. Intendiert ist ein Durchdringen der Sammlungen mit zeitgenössischen Formen des Zugangs. Der wichtigste programmatische Schwerpunkt wird deutlich: die intensive Einbeziehung der Künstler in alle Museumsaktivitäten. Noever hat immer wieder scharfe Formulierungen gefunden, wenn Künstler bei Ausstellungsinszenierungen zu Animateuren oder zu bloßen Ingredenzien für das Ausstellungsfertiggericht gemacht wurden. Im MAK sollen die Künstler, »die als wesentliche Kräfte für diese Zeit bestimmend erscheinen«, metaphorisch oder auch buchstäblich »Wohnung, Baustelle und Werkstatt« haben.

Im Herbst 1988 wurde die Abteilung für Gegenwartskunst eingerichtet. »Wir sammeln in erster Linie keine Malerei, sondern wir sammeln aus Grenzbereichen, räumliche Installationen, Architektur im weitesten Sinn.« Ein weiterer Schritt ist das Sam-

The 19th century museum as a place of preserving fossilised ways of looking and thinking has long since become outmoded."

It is above all a question of creating new spatial qualities. That, too, is not intended in a purely architectural sense: the museum should be a place of intellectuality, a place of confrontation, research and contemplation, at all events a place of the present. This results in the programmatic turning of attention to contemporary art. "The booster detonations occur in art and not in 'industrial design'. There is no applied art without art."

An apparent conflict of interests is developing between tradition (the care and continuation of the valuable collection) and the programmatic orientation to the present (new focus of the collection: contemporary art, with the emphasis on exhibition activities). The collections should be made accessible, exhibited in a new, more meaningful way. "But much more energy should also be spent on the areas of academic studies and research. That means that existing objects are worked on, used and researched from new aspects and in new contexts." This primarily means that information is gathered. The intention is to make all the collections accessible through contemporary approaches. The most important programmatic focus is becoming clear: intensive involvement of the artists in all the museum's activities. Time and again, Noever has made cutting remarks about artists being used as animators, or simply ingredients for the finished 'exhibition meal'. The artists, who "seem to be decisive as the vital forces of our time", should be able to find "a place to live, a building site and a workshop" in the MAK (metaphorically speaking – or even literally-speaking).

In autumn 1988, the department for contemporary art was installed. "We collect in the first place not paintings but works of art from fringe areas, spatial installations, architecture in the broadest sense." A further step is the collection and production of essential information about important artists and their products. The main activities of the new/old museum are exhibitions, publications, symposia, lectures

Dachoberlicht über dem zentralen Innenhof
Skylight over the central courtyard

Peter Noever, Detail Terrassenplateau
Peter Noever, detail of the terrace

Torbogen, zukünftiger Buchladen,
Entwurf von SITE/James Wines
Arch, future bookshop, designed by
SITE/James Wines

Dachoberlicht über dem zentralen Innenhof
Skylight over the central courtyard

meln und Produzieren essentieller Informationen über bedeutende Künstler und ihre Produkte. Die Hauptaktivitäten des neuen alten Museums sind Ausstellungen, Publikationen, Symposien, Vorträge und Filmvorführungen, die sich spezifisch mit zeitgenössischen Strömungen auseinandersetzen. Auch das alte Museum für Kunst und Industrie hatte ein vielfältiges Veranstaltungsprogramm, auch hier wird eher das Bemühen um eine Intensivierung und Neustrukturierung deutlich als ein radikaler Bruch oder das ersatzlose Auflassen ehemaliger Aktivitäten.

Der Umgang mit den Sammlungen ist ein Grundelement der Definition des Hauses. »Wichtig ist das Demonstrieren einer klaren Vorstellung. Man kann nicht immer weitersammeln. Es geht nicht darum, Vollständigkeit anzustreben, Lücken zu schließen. Das Fragmentarische ist immer das Interessantere.« Noever bringt das Beispiel des Archivs der Wiener Werkstätte. Hier steht dem Museum eine repräsentative Sammlung eines kunstgeschichtlichen Phänomens zur Verfügung, die wie viele andere Teilbereiche der Sammlung noch lange nicht vollständig aufgearbeitet ist. »Ich würde sagen, die Sammlung der Wiener Werkstätte ist abgeschlossen, man könnte natürlich in 500 Jahren zu diesem Thema noch weiter sammeln.« Es können also Sammlungen abgeschlossen werden. Mit dem Entschluß zum Erwerb der Bugholzmöbel-Kollektion der Sammlung Vegesack wurde 1986 aber auch demonstriert, daß das Sammeln exemplarischer Produkte früherer Epochen weiter zur Museumsstrategie gehört. Aber dieser Punkt der Sammlungsfortführung oder Schwerpunktverlagerung ist sicher auch weiterhin Anlaß für Diskussion und Kontroversen. Die Energie soll jetzt stärker auf die Bereiche Wissenschaft und Forschung verlagert werden. »Es gilt, zentrale und historische Begriffe der Kunstgeschichte thematisch zu untersuchen, sie einer kritischen Theorie gegenüberzustellen, um auch in diesem Bereich einen Prozeß der ›theoretischen Neugierde‹ einzuleiten.«

»Museum im Aufbruch«

Die Umstrukturierung des MAK erfolgt in

and film shows which deal specifically with contemporary trends. The old *Museum für Kunst und Industrie* ('Museum for Art and Industry') also used to have a varied programme of events; and here, too, it is the attempt at intensification and restructuring that becomes apparent, rather than a radical break with former activities or a move to abandon them without having anything replace them with.

The treatment of the collections is a fundamental part of defining the museum. "What is important is to demonstrate a clarity of concept. One cannot always just continue to collect. It is not a matter of striving for completeness, of filling gaps. The fragmentary aspect is always the more interesting one." Noever gives the example of the archive of the Vienna Workshops, where the museum has a representative collection of this phenomenon in the history of art at its disposal; like many other partial areas of the collection, it has still not been exhaustively dealt with. "I would say that the Vienna Workshops collection is complete, although it would of course still be possible to collect works from this area even in 500 years time." Thus collections can be completed. However, the decision to acquire the collection of bent-wood furniture from the Vegesack Collection in 1986, demonstrated that collecting exemplary products from earlier periods still forms part of the museum's strategy. Nevertheless, this question of whether to continue a collection or shift its emphasis elsewhere certainly continues to be a subject of discussion and controversy. More energy should now be spent on the fields of academic studies and research. "It is a matter of thematically investigating the central and historical concepts of art history, studying them from the point of view of critical theory, so as to introduce a process of 'theoretical curiosity' into this field too."

"New Museum Departures"

The work of restructuring the MAK is being carried out in an atmosphere of programmatic transparency (with all the accompanying media attention). This manner of proceeding should be seen as a component

einer programmatischen Transparenz (und der damit verbundenen Medienpräsenz). Diese Vorgehensweise ist als Bestandteil der Neuerungsstrategien zu sehen. Band I und II der Manuskripte des MAK, »Museum im Aufbruch«[4], liegen derzeit vor. »Um sich die geeignete Ausgangsbasis für eine offensive und professionelle Museumsarbeit zu schaffen, wurden die baulichen, betriebswirtschaftlichen, organisatorischen und personellen Grundlagen des MAK überprüft, in Form von Studien, die zwar die Gegebenheiten des österreichischen Museums für angewandte Kunst zum Gegenstand hatten, aber beispielhaft auch für die anderen Bundesmuseen und letztendlich für die gesamte österreichische Museumslandschaft Gültigkeit haben sollen.«[5]

Bereits zwei Monate nach Noevers Antritt als Direktor wurde die Studie »Bestand und Neuordnung« in Auftrag gegeben: eine kritische Bestandsaufnahme der baulichen und inhaltlichen Situation des Museums. Es wurden von einer Reihe von Spezialisten (von der Haustechnik bis zur Architektur) Bedingungen und Vorschläge für eine bauliche Sanierung erarbeitet. Die Studie war Grundlage für den eigentlichen Umbau. Bauliche Entscheidungen können hier nachvollzogen werden: Durch den Neubau eines Tiefspeichers werden Räume als Ausstellungsflächen frei, die über die Jahre zu Depots zugewachsen waren. Auch hier erfolgte eine Rückführung auf ursprünglich gewollte Funktionsebenen. Der Umbau wird nicht als verschleierter Revitalisierungsversuch der alten Baumasse verstanden. An der alten Bausubstanz sollten keine Verletzungen entstehen, eine nostalgische Fassadenkosmetik wurde ebenfalls abgelehnt. »Es ist noch nicht einmal eine einzige Tür rekonstruiert worden.«

Es folgte 1987 Band II der MAK-Manuskripte, die »Dienstleistungsstudie«, eine Studie über resonanz- und einnahmensteigernde privatwirtschaftliche Dienstleistungen. »Die Studie war nicht nur die Grundlage für eine Reihe privatwirtschaftlicher Initiativen, die das MAK in der Folge im Rahmen seines Förderungsvereins, der ›Gesellschaft für österreichische Kunst‹ setzte, sondern sie hat vielmehr in entscheidendem Maße die Einführung der sogenann-

part of the renovation strategy. Volumes I and II of the manuscripts of the MAK, *Museum im Aufbruch* ('New Museum Departures')[4] are now available. "In order to create a suitable basis for professional museum work, one which takes the offensive, studies were carried out into the underlying foundations of the MAK with regard to its architecture, management, organisation and personnel. Although their subject was indeed the affairs of the Museum of Applied Art, they should nevertheless also serve as examples for the Federal museums and, finally, for the Austrian museum landscape in general."[5] Only two months after Noever started as Director, the study *Bestand und Neuordnung* ('The Collections and Reorganisation') was commissioned, being a critical inventory of the situation with regard to the museum's architecture and collections. A number of specialists (in fields ranging from service and equipment engineering to architecture) were employed to work out prerequisites and proposals for renovation of the building. The study became the basis for the actual alterations. Architectural deliberations resulted in the decision to construct a new underground storeroom, so that those rooms which over the years had come to be used as depots would be free to serve as exhibition areas. Here too there was a return to the levels of function which had been originally desired. The conversion is not to be understood as a veiled attempt at the revitalisation of old architectural material. No damage was to be done to the old architectural substance, and nostalgic cosmetic treatment for the facades was also rejected. "Up until now, not one single door has been reconstructed."

In 1987 followed Volume II of the MAK manuscripts, *Dienstleistungsstudie* ('Services Study'), a study of services in the private sector which could bring an increased response and income. "The study not only formed the basis for a series of initiatives in the private sector, which MAK subsequently undertook within the framework of the Society for Austrian Art, its association for the promotion of the arts, but also influenced and accelerated to a decisive degree the introduction of so-

Detail der Lichtdecke
Detail of the skylight

Detail der Stufen zum Terrassenplateau
Detail of the steps leading to the terrace

ten Teilrechtsfähigkeit der Bundesmuseen beeinflußt und beschleunigt. Vom Gesetzgeber wurde den Bundesmuseen mit 1. Juli 1989 zugestanden, in einem genau definierten Rahmen privatwirtschaftlich tätig zu werden und die Erlöse aus dieser Tätigkeit ›zur Erfüllung ihrer Zwecke‹ zu verwenden.«[6] Ohne dieses Gesetz der Teilrechtsfähigkeit von 1987 wären wesentliche Änderungen in den Arbeitsstrukturen nicht möglich gewesen. Schwierigkeiten bei der notwendigen Neudefinition der Aufgabenbereiche liegen auch im Dienstrecht und in den zementierten verbeamteten Strukturen. Auf Grund dieser und der dritten Studie von Christian Reder, »Neue Sammlungspolitik und Neue Arbeitsstruktur«, hat sich ein Reformbeirat gebildet, der bis Ende 1992 ein Konzept für die neue Organisation des Hauses erarbeiten soll. Die neu zu verteilenden Rollen orientieren sich an der Doppelstruktur des Hauses: den Daueraufgaben (Sammlungen) und den verstärkt projektorientierten Organisationsformen. Bisher abzusehen ist, daß in der Organisationsstruktur eine zweite Ebene zwischen Direktor und Museumsmitarbeitern einzuziehen ist, die Ebene je eines »senior curators« für die Sammlungen und für Austellungen.

Es ist hier nicht möglich, auf die Problemstellungen und die Vorschläge zu einer Neuorientierung im Detail einzugehen. Es erschien aber wichtig, darauf hinzuweisen, daß die neue Definition des Museums bis in diese Ebene der betriebsstrukturellen Verflechtungen reicht. Die Studien des MAK sind wesentlicher Teil der Neuerungsdynamik: Information, Auseinandersetzung, Kontroverse, einschließlich des Risikos der Öffentlichkeit. Die skeptischen und kritischen Stimmen gegenüber der Neugestaltung des Museums kommen ebenfalls zu Wort, sie werden am Schluß von Band III eher kursorisch gesammelt präsentiert.

»Transformation eines Ortes«[7]

Im April 1990 ist der Tiefspeicher fertiggestellt worden. »Hiermit steht dem MAK eine zusätzliche Nutzfläche für die Sammlungsbestände von 3.400 m² zur Verfügung. Kunstobjekte sind nach den neuesten in-

called partial legal responsibility for the Federal museums. On 1st July 1989 the legislator allowed the Federal museums to become active, within exactly defined limits, in the private business sector and to use the proceeds of this activity for the "accomplishment of its own aims".[6] Without the 1987 law relating to partial legal responsibility, essential changes in the working structure would not have been possible. There are also difficulties with the necessary redefinition of the scope of responsibilities in employment law and in the rigid structures relating to permanent official posts. On the basis of this and the third study by Christian Reder, *Neue Sammlungspolitik und Neue Arbeitsstruktur* ('New Collecting Policy and New Working Structure'), a reform committee was established to elaborate a concept for the reorganisation of the museum by the end of 1992. The new roles to be allotted are oriented to the twofold structure of the museum: the permanent responsibilities (collections) and the increased project-oriented forms of organisation. So far, it is foreseen that a second level will be introduced into the organisational structure, between the director and the employees of the museum, that of two 'senior curators', responsible for the collections and for exhibitions respectively.

It is not possible here to enter into more detail concerning the problems of reorientation and the proposals for their solution, although it is important to point out that the redefinition of the museum extends to the level of the interconnections within the organisational structure. The studies of the MAK are an essential part of the dynamics of renewal: information, confrontation, controversy and even the hazard of publicity. Those voices which are sceptical and critical towards the museum's reorganisation are also allowed their say, and a collection of their views are presented at the end of Volume III.

"Transformation of a Location"[7]

In April 1990 the underground storage area was completed. "With this, the MAK has an additional area of 3,400 m² at its disposal for the contents of the collection. Art objects

Tiefspeicher, fertiggestellt 1990
Underground storage area, completed 1990

ternationalen Erkenntnissen bezüglich Klimatechnik, Archivierung und Sicherheit gelagert«.[8] Durch die baulichen Maßnahmen im Keller und Tiefspeicherbereich ist auch die Einrichtung einer Studiensammlung möglich geworden. Sie wird materialbezogen (gemäß der Arbeitsstruktur des Hauses) und seriell präsentiert werden. Es wird ein Café geben (Hermann Czech), einen neuen Lesesaal der Bibliothek (Aichwalder/Strobl), eine Buchhandlung mit einem von den Öffnungszeiten des Museums unabhängigen Eingang: Tor zum Stubenring (Architektengruppe Site, New York). Die Einbeziehung der Gartenanlage in den Ausstellungs- und Museumsbetrieb stellt eine weitere wesentliche Erweiterung dar: das Tor zum Garten (Walter Pichler), das Terrassenplateau (Peter Noever). Außerdem wurde die MAK-Galerie eingerichtet und ein Verbindungstrakt zwischen dem Museum am Stubenring und dem Ausstellungsgebäude von Ludwig Baumann in der Weiskirchnerstraße von Sepp Müller errichtet. Müller (einer der Autoren von »Bestand und Neuordnung«) ist auch der verantwortliche Architekt für den gesamten Umbau.

Die Neuaufstellung der Schausammlungen

Die Neuerung, die vielleicht am deutlichsten die gegenwartsbezogene Grundausrichtung des MAK dokumentiert, ist die Idee der künstlerischen Interventionen in den Schausälen im Gebäude am Stubenring. Die Sammlungen des Hauses sind materialbezogen strukturiert. Bis zur ersten Neuaufstellung 1988 war diese Vorgehensweise auch bei den Schausammlungen maßgebend. Nun wurde einer Objektschau nach Epochen der Vorzug gegeben. Die Neuaufstellung nach dem Umbau erfolgt weitgehend chronologisch. Diese Vorgangsweise wird gleichzeitig durch ein inhaltliches Kriterium gebrochen: Kein möglichst vollständiger Überblick über die Epochen wird angeboten, sondern das Museum stellt seine Stärken aus, seine exemplarischen »Highlights«. Außerdem ist auch bei den Schausammlungen an möglichst flexible Lösungen gedacht, die häufigen Objektwechsel zulassen.

are stored in accordance with the latest international knowledge as regards air-conditioning technology, archive records and security."[8] The building measures undertaken in the cellar and underground storage areas have meant that it has also become possible to set up a study collection. This will be arranged according to materials (following the general working organisation of the museum) and presented serially. There will be a cafe (Hermann Czech), a new reading room in the library (Aichwalder/Strobl), and a bookshop which is independent of the museum opening times, with its own separate entrance: the door on to Stubenring (SITE architects' group, New York). The inclusion of the garden complex in the public exhibition and museum work represents another important step; the new designs here are the door to the garden (Walter Pichler), and the terrace plateau (Peter Noever). The MAK Gallery was established, and a connecting block, designed by Sepp Müller, between the museum on the Stubenring and Ludwig Baumann's exhibition building in the Weiskirchnerstrasse, has already been finished. Müller (one of the authors of *Bestand und Neuordnung*) is also the architect responsible for the conversion work as a whole.

The Reorganisation of the Public Collections

The innovation which most clearly documents the fundamental contemporary orientation of the MAK is the idea of artistic participation in the design of the exhibition rooms in the building on the Stubenring. The museum's collections are organised according to materials. Until the first reorganisation in 1988 this method also predominated in the collections on exhibition. Then, for the first time in many years, an exhibition of objects grouped according to period was given preference. The arrangement after the conversion will, to a large extent, be chronological. Yet, at the same time, this method will also be broken with, due to the criterion for determining which objects shall be exhibited: the presentation will comprise not a complete review of the centuries, but show the

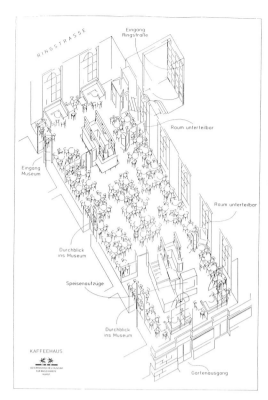

Hermann Czech, neues Museums-Café
Hermann Czech, new museum cafeteria

Neue MAK-Galerie, Ausstellung Kiki Smith, »Silent Work«
New MAK gallery, exhibition Kiki Smith, "Silent Work"

Hermann Czech, Renovierung des Museums-Cafés
Hermann Czech, renovation of the museum cafeteria

Mit der Gestaltung der Neuaufstellung in den Schausälen wurden Künstler beauftragt. Sie werden ihre je individuellen Vorstellungen entwickeln, wie die wichtigsten Objekte der permanenten Sammlungen zu präsentieren sind. Bewußt wurden – bis auf das Designer/Künstler-Duo Eichinger oder Knechtl – keine Architekten, Designer oder Ausstellungsgestalter für diese Aufgabe ausgewählt. Die beteiligten Künstler stehen zum ersten Mal einer solchen Aufgabe gegenüber. Wieder geht es um die Aktualisierung historischer Objekte, um die Verbindung von Tradition mit aktueller Gegenwart. »Die angewandte Kunst hat nur Sinn, wenn sie von aktueller Kunst interpretiert wird«, ist eine der programmatischen Aussagen von Noever. Hier geschieht eine Verbindung von alt und neu auf einer risikoreichen, sehr direkten Ebene. »Es gibt die Fehlmeinung, daß alte Dinge auf jeden Fall zusammenpassen. Dabei gibt es immer Widersprüche. Immer prallen die verschiedensten Dinge aufeinander, die nicht zusammenpassen. Schon jetzt ergibt sich im Haus folgende Situation: Biedermeiermöbel stehen in Räumen historistischer Renaissancearchitektur. Warum sollten dann nicht Künstler mit ihrer heutigen Sicht in den Räumen Eingriffe vornehmen? Das ist kein radikalerer Akt als diese Mischung früherer Epochen.« Leitgedanke ist wieder die neue Qualität von Räumen und eine produktive Komplexität von Situationen. »Künstler denken viel analytischer, sie versuchen das Wesen einer Sache herauszuarbeiten, sie arbeiten inhaltlich.« Natürlich konnte es nicht die Aufgabe der Künstler sein, originelle Vitrinen zu entwerfen, vielmehr geht es um ein sensibles Neudurchdringen der Bestände, damit die historischen Sammlungen durch möglichst unterschiedliche Gesichtspunkte zum Leben erweckt werden. »Künstler haben großen Respekt vor den Dingen und sind gleichzeitig an einer Transformation und an Fragen der Präsentation interessiert.« Bisher scheint das Experiment – zumindest in den intensiven interaktiven Prozessen – zu gelingen. Die Künstler haben sich eingehend mit »ihren« Objekten auseinandergesetzt, die ihnen von den zuständigen Kustoden (die auch die Objektauswahl treffen) nahegebracht

museum's strengths, its unique highlights. Furthermore, it is intended to adopt the most flexible solutions possible for the public collections, so as to allow for frequent changes of objects.

Artists have been commissioned to design the reorganisation of the exhibition halls. They will all develop their own individual ideas of how the most important objects in the permanent collections should be presented. As a deliberate policy, no architects, designers or exhibition organisers were selected for this task, with the exception of the designer/artist-duo Eichinger or Knechtl. For the artists involved it is the first time that they have been confronted with such a task. Once again, it is a question of bringing historic objects up to date, of combining tradition with what is contemporary. "Applied art is only justified when it is interpreted by contemporary art", is one of Noever's programmatic statements. Here, the relationship between the old and the new is on a most hazardous and very direct level. "There exists the mistaken opinion that old things fit together regardless of anything else. However, there are always contradictions. The most varied things are always clashing with one another. Even at present there is the following situation: Biedermeier furniture is standing in rooms decorated in a historicistic Renaissance style. Why, then, should artists not design the rooms from a present-day point of view? This is not any more radical than such a mixture of earlier periods." The central idea here is once more the quality of the rooms and a productive complexity of situations. "Artists think much more analytically, they attempt to discover the nature of a subject, they work on the subject-matter." Of course, it could not be the task of the artist to "design original display cases", rather it is a question of endowing the historical collections with a new and sensitive quality, so that they are brought to life from a variety of standpoints. "Artists have a great respect for objects, and at the same time they are also interested in transformation and questions of presentation." Up until now, the experiment seems to have been successful, at least in the intensive, interactive processes which are going on. The artists have made in-depth

wurden. Dann haben sie ein Konzept zur Präsentation der Objekte ausgearbeitet. Da es sich hier noch um ein »work in progress« handelt, erscheint es nicht sinnvoll, die bisher vorliegenden Künstlervorschläge zu diskutieren. Eine Auflistung ihrer Zuordnung zu den verschiedenen Epochen soll hier genügen. Die Auswahl der Künstler erfolgte intuitiv, subjektiv.

Saal IV: Günther Förg, München: Romanik, Gotik, Renaissance, Kurator: Angela Völker; Saal III: Donald Judd, Marfa/Texas: Barock, Rokoko, Klassizismus, Kurator: Christian Witt-Dörring; Saal V: Franz Graf, Wien: Barock, Rokoko (Spitzen und Gläser), Kurator: Völker; Saal VI: Jenny Holzer, New York: Empire, Biedermeier, Kurator: Witt-Dörring; Saal VII: Barbara Bloom, New York: Historismus, Jugendstil (Bugholzmöbel), Kurator: Witt-Dörring; Saal VIII: Gang Art, Wien: Orient, Kurator: Völker, Saal IX: Manfred Wakolbinger, Wien: Architektur, Design, Kurator: Brigitte Huck; Saal X: Eichinger oder Knechtl, Wien: Jugendstil, Art Deco, Kurator: Waltraud Neuwirth; Saal XI: Heimo Zobernig, Wien: Wiener Werkstätte, Kurator: Elisabeth Schmuttermeier; Saal XII: Peter Noever: Gegenwartskunst.

»Das Museum als kulturelle Zeitmaschine«[9]

Die Symposien, die das MAK immer wieder als »schöne Parallelaktionen«[10] veranstaltet, sind auch ein Zeichen für seine Neuorientierung. Die Schwerpunktthemen dieser Veranstaltungen sind gleichzeitig Interpretations- und Argumentationshilfen bei eigenen Aktivitäten und in aktuellen Kontroversen.

Abschließend seien hier einige Statements zur Phänomenologie des Museums vom vorletzten Tag des Symposions »Das Museum als kulturelle Zeitmaschine« zitiert (in Form einer Kurzmitschrift[11]). Eine zusätzliche deskriptive Ebene, um besonders die informellen Aktivitäten des MAK zu beschreiben, die über eine baulich architektonische Neuorientierung hinausgehen.

Beat Wyss (Zürich) äußerte fünf Thesen zur Frage, was das Museum einmal war: 1. Die Geburt des bürgerlichen Museums ereignete sich nach der Liquidation des

studies of 'their' objects, informed about them by the respective custodians (who also select the objects). Then they elaborate a concept for the presentation of the objects. Since it is here a matter of work in progress, it does not seem very sensible to discuss the proposals that the artists have made so far. A list of the various periods to which they have been assigned should suffice for the present purposes. The selection of the artists was made on an intuitive, subjective basis.

Room IV: Günther Förg, Munich: Romanesque, Gothic, Renaissance. Curator: Angela Völker; Room III: Donald Judd, Marfa/Texas: Baroque, Rococo, Classicism. Curator: Christian Witt-Doerring; Room V: Franz Graf, Vienna: Baroque, Rococo (lace and glass). Curator: Völker; Room VI: Jenny Holzer, New York: Empire, Biedermeier. Curator: Witt-Doerring; Room VII: Barbara Bloom, New York: Historicism, Jugendstil (bent-wood furniture). Curator: Witt-Doerring; Room VIII: Gang Art, Vienna: Orient. Curator: Völker. Room IX: Manfred Wakolbinger, Vienna: architecture, design. Curator: Waltraud Neuwirth; Room X: Eichinger or Knechtl, Vienna: Jugendstil, Art Deco. Curator: Waltraud Neuwirth; Room XI: Heimo Zobernig, Vienna: Vienna workshops. Curator: Elisabeth Schmuttermeier; Room XII: Peter Noever: contemporary art.

"The Museum as a Cultural Time Machine"[9]

The symposia which the MAK time and again organises as "good parallel actions"[10] are also a sign of its reorientation. At the same time, the main themes of these events help in the interpretation and discussion of its own activities and current controversies. Finally, here are a few statements (in the form of a short record) about the phenomenology of the museum from the penultimate day of the symposium The Museum as a Cultural Time Machine.[10] In providing an additional, descriptive level, it becomes possible to describe especially those informal activities of the MAK which go beyond constructional and architectural reorientation.

Beat Wyss (Zurich) offered five theses on

Symposion, *Das Museum als kulturelle Zeitmaschine*, 1990
Symposium, *The Museum as a Cultural Time-Machine*, 1990

Königtums. Die erste Ausstellung der Besitztümer der französischen Könige and 1793 nach der Enthauptung des Bürgers Louis Capet im Louvre statt. Es handelte sich hier um eine Enteignung des Absolutismus.

2. Das Museum funktionierte als ästhetische Kirche, nach der Revolution erfolgte ein Entleerungsprozeß aller traditionellen öffentlichen Räume (»jakobinische Peristaltik«). Nachdem die Revolution zum Teil durch einen blühenden Kunsthandel finanziert wurde, entstanden (zunächst leere) Räume für eine neue Kunstreligion. Ein Hinweis auch für die Debatte über eine adäquate Museumsarchitektur: »Das Museum ist immer auch ein Denkmal und kann in diesem Sinn leer sein. Es ist der Raum, in dem sich das Volk als Souverän fühlt.«

3. Das Museum als nationale Bundeslade. Trotz bürgerlichem Druck seit Beginn des 19. Jahrhunderts waren die Herrscher nicht gewillt, Kunstschätze aus ihren Residenzen öffentlich zugänglich zu machen. Erst als nach der Niederlage Napoleons der preußische Kulturbesitz zurückkkam, erfolgte ein Zugeständnis an den Patriotismus, die Werke wurden nicht wieder in den Wohnzimmern der Herrscher aufgehängt, sondern es wurde ein Museum gegründet.

4. Das Museum als Lehrpfad der Geschichte. Das erste Museum in Preußen, das von Schinkel erbaute Alte Museum in Berlin, verkörperte den Typus des chronologischen Menschheitsmuseums. Hier wurden der Stammbaum des Bürgertums und gleichzeitig dessen Legitimierung geliefert.

5. Heute erscheint das Museum als Abdankungshalle liquidierter Tradition, als Altenasyl. »Im Museum trauert der moderne Sachzwang über seine Unerbittlichkeit.« Fazit heute: das Bürgerliche, das Nationale, das Patriotische sind verdampft. Niemand ist sich dessen bewußt, daß das Museum ein bürgerlich-kulturrevolutionärer Akt war. Nur die These der ästhetischen Kirche greift heute noch, das Museum ist eine säkularisierte, bevölkerte Wallfahrtskirche. Gleichzeitig ist eine Refeudalisierung der Kultur zu beobachten. Die Zeitmaschine läuft rückwärts, die Sansculottes tragen die geraubten Schätze rückwärts ins

the question of what the museum once was: 1) The birth of the middle-class museum occurred after the liquidation of kingship. The first exhibition of the possessions of the French kings took place in the Louvre in 1793, after the beheading of the burgher Louis Capet. The main interest here is in dispossessing Absolutism. 2) The museum functions as an aesthetic church; after the revolution there occurred a process of the evacuation of all traditionally public spaces ('Jacobin peristalsis'). Since the revolution was partly financed by a flourishing art trade, new spaces (at first empty) emerged for a new religion of art. A hint, too, for the debate concerning appropriate museum architecture: "The museum is always also a monument and in this sense can be empty. It is the space in which the people feels itself sovereign." 3) The museum as a national Ark of the Covenant. Despite middle-class pressure since the beginning of the 19th century, the ruling class was not willing to make the art treasures in their residences publicly accessible. Only when the Prussian cultural possessions were returned after the defeat of Napoleon did they make a concession to patriotism; instead of rehanging them in the living rooms of the ruling class, a museum was founded. 4) The museum as a path of instruction in history. The first museum in Prussia, the Alte Museum built by Schinkel in Berlin, embodied a kind of chronological 'museum of mankind'. It presented the genealogical tree of the bourgeoisie and, at the same time, its legitimacy. 5) Today the museum appears to be a retirement hall for liquidated traditions, a refuge for what is old. "In the museum, the modern compulsion for facts laments its inexorability." To take stock today: what is bourgeois, nationalistic and patriotic has evaporated. Nobody is aware of the fact that the museum was a bourgeois, counter-revolutionary act. Only the thesis of the aesthetic church is still effective today; the museum is a secularised, crowded church of pilgrimage. At the same time, one can observe a refeudalisation of culture. The time machine is running backwards, the *sans culottes* carry the stolen treasures back to the castle. If the advanced 'club culture' was a "cultural Rütli field", then the present-day

Schloß zurück. Wenn die entwickelte Vereinskultur eine »kulturelle Rütliwiese« war, so sind die heutigen Strukturen des Kultur-Sponsoring dem aufgeklärten Absolutismus gleichzusetzen.

Hermann Lübbe (Zürich) formulierte zwei Thesen zum Thema Historisierung: Erstens: Es hat noch nie eine kulturelle Gegenwart gegeben, die so sehr vergangenheitsbezogen gewesen wäre wie unsere eigene. Früher fand ein kulturelles Recycling statt: Die Ruinen vergangener Epochen wurden als Baumasse für neue Konstruktionen benutzt. Erst in unserem Jahrhundert versuchen die Denkmalschützer die Präsenz dessen, woran unsere Erfahrung mit der Kontinuität anknüpft, zu retten, um einen Vertrautheitsschwund aufzuhalten. Zweitens : Nichts hat die Musealisierung, speziell der Kunst, mehr gefördert als die avantgardistische Orientierung der Kunst. Es gibt immer mehr unterscheidbare und deklarierte Kunststile in immer kürzerer Zeit. Ein Beschleunigungseffekt des Avantgarde-Prinzips ist zu beobachten, dadurch wird die Veraltensrate erhöht. Moderne Kunst erzeugt ständig veraltete Kunst.

Peter Sloterdijk (München) verweist auf das Museum als mentale Institution, als Denkform des Evolutionismus und Historismus. Erstens: Das moderne Selbst braucht zu seiner eigenen Konstitution und zu seiner Regeneration so etwas wie ein »Uterodrom«, eine Kuppel als Inbegriff aller Projektionsräume. Verweis auf die These des Religionsphilosophen Klaus Heinrich, daß das Museum als modernes Äquivalent der Grabeshöhle funktioniert, in dem sich die Menschen in einem Augenkontakt (»Auge zu Augenhöhle«) der Kontinuität zwischen den Geschlechtern vergewissert haben. Zweitens: Das moderne Museum ist so, wie es ist, wie wir inmitten eines gewaltigen Strukturwandels des Todes leben. Aber das Veralten ist nur ein Problem, wenn das Produkt keine echte Gegenwart hat, wenn – wie bei der heroischen Avantgarde – die Ablösung der Künstlergeneration nicht stattfindet in »einer direkten Auseinandersetzung einer lebenden Generation und einer Generation von lebenden Toten«. Nur in der Diskussion mit autoritativen Toten kann so

structures of cultural sponsoring can be equated with enlightened absolutism.

Hermann Lübbe (Zürich) formulated two theses on the theme of historicisation: 1) Never has a contemporary culture been so very closely connected to the past as our own now is; formerly, a kind of cultural recycling took place, with the ruins of past ages being used as building material for new constructions. Only in our century have the preservers of historical monuments attempted to save those things which provide our experience with a sense of continuity, in order to halt an ever-increasing loss of familiarity. 2) Nothing has been furthered more by 'museumisation', especially that of art, than the avantgarde orientation of art. There is an increasing number of different and declared styles of art emerging over ever shorter periods of time. An acceleration effect can be observed in the avantgarde principle; it increases the rate at which something becomes out-of-date. Modern art is constantly producing art which is already out-of-date.

Peter Sloterdijk (Munich) draws attention to the museum as an intellectual institution, as a way of thinking which belongs to evolutionism and historicism. 1) The modern self needs something like an 'uterodrom', a cupola as the epitomy of all projection rooms. Mention of the thesis put forward by the philosopher of religion, Klaus Heinrich, that the museum serves as the modern equivalent of the grave-pit, in that people reassure themselves in a moment of eye-contact ("eye to eye-socket"), of the continuity between the sexes. 2) The modern museum is the way it is because we live in the midst of a powerful change in the structure of death. But being out-of-date is only a problem if the product does not have any present moment, if – as was the case with the heroic avantgarde – the act of relieving the old artistic generation does not occur as a direct confrontation between a living generation and a generation of the 'living dead'. 3) Today, people are subject to a synchronistic world in an inner cupola. "And that is the actual function of the museum as far as the dimension of exhibition theory is concerned." The museum as a cultural-historical institution is some-

Peter Noever, Terrassenplateau
Peter Noever, the terrace

etwas wie eine lebendige Dialektik des Generationswechsels stattfinden. Drittens: Heute werden die Menschen in der inneren Kuppel einer Synchronwelt unterworfen. »Und das ist die wirkliche Funktion des Museums in seiner ausstellungstheoretischen Dimension.« Das Museum als kulturhistorische Institution ist etwas ganz anderes. Viertens: Heute strahlt nicht mehr die Werkmacht/Werknatur von der Wand, die künstlerische Potenz, sondern der Geldwert des Bildes. Die dämonische Synchronisationskraft des Geldes und des Wertes erzeugt auch in den Subjekten einen spezifischen Reflex: das Museum wird zum Weltganzen. Es ergibt sich die neognostische Situation, in der eine bereits erschlossene Welt zu einer gleichmäßig bedeutungsentleerten Welt wird. Das Museum ist so kein Lehrpfad mehr zu einer Selbsterfahrung, sondern der Inbegriff der Dinge, von denen man zuverlässig weiß, daß sie einen nichts angehen.

Siegfried Gohr (Köln): Die Krise des Museums liegt im Verschwinden der kunsthistorischen Maßstäbe und deren Ersatz durch Erfolg. Das Avantgarde-Museum hat sich abgesetzt von dem Museum des 19. Jahrhunderts, dem Louvre etwa. Er widerspricht Lübbe: Avantgarde-Kunst ersetzt nicht das Alte durch etwas Neues, sondern setzt das Alte anders ein. Der Rückgriff geschieht nicht nur auf die Künstlergeneration davor, sondern kann sich über Jahrhunderte spannen. Erst jetzt in den achtziger Jahren ist das Museum der Avantgarde mit seinem weitgehend aufklärerischen Impuls in die Defensive geraten. Aus Amerika kommt das Bild des Museums als sozialer Versammlungsort. Aber das Kunstwerk (und es wird zu wenig von den Kunstwerken selbst gesprochen) muß als eine Kategorie dessen, was man erfahren kann, beibehalten werden, es gehört zu unserem Lebenshaushalt, nicht nur in seiner verarbeiteten Form über Soziologie und Historie. Wenn dieses Aufstrahlen, dieses Wiederkehren von Eindrücken und Erlebnissen, aufgegeben wird, dann haben wir es tatsächlich mit einer Verwahranstalt für wertvolle oder bessere Gebrauchsgegenstände zu tun.

thing very different indeed. 4) Today, it is no longer the power and nature of the work of art, its artistic potency, which radiates from the wall, but the monetary value of the painting. The demonic synchronising power of money and value produces a specific reflex in the subjects as well: the museum becomes the whole world. The result is a neo-gnostic situation, in which an already developed world gradually becomes a world devoid of significance. The museum is thus not a path of instruction leading to self-experience, but the epitomy of things which one knows for certain do not concern one at all.

Siegfried Gohr (Cologne): The crisis of the museum is due to the fact that art historical standards have disappeared and been replaced by the standard of success. The avantgarde museum is different to the museum of the 19th century, that of the Louvre, for example. He contradicts Lübbe: avantgarde art does not replace the old with the new, but employs the old in a different way. This happens not only with respect to the previous generation of artists, but can also span centuries. Only now, in the 1980s, has the museum of the avantgarde gone on the defensive with its far-reaching impulse to enlighten people. From America there has arrived the image of the museum as a place for social gathering. But the work of art (and too little is said of the work of art itself) must be retained as a category of what can be experienced; it is part of our balance of life, and not only in a reworked form via sociology and history. If we surrender this glow, this recurrence of impressions and experiences, then we really will be dealing simply with an institution for the preservation of valuable or better-quality everyday objects.

"Tradition and Experiment"[11]

To conclude, two pictures: *Domestication of a Pyramid* by Magdalena Jetelova was on exhibition in the columned hall of the MAK until mid-July 1992. Her spatial installation becomes an ambivalent sign on the MAK building site (where exhibition activities are continuing notwithstanding). Has something which was buried been partly excavated, or is something new beginning

»Tradition und Experiment«[11]

Zwei Bilder zum Schluß: In der Säulenhalle des MAK war bis Mitte Juli 1992 die »Domestizierung einer Pyramide« von Magdalena Jetelová zu sehen. Auf der Baustelle MAK (bei synchron weiterlaufenden Ausstellungsaktivitäten) wurde ihre Rauminstallation zu einem ambivalenten Zeichen. Ist etwas Verschüttetes halbausgegraben oder beginnt etwas Neues das Alte zu verdecken? Und ein zweites Bild: in den Publikationen des MAK zur Geschichte des Hauses taucht immer wieder ein Photo auf mit der Legende: »Ausgegrabener Pfahl nach der Belastungsprobe für den Neubau Weiskirchnerstraße von Ludwig Baumann, 1906«. Auch hier setzt die Vieldeutigkeit auf der Bild- und Sprachebene Assoziationen in Gang: ein Objekt, ein riesiger Holznagel, dessen Funktion nicht eindeutig ablesbar ist. Er scheint gleichzeitig für Neukonstruktion und Rückbesinnung auf althergebrachte Bewertungsstrategien zu stehen: die Belastungsprobe des Neuen – ein Experiment.

Anmerkungen:

1 Titel des ersten Pressegesprächs der Direktion Noever im Möbeldepot am 2. Februar 1987.
2 Alle Zitate von Peter Noever, auf die nicht anders verwiesen wird, sind einem Gespräch mit der Autorin vom 23. Juni 1992 entnommen.
3 Titel einer Informationsschrift des Österreichischen Museums für angewandte Kunst. Hrsg. von Peter Noever, Wien 1986.
4 Ein Museum im Aufbruch, Manuskripte des MAK, Bd. 2: Christian Reder, Dienstleistungsstudie, Wien 1991; Bd.3 Christian Reder, Neue Sammlungspolitik und neue Arbeitsstruktur, Wien 1991; der erste Band, Florian Reichmann, Gustav Dreher, Bestand und Neuordnung, liegt vorerst nur als Manuskript vor.
5 Peter Noever: Vorwort in Bd. 2 Museum im Aufbruch (Anmerkung 4)
6 Ebda.
7 Titel des Pressegesprächs, 3. Februar 1992
8 Ebda.
9 »Das Museum als kulturelle Zeitmaschine«, eine Veranstaltung des Österreichischen Museums für angewandte Kunst, Wien, vom 12. bis 14. Oktober 1990, veröffentlicht in: »Kunstforum«, Bd. 111, Januar/Februar 1991, S. 203–251.
10 Jan Tabor in »Falter« Nr. 27/92, S. 24
11 Tradition und Experiment, Das Österreichische Museum für angewandte Kunst, Wien, Salzburg-Wien 1988

to discover what is old? And a second picture: time and time again in the MAK's publications on the history of the museum there appears a photograph with the legend: *Foundation pile excavated after the load test for Ludwig Baumann's new building in Weiskirchnerstrasse, 1906.* Here, too, ambiguity on the pictorial and linguistic level triggers off associations: an object, a huge wooden nail, its function not clearly discernible. Yet, at the same time, it seems to stand for reconstruction, and for reflection on traditional evaluation strategies: the load test of the new – an experiment.

Notes:

1 Title of the Noever direction's first press conference, held in the furniture depot on 2nd February 1987.
2 All the quotes from Peter Noever, when not otherwise indicated, are taken from an interview with the present author on 23rd June 1992.
3 Title of an information leaflet of the Österreichische Museum für angewandte Kunst, ed. Peter Noever, Vienna 1986.
4 *Museum im Aufbruch,* Vol. 2: Christian Reder, 'Dienstleistungsstudie', Vienna 1991; Vol. 3: Christian Reder, 'Neue Sammlungspolitik und Neue Arbeitsstruktur', Vienna 1991; the first volume (Florian Reichmann, Gustav Dreher: Bestand und Neuordnung) is at present only available in manuscript form.
5 Peter Noever: Foreword in Vol. 2 of *Museum im Aufbruch* (s. note 4).
6 Ibid.
7 Title of a press interview, 3rd February 1992.
8 Ibid.
9 *Das Museum als kulturelle Zeitmaschine,* an event organised by the Austrian Museum for Applied Art, Vienna 12th-14th October 1990, published in Kunstforum, Vol. 111 January/February 1991, p. 203-251.
10 Jan Tabor in Falter No. 27/92 p. 24.
11 *Tradition und Experiment,* Österreichisches Museum für angewandte Kunst, Salzburg-Vienna 1988.

Ausgegrabener Pfahl nach der Belastungsprobe für den Neubau an der Weißkirchnerstraße, 1906
Post excavated after the load test for the new building in Weißkirchnerstraße, 1906

Caterpillar bei der Auskofferung der Säulenhalle
Excavator during renovation

PROJEKTE VON KÜNSTLERN UND ARCHITEKTEN

IM RAHMEN DER MAK-GENERALSANIERUNG

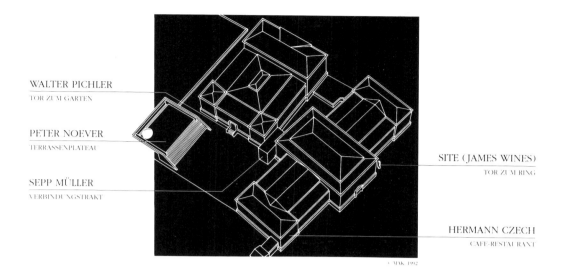

WALTER PICHLER
TOR ZUM GARTEN

PETER NOEVER
TERRASSENPLATEAU

SEPP MÜLLER
VERBINDUNGSTRAKT

SITE (JAMES WINES)
TOR ZUM RING

HERMANN CZECH
CAFE-RESTAURANT

© MAK 1992

NEUAUFSTELLUNG DER MAK-SCHAUSAMMLUNG

RAUMKONZEPTION

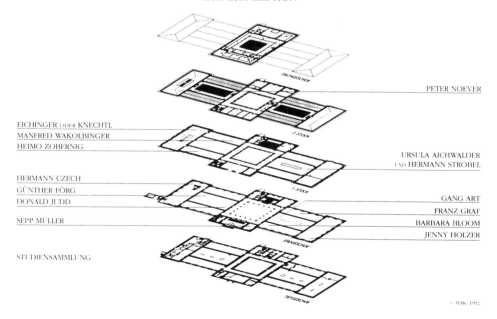

PETER NOEVER

EICHINGER ODER KNECHTL
MANFRED WAKOLBINGER
HEIMO ZOBERNIG

URSULA AICHWALDER
UND HERMANN STROBEL

HERMANN CZECH
GÜNTHER FÖRG
DONALD JUDD

SEPP MÜLLER

GANG ART
FRANZ GRAF
BARBARA BLOOM
JENNY HOLZER

STUDIENSAMMLUNG

© MAK 1992

Projekte von Künstlern und Architekten, Neuaufstellung der Schausammlung
Projects by artists and architects, new designs for the exhibition rooms

Hermann Czech, Neues Museums-Café, Modell
Hermann Czech, new museum cafeteria, model

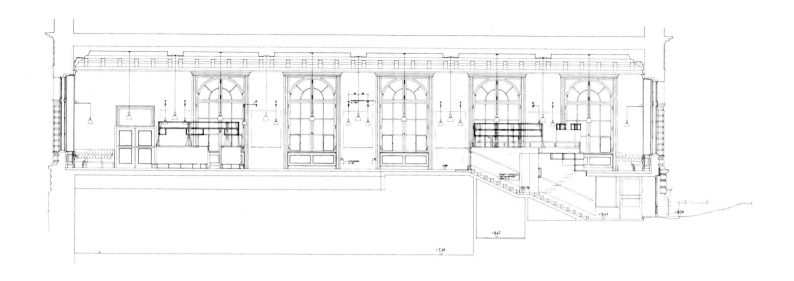

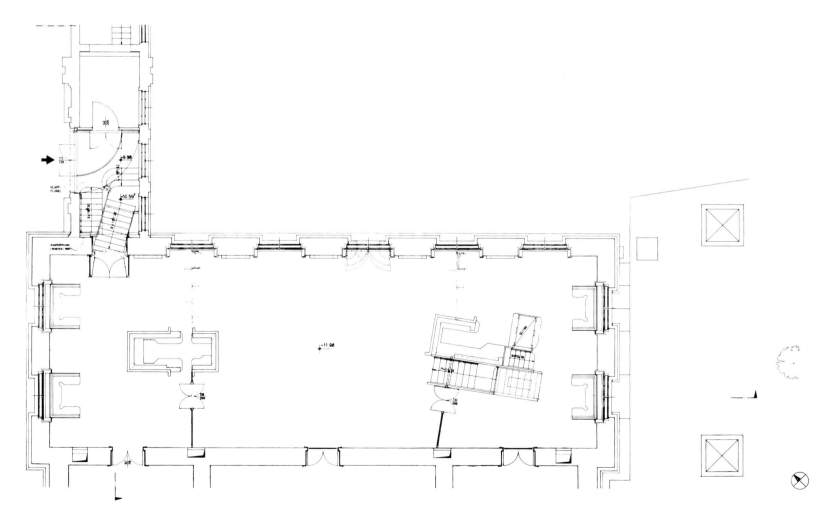

Hermann Czech, Neues Museums-Café, Grundriß und Schnitt
Hermann Czech, new museum cafeteria, floor plan and section

Sepp Müller, Verbindungstrakt, Modell
Sepp Müller, connecting building, model

Sepp Müller, Verbindungstrakt
Sepp Müller, connecting building

Peter Noever, Terrassenplateau, Modell
Peter Noever, terrace, model

Peter Noever, Terrassenplateau
Peter Noever, the terrace

Walter Pichler, Das Tor zum Garten, Modell
Walter Pichler, door to the garden, model

Walter Pichler, Das Tor zum Garten
Walter Pichler, door to the garden

SITE, Neuer Museums-Buchladen, Modell
SITE, new museum bookshop, model

SITE, Neuer Museums-Buchladen
SITE, new museum bookshop

Das Österreichische Theatermuseum

Oskar Pausch

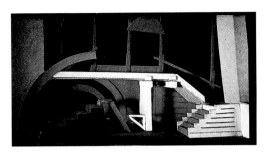

Bühnenbild
Stage set

Das Österreichische Theatermuseum ist eine der wichtigsten Dokumentationsstätten des Art du Spectacle: »... manuscripts, documents, scene und costume designs, paintings, sketches and autographs pertaining to the history of the theater in Vienna and Austria. Over 1.200.000 items – the largest theater collection in the world.« (Wallace Dace, *National Theaters in the larger German and Austrian Cities,* New York 1981). In krassem Gegensatz zur internationalen Reputation stand ein jahrzehntelanges räumlich-organisatorisches Provisorium: die Institution war auf verschiedenste Räumlichkeiten im Bereich der Hofburg aufgesplittert, was eine eigene Ausstellungspolitik faktisch unmöglich machte. Nolens volens lagen die Akzente auf Sammeln und Bewahren, und es war nur konsequent, daß unser Museum seit der Gründung im Jahr 1922 bis 1991 als »Theatersammlung« ein Teil der Österreichischen Nationalbibliothek war.

Die Übersiedlung in das neuadaptierte Palais Lobkowitz hat dieses Aschenbrödeldasein mit einem Schlag erledigt, und zwar aus mehreren Gründen:

Erstens: das neue Haus ist einer der edelsten Profanbauten Wiens und auch kulturhistorisch – vor allem als Ort von Beethoven-Uraufführungen – besonders attraktiv. Seine Lage zwischen Staatsoper, Albertina und Österreichischer Nationalbibliothek ist museumsstrategisch ideal.

Zweitens war es möglich, die Raumstruktur des Barockpalais ohne jede bauliche Änderung für Studien- und Dokumentationszwecke (Lesesaal, Magazine usw.), vor allem aber für die elastischen Erfordernisse eines modernen Ausstellungsbetriebes zu nutzen. Für Expositionen stehen mindestens vier Areale zur Verfügung. Beispielsweise präsentiert sich unsere Institution mit einem Gang durch die Theatergeschichte, wobei es weniger um ein theatralisches Kulinarium als um die Wieder-

The Austrian Theatre Museum

Oskar Pausch

The Austrian Theatre Museum is one of the most important documentation centres of the *art du spectacle:* "... manuscripts, documents, scene and costume designs, paintings, sketches and autographs pertaining to the history of the theatre in Vienna and Austria. Over 1,200,000 items - the largest theatre collection in the world." (Wallace Dace: *National Theaters in the Larger German and Austrian Cities,* New York 1981). In complete contrast to this international reputation, the accommodation and organisation of the museum was subject to a makeshift arrangement for decades; the institution was divided up among a variety of premises around the Hofburg, making any exhibition policy of its own practically impossible. *Nolens volens,* the emphasis lay on collection and conservation, and thus it was only logical that, as a theatre collection, our museum should have remained part of the Austrian National Library from its founding in 1922 until 1991.

The move to the newly adapted Palais Lobkowitz ended this cinderella existence at a stroke, and indeed in several ways:

First of all, the new house is one of the noblest secular buildings in Vienna, as well as being particularly attractive on account of its cultural history, e.g. as the place where works by Beethoven were first performed. Its location is also ideal from the point of view of 'museum strategy'.

Secondly, it was possible, without having to undertake any architectural changes, to utilise the spatial structure of the Baroque palace for the purpose of providing study and documentation facilities (reading room, storeroom etc.) and above all for the flexible requirements of a modern exhibition service. At least four areas are available for exhibitions. To take an example: our institution provides a journey through theatre history, yet it is less concerned to provide a theatrical titillation than to reproduce the theatre's strong emotional attraction, with original exhibits

gabe der stark emotionalen Reize des Theaters geht, mit Originalen vom Barock bis zu Wieland Wagner. Modernste Technik schafft die innovative Klammer dieser Auswahl – unter anderem eine interaktive Bildplatte. Wohl überhaupt zum erstenmal wurde auch ein Theatermuseum für Kinder eingerichtet, ein Ort, an dem das Wesen des Theaters in sinnlich-spielerischer Weise vermittelt werden soll – »learning by doing« ist die Devise. Der Kernpunkt musealer Aktivitäten befindet sich naturgemäß aber rund um den Eroica-Saal: Hier dient eine Kette repräsentativer Räume längerwährenden Großausstellungen mit umfassender Thematik.

Drittens: Zu allen Möglichkeiten für Dokumentation und Präsentation bietet das Palais Lobkowitz auch ideale Voraussetzungen für diverse Veranstaltungen. Ein exklusives Angebot ist der Eroica-Saal, der Große Hof ist im Sommer idealer Rahmen für alle Formen des Art du Spectacle, ein eigener Gedenkraum dient Aufführungen von Richard Teschners berühmtem Puppentheater, ein multifunktionaler Saal für Kinovorführungen, Vorlesungen, Symposien usw. Diese Nutzungsvielfalt soll zu den Hauptarbeitsbereichen Sammeln und Präsentieren auch das Produzieren stellen – eine neue Herausforderung für das »schönste Theatermuseum der Welt«.

Die große Akzeptanz des am 26. Oktober 1991 neueröffneten Österreichischen Theatermuseums macht Mut zu neuen Plänen. So ist in kürzester Zeit ein Kommunikationsbereich, etwa ein Kaffeehaus, zum Desiderat geworden, eine Überdachung des Großen Hofes böte ganzjährige Spiel- und neue Ausstellungsmöglichkeiten. In diesem Konnex sei nicht unerwähnt, daß selbst die kleinste bauliche »Nachjustierung« zum denkmalschützerischen Problem werden kann.

Völlig neue Perspektiven schafft naturgemäß auch die für unseren Aufgabenbereich so entscheidende Entwicklung der Medien. Eine AV-Bank ist im Aufbau, sie wird aus ökonomischen Gründen nur arbeitsteilig agieren können, etwa mit dem Museumsquartier und selbstverständlich auch im Expositionsbereich. Ausstellungen und Veranstaltungen müssen erwerbungspolitisch genutzt werden.

ranging from the Baroque to Wieland Wagner. The most modern technology creates the innovative setting for this selection, including, among other things, an interactive pictorial video disc.

We have also created what is probably the first ever theatre museum for children, a place where the nature of the theatre can be communicated in a sensuous and playful way - where 'learning by doing' is the motto. Naturally enough, our museological activities are concentrated around the Eroicasaal. Here a series of stately rooms provide space for long-term, large-scale exhibitions on a comprehensive theme.

Thirdly, in addition to all its possibilities for documentation and presentation, Palais Lobkowitz also offers ideal conditions for a variety of other events. Although the Eroicasaal is a rather exclusive room, the Great Courtyard provides an ideal setting for all forms of the *art du spectacle* in summer, while a separate commemorative room serves for performances of Richard Teschner's famous puppet theatre and a multi-functional room for film shows, lectures, symposia etc.. This varied utilisation should add to our main areas of activity, namely collection and presentation, also those of production and performance – a new challenge for the "most beautiful theatre museum in the world".

The wide acceptance that the Austrian Theatre Museum has gained since being opened on 26th October 1991 is a source of encouragement for new plans. Thus, in the shortest possible time, some kind of communication area, for example a coffeehouse, has already become a desideratum, while roofing over the large courtyard would make it possible to stage performances and new exhibitions all the year round. In this connection, it should also be mentioned that even the smallest architectural 'readjustment' can, for us here, become a matter involving problems of the preservation of historical monuments.

Completely new perspectives have been created by the developments in media technology, which are of course also decisive for our area of activity. An A.V. databank is being built up, although for economic reasons it will only be possible to employ it on a shared basis.

Wo fängt das Museum wirklich an, wenn schon das Gebäude selbst ein Stück museale Architektur darstellt? Ein großer Teil der österreichischen Museen ist in historisch bedeutsamer Bausubstanz untergebracht. Die historische Bausubstanz als bedeutender Kulturträger per se erfährt eine zusätzliche Dimension durch die Transformation in ein Museum und durch die Überlagerung mit den neuen Inhalten.

Das Palais Dietrichstein-Lobkowitz in Wien in seiner neuen Funktion als Theatermuseum symbolisiert diese Transformation historischer Bausubstanz: dadurch erscheint seine Bau- und Kulturgeschichte fast ebenso interessant wie die neue »Funktion«.

(A. S.)

Where does the museum really begin, if the building itself already represents a piece of museum architecture? A great many Austrian museums are housed in buildings whose architectural substance is of great historic significance. As an important vehicle of the cultural heritage per se, *this historic architectural substance acquires a further dimension if the building is then transformed into a museum and receives new contents.*

In its new role as the Theatre Museum, Vienna's Palais Dietrichstein-Lobkowitz typifies such a transformation of historic architectural substance. For this reason, the architectural and cultural history of this building are almost as interesting as its new 'function'.

(A. S.)

Das Österreichische Theatermuseum im Palais Dietrichstein-Lobkowitz

Wilhelm Georg Rizzi

Das Österreichische Theatermuseum ist in einem dem Kulturleben Wiens mit seinem Schwerpunkt auf Musik und Theater seit alters her in besonderer Weise verbundenen Objekt untergebracht, das mit seiner Tradition und der optischen Kultur seiner Erscheinung prädestiniert ist, dem Anspruch als Kulturbauwerk Rechnung zu tragen. Innerhalb der Museums-Positionen steht dieses Beispiel nicht nur für sich, sondern auch stellvertretend für die in einer Stadt mit Geschichte immer auch legitime Präsentation in künstlerisch, kulturell und historisch bedeutenden Baulichkeiten, und für den Versuch, sowohl der Tradition als auch – im Inneren – den Anforderungen der zeitgenössischen Entwicklung gerecht zu werden. Fast genau dreihundert Jahre nach Baubeginn des Palais Dietrichstein-Lobkowitz hat dieses, nach gründlicher Instandsetzung und Revitalisierung durch den österreichischen Staat, als Theatermuseum im Vorjahr wieder seine Pforten geöffnet. Der inhaltliche Konnex zur neuen Funktion ist durchaus mehrschichtig: Zum einen durch den in-

The Austrian Theatre Museum in Vienna's Palais Dietrichstein-Lobkowitz

Wilhelm Georg Rizzi

The Austrian Theatre Museum is housed in a building which has long been connected in a special way with the cultural life of Vienna, revolving as it does around music and theatre. With its tradition and the optical refinement of its appearance, it is a building predestined to assert its architectural pretensions. It is one of the MUSEUM POSITIONS not solely on its own account, but also as the representative of many other artistically, culturally and historically important buildings always deserving of presentation in a city so full of history. Furthermore, it represents the attempt to do justice both to tradition and - inside the building - to the demands of contemporary developments. Almost exactly three hundred years since its construction began, Palais Dietrichstein-Lobkowitz reopened its portals once again last year, after thorough renovation and revitalisation, as the Theatre Museum. The relationship between the contents of the building and its new function is multi-layered: on the one hand, the theatrical character of this Baroque *Gesamtkunstwerk* has meant that the

szenierenden Charakter des barocken Ge-
samtkunstwerks, der Bauwerk und Ausstattung seit ehedem als Bühne und Kulisse
theatralischen Geschehens gesehen hat;
zum anderen durch das besondere Enga-
gement für Musik und Theater, das die seit
1745 im Palais residierende Familie Lobkowitz durch Generationen auf das engste
mit der Kultur der Metropole verbunden
hat. Unter Franz Joseph Maximilian Fürst
Lobkowitz, dem Hoftheaterdirektor und
begeisterten Mäzen Ludwig van Beethovens, gelangte 1804 dessen dritte Symphonie, die sogenannte Eroica, im Festsaal
des Stadtpalastes erstmals, im privaten
Kreis, zur Aufführung. Zahlreiche kon-
zertante und musiktheatralische Veranstaltungen machten das Haus besonders
unter Franz Joseph Maximilian und seinem Sohn Ferdinand Joseph zu einem
Zentrum kulturellen Lebens.

Das Palais und seine Ausstattung haben die
Fürsten Lobkowitz von ihren Vorgängern
weitestgehend unverändert übernommen,
in der repräsentativen Hauptraumfolge
vom Portal zum Festsaal ist es im Inneren
auch heute noch getreu erhalten. Das
Palais Dietrichstein-Lobkowitz ist der erste
bedeutende barocke Stadtpalast Wiens
nach 1683 und seiner Genese nach das
Produkt einer komplexen Planungs- und
Baugeschichte, in der die Konzepte mehrerer Künstler einander überlagern und
wechselseitig bedingen. Untersuchungen
am Bauwerk – gelegentlich der in den
letzten Jahren durchgeführten Gesamtin-
standsetzung vorgenommen – und die Ergebnisse ergänzender Archivforschungen
bereichern heute unser Wissen um wich-
tige Erkenntnisse, aus denen sowohl für
die Stellung innerhalb der Entwicklungs-
reihe der Wiener Palastarchitektur als auch
für die Beurteilung der Architektenfrage
merkliche Akzentverschiebungen resul-
tieren.

Bekannt ist, daß der Bauherr, Philipp
Sigmund Graf von Dietrichstein, vier alternative Projekte eingeholt hat; der aus diesen hervorgegangene Ausführungsent-
wurf ist nach Vergrößerung der Bauparzelle und vor allem durch Modernisie-
rungsmaßnahmen erheblich verändert
worden, wobei glücklicherweise alle Pha-
sen der Genese durch Planmaterial weitge-

building and its decoration has always been
regarded as a stage and backdrop for
theatrical events; on the other hand, the
family Lobkowitz, who resided in the Palais
from 1745 onwards, were particularly
involved with music and theatre, and that
closely bound the family to the cultural life
of the metropolis for generations. In 1804,
during the reign of Franz Joseph Maximilian, Prince Lobkowitz, who was director of
the court theatre and an enthusiastic patron
of Beethoven, succeeded in staging the first
performance, for a private circle, of the
latter's Third Symphony, the so-called
'Eroica', in the banqueting hall of this town
palace. As a result of the numerous musical
performances that were held there, the
house became widely known as a centre of
cultural life, especially during the reigns of
Franz Joseph Maximilian and his son, Ferdinand Joseph.

The Lobkowitz Princes maintained the
Palais and its decoration very largely unchanged from the state in which they
received it from their predecessors, and
even today the prestigious main sequence
of rooms from the portal to the banqueting
hall has been preserved in its original state.
The Palais Dietrichstein-Lobkowitz was
the first important town palace to be built
in Vienna after 1683 and, according to the
story of its genesis, it is the product of a
complex planning and building history in
which the conceptions of several different
artists overlay and reciprocally influence
one another. Today, investigations of the
building, undertaken during the total renovation which has been carried out over
the past few years, together with the results
of archive research, have granted us important new perceptions and improved our
knowledge of its history, and this has resulted in notable shifts of emphasis, both as
regards the building's position within the
development of Viennese palace architecture, and the question of its architect.
What we do know, is that the man for whom
it was built, Count Philipp Sigmund of
Dietrichstein, had plans drawn up for four
alternative projects. The design which
eventually emerged from these was considerably altered after enlargement of the
property and, more particularly, due to
modernisation measures. We are fortunate

Johann Bernhard Fischer,
Portalentwurf Palais Lobkowitz
Johann Bernhard Fischer, design for the portal,
Palais Lobkowitz

hend vollständig dokumentiert sind. In seinem Gesamtausmaß setzt sich der Baugrund aus drei Parzellen zusammen. Voraussetzung für die Errichtung eines zeitgemäß-repräsentativen Bauwerks war zunächst der Ankauf des Felßschen Freihauses, das neben der Seite an der Augustinerstraße etwa die halbe Frontlänge der späteren Hauptfront am damaligen Schweinmarkt einnahm. Der Kaufkontrakt mit der Witwe des Freiherrn Colonna von Felß datiert vom 10. März 1687. Nur wenig später, am 18. April 1687, kommt der Zuerwerb des im Besitz des Dorotheerklosters befindlichen sogenannten Badhauses und damit ein dem frühbarocken Ideal der Breitenlagerung eines Stadtpalastes entsprechendes Grundstück zustande. Der Ausschnitt aus der Stadtkarte von Suttinger 1683 zeigt die Situation mit den damals bestehenden Baulichkeiten, wobei – ebenso wie bei Steinhausen 1710 – die unregelmäßig verlaufende hintere Grundstücksgrenze und das erst am 23. April 1691 erworbene »Prevostsche Stöckl« nicht berücksichtigt sind.

Wurden bisher stets die Jahre 1685–1687 als Bauzeit des Palais angegeben, so muß diese nunmehr beträchtlich verschoben werden, wobei das Frühjahr 1687 als Terminus post quem für die frühesten Planungsarbeiten anzusehen ist. Dieser ersten Planungsphase sind demgemäß all jene in einem Klebeband in gräflich Harrachschem Besitz befindlichen Projekte zuzuzählen, die noch nicht die Grundstückskorrektur von 1691 berücksichtigen. In ihrer baukünstlerischen Qualität unterschiedlich, sind sie dennoch insgesamt durch ihre entwicklungsgeschichtliche Stellung an der Schwelle zum Hochbarock und als Dokumente für die Situation in Wien vor dem folgenreichen Eintreffen Fischers von Erlach und Domenico Martinellis einer näheren Betrachtung wert.

Während drei Projekte eine grundsätzlich ähnliche Anordnung der Trakte um zwei unterschiedlich dimensionierte quergelagerte Höfe und eine 17achsige Hauptfassade am Schweinmarkt so wie die späteren Ausführungen aufweisen, stellt der »Plan über das Wiennerische Haus von Strudel« eine abweichende Gebäudeorganisation mit einem großen repräsentativen

enough to have planning material which provides almost complete documentation of all phases of the building's genesis. In its full extent the site consists of three different plots of land which have been combined. The first step towards the erection of what was at that time a prestigious modern building, was the purchase of the *"Felß'schen Freihaus"* ('house of the Felß' family'), which took up about half the length of what was later to become the main facade, in the former Schweinmarkt, and which on one side looked onto the Augustinerstrasse. The contract of purchase was concluded with the widow of Baron Colonna von Felß, dated 10th March 1687. Not long afterwards, on 18th April 1687, followed the further purchase of the so-called Bathhouse, which was in the possession of the Monastery of St. Dorothy. This produced a piece of ground corresponding to the early Baroque ideal of what the width of a city palace ought to be. A detail of Suttinger's 1683 map of the city shows the location of the buildings which existed at that time. As on Steinhausen's map of 1710, neither the irregular course of the border at the back of this piece of ground, nor the "Prevost'sche Stöckl" ('small plot of land belonging to the Prevost family'), which was first purchased on 23rd April 1691, had yet been taken into consideration.

If the date of construction of the Palais always used to be given as 1685-1687, it has since been considerably revised, and Spring 1687 is now regarded as the date *post quem* for the earliest planning work. To this first planning phase belong all those projects which are to be found in an album in the possession of the Counts of Harrach, which does not yet include the property changes of 1691. Varied in their architectural quality, they nevertheless merit examination, on account of their place in developmental history (i.e. on the threshhold of the High Baroque) and because of their role in documenting the situation in Vienna before the momentous arrival of Fischer von Erlach and Domenico Martinelli. Three of the projects show a fundamentally similar arrangement of the parts of the building around two transverse courtyards of different dimensions, and a main facade

Mittelhof und je einem seitlichen, in die Tiefe reichenden Lichthof vor. Das Hauptgeschoß zeigt eine in Trakttiefe durchgehende Zimmerflucht, die durch das Schachttreppenhaus unterbrochen wird. Der anschließende, über dem Vestibül angeordnete zentrale Saal erstreckt sich über drei Achsen und bezieht innerhalb der mittigen Hauptraumgruppe Licht auch von der Hofseite. Links, im Quertrakt zwischen den Höfen, ist offenbar die Galerie zu erkennen; die übrigen Räume dienten wohl dem Wohnbedarf der Herrschaft. Für die offenbar im Mezzanin untergebrachte Dienerschaft und zur Beheizung der Öfen sind zwei Wendeltreppen in den Lichthöfen angeordnet. Im Erdgeschoß finden sich ausgedehnte Wirtschaftsräume und Stallungen, die großteils von den Höfen zugänglich sind. Eine besondere Gestaltung ist für den großen Hof anzunehmen, dessen Rückwand eine Brunnennische in der Hauptachse aufnimmt.

Eine stärker retardierende Auffassung vertritt ein Projekt, dessen Urheber am Fassadenplan zwar vermerkt, infolge der Wurmlöcher heute jedoch nur mehr bruchstückhaft zu entziffern ist. Dieser Plan über das »... Haus von Mr. ... tien« stammt wohl von einer zünftisch geschulten Hand, was besonders an der mangelnden Klarheit des Grundrißbildes deutlich wird. Stimmt die Disposition mit 17achsiger Fassade, Mitteleingang, großem und kleinem Hof und der Lage der Hauptstiege dazwischen im großen mit der Ausführung überein, so sind die Lösungen im Detail recht unbekümmert. Wenig repräsentativ ist auch die Zugangssituation mit eher schmaler Einfahrt und seitlich versetzter Hauptstiege. Insgesamt atmet der Grundriß eher den Charakter der Paläste der »Prämerzeit«. Auffallend ist, daß sowohl die Situierung der Stallungen als auch die beiden Wendeltreppen dann ziemlich getreu bei Tencala wiederkehren.

Ein weiteres Projekt ist nur in zwei Grundrissen erhalten, denen eine ausführliche »Reflexion über das Gebäude« samt Angabe der Raumwidmungen beigefügt ist. Die alte Bezeichnung »de Paris« läßt an eine jener für barocke Bauplanungen auch in der Wiener Szene durch ihren befruchtenden

with 17 units overlooking the Schweinmarkt. Yet, as the subsequent construction demonstrates, the "Plan for the Viennese house of Strudel" envisages a differently organised building, with a large and prestigious central courtyard and deep air wells on either side. The main floor displays a continuous suite of rooms which extends to the end of the building and is only interrupted by the shaft of the stairwell. The adjoining central hall, positioned above the vestibule, extends for the length of three units and, being within the central group of rooms, also receives light on the courtyard side. On the left, in the transverse block between the courtyards, the gallery can be discerned, while the remaining rooms were probably intended to meet the owners' living requirements. In the air wells were two spiral staircases for the use of the servants, whose quarters were evidently on the mezzanine floor, and for heating the stoves. The ground floor has extensive service rooms and stables, most of which are accessible from the courtyards. A special design must be presumed for the large courtyard, the rear wall of which has a fountain niche in its main axis.

A more emphatically regressive conception is represented by a project whose author is noted on the facade plan, even if only fragments of the name can be deciphered today, due to the worm-eaten condition of the paper. This plan for the "...Haus von Mr. ...tien" was probably drawn by a hand which had been trained by the guild, as is evident from the lack of clarity of the ground plan. Although the layout, with its 17-unit facade, central entrance, and large and small courtyards with the main stairs located between them, generally agrees with what was subsequently constructed, the details of the solutions are very careless. The access situation is also less than prestigious, with a rather narrow entrance and the main stairway transferred to the side. In all, the ground plan tends to take on the character of the palaces of the 'Prämerzeit'. Both the positioning of the stables and the two spiral staircases then recur fairly faithfully in Tencala.

Another project is only preserved in two ground plans, one of which is an extensive "Reflection on the building" and includes

Einfluß bedeutsamen »Korrespondenz-Architekturen« denken.

Oft handelt es sich dabei um Idealkonzepte für überall und nirgendwo, die dem Bauherrn als Informationsquelle über aktuelle Trends der Baukunst trotz mangelnden Realitätsbezugs unverzichtbar waren.

Das für die Ausführungsplanung bestimmte vierte Projekt stammt vom kaiserlichen Hofingenieur Giovanni Pietro Tencala, wie sich aus Stilkritik, Vergleichen der technischen Faktur der Zeichnungen und der mit barocker Schrift bezeichneten Fassade »Erster Abriß von Mr. Tincala« mit Sicherheit ergibt; daran ändert auch nichts, daß dieser Fassadenplan – entgegen seiner Bezeichnung – erst der zweiten Stufe der Tencala-Planung angehört. Das klare, graphisch ansprechende Planbild zeigt die Handschrift eines erfahrenen Architekten, die denn auch in der Detailbehandlung zutage tritt. In Bissone am Luganer See geboren, ist Tencala seit 1658 in Wien nachzuweisen, zunächst als »Sozius« des kaiserlichen Hofingenieurs Philiberto Lucchese und, nach dessen Tod 1666, sodann bis 1699 selbst in dieser Funktion. Mit sicherem Gefühl für Maß und Proportion erscheinen die Trakte um die beiden Höfe angelegt, axial symmetrisch gegliedert und zentral über Einfahrt, Halle und Stiegenhaus erschlossen. Seitliche Einfahrten gibt es bei diesem Projekt noch nicht. Wie in der späteren Ausführung ist die Treppe in drei Läufen um einen offenen Kern gelegt. Der große Saal im Hauptgeschoß nimmt die drei Mittelachsen ein, die durch einen sehr flach vorgezogenen Risalit und durch Lisenen besonders hervorgehoben sind. Paradezimmer und Wohngemächer bleiben wiederum auf die Beletage beschränkt; eine Sala terrena – an den Wandnischen kenntlich – ist an der Ecke zur Augustinerstraße vorgesehen. Die Stiegenhaushalle mit der großen Bogennische gegenüber der Einfahrt ist zum Hof hin offen, ihr antwortet die Arkatur vis-à-vis, die den wohl noch vom Vorgängerbau stammenden Trakt an der Augustinerstraße in das regulierte Achsensystem des neuen Palastes einbindet. Auch im kleinen Hof – er nimmt die Wagenschuppen und Stallungen auf – sind die Schmalseiten in Bogen geöffnet.

details of the rooms' intended functions. The old term 'de Paris' makes one think of that 'correspondence architecture' which was so important for Baroque planning, in Vienna as elsewhere, due to the fruitful influence it exerted. The often idealised designs for everywhere and nowhere were, despite their lack of reality, indispensable to building clients as sources of information about current architectural trends.

The fourth project intended for final planning was designed by the engineer at the Imperial court, Giovanni Pietro Tencala, as can be established with certainty from stylistic criticism, comparisons of the drawings' technical calculations and from the description, in Baroque handwriting, of the facade as the "First outline by Mr. Tincala" (although that does not alter the fact that this plan for the facade – as opposed to its description – only belongs to the second stage of the Tencala design). The clear, graphically attractive drawing bears the trademark of an experienced architect, and that also emerges from the treatment of the details. Born in Bissone, on Lake Lugano, Tencala's presence in Vienna is attested from 1658 onwards, at first as the 'partner' of the engineer to the Imperial Court, Philiberto Lucchese, and then, from the latter's death in 1666 until 1699, in the same function himself.

With a sure sense of measurement and proportion, the layout of the blocks around the two courtyards seems to be arranged in an axially symmetrical manner, with the hall and the staircase centrally developed above the entrance. There are still no side entrances in this project. As in the construction carried out later, the stairs are arranged in three flights around an open core. The large hall on the main floor takes up the three central axes, which are particularly emphasised by means of a very flat projection and pilaster strips. Audience rooms and residential chambers are once again restricted to the first floor; a *sala terrena* – recognisable by its wall niches – is provided at the corner with Augustinerstrasse. The staircase hall, with its large arched niche opposite the entrance, is open towards the courtyard, and is balanced by the arcade vis-à-vis, which integrates the block on the Augustinerstrasse (probably

Indem Tencalas Projekt eine gezielte Auswahl von Planungsideen der vorbesprochenen Entwürfe zusammenfaßt, ist davon auszugehen, daß der Bauherr – im Sinne des gewählten Verfahrens, durch mehrere Planungsaufträge unterschiedliche Varianten zur Lösung der Bauaufgabe kennenzulernen – das entscheidende Wort bereits gesprochen hat. Tencala ist daher nicht als Teilnehmer der »Konkurrenz«, sondern als Redaktor der unterschiedlichen Planungsergebnisse zu sehen; der Erfahrung eines Hofarchitekten konnte die schwierige Aufgabe: fremde Vorgaben und eigene Inventionen nahtlos miteinander zu verknüpfen, denn auch anvertraut werden. Vergleicht man etwa den Fassadenplan Strudels mit Tencalas »Abriß«, so ergibt sich, daß die Gliederung in Portal- und Geschoßteilung und in den alternierenden Fenstern des piano nobile grundsätzlich übereinstimmen; auch Strudels Dachauszug kehrt bei Tencala als Dachloggia, noch nicht in die rechte Form gebracht, wieder. Wie nachhaltig gerade Strudels Fassade die weitere Planung beeinflußt, zeigen die Seitenportale, die erst wieder in Tencalas zweiten Entwurf Eingang finden und auch dort – wie bei Strudel – noch keine praktische Funktion erfüllen.

Aus der Plandarstellung ergibt sich eindeutig, daß der Bau – offenbar von Beginn an – nicht nach Tencalas erstem, sondern nach dem überarbeiteten zweiten Projekt, das mit der Stiege bis hart an die Grundgrenze rückt, geführt worden ist. Angesichts des zu diesem Zeitpunkt offenbar nicht allzuweit gediehenen Baufortschritts dürfte mit den Arbeiten erst 1689/90 begonnen worden sein; beide Tencala-Entwürfe sind vielleicht nur wenig früher, in knapper Folge und zeitlichem Abstand zu den übrigen Projekten, entstanden.

Der Ankauf des Prevostschen Stöckels ermöglicht die Anordnung eines Prunkstalls, der, von der Halle zugänglich, halbkreisförmig in die Tiefe der Parzelle vorstößt. Der hauptsächliche Vorteil ergibt sich in der umlaufenden Korridorerschließung, die die Kommunikation im Haus wesentlich verbessert.

In dieser überarbeiteten Projektstufe scheint auch die Idee des Mittelrisalits klarere Kontur anzunehmen. Allem Anschein

deriving from an earlier building) into the regulated axial system of the new palace. In the little courtyard which continues the coach-house and stable, the narrow sides are also open in arches.

Since Tencala's project brings together a deliberate selection of planning ideas from the previously discussed designs, one may presume that the building client had already spoken the final word - in the sense of having completed the favoured method of becoming acquainted with various possibilities for solving the architectural problems involved by commissioning several different designs. Tencala is therefore not to be seen as a participant in the 'competition', but as the editor of the results of the various designs; his experience as a court architect enabled him to deal with this difficult task: to be entrusted with smoothly combining others' indications and his own inventions. If one compares, for example, Strudel's facade plan with Tencala's 'outline', the result is that the division according to portals and floors and the arrangement of the alternating windows on the *piano nobile* are in fundamental agreement; even Strudel's roof drawing returns in Tencala's work as a roof loggia. The lasting influence of Strudel's facade on the subsequent planning can be seen in the side portals, which are only reintroduced in Tencala's second design; and even there – just as in Strudel's work – they still do not fulfil any practical purpose.

It becomes clear from the indications of the drawing that construction – obviously from the very beginning – did not proceed according to Tencala's first project, but according to the reworked second one, in which the staircase is shifted back almost to the edge of the property. Since, at this point in time, work had obviously not progressed very far, building must have only begun in 1689/90. Perhaps the two Tencala designs originated just a little bit beforehand, in close succession and only shortly after the other projects.

The purchase of the *Prevost'sche Stöckel* made it possible to lay out a magnificent stable which was accessible from the hall and protruded deep into the property in semi-circular form. The main advantage

Josef Emanuel Fischer von Erlach, Zeichnung des Palais Dietrichstein
Josef Emanuel Fischer von Erlach, drawing of Palais Dietrichstein

nach handelt es sich dabei um den ersten Mittelrisalit auf Wiener Boden; dementsprechend unsicher in der Ponderierung nimmt sich denn auch die Fassade aus, deren dreiachsige Mitte nur mit der Kopflast der Dachloggia der siebenachsigen Flanken Herr werden kann.

Tencala gestaltet die Seitenflügel als »stabilisierte Systeme«, mit axialen Portalen, die gleichsam als in sich geschlossene Einheiten dem horizontalen Bewegungsdrang entgegenwirken. Wie der Mittelrisalit sind allerdings auch die Seitenportale zu schwächlich geraten, um ihrer Aufgabe wirklich gerecht zu werden. Im übrigen läßt das Fassadenkonzept mit seiner Nutzung und Bänderung, welche die Tektonik und Bewegungsrichtung der Lisenen weitgehend entwertet, noch das überkommene Bemühen um dichte Durchgliederung und ornamentale Gestaltung der Wandflächen erkennen. Die Dominanz des Piano nobile ist dabei durch die stark vortretenden Fenster mit den Bogen- und Dreieckgiebeln gewahrt, die sich wie die Portale von der kleinteiligen Textur der Fassade deutlich abheben. Das Mezzanin erscheint mit übereinandergestellten Konsolen, Festons und ornamentalem Schmuck plastisch stark verlebendigt, um die optische Last des schattenden Daches aufzunehmen. Instrumentar und Formensprache des Frühbarock stecken dem Architekten sichtlich noch tief in allen Gliedern; der wesentliche Schritt zum Palast des Hochbarock, die Ausbildung des Mittelrisalits, ist dennoch vollzogen, die Verfeinerung erfolgt sodann in der nächsten Stufe.

Diese – letzte – Stufe der Planung ist durch Grundrißpläne und das ausgeführte Bauwerk selbst dokumentiert, wobei sich die Änderung im Hausinneren im wesentlichen auf die Wiederaufnahme der bereits im ersten Projekt enthaltenen Brunnennische in der Einfahrtshalle beschränkt. Von eminenter Bedeutung ist die Korrektur der Fassade durch Ausdehnung des Mittelrisalits auf sieben Achsen. Damit verschiebt sich die Gewichtung wesentlich hin zur Mitte, der Risalit dominiert nun an Breite über die fünfachsigen Seitenflügel und hält gleichzeitig mit dem Gewicht seiner Erscheinung die in sich geschlossenen Teile wieder zusammen.

resulted from the development of a circular corridor, which considerably improves communications in the house.

At this reworked stage of the project, the idea of the central projection also seems to acquire clearer contours. According to all appearances, this was the first central projection in Vienna; consequently, the facade looks correspondingly uncertain in the background, and its three-unit centre can only master the seven-unit sides by means of the topheavy roof loggia.

Tencala designed the side wings as a "stabilised system", with axial portals which, as self-enclosed units, contrast with the horizontal urge to movement. However, like the central projection, the side portals also become too weak to really be able to do their job. Incidentally, the design of the facade, with its fluting and banding, which largely devalues the tectonics and direction of movement of the pilaster strips, can still be recognised as a traditional striving for the tight subdivision and ornamental design of the wall areas. Following this, the dominance of the *piano nobile* is preserved by the extremely prominent windows with arched trianglular gables, which, like the portals, stand out distinctly from the smallscale texture of the facade. The mezzanine floor seems to come to life in a powerfully plastic way, with consoles, festoons and ornamental decoration taking up the optical burden of the shading roof. The instrumentation and formal language of the Early Baroque obviously still permeate the architect's work; the essential step towards the palace of the High Baroque, namely the development of the central projection, is nevertheless complete, and its refinement then follows in the next stage.

This – the last – stage of the design is documented by ground plans and by the finished building itself, with changes to the inside of the house essentially limited to the readoption of the fountain niche which had already been included in the first project. Of eminent significance is the correction of the facade by the extension of the central projection to seven units. This means that the weight is shifted towards the centre, with the projection now dominating the width of the five-unit side wing and, at the same time, once again holding

Über die weiteren Eigentümer bis zur Erwerbung durch die Familie Lobkowitz 1745 herrschte komplette Ungewißheit, bis sich unter dem im Zuge der Restaurierung zur Neuvergoldung abgenommenen Wappenschild im Stein das Wappen der Familie Althan fand. Die erst später zugänglichen Archivalien aus dem Lobkowitz-Archiv in Leitmeritz haben schließlich bestätigt, daß der Palast 1724 durch Kauf an Gundacker Graf von Althan gekommen ist. Mit der Oberaufsicht über das gesamte kaiserliche Bauwesen betraut, also Hofbaudirektor und oberster Baubeamter des Habsburgerreiches, kommt Althan die wichtigste Rolle bei der Prägung des Reichsstils unter Karl VI. zu. Gleichzeitig Oberinspektor der neu gegründeten kaiserlichen Maler- und Bildhauerakademie sowie der kaiserlichen Bildergalerie ist Althan unbestrittene Autorität in Sachen Kunst schlechthin. Diesem gehobenen Anspruch muß daher auch der Althansche Stadtpalast nachkommen, dessen Größe und Nähe zur Hofburg die bedeutende Stellung seines Besitzers bei Hof eindrucksvoll unter Beweis stellt. Es ist ein Zeugnis sowohl für das Kunstverständnis des Hofbaudirektors als auch für die ein Vierteljahrhundert nach ihrer Entstehung selbst höchstem künstlerischem Anspruch genügende Architektur.

Die von Althan vorgenommene Änderung am Äußeren ist bemerkenswert geringfügig, sie betrifft die plastische Gruppe der Wappenhalter am Mittelfenster über dem Portal. Ob die Saalfenster schon damals oder erst unter Lobkowitz ihre heutige Bogenform, die anstelle der schweren Segment- und Dreieckgiebel auch eine bessere Belichtung bringt, erhalten haben, ist ungewiß, ein Zusammenhang mit den Maßnahmen im Hausinneren gleichwohl wahrscheinlich.

Damals hat der Festsaal die bestehende Struktur mit den hofseitig geschlossenen Fenstern und seine Ausstattung erhalten; allein der Stuckmarmor ist 1845 von Moosbrugger neu angefertigt worden. Das Wichtigste ist die gemalte Decke, deren hohes Muldengewölbe mit den straßenseitig einschneidenden Mezzaninfenstern eine Quadratur mit in die Tiefe gestaffelten Feldern und Kassetten, ganz nach bolognesischer Art, zeigt. Die figuralen Partien sind hier

together the self-enclosed elements by the weight of its appearance.

Complete uncertainty reigned about the subsequent owners (prior to the purchase by the Lobkowitz family in 1745), until the coat of arms was taken down for regilding in the course of restoration work, when the arms of the Althan family were discovered in the stone. The records from the Lobkowitz archive in Leitmeritz, which only became accessible later on, finally confirmed that the palace entered the possession of Count Gundacker von Althan, who purchased it in 1724. Superintendant of the whole of the Imperial building trade, (that is, as court building director and chief construction official of the Habsburg Empire), Althan had a most important role in determining the Imperial style under Karl VI. At the same time chief inspector of the newly founded Imperial Academy for Painters and Sculptors, and of the Imperial Picture Gallery, Althan was an undisputed authority on matters of art. This elevated claim must therefore also apply to the Althan town palace, whose size and proximity to the Hofburg impressively demonstrates its owner's important position at court. It is a testament both to the court building director's appreciation of art and to a work of architecture which still matched the highest artistic standards even a quarter of a century after it was built.

The change which Althan made to the outside is a remarkably minor one, concerning the group of arms bearers at the central window above the portal. It is uncertain whether the hall window had already received the arched form which it has today, or only received it under Lobkowitz. Replacing the heavy segmental pediments, the arched form provided better lighting, and it is equally probable that it is connected with the measures undertaken to the inside of the house.

It was at this time that the banqueting hall received its present form, including the windows (which are closed on the courtyard side) and the decoration; only the stucco marble was remade by Moosbrugger in 1845. The most important feature is the painted ceiling, whose high trough-vaulting, with the steep mezzanine windows on the street side, displays a quadratura with

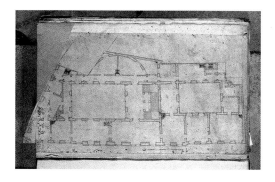

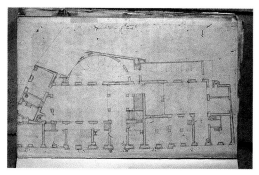

Johann Bernhard Fischer und Tencala-Werkstatt, Palais Dietrichstein, Erdgeschoß und 1. Obergeschoß
Johann Bernhard Fischer and Tencala office, Palais Dietrichstein, ground floor and 1st floor

nicht wie üblich ebenfalls in Fresko, sondern in der französischen Marouflage-technik, als Ölbilder auf Leinwand, mit Kolophonium an die Decke und in die Wölbekehle geheftet. Im Mittelfeld ist der Ruhm verkündende Fama-Engel dargestellt, an den sich ein Genius mit Malerpalette und Farbpinsel schmiegt. Auf den Bildern der Randzone sind Allegorien der Ingenieurbaukunst, der Meß- und Gartenkunst, von Musik und Poesie, Optik und Geographie, schließlich der Einblick in ein Maler- und Bildhaueratelier der Akademie und deren jährliche Preisverleihung zu sehen. Es handelt sich, wie Haberditzl festgestellt hat, um eine Allegorie der 1726 gegründeten kaiserlichen Maler- und Bildhauerakademie, entworfen und ausgeführt von ihrem ersten Direktor Jakob van Schuppen, und sohin um eine Huldigung an das Oberhaupt dieses Institutes, Gundacker von Althan, der uns heute als Auftraggeber bekannt ist. Da die Akademie viele Jahre im Althanschen Haus in der Seilergasse untergebracht war, darf vermutet werden, daß der Saal im Palais auch als Festsaal der Akademie gedient hat.

Weitere Bezüge zur Person des Auftraggebers sind nicht zu übersehen: als Kommandant der Festung Raab durch den Festungsplan dieser Stadt und durch die Darstellung des Grundrisses eines Gartenpalastes, bei dem es sich nach Lage der Dinge offenbar um das im Frühjahr 1729 erstellte Projekt des Anton Erhard Martinelli für die von Althan angekaufte Liegenschaft an der Ungargasse handelt. Diese noch an einen Altbestand gebundene Planung war nur ganz kurz aktuell und wurde durch das – leider nur mehr aus den Stichen Salomon Kleiners bekannte – Ausführungsprojekt Fischers des Jüngeren ersetzt.

In der Repräsentationsraumfolge zwischen Portal und Saal hat Althan noch einen weiteren bemerkenswerten Akzent gesetzt: Der Herkules-Brunnen in der Halle des Vestibüls muß damals entweder neu geschaffen oder – wahrscheinlicher – umgestaltet worden sein. Die mit tropfsteinähnlichem Grottenwerk ausgekleidete Nische zeigt den auf eine Keule gestützten Herkules, mit Löwe und Stier, gekrönt durch einen weiblichen Genius. Bei der Restaurierung hat sich gezeigt, daß die in

staggered fields and boxes in perspective, quite in Bolognese fashion. The figural parts are here not executed as the usual frescoes, but with the French *marouflage* technique, as oil paintings on canvas, attached with colophonium to the ceiling and to the valley of the vaulting. In the central field is a representation of the Angel of Fame proclaiming fame, against whom nestles a genius with a painter's palette and brush. In the pictures around the edges are allegories of the sciences of engineering, surveying, optics and geography, as well as of the arts of music, poetry and gardening; finally, there can also be seen the view of one of the studios for painters and sculptors at the Academy, and the annual prize-giving ceremony held there. As Haberditzl has established, this is an allegory of the Imperial Academy for Painters and Sculptors, founded in 1726, designed and executed by its first director, Jacob von Schuppen; it is thus also a tribute to the head of this institute, Gundacker von Althan, whom we know today to have commissioned it. Since the Academy was for many years housed in Althan's residence in Seilergasse, it is suspected that the hall in the Palais might also have served as the Academy's banqueting hall.

One cannot fail to notice other connections to Althan's person: in the plans for the town fortress of Raab when he was its commander; or in the ground plan of a palace with gardens. By all appearances, the latter was obviously the same project which was designed by Anton Erhard Martinelli in 1729, for the property purchased by Althan in the Ungargasse. Still based on the old construction, this design was current for only a short time and was replaced by the project drawn up by Fischer the Younger, which is unfortunately only known today from the engravings of Salomon Kleiner.

Althan added a further, remarkable touch to the sequence of prestigious rooms between the portal and the hall: namely, the Hercules fountain in the vestibule, which at that time must have been either redesigned or – more probably – remodelled. The niche is lined with dripstone-like grotto figures and shows Hercules leaning on his club, with a lion and a bull, and being

Pose und Auffassung direkt dem Herkules Farnese nachempfundene Figur des mythologischen Helden Spuren einer späteren Überarbeitung aufweist. So ist etwa der Kopf angestückt und der Fellschurz dem nackten Körper in Stuckmasse nachträglich aufmodelliert worden. Da gerade der Kopf des Herkules und der geflügelte Genius unverkennbare Züge der Hofbildhauerwerkstatt des Lorenzo Mattielli aufweisen, läßt sich dessen – von Claudia Maué bereits vermutete – Urheberschaft nunmehr zwanglos als Adaptierung und Modernisierung einer in der Nische seit ehedem aufgestellten Brunnenfigur erklären. Daß der den Figuren der Reichskanzlei zum Verwechseln ähnliche weibliche Genius neu hinzugefügt wurde, erhellt zudem eine Zeichnung des seit 1730 in Wien weilenden Mattielli-Schülers Johann Wolfgang van der Auwera, welche die Komposition nicht in der endgültigen Fassung, sondern noch mit der früher offenbar axial aufgestellten Herkules-Figur wiedergibt. Als kaiserlicher Hofkünstler unterstand Lorenzo Mattielli ebenso wie der Hofarchitekt Fischer von Erlach unmittelbar dem kunstsinnigen Hofbaudirektor, der sich verständlicherweise auch privat ihrer Meisterschaft bediente.

An der übrigen Ausstattung von Vestibül und Stiegenhaus hat Althan nichts geändert, denn das schwere Stuckwerk des tonnengewölbten Eingangs und der arkadierten Halle verrät eine noch merklich dem Frühbarock anhängende Hand. Der in seinem Charakter völlig andersartige Stuck in den von toskanischen Säulen getragenen Stiegenhausgewölben hingegen gehört mit seinen großspiraligen Akanthusranken Mitte der 1690er Jahre zu den frühesten Beispielen hochbarocker Ausstattungskunst auf Wiener Boden. Daß auch hier, im Hausinneren, eine in den Supraporten, Nischen und Eckkartuschen noch erhaltene Erstausstattung plötzlich in gewandelter Formvorstellung Fortsetzung gefunden hat, entspricht vollkommen dem am Außenbau konstatierten Eingreifen Fischers. Es ist die eigentliche Geburtsstunde des Wiener Barocks, des Heldenzeitalters der österreichischen Kunst.

crowned by a female genius. The restoration showed that the figure of the mythological hero, which is directly based on Hercules Farnese, displays traces of later reworking. The head, for instance, has been added separately and the sheepskin loincloth was modelled on to the naked body in pieces of stucco later. The head of Hercules and the winged genius show unmistakeable signs of having been executed in the studio of the court sculptor Lorenzo Mattielli, and this attribution – already postulated by Claudia Maué – can now also be accepted with certainty for the adaptation and modernisation of a fountain figure which had long since been in the niche. Furthermore, the fact that a female genius, confusingly similar to the figures in the Imperial Chancery, was added later, is elucidated by a drawing by Mattielli's pupil, Johann Wolfgang van der Auwera, who lived in Vienna from 1730 onwards. The sketch reproduces the composition not in its final version but with the earlier figure of Hercules, evidently set up axially. As an artist at the Imperial court, Lorenzo Mattielli, like the court architect Fischer von Erlach, was subordinate to the artistically-minded Court Director of Building, who, understandably enough, also availed himself of these masters' services directly for private commissions.

Althan changed nothing else of the decoration of the vestibule and staircase, for the heavy stucco of the tunnel-vaulted entrance and the arcaded hall betray a hand which adheres noticeably to the early Baroque. In contrast, the staircase vaulting, (which is borne by Tuscan pillars) displays a section which is completely different in nature, belonging, with its large spiralling acanthus tendrils from the mid-1690s, to the earliest examples of High Baroque decorative art in Vienna. The fact that here, in the interior of the house, the earliest decoration, which still survives in the sopraportes, niches and corner cartouches, is suddenly continued with a very different formal approach, in complete accord with those of Fischer's additions which have been noticed in the external structure. It is the actual birth of Viennese Baroque, of the heroic age of Austrian art.

Palais Lobkowitz nach der Renovierung (Karl und Eva Mang), Österreichisches Theatermuseum
Palais Lobkowitz after renovation (Karl and Eva Mang), Austrian Theatre Museum

Theatermuseum, großer Innenhof für Freiluftaufführungen
Theatre Museum, large courtyard for open air performances

Eingangshalle mit Ausstellungsobjekten
Entrance hall with museum exhibits

Stiegenhaus mit Ausstellungsobjekten
Staircase with museum exhibits

Ausstellungsraum
Exhibition room

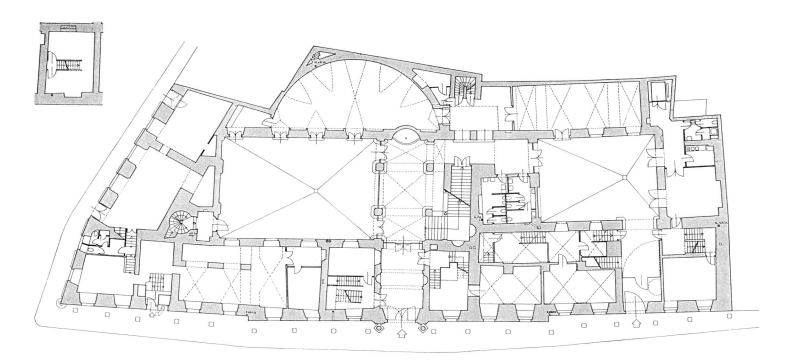

Erdgeschoß des renovierten Theatermuseums
Ground floor of the renovated Theatre Museum

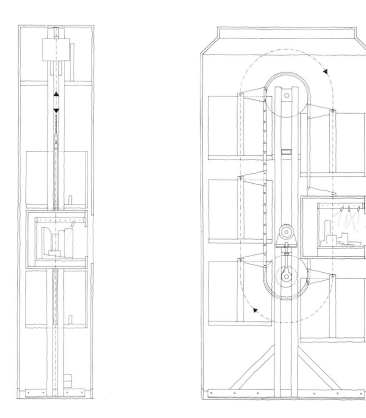

Präsentationstechnik für Bühnenbilder
(links »Aufzug«, rechts »Paternoster«)
Presentation technique for models of stage sets
(left 'elevator', right 'paternoster lift')

Museumspositionen

Peter Rebernik

Museum Positions

Peter Rebernik

Technisches Museum Wien, Luftbild, vor 1988
Technical Museum of Vienna, aerial photograph,
pre-1988

Was soll uns heute ein technisches Museum, wo doch die bubenhaft-begeisternde Unschuld der Utopie des technischen Fortschritts mit Exxon-Valdez, Challenger und Tschernobyl verloren wurde? Leuchtende Augen über monströse Verkehrssysteme, Raumfahrt oder Kommunikationstechnologie hervorrufbar machen?

Aber: Kann oder soll ein technisches Museum deshalb den Menschen als Werkzeugmacher, als Planer, Entwickler, Denker, Realisierer, als Benützer von Technik und Wissenschaft verleugnen?

Museen als Kulturinstitutionen sind Spiegel unserer selbst in die Vergangenheit und Zukunft und schlagen jene Saiten in uns an, deren Vibrieren wir zur Lebensintensität nützen.

Das Museum will den Blick in den Spiegel menschlicher Wesenheit schöpferisch fördern.

Das Museum – nicht das Museale – sondern das Dynamisch-Darstellende und Dramatisch-Präsentierende – erlaubt sich, einzugreifen in die Welt, nimmt sich heraus, ein Spiegel mit besonderem Rahmen zu sein, vergilt Unverständnis mit Stille und menschliches Suchen mit Offenstellen neuer Wege.

Aus der Gegenüberstellung von Verschiedenem erkennt der Mensch seinen eigenen multichromatischen Eigenschaftsraum, erfreut sich daran, fürchtet sich davor und versucht ihn und damit sich selbst als ein Ganzes zu verdrängen.

Die Reaktion auf Versuche zur kulturellen Destabilisierung kennzeichnet uns:

Wir, Spießer-Bürger, antworten mit einerseits gewollt harmonisierenden und andrerseits das Andere in uns und in anderen verdammender Eindimensionalität des einmal gefundenen und ängstlich bewahrten Weges.

Wir, liberale Bürger, vereinnahmen bereichert das fremde Gedankengut, schmükken unseren Lebensweg mit fremden Blüten, ohne ihn jedoch wesentlich zu verlassen.

Wir, Nicht-Bürger, werden aus der Bahn

What is the point of a Technical Museum, when the boyishly enthusiastic innocence of the utopia of technical progress disappeared with Exxon-Valdez, Challenger and Chernobyl? Eyes sparkling at monstrous traffic systems, space travel or communication technology?

Nonetheless: can or should a technical museum for that reason deny human beings as toolmakers, planners, developers, thinkers, manufacturers, as users of technology and science?

Museums as cultural institutions are reflections of ourselves in the past and the future, and strike chords within us whose vibrations we use to intensify our lives.

The museum wants to help people in a creative way to look into the mirror of human wisdom.

The museum – not in its role as a guardian of the past, but rather in its dynamic representational and dramatic presentational aspects – allows itself to intervene in the world, has the presumption to act as a mirror in a special frame, repaying incomprehension with silence and the human search with newly opened paths.

By comparing things which are different, man recognises his own polychromatic sphere of qualities and rejoices at this prospect, but becomes afraid of it, attempts to repress it and in doing so represses himself as a whole.

We are characterised by our reactions to attempts at cultural destabilisation:

We middle-class citizens answer with the one-dimensionality of people who once found the path and have anxiously preserved it, on the one hand harmonising deliberately yet, on the other hand, condemning the 'other' both within ourselves and within others.

We liberal citizens enrich ourselves by absorbing the foreign intellectual tradition, adorning our lives' path with the blossoms of others; without, however, essentially departing from it.

We non-citizens are thrown off course and our lives are changed.

geworfen, unser Leben wird verändert. Für wen sollte im Museum gearbeitet und dargestellt, dargeboten werden? Lebensbehübschend, als sakrales Reservat für Unbetroffene, Untreffbare? Spielen Museen belanglos-unterhaltendes Revuetheater mit schön drapierten Objekten? Oder schnitzen Museen gleichsam an hart gespannten Bögen mit Pfeilen, die so manchen treffen sollen?

Museen stellen gegenüber. Stellen dar. Plazieren das Ungeheure, das Erst- oder Einmalige ungewollt in bequem spazierbaren Räumen. Verniedlichen scheinbar die Vergangenheit durch beleuchtete, geschlossene Vitrinen und akademische Erklärungen.

Für den Gelangweilten und den in Wahrheit Unbetroffenen bleibt die kulturelle Erbauung eine Vergnügung für verregnete Tage. Für andere ein Ausflug zu unentdeckten Teilen seines eigenen Wesens.

Museen machen die Menschheit begehbar.

For whom should the museum do its work, representing and presenting things? Prettifying life, as a sacred reserve for people who are unaffected, unreachable? Are museums performing an entertaining but trivial theatre revue, with beautifully draped objects? Or are museums carving away, as it were, at a tightly-drawn bow and arrows, aiming to let fly at someone or other?

Museums confront. Represent. Inadvertently place what is prodigious, new or unique in rooms one can comfortably walk around. Would seem to trivialise the past with illuminated, locked showcases and academic explanations.

For people who are bored or those who really are unaffected, cultural edification is still a pleasure for rainy days. For others it is a trip to undiscovered parts of their own being.

Museums make humanity accessible.

Technisches Museum Wien, Großer Ausstellungsraum, Vorführung
Technical Museum of Vienna, large exhibition hall, guided tour

Technisches Museum Wien – Zur Funktion

Brennig, Christen, Stepanek, Thetter, Wimmer

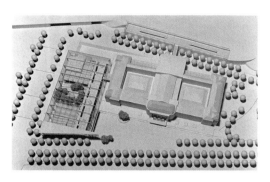

Wettbewerb Erweiterung Technisches Museum Wien, 1. Preis, 1990: Architektengruppe Brennig, Christen, Stepanek, Thetter, Wimmer Competition for the extension to the Technical Museum of Vienna, 1st prize 1990: architectural team Brennig, Christen, Stepanek, Thetter, Wimmer

Ein architektonisch und energietechnisch innovatives Bauvorhaben ist der Neubau des Technischen Museums, der von der Architektengruppe »Atelier in der Schönbrunner Straße« in Wien entworfen wurde. Die Modellaufnahmen zeigen das Gebäude, in dem sehr gut im hinteren Bereich (langgestreckte Bebauung) Büros und Schulungsräume erkennbar sind, während im vorderen linken Bereich ständige Ausstellungsflächen untergebracht werden.

Im mittleren, vorderen Bereich ist in der Halle eine Baumgruppe erkennbar, die zur Zeit auf dem Baugelände steht und erhalten werden soll. Im rechten, vorderen Bereich ist eine Fläche für Wechselausstellungen oder Großprojekte vorgesehen. Den rechten Abschluß (dreieckige Gebäudestruktur) des Gesamtkomplexes bildet ein Baukörper, der Restaurants und Verweilzonen aufnimmt. In einem ersten Ansatz wurde durch das Ingenieurunternehmen O. Arup, London, ein ökologisches Konzept zum Teil passiver, zum Teil aktiver Maßnahmen entwickelt, das in den Schema-Bildern dargestellt ist.

Dieses Konzept geht von einer äußeren Doppelhülle des gesamten Baukörpers aus, ähnlich den Gebäuden, die in der Vergangenheit mit sogenannten Klimahüllen ausgerüstet wurden. Eine äußere Glashaut und eine dahinterliegende, innere Glashaut umhüllen somit die eigentlichen Nutzflächen einschließlich des Gartens mit den bestehenden Bäumen. Es wurde bei diesem Konzept davon ausgegangen, daß die Einwirkungen von außen zwischen den beiden Glashüllen soweit als möglich eliminiert werden, um die gebäudeinneren Nutzbereiche soweit als möglich abzuschirmen. Hieraus ergibt sich zwangsläufig die Notwendigkeit, den gesamten Gebäudekomplex, ähnlich wie beim Technologiepark in Duisburg, über das ganze Jahr hinweg lufttechnisch zu behandeln, das heißt zu heizen oder zu kühlen.

Technical Museum of Vienna – On function

Brennig, Christen, Stepanek, Thetter, Wimmer

The new building of the Technical Museum in Vienna was designed by the group of architects "Atelier in the Schönbrunnerstrasse", Vienna. It is an innovative project as far as its architecture and energy technology is concerned. The photographs of the model show us the building, with the offices and training rooms easily visible in the background (elongated building), and the areas where the permanent exhibitions will be housed in the foreground, to the left. In the hall in the centre of the foreground can be seen a group of trees which at present stands on the building site and which it is intended to preserve. In the foreground, right, is an area for temporary exhibitions or large-scale objects. The right end (triangular structure) of the whole complex is composed of an architectural envelope which includes restaurants and relaxation areas. In a first estimate, the firm of engineers O. Arup, London, developed an ecological concept involving partly passive, partly active measures, and these are represented in the diagrams.

This concept proceeds from the external double envelope of the construction as a whole, similar to that of buildings which were fitted with so-called air-conditioning envelopes in the past. An outer glass skin and a inner glass skin located behind it envelope in this way the actual utilisable area, including the garden with the existing trees. On the basis of this concept it was assumed that the influences penetrating between the two glass envelopes from outside would be largely eliminated, allowing the utilisable area on the inside of the building to be screened off as much as possible. As a matter of course, this resulted in the necessity of employing ventilation and air-conditioning technology for the whole building complex (i.e. to heat or cool it) all the year round, as in the case of the Technology Park in Duisburg.

The diagrams show the hall in operation in

Die Schemazeichnungen zeigen den Betrieb der Halle im Winter und im Sommer. Wie beide Darstellungen ausweisen, werden auch hier neben den passiven Maßnahmen aktive ökologische Maßnahmen eingesetzt, um den Primärenergiebedarf (Heiz- und Kälteenergie) so klein als möglich zu halten. Hiebei jedoch ist fraglich, ob Grundwasser zur direkten Kühlung des Gebäudes eingesetzt werden kann, da dies in der Regel heute weitestgehend verboten wird.

Nach eingehender Diskussion des ersten ökologischen Konzepts wurde nicht zuletzt auch aus Gründen der Notwendigkeit, Investitionskosten zu sparen, durch uns gemeinsam mit Univ.-Prof. Klaus Daniels, München, eine neue Planungsphilosophie entwickelt. Diese besagt, daß anstatt der Zweischaligkeit des Gebäudes lediglich eine Einschaligkeit vorzusehen ist und das gesamte Gebäudekonzept so angelegt werden sollte, daß sich das Haus im Sommer und im Winter ähnlich verhält wie ein Mensch, der sich im Sommer sehr leicht und luftig kleidet und im Winter einen Wintermantel überzieht.

In den Schemata wird diese Philosophie bildhaft dargestellt. Im Winter wird die einfach verglaste, äußere Glashülle weitestgehend geschlossen, um passive Wärmegewinne nutzen zu können. Eine natürliche Durchlüftung des Hallenraumes mit Bäumen erfolgt nur insoweit, daß einmal hygienische Raumverhältnisse entstehen und weiterhin eine Überheizung dieses Raumbereiches vermieden wird. Dabei wird davon ausgegangen, daß zur Erhaltung der bestehenden Bäume im zentralen Hallenbereich im Winter maximal Temperaturen von +12 °C entstehen dürfen, so daß der Jahresrhythmus für diese Pflanzen nicht eingeschränkt wird und somit keine irreparablen Schäden entstehen. Die ständige Ausstellungsfläche in der linken Seite des Gebäudes ist im wesentlichen umhüllt (Haus-in-Haus-Lösung) und kann somit ausreichend beheizt und gelüftet werden. Offene Ausstellungsbereiche, die in direkter Verbindung mit dem Grün des Gebäudes stehen, sollen durch eine Warmluftheizung von unten nach oben beheizt und gegebenenfalls unterstützend mit Infrarotstrahlern ausgerüstet werden. Unter

both winter and summer. As the two representations demonstrate, here too, active as well as passive ecological measures will be applied, in order to keep the requirements for primary energy (hot and cold energy) as low as possible. However, it is questionable whether or not ground water can be used to cool the building directly, since in general this is largely prohibited today.

After extensive discussion of the first ecological concept, we developed a new planning philosophy, not least on account of the necessity to reduce investment costs (in conjunction with Prof. Klaus Daniels, Munich). It involved providing only one envelope for the building instead of two, and laying out the whole complex in such a way as to enable the museum to behave in winter and summer like a human being, who wears light and airy clothes in summer and an overcoat in winter.

This philosophy is represented pictorially in the diagrams. In winter, the simply glazed, outer glass envelope is closed as far as possible in order to be able to take advantage of passive heat gains. Natural through-ventilation of the hall containing the trees occurs only to the extent of creating hygienic spatial conditions and avoiding any overheating of the area. In this it is assumed that to keep the existing trees in the central area of the hall in winter requires temperatures of around 12 degrees centigrade, in order to ensure that the trees' annual rhythm is not restricted and no irreparable harm is done. The permanent exhibition area in the left part of the building is to a large extent enveloped (house-in-house solution) and can therefore be sufficiently heated and air-conditioned. Open exhibition areas, which are in a direct relationship to the greenery of the building, will be heated by means of warm-air heating from below and, if necessary, fitted with supplementary infrared panels. Should it be necessary, lightweight folding glass walls will have to screen the greenery room from the exhibition area. The same applies to the area for temporary exhibitions.

In summer, an intensive, natural through-ventilation of the building occurs, simultaneously with the implementation of sun-

Erweiterung Technisches Museum Wien, Modell
Extension to the Technical Museum of Vienna, model

Erweiterung Technisches Museum Wien, Modell
Extension to the Technical Museum of Vienna,
model

Umständen müssen hier leichte Glasfaltwände den Grünraum gegen die Ausstellungsflächen abschirmen. Das gleiche gilt auch für den Bereich der Wechselausstellung.

Im Sommer erfolgt eine intensive, natürliche Durchlüftung des Gebäudes bei gleichzeitigem Einsatz von Sonnenschutzmaßnahmen innerhalb des Gebäudes zur Vermeidung von Überheizungen usw. Auf Grund des Standortes und der zu erwartenden Windgeschwindigkeiten und Windhäufigkeiten ist eine natürliche, ausreichende Durchlüftung in jedem Fall gegeben, wobei an den wenigen Tagen mit Windstille die Thermik im Inneren der glasumhüllten Flächen für eine Durchlüftung sorgt.

Aktive ökologische Maßnahmen, wie bei den vorher gezeigten Beispielen, sind selbstverständlich auch bei diesem Objekt möglich und werden unter Kosten-Nutzen-Gesichtspunkten eingesetzt.

Die Architektur und Planungsphilosophie kann für das Technische Museum wie folgt zusammengefaßt werden.

– Öffne ein Haus im Sommer
– durchlüfte es natürlich so lange als möglich
– schütze die Nutzer gegen intensive Sonneneinstrahlung durch geeignete Maßnahmen
– schließe das Haus im Winter
– gewinne durch die Sonne so viel Wärmeenergie als möglich
– verbessere das Mikroklima im Gebäude durch natürliche Maßnahmen usw.

(Anmerkung des Herausgebers: Der Neubau des Zubaues wurde auf unbestimmte Zeit verschoben.)

protection measures below the outer glass envelope, in order to avoid overheating etc.. Due to the location of the site and the expected frequency and velocity of winds, sufficient natural ventilation will certainly be provided, and on the few windless days it will occur by means of the thermal currents in the interior of the glass-enveloped areas.

As the examples outlined above show, it is quite possible to apply ecological measures in the case of such a building as this too, and to implement them cost-effectively.

The architecture and planning philosophy for the Technical Museum can be summarised as follows:

Open a building in summer – ventilate it naturally for as long as possible – protect the users against intensive sun radiation by taking appropriate measures – close the building in winter – gain as much heat energy as possible form the sun – improve the micro-climate in the building by taking natural measures etc.

(Editor's note: The construction of a new museum's wing has been postponed.)

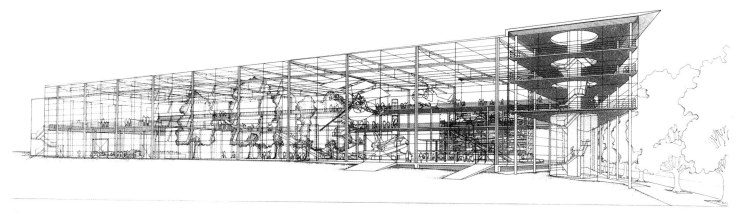

Perspektive Erweiterung Technisches Museum Wien, 1992
Perspective drawing, extension to the Technical Museum of Vienna, 1992

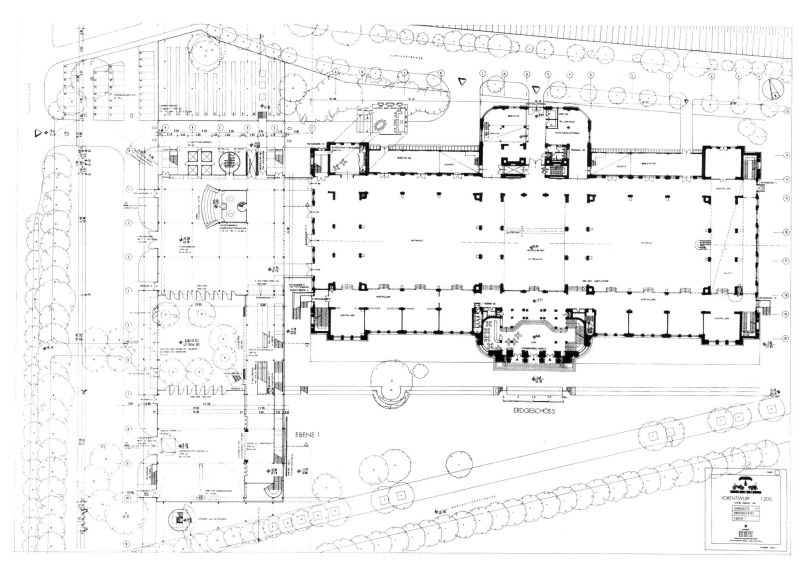

Altbau und Neubau (links), Erdgeschoßplan
Existing building and new extension (left), ground floor plan

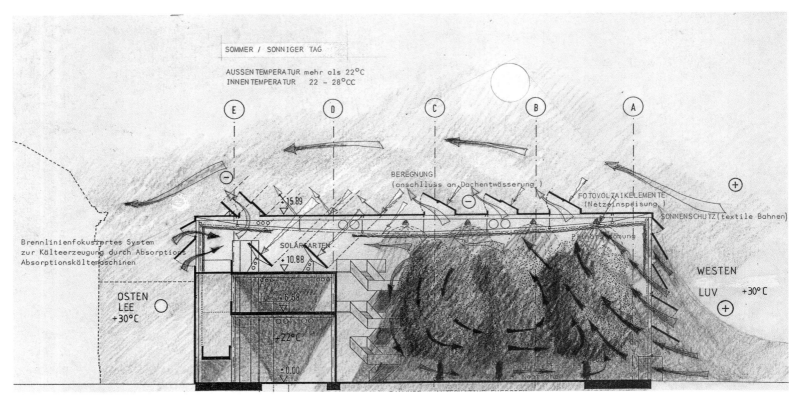

Ökologisches Konzept, Sommer, sonniger Tag
Ecological concept, summer, sunny day

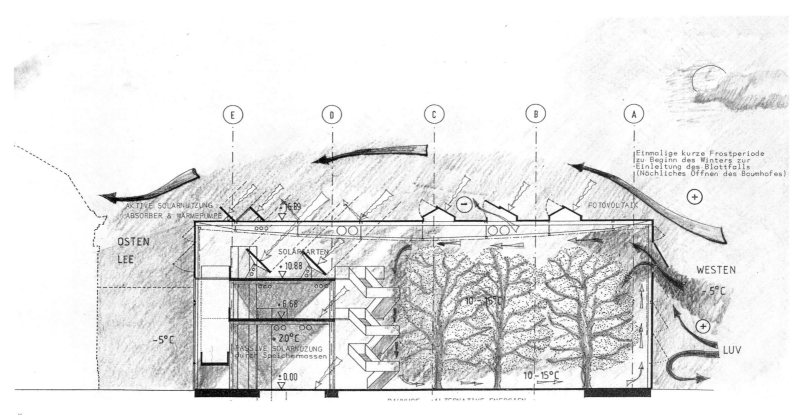

Ökologisches Konzept, Winter
Ecological concept, winter

Ansicht des neuen Museumsflügels, Modell
View of the new wing of the museum, model

Altbau und neuer Museumsflügel, Modell
Existing building and new wing of the museum, model

Neuer Museumsflügel, Innenraum
New wing of the museum, interior

Neuer Museumsflügel, Modell
New wing of the museum, model

Ein »Stadtfragment« für ein Kunstkonzept – oder Ein »Raum-Kunst-Konzept«

Wolfdieter Dreibholz

Nach allen Erfahrungen braucht neue Kunst neue Räume und schaffen neue Räume neue Kunst und neues Publikum. Dafür gibt es positive Beispiele vom Ennstal in der Steiermark bis Paris, vom »culturcentrum wolkenstein« – einer regionalen Kulturinitiative in der Steiermark – bis zum Centre Pompidou in der französischen Metropole.

Im Zusammenhang mit dem steigenden Interesse, das zeitgenössischer bildender Kunst entgegengebracht wird, hat in den achtziger Jahren eine internationale Dezentralisierungstendenz bei Ausstellungshäusern und Museen eingesetzt. Dezentralisation bedeutet heute nicht mehr nur konkrete kulturpolitische Regionalisierung, sondern drückt das gleichwertige Verhältnis der gewachsenen kulturhistorischen Landschaften in einem großen europäischen, übernationalen Kontext aus. Das Europa der Zukunft wird auch ein Europa der Regionen sein.

Graz und die Steiermark haben sich entschlossen, an diese bereits fortgeschrittene Entwicklung mit einem Ausstellungshaus überregionalen Zuschnitts anzuschließen. Die Forum-Stadtpark-Bewegung, der Steirische Herbst und die Trigon-Idee, kulturell bedeutende Initiativen der Moderne, haben das Vorfeld für diese Entscheidung aufbereitet.

Die Notwendigkeit eines Neubaus ergab sich in Graz aus mehreren Gründen. Einerseits ist die Neue Galerie im Palais Herberstein räumlich überlastet. Es wird dort möglich sein, nach dem neuesten Raumgewinn und mit einer eventuellen Hofüberdachung einen anspruchsvollen Museumsbetrieb weiterzuführen. Gewisse Vorhaben sind in dem alten Barockpalais aber auf die Dauer nicht unterzubringen. So fehlt es in Graz an einer großen, zusammenhängenden Ausstellungsfläche. Das machte es bisher unmöglich, eine vom Umfang her wirklich bedeutende Schau –

A "City Fragment" for an Art Concept, or an "Space Design Concept"

Wolfdieter Dreibholz

Experience tells us that new art needs new spaces and that new spaces create new art and a new public. Positive examples of this exist everywhere: from Ennstal in Styria to Paris, from the *culturcentrum wolkenstein* (a regional cultural initiative in Styria) to the Centre Pompidou in the French metropolis.

The 80s saw the start of an international trend towards the decentralisation of exhibition houses and museums, in connection with the increased interest shown in the contemporary visual arts. Today, decentralisation no longer means simply the actual regionalisation of arts policy, but is an expression of the equal standing of developed cultural-historical landscapes in a large-scale supra-national European context. The Europe of the future will also be a Europe of regions.

Graz and Styria have decided to join this already advanced development with an exhibition house of international calibre. The Forum Stadtpark movement, the Steirische Herbst and the Trigon concept, all of them culturally important modernist initiatives, have helped to prepare the ground for this decision.

The necessity for a new building in Graz has arisen for a number of reasons. On the one hand, the Neue Galerie in Palais Herberstein is overtaxed spatially. The latest spatial gains and perhaps a new roof over the courtyard will make it possible to continue to run a museum of high standards there. Yet, from a long-term point of view, certain projects cannot be housed in the old Baroque palace. Thus Graz lacks a large integrated exhibition space. Up until now, this has made it impossible for the provincial capital of Styria to host any exhibition of real importance as far as size is concerned - whether traditional or modern. Up until now, large exhibitions have regularly by-passed Graz. The patchwork of the Trigon Biennale exhibitions in the

ob traditionell oder modern – in die steirische Landeshauptstadt zu bringen. Große Ausstellungen sind bisher an Graz regelmäßig vorübergegangen.

Das Trigon-Haus wird sein Wirkungsgebiet in konzentrischen Kreisen sehen müssen, erstens in der Steiermark und Österreich, zweitens in einem Mitteleuropa, das auf sinnvolle Weise seit Jahrzehnten gewachsene kulturpolitische Verbindungen weiterführt, ohne drittens im Rahmen der Möglichkeiten den internationalen Kontext zu übersehen.

Das Projekt der Architekten Schöffauer, Schrom und Tschapeller, das in einem internationalen Wettbewerb preisgekrönt wurde, bietet im Vergleich zu Ausstellungshäusern im Ausland in verwandter kulturgeographischer Situation die angemessenen und notwendigen Ausstellungsflächen. Die Struktur des projektierten Gebäudes – ein »Stadtfragment« (so ein Juror) – und seine Interpretation als Haus für Erlebnis und Ereignis dürften dem Gebäude von vornherein überregionales Interesse sichern.

Was seine Funktion anlangt, handelt es sich um ein Haus für moderne bildende Kunst im weitesten Sinne des Wortes, eine Stätte für Ereignisse und Erlebnisse durch Ausstellungen und Vorführungen aller Art. Es muß auf die Zukunft gerichtet sein, offen für alle Entwicklungen, ohne Abkapselungen. Es muß durch Kooperation mit künstlerischen und wissenschaftlichen Personen und Einrichtungen interdisziplinär wirken. Es muß Impulse auffangen und seinerseits ausstrahlen, Empfangs- und Sendestation sein. Bei aller Blickrichtung auf Gegenwart und Zukunft muß es auch möglich sein, vergangene Wurzeln von Entwicklungen zu zeigen, um Gegenwart zu erhellen. Die Verwendung und Präsentation visueller und auditiver, digitaler und elektronischer Medien muß gesichert sein. Einsatz von Photographie, Video und Film, Computergraphik, experimenteller Installation und Aktionen gehören dazu.

Das Haus wird Künstlern und Publikum in gleicher Weise gewidmet sein und muß für beide offen bleiben.

Neue Galerie and the Kunstlerhaus, which may have seemed attractive in the beginning, has since come to create the impression of provincialism.

The Trigon Museum will have to think of its sphere of activity in terms of concentric circles: encompassing first of all Styria and Austria, secondly Central Europe (which has continued to develop its arts connections in a sensible way for many decades), yet without overlooking, thirdly, the international context as far as that is feasibly relevant.

In comparison to exhibition houses abroad in similar cultural and geographical situations, the project designed by the architects Schöffauer, Schrom and Tschapeller, the winners of the international competition, provides all the appropriate and necessary exhibition areas. The structure of the projected building (a "city fragment", as a juror described it), as well as its interpretation as a place of experience and action, ought to assure the museum international interest from the very start.

As far as its function is concerned, it is to be a museum for modern art in the broadest sense of the word, a place for events and experiences organised in the form of exhibitions and presentations of all kinds. It must also be oriented to the future, open to all developments, and avoid encapsulation. It must have an interdisciplinary effect through co-operation with artists and academics and as well as institutions. It must absorb impulses and in its turn communicate them, acting as both a receiving and transmitting station. Despite being oriented towards the present and the future, there must also be the possibility of indicating the past roots of developments, as a way of elucidating the present. The use and presentation of visual and auditory, digital and electronic media technology must be secured. This includes the use of photography, video and film, computer graphics, experimental installations and actions.

The house will be devoted to artists and the public in the same measure and must remain open for both.

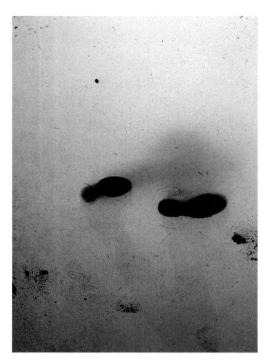

Fußabdruck
Footprints

Zwischen den Stücken

Schöffauer, Schrom, Tschapeller

01	Position	15 24'41" östl. v. Greenwich 47 05'07" nördl. d. Äquators
02	Seehöhe	568 m
03	Niederschlag	838 mm
04	max. Tagesniederschlag	42 mm
05	rel. Luftfeuchte	75% Monatsmittel
06	max. Lufttemperatur	31,6 Grad Celsius
07	min. Lufttemperatur	-13,2 Grad Celsius
08	Sonnenscheindauer h/a.	2045 h

Ich möchte keine Namen nennen. Statt dessen werden gebietsweise Qualitäten entwickelt, die sich in einer sehr reduzierten sprachlichen Terminologie äußern. Es genügt mir zu sagen: dieses Gebiet ist abgeschlossen oder da gibt es eine bestimmte Ansammlung von Licht. In einem Bereich ist die Definition der Luftfeuchtigkeit oder der Temperatur von Bedeutung, dann wieder die Materialkonstanten. Dabei entsteht eine Beschreibung von meteorologischen, geographischen und geologischen Verhältnissen.

1	Grundstücksfläche	ca.	12.714 m²
2	Bebaute Fläche	ca.	6.310 m²
3	Nettogrundrißfläche	ca.	5.688 m²
4	Tara-Grundrißfläche	ca.	622 m²
5	Brutto-Grundrißfläche	ca.	6.310 m²
6	Bruttorauminhalt	ca.	35.900 m³

Der wahre Grund (auf dem hier gebaut werden soll) ist nicht ein Stück, sondern liegt zwischen den Stücken. Die Grundstücke trennenden Linien sind der Grund des Vorhabens. Nicht das Stück. Damit befinden wir uns in einer gegen unendlich konvergierenden Enge. Entweder erfährt das Volumen des Vorhabens die notwendige Verdichtung, oder die Trennlinie expandiert zu dem Raum, der notwendig ist, um das Volumen des Vorhabens aufzunehmen.

7	Versorgung	91 Stück

91 Versorgungseinheiten oder Anschlußstellen für Schwachstrom, Starkstrom, Ton, Bild und Kommunikation werden in einem Netz mit dem Rastermaß von 7 m × 7 m ausgelegt. Diese Zellen sind mit stationären und transportablen Regiepulten verbunden.

8	Versorgung Tageslicht	Tageslichtquotient: Maximalwerte: ca. 4,5%–6,0% Minimalwerte: ca. 2,0%

..., sondern arbeitet in Bereichen mit dem, »das abfällt« mit Resten oder mit Restlicht von anderen Bereichen. Dadurch entstehen vereinzelt »Schattenbereiche« oder differenzierte Helligkeiten, die Produkt der tektonischen Situation sind.

Das Kunstlicht befindet sich auf dem Weg des Sonnenlichts von der Quelle bis zum Aufschlag.

9	Versorgung Kunstlicht	
	Maximalwert:	600 Lux
	Minimalwert:	50 Lux
10	Klima	
	10.1.	
	Fläche: ca.	3.560 m²
	Volumen: ca.	22.083 m³
	10.2.	
	Fläche: ca.	190 m²
	Volumen: ca.	880 m³

Folgende, technisch erzeugte Klimasituationen stehen zur Verfügung:
Temperatur: 17–27 Grad Celsius
Luftfeuchtigkeit: 45%–65%
künstliche Be- und Entlüftung
durchschnittlicher Luftwechsel:
ca. 22.083 m³ × 1,6/h

Temperatur: 18 Grad Celsius konstant
Luftfeuchtigkeit: 45%–55%
künstliche Be- und Entlüftung

11	Vorhandene Bauteile:
	11.1. Stadtmauer:

ca. 1.800 m³ Ziegelmauerwerk
tiefste, nachgewiesene Lage:
ca. –9,00 m unter Niveau
höchster Bereich: ca. +4,70 m über Niveau

Borderlines

Schöffauer, Schrom, Tschapeller

The digits on the left site of what is written here are not about size. They are about a degree of expansion which originates at the very inside of a 'thing' without any interior. Now, look at the place you are at! The 'thing' might be to your left and later to your right. Exactly like those vertical lines on this chart, which separate the territory of numbers from the territory of the words. No digit nor letter dares to touch or to cross those verticals. They are made of chipboard. They are that area which was described above as having no interior, yet there is space between them and there are letters. Imagine those letters growing smaller and smaller to the point where that which seems to be their border, (see the distance you gain from it and how you, or it, approach it again, to be very close to it, to have it right in front of you or at the next moment it covers your rear) is at least the size of the space of what is said between those brackets. They split this sentence in such a way that you cannot remember what was said in the beginning or at the first border of this sentence, nor will you be able to find out what brought you to the point you are at now. This point might be the second border or also that which we call a wall. To bring you back to where you lost sight of the beginning, we have to reduce those letters to a size where that which confines them (and still you are in between) – that which was thin like a line before – grows to an area which still does not have any interior, but gains mass and volume to such a degree that the space you are at now is squeezed together. From now on the place at which you believe you are does not have any interior. You are not at the place you were before. From now on, you are within that which confined the space you were in before. You are within the left margin of this column as you are within the right margin of this column. Thus this text is not only about expansion, it is about contraction and condensation as well. It is also about the change of place and the change of direction. Do the horizontals of this chart behave in a similiar manner to the way the verticals do? Apparently not you, but letters are in between them. They house letters and words like a building gives shelter to people. They behave like walls. They, too, are close to each other. They also behave like frames and they might as well expand to the size mentioned before. But let us look at another case contained by the chart. Suppose those letters would expand. First they would touch on their upper and lower

confinement. Next, they would pass through many confinements, not only those given by this chart. This action could cause serious damage to both, the lines and the letters. (Only one letter would not be affected nor would it affect anything else. Remember the letters we sent across the left margin of this column.) Now, a mutual infection takes place, where the one assumes the qualities of the other without losing its identity or contour. The letters overwrite the lines, whereas the lines are overwritten. The one being on top of the other, or the other being below the one. You might misunderstand this process. You might take it for something which is familiar to you. A situation where there is a line drawn on top of or through the middle of letters. This crossing out (yet again crossing out but not deleting) of letters is not what you should think of. You should not think of the process where you want to eliminate the letters or where you would like to empty them of their interior. In this situation you should not imagine a space or a room without an interior or furniture. (In this situation, that is the place to where this text brought you. In every other situation you should imagine this 'thing' with an inside but without any interior. Remember, this is an area which is familiar to you). This is not what you should concentrate on. Think about the vibration of that which is written here. The way it moves up towards the top only to fall, so to speak, to the bottom. The vibration of the written might also indicate the desire to merge with what is below and what is on top of it. You might sense this weight which is continuously building up, the further you read and the further somebody else has written. Again, you lose control of the situation.

Erdloch
Hole in the earth

Luftaufnahme von Graz mit der Situation des Grundstücks
Aerial photograph of Graz, showing the location of the site

Schnittstellen (Höhenschichtlinien, Bohrpunkte)
Borderlines (contour lines, bore holes)

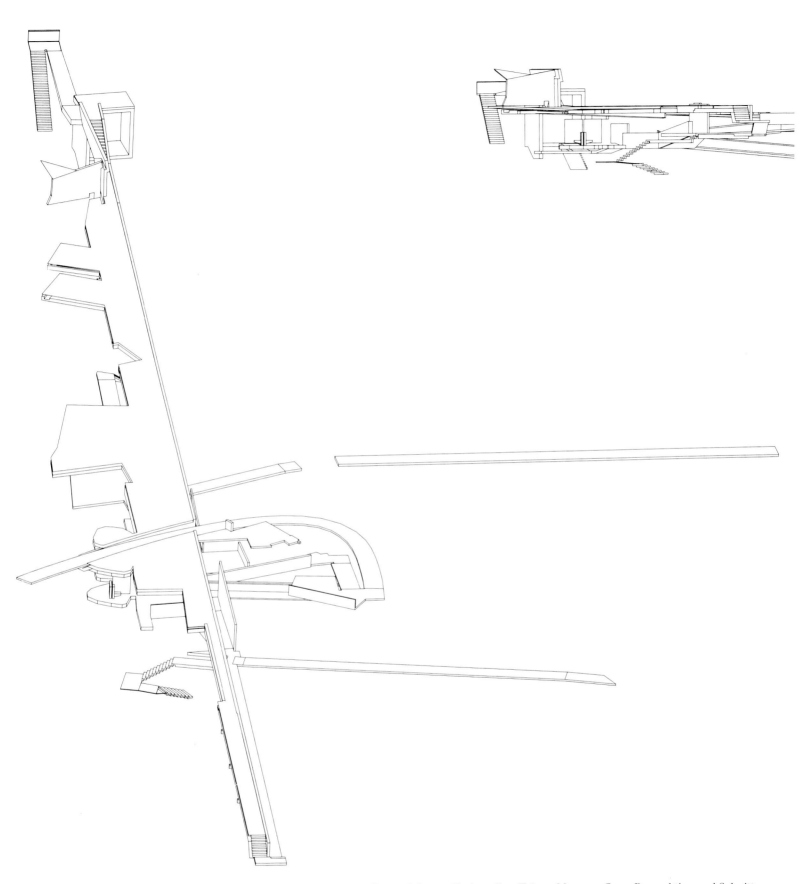

Schöffauer, Schrom, Tschapeller, Trigon Museum Graz, Perspektive und Schnitt
Schöffauer, Schrom, Tschapeller, Trigon Museum Graz, perspective drawing and section

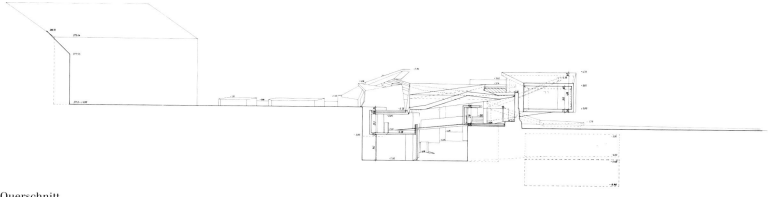

Querschnitt
Section

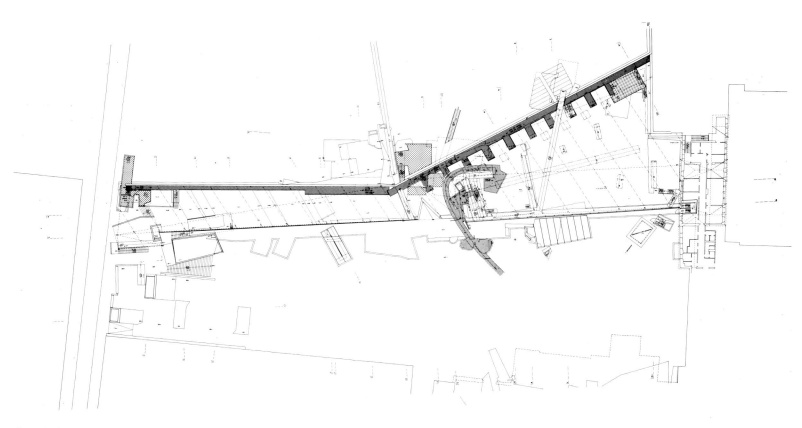

Grundrißplan, Trigon Museum Graz
Floor plan, Trigon Museum Graz

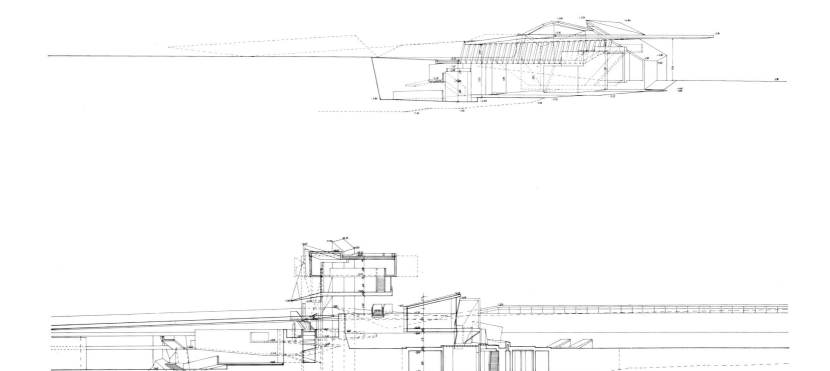

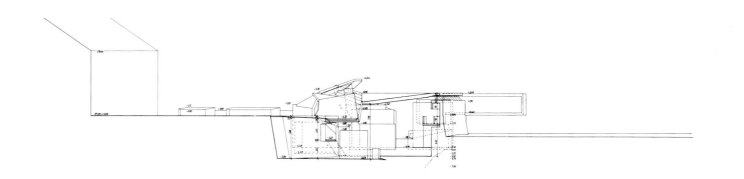

Schnitte durch das Museum
Sections through the museum

Trigon Museum, Modell
Trigon Museum, model

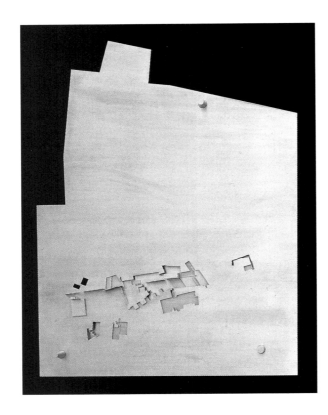
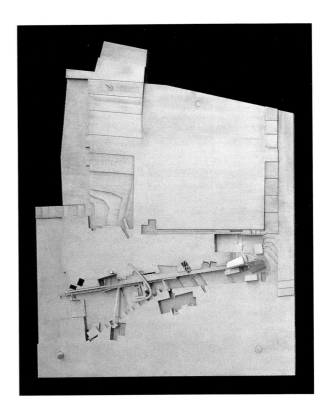
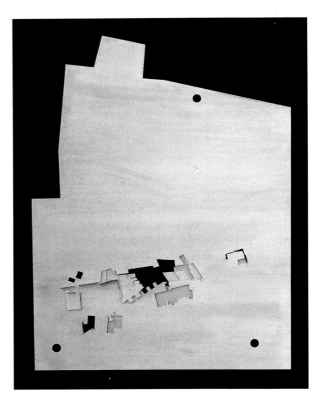

Sequenz von verschiedenen Ebenen des Schichtenmodells
Sequence showing the different levels on a multi-layered model

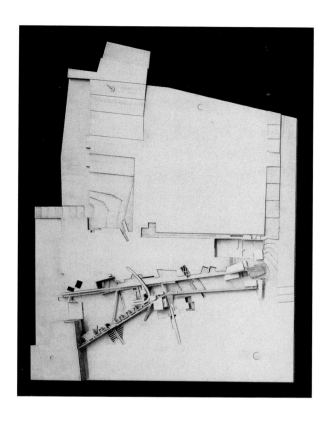
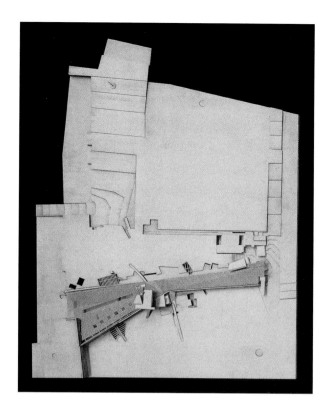
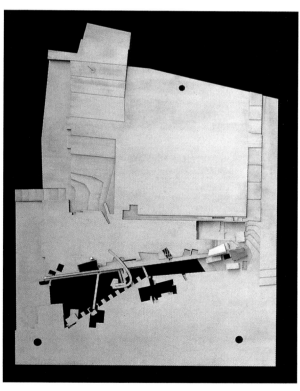

Kurzbiographien

»ATELIER IN DER SCHÖNBRUNNER STRASSE« (seit Mai 1980): Johann Brennig, geboren 1947 in Wien, Studium an der Hochschule für angewandte Kunst in Wien, Mag. arch., Architekt, seit 1980 freischaffender Architekt. – Helmut Christen, geboren 1943 in Wien. Studium an der Technischen Universität Wien, Dipl.-Ing., Architekt, seit 1978 freischaffender Architekt, seit 1982 Universitätsassistent an der Technischen Universität Wien. – Michael Stepanek, geboren 1943 in Wien. Studium an der Technischen Universität Wien, Dipl.-Ing., Architekt, seit 1982 freischaffender Architekt. – Christoph Thetter, geboren 1943 in Wien. Studium an der Technischen Universität Wien, Dipl.-Ing., Architekt, seit 1982 freischaffender Architekt. – Helmut Wimmer, geboren 1947 in Wien. Studium an der Technischen Universität Wien, Dipl.-Ing., Architekt, seit 1981 freischaffender Architekt, seit 1982 Universitätsassistent an der Technischen Universität Wien, 1989 Gastprofessor an der University of Michigan / Ann Arbor, USA.

DIETER BOGNER, geboren 1942, Kunsthistoriker, Publizist und Ausstellungsorganisator. Direktor der Museumsquartier-Errichtungs- und Betriebsges.m.b.H. Wien.

HERMANN CZECH, geboren in Wien. Student bei Konrad Wachsmann und Ernst A. Plischke. Bauten und Ausstellungsgestaltungen, kritische und theoretische Publikationen. 1985 Preis der Stadt Wien für Architektur. 1985-86 Gastprofessor an der Hochschule für angewandte Kunst in Wien. 1988–89 Gastprofessor an der Harvard University, Cambridge, USA. Freiberuflicher Architekt in Wien.

WOLFDIETER DREIBHOLZ, geboren in Wien 1941. Architekturstudium an der Technischen Universität Wien (1959–66). Universitätsassistent an der Technischen Universität Graz (1968–73). 1974–77 Mitarbeiter am Institut für Umweltforschung am Forschungszentrum Graz. Dissertation »Die Internationale Werkbundsiedlung Wien 1932« (1977). Seit 1978 in der Landesbaudirektion der Steiermark tätig, seit 1980 Leitung des Planungsreferates in der Fachabteilung IVa. Seit 1988 Mitglied des Vorstandes im »Haus der Architektur«. Zahlreiche Vorträge im In- und Ausland sowie zahlreiche Artikel in Tages- und Fachzeitschriften.

BIRGIT FLOS, Studium der vergleichenden Literaturwissenschaft in New York. 1982–85 Gastprofessur für Medientheorie an der Hochschule der Künste, Berlin. Ab Herbst 1988 Lehrauftrag für Filmgeschichte an der Filmakademie, Wien. Stadt-, Museums- und Ausstellungskonzepte. Lebt als freie Autorin in Wien.

HANS HOLLEIN, geboren 1934. O. Professor an der Hochschule für angewandte Kunst, Leiter einer Meisterklasse für Architektur. Hans Hollein entwarf das Städtische Museum Abteiberg Mönchengladbach und das Museum für Moderne Kunst, Frankfurt. Hollein hat eine Reihe von Auszeichnungen und Preisen erhalten, u. a. den Großen Österreichischen Staatspreis, 1983, The Pritzker Architecture Prize, 1985, und The Chicago Architecture Award, 1990.

EDELBERT KÖB, geboren 1942 in Bregenz. Studium an der Akademie der bildenden Künste in Wien und an der Universität Wien (1961–65), 1968 Beginn bildhauerischer Tätigkeit. Seit 1974 Professor und seit 1988 Prorektor an der Akademie der bildenden Künste in Wien, Präsident der Wiener Secession (1982–91), seit 1990 Leiter des Kunsthauses Bregenz.

ADOLF KRISCHANITZ, geboren in Schwarzach/Pongau. Studium der Architektur an der Technischen Universität Wien. Seit 1979 freischaffender Architekt in Wien. 1988–89 Gastprofessor an der Technischen Universität München. 1991 Preis der Stadt Wien für Architektur. 1991 Teilnahme an der 5. Architektur-Biennale Venedig. Seit 1991 Präsident der Wiener Secession. 1992 Professor für Entwerfen und Stadterneuerung an der Hochschule der Künste, Berlin.

RUDOLF LAMPRECHT, geboren 1946 in Wien. Architekturstudium TU Wien (1964–72). Mitarbeit im Atelier Hollein (1969–74), Mitarbeit bei Lichtplaner v. Malotki in Köln (1974–77). Seit 1978 freischaffender Architekt in Wien. Tätigkeitsschwerpunkte: Wohnbau-Revitalisierungsprojekte, Präsentation und Beleuchtung von Großausstellungen und Museen.

VITTORIO MAGNAGO LAMPUGNANI, geboren 1951 in Rom. Studium der Architektur an der Universität Rom und in Stuttgart. Dottore in Architettura an der Universität Rom (1983). 1981–83 Columbia University, New York, Forschungsförderung des American Council of Learned Societies. Professur an der Harvard University, Graduate School of Design (1984–85). Seit 1990 Universitätsprofessor an der Staatlichen Hochschule für bildende Künste in Frankfurt am Main. Direktor des Deutschen Architekturmuseums Frankfurt. Umfangreiche Tätigkeit als Ausstellungsmacher, viele Buchpublikationen. Seit 1991 Herausgeber von »DOMUS«.

DANIELLA LUXEMBOURG, Studium der Kunstgeschichte, spezialisiert auf Jüdische Kunst, an der Hebräischen Universität, Jerusalem (1970–76). Hauptkustos des Alten Yishuv Hofmuseums, Jerusalem (1972–75). Kustos von Ausstellungen und Planungs-Koordination, Diaspora Museum, Tel Aviv (1976–82). Codirektorin von Sotheby's in Israel. Tätig als Mitglied von ICOM, Teilnahme an der Ersten Internationalen Museumskonferenz Moskau–Leningrad (1976). Italienisch-Israelisches Kulturstipendium in Rom und im Vatikan (1982).

KARL MANG, geboren 1922 in Wien. Hochschule Wien 1945–48 (Architekturstudium), 1950/51 Rom-Stipendium. Einfamilienhäuser und sozialer Wohnbau (Raumplan), Sakralbauten etc. Flexible Strukturen in Laden- und Ausstellungsbauten. Ausstellungen mit sozialem Hintergrund; Museumsplanungen: Schatzkammer Wien, Österr. Theatermuseum, Modemuseum der Stadt Wien. Schriftstellerische Arbeiten, zumeist in Zusammenarbeit mit Eva Mang.

SEPP MÜLLER, geboren 1927 in Linz. Studium an der TU Wien und an der Akademie der Bildenden Künste – Diplom Meisterschule Holzmeister. Mag. arch. Mitarbeiter bei Roland Rainer 1951–57, seit 1958 freischaffender Architekt in Wien.

PETER NOEVER, geboren 1941 in Innsbruck; Designer, seit 1986 Direktor des Österreichischen Museums für angewandte Kunst, Professor für Museologie an der Hochschule für angewandte Kunst. Seit 1975 Lehrauftrag für »Design-Analyse« an der Akademie der bildenden Künste, Wien. Gründer und Herausgeber der Architekturzeitschrift UMRISS (1982). Publikationen in in- und ausländischen Zeitschriften; Autor und Regisseur von Architektur- und Designfilmen. Zahlreiche Ausstellungen; 1991 erhielt Noever den »PAN Preis für Ausstellungsmacher« des Kunstmagazins PAN.

ORTNER UND ORTNER: Laurids Ortner, geboren 1941 in Linz. Architekturstudium an der TU Wien (1959–65). Mitbegründer der Architekten-, Designer- und Künstlergruppe Haus-Rucker-Co in Wien (1967). Übersiedlung nach Düsseldorf. Einrichtung eines Ateliers Haus-Rucker-Co mit Günter Zam Kelp und Manfred Ortner (1970), Berufung an die Hochschule für künstlerische und industrielle Gestaltung in Linz, bis 1987 Leiter der Meisterklasse für Visuelle Gestaltung. 1987 Berufung an die Staatliche Kunstakademie Düsseldorf als Professor für Architektur. 1987 Gründung des Büros ORTNER ARCHITEKTEN zusammen mit Manfred Ortner in Düsseldorf, Gründung des Büros ORTNER & ORTNER in Wien (1990). – Manfred Ortner, geboren 1943 in Linz. Studium der Malerei und Kunsterziehung an der Akademie der bildenden Künste, Geschichte an der Universität Wien (1961–67). 1971 Übersiedlung nach Düsseldorf. Zusammen mit Laurids Ortner und Günter Zam Kelp in der Gruppe Haus-Rucker-Co, Düsseldorf, als freischaffender Künstler und Architekt tätig. Zahlreiche Vorträge und Gastseminare im In- und Ausland. 1985–86 Dozent für Formgebung an der TH Eindhoven.

OSKAR PAUSCH, geboren 1937 in St. Pölten. Studium an der Universität Wien (Germanistik, Psychologie, Anglistik), Promotion 1962, Eintritt in die Österreichische Nationalbibliothek (1963), ab 1968 Leiter der Bibliothek im Institut für Österreichische Geschichtsforschung. Habilitation an der Universität Wien 1974, Gastdozentur an der Universität Klagenfurt (1977–78), ab 1990 Direktor der Theatersammlung der Österreichischen Nationalbibliothek bzw. des Österreichischen Theatermuseums. Seit 1988 Präsident der SIBMAS (Société Internationale des Bibliothèques et des Musées des Arts du Spectacle). Umfangreiche Publikationen.

WALTER PICHLER, geboren 1936 in Deutschnofen (Südtirol). Studium an der Akademie für angewandte Kunst in Wien. Längere Aufenthalte in Paris (1960) und New York (1963). Ausstellungen u. a. in Wien, Kassel, Hamburg, New York, München, London, Jerusalem und 1982 auf der Biennale in Venedig. 1985 erhielt Pichler den Großen Österreichischen Staatspreis für bildende Kunst.

PETER REBERNIK, geboren 1947 in Graz. Nach Beendigung des Studiums Nachrichtentechnik an der TU Wien Universitätsassistent, danach Einstieg in die Privatwirtschaft (bei Philips in Hilversum/Niederlande, Softwareentwicklung in Österreich). Seit 1987 Direktor des Technischen Museums Wien. Auslandsaufenthalt in Dallas, Texas.

WILHELM GEORG RIZZI, geboren in Wien. Architektur- und Doktoratsstudium, Forschungsassistent, später Fachbeamter und seit 1991 Architekturdirektor im Präsidium des Bundesdenkmalamtes. Forschungsschwerpunkte auf dem Gebiet Architektur- und Baugeschichte, speziell des 18. und 19. Jahrhunderts, dazu zahlreiche wissenschaftliche Publikationen. Universitätslektor für das Fach Historische Gartenanlagen.

DIETER RONTE, geboren 1943 in Leipzig. Studium der Kunstgeschichte, Archäologie und Romanistik in Münster, Pavia und Rom. Dr. phil. Ab 1971 Mitarbeiter der Museen der Stadt Köln, dann Leiter der Graphischen Sammlung des Museums Ludwig in Köln, ab 1979 Direktor des Museums moderner Kunst in Wien. Seit 1989 Direktor des Sprengel Museums Hannover. Veröffentlichungen u. a. über die Kunst des 20. Jahrhunderts. Seit 1980 Lehrverpflichtungen u. a. an der Akademie der bildenden Künste Wien, Hochschule für angewandte Kunst Wien, seit 1990 Universität Hannover.

AUGUST SARNITZ, geboren 1956 in Innsbruck. Studium der Architektur an der Akademie der bildenden Künste, Wien, anschließend Postgraduate Studium der Architekturgeschichte und Architekturtheorie als Fulbright-Scholar am Massachusetts Institute of Technology. Promotion an der Technischen Universität Wien 1983. Architekt und Hochschuldozent für Architekturgeschichte. Seit 1984 Lehrbeauftragter an der Akademie der bildenden Künste. Visiting Professor an der University of California, Los Angeles (1988) und an der Rhode Island School of Design, Providence (1990). Zahlreiche Publikationen zum Thema Architekturgeschichte.

WILFRIED SEIPEL, geboren 1944 in Wien. Studium an den Universitäten Wien und Heidelberg (Klassische Philologie, Alte Geschichte, Indogermanistik, Ur- und Frühgeschichte, Assyriologie) 1963–71. Assistenzprofessor an der Universität Konstanz (1981–83). Direktor der Städtischen Museen Konstanz (1983–85), Direktor des OÖ. Landesmuseums in Linz (1985–90). Seit 1990 Generaldirektor des Kunsthistorischen Museums, Wien.

DIE KÜNSTLERGRUPPE SITE: Alison Sky, studierte Kunst und Literaturwissenschaft und wirkt seit der Gründung von SITE an der konzeptuellen Projektentwicklung mit. Außerdem ist sie Gründerin und Mitherausgeberin der Publikationen von SITE. – Michelle Stone, studierte Psychologie und Soziologie an der New Yorker Universität und ist seit 1970 bei SITE. Sie ist verantwortlich für Verwaltung und Projektkoordination, außerdem Mitherausgeberin und Photographin der Publikationsreihe »On Site«. – Joshua Weinstein, studierte Architektur an der Pratt Institute School of Architecture. Seit 1982 bei SITE, zeichnet er verantwortlich für die konzeptuelle Mitarbeit und die Umsetzung der Ideen in Architektur. – James Wines, studierte Kunst und Kunstgeschichte an der Syracuse University, arbeitete als Bildhauer in den sechziger Jahren in Rom und gründete 1970 mit anderen Künstlern und experimentellen Architekten die Gruppe SITE. Seine Vorträge und Projekte wurden international als experimentelle Architektur diskutiert. Zahlreiche Preise, u. a. Pulitzer Fellowship for Graphic Art (1953), The Ford Foundation Fellowship for Sculpture (1964), The Guggenheim Foundation Fellowship for

Sculpture (1962), The Graham Foundation Fellowship for Critical Writing (1983), The NEA Distinguished Designer Award for Architecture (1983). Zahlreiche Bücher, darunter »De-Architecture«, 1988, eine Abhandlung über die Philosophie von SITE. James Wines ist Professor und Dekan für Environmental Design an der Parson School of Design in New York.

NORBERT STEINER, Jahrgang 1942; Architekturstudium an der Technischen Hochschule Wien, Dipl.-Ing. Ab 1972 Mitarbeit im Stadtentwicklungs- und Planungsreferat der Landeshauptstadt München, ab 1975 Leiter der Abteilung »Räumliche Entwicklungsplanung« im Planungsreferat München. Neben der Tätigkeit im Planungsreferat Konsulententätigkeit bei Wohnbauprojekten in den USA sowie bei der Entwicklung der Hauptstadtregion im Oman. Seit 1987 Vorstandsvorsitzender der »Niederösterreichischen Landeshauptstadt Planungsgesellschaft m.b.H.« in St. Pölten, der die für die Entwicklung der jungen niederösterreichischen Landeshauptstadt zur vollwertigen Metropole erforderlichen Maßnahmen obliegen. Dazu zählen insbesonders die Planung von städtebaulichen Lösungen, die dafür notwendige Grundstücksbeschaffung, die Erarbeitung von Finanzierungsplänen sowie die Projektierung und Errichtung aller wichtigen Hauptstadtbauten.

SSTT-Büro: Schöffauer (Friedrich W.), Schrom (Wolfgang), Tschapeller (Wolfgang). Zusammenarbeit zum Zweck der Planungsarbeit – Trigon/Pfauengarten ab 1988.

MARIO TERZIC, geboren 1945 in Feldkirch, Vorarlberg. Seit 1991 Professor an der Hochschule für angewandte Kunst Wien, Leiter der Meisterklasse für Grafik. Ausstellungen in Wien, Paris, Basel, Frankfurt, New York. Künstlerische Reisen. Preis der Stadt Wien 1989. Veröffentlichungen seiner Arbeiten in mehreren Buch-Publikationen.

HERWIG ZENS, geboren 1943 in Himberg bei Wien. Studium an der Akademie der bildenden Künste, Wien (Elsner, Boeckl), 1961–67. Seit 1987 Professur an der Akademie der bildenden Künste, Wien. Förderungspreis des Landes Niederösterreich (1972). Förderungspreis des Landes Wien (1982). Seit 1966 durchgehende Ausstellungstätigkeit im In- und Ausland. Mehrere Veröffentlichungen im kunstpädagogischen Bereich. Diverse Videofilme.

PETER ZUMTHOR, geboren 1943 in Basel. Lehre als Möbelschreiner; Fachklasse für Innenarchitektur an der Schule für Gestaltung, Basel; Architecture and Interior Design, Pratt Institute New York; 1968–78 Bauberater und Siedlungsinventarisator, Kant. Denkmalpflege Graubünden; 1978 Lehrauftrag an der Universität Zürich. Seit 1979 selbständiger Architekt; 1988 Gastprofessor am SCI-ARC, Santa Monica, Los Angeles; 1989 Gastprofessor an der Technischen Universität München.

Biographies

ATELIER IN SCHÖNBRUNNER STRASSE (since May 1980): Johann Brennig. Born in 1947 in Vienna. Studied at the School of Applied Art in Vienna. Mag. arch. Architect. Since 1980 freelance architect. – Helmut Christen. Born in 1943 in Vienna. Studied at the Technical University of Vienna. Dipl.-Ing. Architect. Since 1978 freelance architect. Since 1982 university assistant at the Technical University of Vienna. – Michael Stepanek. Born in 1943 in Vienna. Studied at the Technical University of Vienna. Dipl.-Ing. Architect. Since 1982 freelance architect. – Christoph Thetter. Born in 1943 in Vienna. Studied at the Technical University of Vienna. Dipl.-Ing. Architect. Since 1982 freelance architect. – Helmut Wimmer. Born in 1947 in Vienna. Studied at the Technical University of Vienna. Dipl.-Ing. Architect. Since 1981 freelance architect. Since 1982 university assistant at the Technical University of Vienna. In 1989 Visiting Professor at the University of Michigan / Ann Arbor, USA.

DIETER BOGNER. Born in 1942. Art historian, journalist and exhibition organiser. Director of the Museumsquartier-Errichtungs- und Betriebsges. m.b.H (Limited liability company for the construction and operation of the Museum Quarter).

HERMANN CZECH. Born in Vienna. Student of Konrad Wachsmann and Ernst A. Plischke. Designs for buildings and exhibitions, critical and theoretical publications. 1985 City of Vienna Prize for Architecture. 1985–86 Visiting Professor at the School of Applied Art in Vienna. 1988–89 Visiting Professor at Harvard University, Cambridge, USA. Freelance architect in Vienna.

WOLFDIETER DREIBHOLZ. Born in Vienna in 1941. Study of architecture at the Technical University of Vienna (1959–66). University assistant at the Technical University of Graz (1968–73). 1974–77 employed by the Institute for Environmental Research at the Graz Research Centre. Dissertation *The International Werkbund Housing Estate in Vienna, 1932* (1977). Since 1978 active in the Building Department of the Styrian Provincial Government, since 1980 Director of the Planning Section of Department IVa. Since 1988 member of the executive board of the House of Architecture. Numerous lectures in Austria and abroad, as well as articles in daily newspapers and professional journals.

BIRGIT FLOS. Studied comparative literature in New York. 1982–1985 Visiting Professor for Media Theory at the Berlin School of Art. Since 1988 Professor for Cinema History at the Vienna Film Academy. Conceptual design for urban planning, museums and exhibitions. Lives as freelance author in Vienna.

HANS HOLLEIN. Born 1934. Professor of Architecture at the Academy of Applied Arts, Vienna. Prof. Hollein has designed the Municipal Museum Abteiberg, Mönchengladbach, and the Museum of Modern Art, Frankfurt. Prof. Hollein has received many prestigious awards, including the Grosser Österreichischer Staatspreis, 1983, The Pritzker Architecture Prize, 1985, and The Chicago Architecture Award in 1990.

EDELBERT KÖB. Born in 1942 in Bregenz. Studied at the Academy of Fine Arts in Vienna and at the University of Vienna (1961–65). Began to work as a sculptor in 1968. Since 1974 Professor at the Academy of Fine Arts in Vienna, since 1988 Vice-Chancellor there. President of the Vienna Secession (1982–91). Since 1990 Director of the Kunsthaus Bregenz.

ADOLF KRISCHANITZ. Born 1946 in Schwarzach/Pongau. Studied architecture at the Technical University of Vienna. Since 1979 freelance architect in Vienna. 1988-89 Visiting Professor at the Technical University in Munich. 1991 City of Vienna Prize for Architecture. In 1991 participated at the 5th Venice Architecture Biennale. Since 1991 President of the Vienna Secession. 1992 Professor for Design and Urban Redevelopment at the School of Fine Arts, Berlin.

RUDOLF LAMPRECHT. Born in 1946 in Vienna. Studied architecture at the TU Vienna (1964–72). Worked at Atelier Hollein (1969–74), and with the lighting designer Malotki in Cologne. Since 1978 freelance architect in Vienna. Main areas of activity: housing renovation projects, presentation and illumination of large-scale exhibitions and museums.

VITTORIO MAGNAGO LAMPUGNANI. Born in 1951 in Rome. Studied architecture at the University of Rome and in Stuttgart. *Dottore in Archittetura* at the University of Rome (1983). 1981-83 research sponsorship from the American Council of Learned Societies at Columbia University, New York. Professorship at the Graduate School of Design, Harvard University (1984-85). Since 1990 Professor at the School of Fine Arts in Frankfurt am Main. Director of the German Museum of Architecture in Frankfurt. Wide experience as exhibition organiser, many book publications. Since 1991 editor of DOMUS.

DANIELLA LUXEMBOURG. Studies in Art History, specialising in Jewish art, Hebrew University, Jerusalem (1970–76). Chief curator of the Old Yishuv Court Museum, Jerusalem (1972–75). Curator of exhibitions and co-ordinator of textual planning, Diaspora Museum, Tel Aviv (1976–82). Co-director of Sotheby's Israel. Member of ICOM. Representative at the First International Museum Conference Moscow/Leningrad (1976). Italian Israel Cultural Scholarship Recipient to Rome and the Vatican (1982).

KARL MANG. Born in 1922 in Vienna. Studied architecture at the University of Vienna 1945–1948. 1950/51 Fellowship in Rome. Single-family housing and publicly assisted housing (spatial plan), religious buildings, etc. Flexible structures for shops and exhibition buildings. Exhibitions with social background. Museum designs: Vienna Treasury, Austrian Theatre Museum, Fashion Museum of the City of Vienna. Author of several books, mostly in collaboration with Eva Mang.

SEPP MÜLLER. Born in 1927 in Linz. Studied at the TU Vienna and at the Academy of the Fine Arts, Vienna. Diploma Master-class Prof. Holzmeister. Mag. arch. Worked for Roland Rainer 1951–57. Since 1958 freelance architect in Vienna.

PETER NOEVER. Born in 1941 in Innsbruck. Designer, since 1986 Director of the Austrian Museum for Applied Art and Professor for Museology at the School of Applied Art. Since 1975 Professor for Design Analysis at the Academy of Fine Arts in Vienna. Founder and editor of the architectural journal UMRISS (1982). Publications in Austrian and foreign journals. Author and director of films on architecture and design. Numerous exhibitions. In 1991 Noever received the PAN Prize for Exhibition Organisers, sponsored by the art magazine PAN.

ORTNER AND ORTNER: Laurids Ortner. Born in 1941 in Linz. Studied architecture at the TU Vienna (1959–65). Co-founder of the team of architects, designers and artists, Haus-Rucker-Co, in Vienna (1967). Moved to Düsseldorf. Set up a Haus-Rucker-Co studio with Günter Zam Kelp and Manfred Ortner (1970). Appointed Professor at the School of Artistic and Industrial Design, Linz. Until 1987 head of the Master-class in Visual Design. In 1987 appointed Professor of Architecture at the Academy of Art in Düsseldorf. In 1987 opened, together with Manfred Ortner, the office ORTNER ARCHITEK-TEN in Düsseldorf, and in 1990 the office ORTNER & ORTNER in Vienna. – Manfred Ortner. Born in 1943 in Linz. Studied painting and art education at the Academy of Fine Arts, history at the University of Vienna (1961–67). In 1971 moved to Düsseldorf. Works as freelance artist and architect, and in the group Haus-Rucker-Co, in collaboration with Laurids Ortner and Günter Zam Kelp. Numerous lectures and seminars in Austria and abroad. 1985–86 Professor for Design at the Technical University of Eindhoven.

OSKAR PAUSCH. Born in 1937 in St. Pölten. Studied at the University of Vienna (German studies, psychology, English studies), graduating in 1962. Joined the Austrian National Library (1963), after 1968 Director of the Institute for Austrian Historical Research. Habilitation as university lecturer at the University of Vienna in 1974, Visiting Professor at the University of Klagenfurt (1977–78). Since 1990 Director of the Theatre Collection of the Austrian National Library and Austrian Theatre Museum. Since 1988 President of SIMBAS (Societé Internationale des Bibliotheques et des Museés des Arts du Spectacle). Extensive publications.

WALTER PICHLER. Born in 1936 in Deutschnofen (South Tyrol). Studied at the Academy of Applied Art in Vienna. Extended visits to Paris (1960) and New York (1963). Exhibitions in Vienna, Kassel, Hamburg, New York, Munich, London, Jerusalem and at the 1982 Venice Biennale. In 1985 Pichler was awarded the Austrian State Prize for Fine Art.

PETER REBERNIK. Born in 1947 in Graz. After completing his studies in communication engineering at the Technical University of Vienna, worked as university assistant, before entering the private industry sector (Philips in Hilversum/ Holland, software development in Austria). Since 1987 Director of the Technical Museum of Vienna. Study visit abroad in Dallas, Texas.

WILHELM GEORG RIZZI. Born in Vienna. Study of architecture, doctorate, research assistant. Later joined the civil service as a technical specialist, since 1991 architectural director in the executive commitee of the Austrian Federal Office for the Preservation of Historical Monuments. Research in the field of architectural and building history, specialising on the 18th and 19th centuries, numerous scientific publications. University lecturer in the study of historical gardens.

DIETER RONTE. Born in 1943 in Leipzig. Studied art history, archaeology and Romance languages and literature in Münster, Pavia and Rome. Dr. phil. In 1971 employed by the Museum of the City of Cologne, before becoming Director of the Graphic Art Collection at the Museum Ludwig in Cologne, and in 1979 Director of the Museum of Modern Art in Vienna. Since 1989 Director of the Sprengel Museum in Hannover. Many publications, in particular on 20th century art. Since 1980 lecturer at the Academy of the Fine Arts in Vienna, the School of Applied Art in Vienna and, since 1990, at the University of Hanover.

AUGUST SARNITZ. Born in 1956 in Innsbruck. Studied architecture at the Academy of Fine Arts in Vienna, followed by a post-graduate study in the history of architecture and architectural theory as a Fulbright Scholar at the Massachusetts Institute of Technology. Doctorate at the Technical University of Vienna in 1983. Architect and university lecturer in the history of architecture. Since 1984 lecturer at the Academy of Fine Arts. Visiting Professor at the University of California, Los Angeles (1988) and at the Rhode Island School of Design, Providence (1990). Numerous publications on architectural history.

WILFRIED SEIPEL. Born in 1944 in Vienna. Studied at the universities of Vienna and Heidelberg (classical philology, ancient history, Indo-Germanic studies, prehistory and primitive history, Assyriology) 1963–1971. Assistant Professor at the University of Constance (1981–83). Director of Constance Municipal Museums (1983–85), Director of the Upper Austrian Regional Museum in Linz (1985–90). Since 1990 General Director of the Kunsthistorische Museum, Vienna.

SITE ARTISTS' GROUP: Alison Sky. Studied art and literature. She has worked on conceptual project development since the foundation of SITE. She is also the founder and co-editor of publications by SITE. – Michelle Stone. Studied psychology and sociology at New York University. She has been with SITE since 1970, is responsible for administration and project coordination, and is co-editor and photographer for the publication series *On Site.* – Joshua Weinstein. Studied architecture at the Pratt Institute School of Architecture. With SITE since 1982, he is responsible for conceptual collaboration and the translation of ideas into architecture. – James Wines. Studied art and art history at Syracuse University, worked in Rome as a sculptor in the 60s and founded the group SITE in 1970, together with other artists and experimental architects. Numerous prizes, including the Pulitzer Fellowship for Graphic Art (1953), the Ford Foundation Fellowship for Sculpture (1964), the Guggenheim Foundation Fellowship for Sculpture (1962), the Graham Foundation Fellowship for Critical Writing (1983), the NEA Distinguished Designer Award for Architecture (1983). Numerous books, including *De-Architecture* (1988), a treatise on the philosophy of SITE. James Wines is Professor and Dean at the Department for Environmental Design at the Parson School of Design in New York.

NORBERT STEINER. Born 1942, Architectural studies at the Technical University of Vienna, Dipl.-Ing. From 1972 employed in the Town Development and Planning Department of the state capital Munich. From 1975 Head of the "Regional Development Planning" section of Munich's Town Planning Department. In addition to the activities in the planning department, consultancy for housing projects in the USA and the development of the main city region in Oman. Since 1987 Chairman of the Executive Board of the "Niederösterreichische Landeshauptstadt Planungsgesellschaft mbH" in St. Pölten, which is responsible for the measures required to develop the young capital city of the province of Lower Austria into a full-scale metropolis. The emphasis is on town planning solutions, acquiring the land required for their implementation, financial planning, and planning and erecting all of the important structures in the capital.
(translation: All Languages)

SSTT OFFICE: Schöffauer (Friedrich W.), Schrom (Wolfgang), Tschapeller (Wolfgang). Collaboration with the aim of planning work – since 1988 for Trigon / Pfauengarten.

MARIO TERZIC. Born in 1945 in Feldkirch, Vorarlberg. Since 1991 Professor at the School of Applied Art in Vienna, head of the Master-class for graphic art. Exhibitions in Vienna, Paris, Basle, Frankfurt, New York. Artistic travels. Prize of the City of Vienna, 1989. His work has appeared in diverse book publications.

HERWIG ZENS. Born in 1943 in Himberg near Vienna. Studied at the Academy of the Fine Arts in Vienna (Elsner, Boeckl), 1961-1967. Since 1987 Professor at the Academy of Fine Arts in Vienna. Fellowship Prize of the Province of Lower Austria (1972). Fellowship Prize of the Province of Vienna (1982). Since 1966 constant exhibitions in Austria and abroad. Several publications on the teaching of art. Diverse video films.

PETER ZUMTHOR. Born 1943 in Basle. Apprenticeship as cabinet-maker. Class for interior decoration at the School of Design in Basle. Architecture and Interior Design, Pratt Institute, New York. 1968–78 construction advisor and housing estate inventory controller at Provincial Department of Preservation of historical monuments, Graubünden. In 1978 lecturer at the University of Zurich. Since 1979 freelance architect. In 1988 Visiting Professor at SCI-ARC, Santa Monica, Los Angeles. In 1989 Visiting Professor at the Technical University of Munich.